THE PUBLIC SCHOOLS OF CHICAGO

THE
PUBLIC SCHOOLS
OF
CHICAGO

A Survey

for the Board of Education of the

City of Chicago

by ROBERT J. HAVIGHURST

THE BOARD OF EDUCATION OF THE

CITY OF CHICAGO

Chicago 1964

Contents

Introduction

This is a time of change in public education, more fundamental and widespread than the changes in any other period during the 20th century. In such a time it is inevitable that there should be much searching inquiry into the educational systems of the country. Philadelphia has a survey going on this year. New York, Detroit, Los Angeles, Miami and Baltimore, to name only a few, have Citizens Committees which have made or are currently making studies of the effectiveness of their schools.

Background of the Chicago Survey

The first and only previous Chicago survey was made in 1931–32, at a time when the Great Depression had reduced tax collections to a point where the amount of money available for schools was substantially less than the amount included in the budget the Board of Education had adopted. Reduction of expense was necessary, and one of the purposes of the survey was to advise the Board where it could cut costs with the least damage to the education of children and youth. The survey also had the usual positive purposes of studying the educational program, school organization, business management, buildings, and personnel. Very few of the recommendations for positive development were followed, since the recovery from the

1

financial difficulties of the 1930's was slow. This survey was directed by Professor George D. Strayer of Columbia University.*

During the 1930's and the early 1940's the Chicago schools muddled through, with some flashes of creative work. However, there were difficulties of administration which aroused a great deal of local citizen protest as well as investigations by the National Education Association and the North Central Association of Colleges and Secondary Schools. At the close of World War II the Superintendent resigned and several members of the Board of Education withdrew, clearing the way for a reorganization which restored public confidence and which increased the power of the Superintendent so as to give him authority over both educational and business matters in the system, together with the title of General Superintendent.

Herold C. Hunt became General Superintendent in 1947. In 1953 he resigned to join the faculty of Harvard University, and Benjamin C. Willis succeeded him. Under these two men the school system has grown tremendously. The postwar increase of births affected the schools first in 1952, but in-migration of low-income people with large families had already pushed up school enrollments to the point that many schools were on double shift at the beginning of the 1950's. A great building program was carried out, and this eliminated the double shift by 1963.

About 1960 there arose a public concern over the school program. Changes in the socioeconomic composition of the city, as well as new developments in methods of teaching and problems of de facto segregation, contributed to this often controversial discussion. This happened in all the northern industrial cities which had received substantial numbers of Negro workers from the South after the war. At the same time there were searching questions about the school program for all pupils, due to the atmosphere of criticism which political, economic, and scientific events of the 1950 decade produced. The big cities were all having "growing pains" related not to their own physical growth but rather to their deterioration combined with the growth of their suburbs.

---

*George D. Strayer, *Report of the Survey of the Schools of Chicago, Illinois.* 4 volumes. (New York: Bureau of Publications, Teachers College, Columbia University, 1932).

In Chicago, the Board of Education authorized a School Survey, and on November 22, 1961, the President of the Board, Mr. Clair Roddewig, appointed a Survey Committee consisting of Mr. Fairfax Cone, Mr. Thomas Marshall, and Mr. Thomas Murray. Mr. Bernard Friedman was later added to this Committee. On this occasion, the Superintendent said:

> . . . I subscribe wholeheartedly to the suggestions made today by the President of the Board of Education with respect to a thorough survey. I have participated in surveys in other school systems, and have served during the time of exhaustive surveys involving many people. I would like the record to show at this time, which is an appropriate time for me to comment, that I not only have no objection but I, in fact, welcome an exhaustive clear-cut study by responsible people of any and all aspects of this school system.
>
> I welcome a carefully designed, all inclusive study, not to satisfy any individual or group but to insure in the years ahead that the public schools in this city may make the maximum contribution to every individual enrolled in elementary school, high school, vocational school, college, evening school, summer school and every other facet of the program of education and that always attention be given to efficiency, economy and foremost the quality of education.

The Board's Survey Committee spent more than a year discussing the proposed Survey with a number of educators who might conceivably take charge of it. There was some question about the scope of the Survey, and just how it should be related to the administration of the Chicago schools. Eventually the Survey Committee concluded that it should have a broad scope, covering all major aspects of instruction in the schools.

The Survey Committee called on Professor Havighurst on April 14, 1963, and asked him to direct the Survey. He had planned to be out of the country in 1964, but he reconsidered and agreed to carry on the Survey.

His appointment was announced on April 22, and ran into opposition. Superintendent Willis in a statement of May 22, 1963, told the Board of Education that he had not been adequately consulted concerning the choice of a director and the design of the Survey.

Discussions which followed resulted in the formation of a Survey Committee of three people, including Mr. Havighurst, Mr. Willis, and a third person to be selected by them. The action of the Board of Education on May 28 was as follows:

> The Committee of the Whole has received the report of the Survey Committee and makes the following recommendations to the Board:
> 1. A survey of the Chicago Public Schools shall be instituted under the direction of a Committee of Three.
> 2. The Committee shall consist of Dr. Robert J. Havighurst, Dr. Benjamin C. Willis, and a third person to be selected by them at the earliest possible date.
> 3. Dr. Robert J. Havighurst shall serve as Chairman of this Committee.
> 4. The Committee shall proceed immediately with the first stage of the survey, which will be a design of the survey, and upon completion of the design shall report it back to the entire Board for further direction; that in the preparation of this design the Committee shall utilize the facilities, the Associate Superintendents and the staff of the Board of Education.
> 5. That the Committee also proceed with such fact-gathering activity or other groundwork as may be determined to be useful at this preparatory stage.

A third member of the Committee was chosen at once, Dean Alonzo G. Grace of the College of Education at the University of Illinois. The Committee met several times during the autumn and produced a *Design for a Survey of Public Education in Chicago,* which was approved by the Board of Education on December 3, 1963, with a budget of $140,000 for basic expenses plus the cost of possible studies to be made on contract by outside agencies, and the cost of printing and distribution of the final report.

In the Design, it was agreed to study a wide range of areas within the program and the organization of the Chicago Public Schools. These areas are not reported here because this Report deals with them and they can be seen with a glance at the Table of Contents.

The panel on problems of integration. During the time that the Survey was being discussed and planned, a lawsuit was brought against the Chicago Public Schools charging that racial segregation was being practiced. This particular suit was dropped in the summer of 1963 after the Board of Education appointed a panel of five "to analyze and study the school system in particular regard to schools attended entirely or predominantly by Negroes, define any problems that result therefrom, and formulate and report to this Board . . . a plan by which any educational, psychological, and emotional problems or inequities in the school system that prevail may best be eliminated." Since this panel was at work while the Design of the Survey was being drawn up, the Design did not consider the issue of racial balance in the schools specifically. The Design stated, "In the light of the panel's report, when it is completed, the Survey will deal constructively with this area."

The panel reported at the end of March, 1964 (the Hauser Report). The Survey does deal with problems of racial balance in Part IV, building upon the panel report. Among other recommendations, the panel proposed that a Citizens Committee be formed to work with the Board and the General Superintendent on problems related to school integration. Such a Committee was appointed in the summer of 1964.

Procedure of the Survey

There are two general ways by which a school survey can be made. One is the traditional method by which an outside, *independent survey organization* comes in and examines the schools, with the cooperation and support of the Superintendent and his staff. This was the method adopted for the 1932 Survey, in which the Board of Education formally agreed ". . . to give access to all records and to provide for such cooperation of the superintendent of schools and other administrative officers and of principals and teachers in the schools in assembling data as might be necessary for the conduct of the study."

The other possible procedure is a rather close cooperation between the outside surveyors and the administration and staff of the school system. The survey in this case would be planned cooperatively, and the outsiders coming in to examine the schools would act as consultants to the staff as well as critics and evaluators of what they observed. This procedure might be called a *self-survey*.

The procedure actually recommended in the Design lay between the two clear-cut alternatives. It set up a three-man Survey

Committee, consisting of Mr. Havighurst as Chairman, Mr. Grace, and Mr. Willis, with the following responsibilities:

> to maintain a general overview of the Survey;
> to hear progress reports from the Director approximately
>   once a month and to discuss them critically;
> to supervise preparation of the final report;
> to be a policy committee for all policy decisions.

The actual work of the Survey was to be done by three groups of people:

1. The Survey staff, consisting of Director and Survey staff associates.
2. Outside consultants, people who are experts in various aspects of educational practice and theory. They would observe critically and write reports, with recommendations for improvement. Their reports would go to the Director and through him to the Survey Committee. Some consultants might work closely in an advisory capacity to school staff study groups.
3. School staff study groups, consisting of teachers, principals, specialists, and administrators on the staff of the Chicago Public Schools. They would make self-studies of present practices and innovations in the Chicago schools, and would make recommendations for improvement. They would be appointed by the General Superintendent. They might use consultants provided by the Survey Director, if they wished to do so.

With this Design, the Survey got under way in December, 1963. The Board of Education appointed Mr. Havighurst as Director.

The actual procedure of the Survey veered away from the second alternative toward the first, or independent survey procedure. This happened during the first three months of the Survey. The Survey Committee held three meetings in December and January, during which time eight staff study committees were organized. (Four more were added later.) At the same time a list of outside consultants was discussed, and the Director proceeded to employ consultants and get them to work. Also, several Survey staff members were appointed.

After January, the Superintendent did not attend any Survey Committee meetings until September 21. One or two meetings were held each month, with Mr. Grace and Mr. Havighurst in attendance. The Survey Committee conducted its business with two members present, plus Dr. Arthur Lehne, Assistant Superintendent, who was the Superintendent's representative without a vote. Mr. Lehne was appointed by the Superintendent to be in charge of liaison with the Survey Committee. He and his staff arranged all appointments and visits to schools by the Survey staff and consultants, and secured information and data which were requested by the Director and his staff. Mr. Lehne's work was highly efficient and satisfactory.

During the first weeks of activity by the school staff study committees, the first two or three outside consultants entered into active cooperation with the committees, and one consultant attended a meeting of one of the staff study committees. Thereafter, this relation was broken off by the chairmen of the staff study committees. They had no formal connection with Survey consultants or Survey staff members. Their reports came to the Survey staff only through the office of Mr. Lehne.

The Director and the Superintendent did not have any face-to-face discussion about the Survey between February and September. Thus the Survey became in fact an independent survey, conducted by the Director with the advice and assistance of Mr. Grace, the other member of the Survey Committee. Mr. Grace acted as an advisor to the Director and also as coordinator of the section of the Survey dealing with the Chicago Teachers College and the Chicago Junior College. The Superintendent did not discuss with the Survey Committee findings of the Survey or recommendations to be made. He did not influence the recommendations. He facilitated the conduct of the Survey through his deputy, Mr. Lehne.

On September 21, the Survey Committee including Mr. Willis met briefly and agreed upon a procedure for completing the Survey Report. The Director was to prepare the report and to send it to the printer according to a rigorous schedule which would have the report in print by November 11. The Director was to provide copies of the report in proof to Mr. Willis and Mr. Grace. Any comments they might make would be considered by the Director in correcting the proof. It was expected, particularly, that they would point out any errors in fact which might have crept into the manuscript.

Dean Grace, acting as a member of the Committee, discussed the general structure of the Survey Report, and the major recommendations to be made. He saw and commented on many, but not all, of the chapters in manuscript. The responsibility for the Survey Report rests clearly on the Director, though the recommendations represent a consensus of consultants and Survey staff.

The conduct of the Survey

The work of the Survey was done mainly by outside consultants and by Survey staff members. The consultants have been named in the chapters to which they contributed, and they are brought together here in the following list.

Charles Allen, Professor of Education, University of Illinois

R. Bruce Allingham, Superintendent, Willowbrook and York Community High Schools, Villa Park, Illinois

Walter Barbe, Chairman, Department of Special Education, Kent State University, Ohio

George Beauchamp, Professor of Education, Northwestern University

Emma Birkmaier, Professor of Education, University of Minnesota

Eli Bower, Staff Member, Research Utilization Branch, National Institute of Mental Health

Edward Brice, Director, Adult Education Branch, Department of Health, Education and Welfare, Washington

Leon Carnovsky, Professor, Graduate Library School, University of Chicago

Dorothy Carr, Supervisor of Special Education, Los Angeles City Schools

Wells F. Chamberlin, Associate Professor of Romance Languages, University of Chicago

George W. Denemark, Dean, School of Education, University of Wisconsin-Milwaukee

Robert L. Ebel, Professor of Education, Michigan State University

Dorothy M. Fraser, Professor of Education, City University of New York

Robert A. Henderson, Chairman, Department of Special Education, University of Illinois

Cyril O. Houle, Professor of Education, University of Chicago

Phillip Jones, Professor of Mathematics, University of Michigan

LeRoy Knoeppel, Superintendent, Proviso Township High Schools, Maywood, Illinois

Arthur Livermore, Deputy Director of Education, American Association for the Advancement of Science

Alvin Loving, Professor of Education, University of Michigan

Warren C. Lovinger, President, Central Missouri State College

Leland Medsker, Professor of Education, University of California

Lloyd Michael, Superintendent, Evanston Township High School, Evanston, Illinois

Walter J. Moore, Professor of Education, University of Illinois

Gordon Mork, Professor of Education, University of Minnesota

Jeanne L. Noble, Associate Professor of Education, New York University

Charles E. Olmsted, Chairman, Department of Botany, University of Chicago

George W. Overton, Attorney, Overton, Marks, Schwartz, Chicago

John R. Palmer, Associate Professor of Education, University of Illinois

George Philips, Director of Management Research, Illinois Institute of Technology

William D. Phillips, Associate Professor of Education, DePaul University, Chicago

H. Alan Robinson, Assistant Professor of Education, University of Chicago

Edward Roeber, Professor of Education, University of Michigan

Bruce E. Shear, Director of Pupil Personnel Services, New York State Department of Education

J. Richard Smith, Assistant Superintendent, Adult Education, Los Angeles City Schools

Daniel Tanner, Associate Professor of Education, Northwestern University

Thomas Van Sant, Assistant Superintendent, New York Public Schools

Paul Witty, Professor of Education, Northwestern University

Lorne Woollatt, Associate Commissioner for Research, New York State Department of Education

Survey staff members
Jerome M. Ziegler, Associate Director
Elizabeth L. Murray, Special Consultant

Staff Associates
Wade Arends, Lecturer, Chicago City Junior College
Ida Cress, Kindergarten teacher, Chicago Public Schools
Albert Cunningham, Teacher, Chicago Public Schools
Russell Doll, Teacher, Chicago Public Schools, and Research Assistant, University of Chicago
Kenneth Haygood, Staff Associate, Center for the Study of Liberal Education for Adults
Daniel Levine, formerly Teacher in the Chicago Public Schools, now Assistant Professor of Education, University of Missouri at Kansas City
Thomas Moorefield, Research Assistant, University of Chicago, and now Supervisor of Special Projects, Kansas City (Mo.) Public Schools
Lionel Orlikow, Graduate Student, University of Chicago

These people worked full-time or part-time for periods varying from a few weeks to 12 months.

Table 1 shows how many schools were visited by outside consultants and by staff members. Usually a visit occupied a half day or a full day, and occasionally more than one day. During a school visit, generally from three to six teachers were interviewed or their classes visited, and the principal or assistant principal or both were interviewed. Thus slightly over one-fourth of the elementary schools were visited, two-thirds of the general high schools, and all of the vocational high schools and Junior College and Teachers College buildings. About 800 different elementary school teachers were interviewed or observed, and about 500 high school teachers. In addition, a Teacher Questionnaire was sent to all teachers and responses were received from 70 percent of them.

During the last weeks of the Survey most of the School Staff Study Reports became available, and they have been used in the preparation of the Survey Report as indicated in the text.

Table 1
Numbers of schools visited

	Survey staff		Consultants		
	No. of visits	No. of schools	No. of visits	No. of schools	No. of different schools
Elementary schools	116	75	92	70	119
General high schools	62	25	85	33	34
Vocational high schools	26	10	15	6	10
Junior College	20	8	2	2	8
Teachers College	6	3	15	3	3

The actual writing of the Report has been the responsibility of the Director, aided by Mr. Ziegler and Mrs. Murray, each of whom took major responsibility for writing two or three chapters. Reports of the outside consultants have been used liberally, though only two of them have been printed in their entirety, namely, the chapter on Adult Education in Chicago and the supplement on the Study of Selected Chicago High Schools. When blocks of a consultant's report have been quoted, the text indicates this. But much of the text consists of paraphrases of sections of consultants' reports and recommendations. Where the names of consultants do not appear, the work of summarizing and of writing was done by the Survey staff and Director.

* * *

The use of the Survey Report

We have written this Report essentially as a document to be studied as well as a basis for action. It is not something to be adopted in a formal manner, or to be rejected. It is something to be considered. A good many people with expert knowledge and much experience have given their advice, based on what they have seen in the schools. Their recommendations should be considered not only by the members of the Board of Education, but also by the staff of the school system and by interested parents and citizens. The Citizens Committee appointed by the Board to help interpret and implement the Hauser Report may wish to study the Report.

Since the Report contains some urgent recommendations for action, I hope that such action will be taken by the Board of Education and by the school administration and staff within a reasonable time.

Possibly the Board of Education might divide the Report into two major parts, for separate consideration and action. One part would deal with *Priorities and Costs.* Here the Board would decide what major new expenditures it wants to make and to explain to the public, and with what priorities. The other part would deal with the *Internal Organization and Administration of the Schools.* Here the Board would describe what changes it wants to see and work out a timetable for such changes.

There is an urgency about the situation in Chicago that requires action as soon as is reasonably possible. Perhaps the Board of Education might set the month of March, 1965, as the time to take action.

Robert J. Havighurst

I

How Good Are the Schools?
The Quality of Education

Consideration of quality is important and crucial in any survey of public schools. A major purpose of this survey is to seek answers to questions about the quality of Chicago's public schools. The answers should be more than a simple yes or no. They should point out the strengths and weaknesses of the program and make constructive suggestions for improvement.

Every school system is changing, partly in order to keep up with social changes in the community and the world, and partly to improve itself. A survey can assist this process. The report of a survey generally focuses on the changes that are desirable, and everybody understands that even the best school should change. Consequently the emphasis of the survey report on desirable changes should not be taken as a criticism of the school program or of the people who work in the schools. The survey may praise the schools for some aspects of the program and criticize them for other things. Such praise or blame will only be a by-product of the more important task.

Nevertheless, this report will be read by many people with the purpose of answering for themselves the question: How good are the Chicago Public Schools? The reader will have to be responsible for his own answer, but this chapter may help him to understand the complexity of the question.

13

What is quality in education?

A wise man once said that a democratic society should want for all of its children the kind of education which the wisest and best people want for their children. This is a good general idea. Chicago should strive to provide for all an education that is equal to what the wisest and best people want for their own children. But the wisest and best people cannot give a simple answer to the question about quality in education.

Although the basic aims of education should be the same for all children, the actual program should differ for different kinds of children, because they have different abilities and different viewpoints on life. Education of good quality has four characteristics:

1. It has a variety of courses, classes, and methods suited to the abilities, interests, and vocational expectations of all kinds of pupils and their families.

2. Pupils become active learners, who want an education and take the initiative in studying.

3. The teaching is done by competent, well-trained, and devoted teachers.

4. The school system is organized and administered for effective teaching and efficient use of resources.

How can quality be judged or measured?

There are several ways by which the quality of education can be judged, and these ways have been followed in the Survey. There are also some ways which are seductively simple and attractive but not workable.

Comparison of test results with other cities? It is natural to suppose that a simple comparison of Chicago with other cities on the achievement test scores made by pupils will provide a basis for judgment. If Chicago pupils are above the national average, then it may be reasoned that Chicago schools are above average. But this conclusion would only be justified if all the other factors that influence school achievement were equal between Chicago and the other cities. The other factors of major importance are innate biological ability and family background.

Most educators believe that inborn biological ability for mental skills is the same for all large social and racial groups, and therefore there is no difference in this factor between Chicago and other cities. But the family background factor may differ tremendously between Chicago and other cities. This will be discussed in detail in Chapter III, and here it is enough to point out the well-known fact that parents with much education give their children a better chance for good school achievement than do parents with little education. Therefore, it would not be fair to compare the achievement of Chicago school children, whose parents average about 10 grades of school, with the achievement of children in a North Shore suburb, whose parents average about 14 grades of school.

But one might suppose that all big cities could be fairly compared, because they all have about the same educational level for adults and the same level in other socioeconomic factors. This is not true. For example, Los Angeles adults averaged 12.1 grades of school in 1960, while Chicago adults averaged 10.0 grades. Los Angeles has within its boundaries many suburban-type communities whose people have high levels of education, while the city limits of Chicago exclude many suburban-type communities. Baltimore, on the other hand, had an average of 8.9 grades of schooling for its adults, and would be at a disadvantage compared with Chicago.

Following this line of reasoning, one might try to compare Chicago, New York, and Detroit on the achievement scores of school children, since all three cities have almost equal educational levels for adults. It happens the Chicago and New York schools used the same Metropolitan Reading Achievement Test with sixth graders in 1963. In both cities the sixth-grade pupils were slightly below the national average for sixth graders. There was very little difference between the New York and Chicago results.

This might lead to the conclusion that the school systems of New York and Chicago are about equally good in the teaching of reading. However, there are several other questions to be asked before accepting this conclusion. It may be that one city has more of its low-ability pupils in special classes, and these classes are not counted in working out the test averages. If one city has more low-ability pupils in regular sixth-grade classes, it will have lower test scores than the other city for this reason. Again, one city may have a higher rate of nonpromotion than the other, in which case it will have more over-age sixth graders. These pupils will have more years in school and therefore will tend to get higher scores than the sixth graders in the city where the promotion policy is less rigorous. Finally, even though the average adult educational level in the two cities is the same, this may not mean that the average educational levels of parents of public school children are the same. In Chicago about half of the white children go to Catholic parochial schools. The parents of these children may have a different educational level than the parents of children in the public schools.

Thus it becomes apparent that a fair comparison of the test scores of two cities can only be made if a carefully designed research study is made, in which all factors which would affect school achievement are known and allowed for. This has not been done, and therefore one cannot fairly judge Chicago schools by comparison of test results with those of other schools, especially since differences in test results are not large.

Comparison with the past? One could judge the quality of Chicago's public schools by comparing the present with the past. One might compare achievement test scores of today with those of 10 or 20 years ago on similar tests. This is difficult, but it has been done in a few places. Generally it is found that there is very little difference in reading and arithmetic achievement between today and an earlier period. But in a city like Chicago the effect of migration to the suburbs of high- and middle-income people might be expected to lower the school achievement levels in Chicago. The Survey did not compare present with past in any systematic way.

Another way of judging quality by comparison with the past is to compare the *conditions* of learning. Class size is an illustration. In 1932, according to the survey of that year, the average number of pupils per teacher was 42 for the first five grades, and 34 in the sixth, seventh and eighth grades. This compares with an average of 32.5 in the elementary schools of Chicago today. Again, the training of teachers may be compared. In 1932 most elementary school teachers did not have a four-year college course. They were graduates of two-year normal schools. Today the vast majority of teachers are college graduates and many have masters' degrees. Another basis for comparison is the physical facilities of the schools—the number of libraries and laboratories and gymnasia, etc. In the Chicago schools progress has been made over the past 30 years in all these respects.

It is clear that the schools are better physically and in other ways than they were a generation ago.

Comparisons within the school system? Many people wonder whether the schools within the Chicago system, and in other big cities, are equally good for all kinds of pupils. Are they as good for children of working-class families as they are for children of white-collar families? Are they as good for Negro as for white children? The Survey has been concerned with this question and has attempted to answer it in some of the later chapters.

For comparisons within the school system, it should be understood that one should not expect the children of all schools to do equally well on achievement tests. The differences in home background in groups of different income and educational levels make it inevitable that children will do better in the neighborhoods of high socioeconomic level.

It might be possible to compare schools in the same or similar neighborhoods. A school with higher test scores might be regarded as superior to a school with lower test scores. Such comparisons are useful, but must be made with caution to make sure that the schools are similar in age distribution, percentages of very slow pupils in regular classes, etc.

Judgments of quality of education which are not based on test scores

It seems clear that the answer to the question about the quality of Chicago schools cannot be based with much assurance on the study of standardized achievement test scores.

There are other ways of judging quality, and they have been used in the Survey. One consists of asking experienced educators to study the schools and to report their judgments and their suggestions for improvement. Also, teachers and principals can be asked how they feel about the schools in which they work, and what suggestions they have for improvement. Finally, the practices and the organization of the Chicago schools can be compared with what is being done successfully elsewhere.

Since good education is different for different types and groups of pupils, it is useful to look searchingly at the educational program for various groups of pupils. This has been done.

For gifted and superior pupils, the Survey has looked at the educational provisions and has tried to evaluate these provisions in Chapter V.

For socially disadvantaged children, we should expect different provisions, and the Survey has tried to evaluate these in Chapter IV.

For mentally and physically handicapped children, other kinds of educational procedures are needed. Evaluation of these procedures has been made by experts in education of the handicapped.

Another way to judge quality is to answer the questions: Are Chicago schools so organized that weaknesses can be recognized with reasonable promptness and corrective action initiated at whatever level such action is necessary? Is there sufficient communication, flexibility, and response to dissatisfaction within the system to make this possible?

How has quality been assessed?

There is no single correct answer to questions about the quality of Chicago schools, or of American schools in general. Some schools may do a good job with bright children and a poor job with slow children; others may do a good job with slow children. The schools are doing well if they are serving well the boys and girls they are intended to serve, and if they are serving well in making the city a good place for all kinds of people to live in.

Contemporary life demands more learning of an academic type than did life a generation or more ago. Therefore the schools, working with families, must teach children more than they have learned in the past. In evaluating the quality of Chicago schools we have kept in mind these increasing demands made by contemporary society upon the schools.

In brief, the Survey has assessed quality in the Chicago Public Schools by three methods.

1. By asking outside experts in various aspects of education to study the Chicago schools and report their findings and conclusions.

2. By assigning members of the Survey staff to observe the schools, interview teachers and administrators, and collect data on the schools.

3. By asking teachers and administrators systematically how they feel about their work and how they think the schools could be improved.

II

The City

To understand the educational problems of Chicago, it is necessary to understand the social and economic characteristics of the people of Chicago. There are a number of things about adults that determine their expectations for the education of their children. For example, the more education a parent has, the more education he wants for his children. In general, people with more than average education, more than average income, and white-collar jobs want their children to finish high school and go to college. Although an increasing number of parents with less than average income and education also want high school and college for their children, many of them are content if their children go to school to the end of compulsory education at age 16.

The socioeconomic level of the City of Chicago has gone down since 1950, as a result of two things. One is that many high-income and high-education people have moved out of the city into the suburbs. The other is that many people of relatively low education and low occupational level have moved into the city, mainly from the rural South.

These facts come out most clearly if we compare the City of Chicago with the suburbs on education and occupational level. Such comparisons can be made with census data for the Chicago

Standard Metropolitan Statistical Area, which consists of the Illinois counties of Cook, Lake, McHenry, Kane, DuPage, and Will.

In Table 1 we compare the median educational level of adults in Chicago with the country as a whole and with the metropolitan area outside of Chicago. The educational level increased substantially for the United States between 1940 and 1950 and between 1950 and 1960. For the City of Chicago the education of the average adult increased 1.1 years between 1940 and 1950, and then increased *slightly* between 1950 and 1960. Thus, Chicago was above the national level in 1940 and 1950, but below the national level in 1960. Meanwhile, the level in the suburban area around Chicago climbed and left Chicago farther and farther behind.

A somewhat better measure of socioeconomic level is given by occupation. What we call the socioeconomic ratio (SER) is a ratio of white-collar to blue-collar workers, that is, of business and professional workers to factory and manual workers. Data on the SER for Chicago are shown in Table 2.* The ratio goes up with increasing proportions of white-collar workers.

Looking at the SER for the United States, we see that this ratio has been increasing since 1940, and especially since 1950. This expresses the fact that the proportion of white-collar jobs in the American economy is increasing while the proportion of blue-collar jobs is decreasing. The SER for the Chicago Metropolitan Area shows a similar increase, and is higher at all three dates than the SER for the U.S.A. as a whole.

In 1940 the City of Chicago was slightly below the average of the metropolitan area. In 1950, the Chicago city SER had increased from .69 to .73, while the total metropolitan area increased from .71 to .77. Clearly, the suburbs were carrying up the metropolitan area total, for they increased from .77 to .86. The city was lagging. The flight of middle-class people to the suburbs was in full course.

But the decade after 1950 saw even greater changes. The City of Chicago decreased in SER from .73 to .69, while the total

---

*Detailed description of the socioeconomic ratio is given in Supplement G. It is computed for males in the labor force, aged 14 and over.

Table 1
Educational level of Chicago adults

*Median grade of school completed
by adults 25 years and over*

	1940	1950	1960
Chicago city	8.5	9.6	10.0
Chicago suburban area	8.9	10.8	12.1
Illinois	8.5	9.3	10.5
U.S.A.	8.4	9.3	10.6

Table 2
Socioeconomic ratios* of the Chicago area

	U.S.A.	Chicago SMSA	Chicago city	Chicago suburbs	Chicago city White	Nonwhite
1940	.66	.71	.69	.77	.75	.17
1950	.71	.77	.73	.86	.84	.18
1960	.82	.92	.69	1.28	.82	.25

*The socioeconomic ratio is a rough ratio of white-collar to manual workers. See Supplement G for detailed description.

SMSA increased from .77 to .92, and the suburbs jumped from .86 to 1.28. The central city was decreasing in average socio-economic level, in the face of a country-wide increase as well as a sharp increase in the Chicago area suburbs.

The racial aspect of this phenomenon is also seen in Table 2 for the City of Chicago. While the SER of white male workers was going up from .75 to .84 and down to .82 between 1940 and 1960, the SER for nonwhites (almost all Negroes) was increasing rapidly, but from a low base, from .17 to .25. Since the proportions of nonwhites in Chicago increased from 8.2 percent in 1940 to 22.9 percent in 1960, it was the in-migration of nonwhites with relatively low occupational level that caused a substantial part of the change in Chicago.

Economic and racial stratification in the Chicago area

The past 20 years have seen an increase of economic and racial segregation in Chicago, as in the other large metropolitan areas of the country. The central cities have gained in their proportions of Negro and working-class residents, while the suburbs have gained in their proportions of middle-class residents. This can be seen for the City of Chicago in Table 3, which reports the socioeconomic ratios for Chicago's 75 local community areas for 1940, 1950, and 1960. A local community area varies in population from 10,000 to 100,000 and has its own shopping centers, churches, and community organizations. It has a sense of being a community, sometimes going back to the time when it was first settled by a particular nationality or economic group. These areas have been placed in four groups according to their predominant socioeconomic composition. Group A consists largely of upper-middle class people, business and professional workers and their families. By contrast, the communities making up Group D consist largely of semiskilled or unskilled workers, and are regarded as slums by other city residents. There were 11 local community areas that were substantially upper-middle class in 1940, and 26, or a third of all the local communities were substantially lower working class. This reflected the large numbers of unskilled workers who lived in the city at that time. The following 10 years saw the

Table 3
Socioeconomic ratios
of the local community areas
of Chicago

Socioeconomic level	*Number of local community areas*		
	1940	1950	1960
A SER 1.5+	11	12	8
B SER .65-1.5	20	28	26
C SER .35-.65	18	20	23
D SER <.35	26	15	18

Table 4
Population of Chicago and suburban area

	City of Chicago		Suburban ring	
	White	*Nonwhite*	*White*	*Nonwhite*
1940	3,115,000	282,000	1,148,000	25,000
1950	3,112,000	509,000	1,512,000	45,000
1960	2,713,000	838,000	2,588,000	82,000
1965	2,579,000	980,000	2,980,000	113,000
1970 (est.)	2,427,000	1,173,000	3,525,000	175,000
1980 (est.)	2,234,000	1,540,000	4,499,000	347,000

Source: U.S. Census and *Population Projections for the Chicago Standard Metro-politan Statistical Area and City of Chicago.* Population Research and Training Center, University of Chicago, 1964.

number of lower working-class areas reduced to 15, while there was a substantial gain, from 20 to 28, in lower-middle class areas. This reflected the decrease of unskilled workers in the labor force, and the increase in white-collar workers. But upper-middle class people were moving to the suburbs in large numbers, leaving the lower-middle class districts to carry the SER up a few points over 1940.

After 1950 the influx of working-class Negroes combined with the stepped-up flight of white-collar people to the suburbs to reduce the SER. The numbers of lower working-class and upper working-class community areas increased, while the numbers of middle-class areas decreased. Thus, since 1950, the City of Chicago has lost middle-class communities and gained working-class communities. Meanwhile, the suburbs have been gaining middle-class communities, though there is also a small number of working-class communities growing up in the suburbs.

To a child growing up in Chicago today this trend of population means that he is more segregated by family socioeconomic status than he would have been if he had grown up in the Chicago area about 1940. At the earlier time, a child in a Chicago school was more likely to have in his school or class children of quite different family background. At present, there are slum areas so large that a child living there never sees children from middle-class homes. The middle-class children for the most part live in the suburbs or on the edges of the city.

Since 1940, many of the working-class communities in Chicago have become largely Negro. In 1940, three of the 44 working-class communities of Chicago (categories C and D of Table 3) had 50 percent or more Negroes. In 1960, 14 of the 41 working-class communities had 50 percent or more Negroes, and eight of these 14 had 90 percent or more Negroes.

In spite of the relatively high degree of segregation of Negroes in Chicago, there is considerably more contact between white and Negro children now than there was in 1940. At that time the number of Negro children in the city and the schools was so much smaller than it is today that there simply was not much chance for many white children to meet Negro children. At the same time, there were many Negro children living a segregated life in the

South who later came to Chicago and other northern cities and came into contact with white children.

Thus there has been a growth of experience of Negro children with whites and of white children with Negroes, in spite of the degree of residential and school segregation that exists today in the northern cities.

The future of the city population

In Chicago, as in several other large cities, a continuation of present population trends might result in a growing, segregated Negro population in the city, together with a decrease in the white population, which will in turn grow rapidly in the suburbs. Furthermore, racial segregation may be accompanied by economic segregation, as high-income people continue to move to the suburbs and low-income people cluster in larger groups in the central city.

Both of these forms of segregation would be undesirable from the point of view of one who believes in democracy. They would also be undesirable from the point of view of one who is interested in the public services of the city—the schools, streets, police, fire department, and parks. With a population of reduced income, the city would find it more difficult to support the public services adequately.

Chicago's chief problem is this: how to keep and attract middle-income people to the central city and how to maintain a substantial white majority in the central city. Present trends lead to a decrease of middle-income people and a decrease of whites in the central city. The task is to change these trends.

Table 4 shows the facts of the recent past with respect to population. It also shows the future, *if present trends continue* without substantial change. But these trends simply represent the attitudes of people concerning desirable places to live. Such attitudes will be changed if the central city becomes a more desirable place in which to live and raise children.

The table shows two main things. First, the future growth of the area will be in the suburbs. The central city will probably not grow very much. We say "probably" because the central city could grow substantially if more people wanted to live in apartment buildings, which do not take as much space per person as do single family dwellings. Thus the central city does have some growth potential. Second, the proportion of Negroes will continue to increase, both in the central city and the suburbs. This is certain, but the rate of increase in the central city will depend upon the rate of increase in the suburbs, and no one knows with any certainty what the latter will be. The estimates of Table 4 are based on assumptions by population experts which are stated in Appendix 2.

The metropolitan area is the basic reality of modern urban life. It is a complex sociocivic organism. Its suburbs could not live without its central city, and its central city is a vital part of the whole. But the central city is sick. Its increasing proportion of low-income residents means it has decreasing tax potential. Its growing Negro population increases the size of the Negro ghettoes. The suburbs will suffer if the central city deteriorates, a fact which many suburban dwellers do not recognize. The cure for the ills of the central city may lie in urban renewal.

Urban renewal. Since World War II Chicago and other big cities have been working at the job of urban renewal, which has several aspects. *Physical* urban renewal consists of clearing out old and run-down buildings and replacing them with modern housing and parks and open spaces. The modern housing may be built by private enterprise and aimed to serve middle- and high-income people, or it may be built by the government and rented at below-cost rents to low-income people.

The middle-income housing can be a force for residential integration and is such a force in several sections of Chicago. Large apartment houses or large blocks of single-family dwellings have been built by private enterprise and sold or rented under policies which promote residential integration.

The low-rent public housing has tended to congregate Negroes in large masses in large housing projects. Although this was not a part of the original housing policy of the Chicago Housing Authority, it has worked out that way. In a few cases, Negro housing projects have been located in predominantly white areas, and the Negro children have therefore gone to integrated schools. Another type of public housing has been suggested but not used appreciably in Chicago. This consists of small one- to six-family units built on vacant or vacated lots in the midst of stable residential areas. If such units were constructed and rented to Negro as well as white families in predominantly white areas throughout the city, they would increase the amount of residential integration. Several predominantly white communities have requested such housing projects, but without success up to now.

Social urban renewal consists in taking advantage of physical urban renewal in a local community area under the leadership of local community organizations to create communities which are attractive to all kinds of people—rich and poor, Negro and white. One sees this concept in action in several areas of Chicago—in the near North Side, in the Hyde Park-Kenwood area, in the area between Congress Circle (the new University of Illinois site) and the Michael Reese-Prairie Shores-Lake Meadows-Illinois Institute of Technology area. These are areas of hope for the future of the central city. One also sees the results of physical urban renewal without social renewal in the great high-rise public housing projects on South State Street, where masses of low-income Negroes are jammed together in segregated areas that present modern concrete walls of resistance to integration.

Physical urban renewal is not an unmixed blessing. The future welfare of Chicago requires that the principles of social urban renewal be applied in future physical renewal.

The city and the school system

The future of the city is bound up with the program of the public schools in two basic ways.

First, the schools help to give the next generation and the present generation of citizens and workers the knowledge and the understanding and the attitudes that make them good, bad, or indifferent citizens, workers, and parents.

Second, the program of the schools is the greatest single factor in the decision of middle-income people to live in the central city or to live in the suburbs, and to live in one section of the city or another.

There are two opposite schools of thought among educators concerning the conduct of public schools in the big city. One may be called the "four-walls" school. The basic principle is to do the best possible job of educating every boy or girl who comes into the school, whoever he is, whatever his color, nationality, IQ or handicap. This means building good school buildings, equipping them well, and staffing them with well-trained teachers. At its best, it means being courteous and friendly to parents and to citizens who are interested in the schools, but making it quite clear to them that the schools are run by professionals who know their business and do not need advice from other people. It means making use of the cultural resources of the city—museums, theaters, orchestras, TV programs—under a system which guarantees the safety of the children and meets the convenience of the teachers.

It means keeping the schools "out of local politics." Staff appointments are to be made on the basis of merit alone, and promotion of staff on the basis of performance. It means a limited cooperation with other social institutions, public and private. The welfare and public aid and public health agencies are asked for help when the schools need it, but they cannot initiate school programs. Youth welfare and delinquency control agencies have their jobs to do, which meet and overlap the work of the schools. On this common ground the schools' administration must have full control of the use of school personnel and school facilities. In the area of training youth for employment, the school system will use the facilities of local business and industry for on-the-job training according to agreements worked out. Over-all policy for vocational education is the responsibility of the school administration under the Board of Education, and local business and industry are not closely related to policy determination in this area.

The four-walls type of school system works for efficiency and economy, and attempts to free the creative teacher to do the best possible job of teaching under good conditions. The community outside of the school is regarded as a source of complexity and of tension-arousal if the boundary between community and school is not clearly defined and respected.

The other school of thought may be called the "urban community" school. The educators who advocate this believe that the big city is in a crisis which has been in force for some years and will last for at least 10 years and requires the active participation of schools in the making and practicing of policy for social urban renewal. This big-city crisis is reflected in feelings of uncertainty and anxiety on the part of parents and citizens. There is danger of a collective failure of nerve which saps the vitality and flexibility of the city's efforts at urban renewal. Parents and citizens of middle income are tempted in this situation to escape to the suburbs, where life seems simpler and safer, especially for children.

The urban community school attempts to act constructively in this crisis by involving the parents and citizens in the decisions about school policy and practice. The educator accepts the frustration of working with people who themselves are confused and uncertain about the schools, believing that the only way to solve the problems of the city is to work on a give-and-take basis with citizens and community organizations.

The urban community school includes the intraschool program of the four-walls school, but differs at important points on the relation of the school to the community.

Those who take the urban community school point of view believe there is no viable alternative. They believe that the four-walls school actually causes some of the problems of the community through its rigid rules about attendance districts and about keeping the public away from the classroom. They believe that the schools by their policies and practices either attract or repel people in the local community. Under present conditions, the typical school system repels people whom the central city cannot afford to lose as citizens. They believe that the present trend toward economic and racial segregation in the metropolitan area will continue, and the central city will lose quality, unless the schools take a more active part in social urban renewal.

III

The City's Youth

In our description of the changing City of Chicago we have seen that the central city has been going down in socioeconomic level since 1950 while the suburbs have been going up.

This change in the adult population throws a great load on the schools, and has effectively lowered the average of school ability in the school population. For example, the average intelligence quotient (IQ) of the elementary school pupils of Chicago has decreased noticeably since 1958, as can be seen in Table 1. This table shows what percent of the total school enrollment was found at various IQ levels. In 1958 there were 53.5 percent of pupils above 100, which is the national average. The average IQ of Chicago elementary school pupils was about 101. Six years later there were 48.7 percent above 100, and the average IQ was just below 100. This is not an alarming decrease, but it shows that the changes in Chicago's adult population are reflected in changes in the school population.

This report will not discuss in any detail the pros and cons of the group intelligence tests as accurate measures of learning ability. They certainly are not completely satisfactory measuring instruments, and we do not take their results to be satisfactory as measures of the "real" learning ability of all children. Many children

Table 1
Intelligence levels of elementary school children in Chicago

IQ	Percent of pupils in grades 1-8 with indicated IQ	
	March 1958	March 1964
140+	.53	.27
130-139	2.04	.96
125-129	2.52	1.53
120-124	4.49	3.60
110-119	17.95	15.69
100-109	25.92	26.59
Below 100	46.55	51.36

Source: *Staff Study Report on Intermediate and Upper Grades of the Elementary Schools.* Chicago Public Schools, 1964.

of working-class families are brighter than the tests indicate. Yet these tests do predict quite well the achievement of children on tests of reading and arithmetic and other school subjects which require verbal intelligence.

The task before the Chicago schools and the schools of other big cities is to make up in some measure for the educational disadvantages which the children of low-income families suffer. Educators are convinced that the schools can compensate to some extent for these disadvantages.

Factors affecting a child's school achievement

There are four factors which determine the level of achievement of a child in school, assuming that he comes to school regularly and does his school work willingly. One of these is the inborn ability or disability of the child. Another is the kind of family life and family training he experiences. A third is the quality of the schooling he gets.

These three factors are roughly equal in importance. It would be hard to say exactly how much of the child's achievement in school is due to one or another of the factors, since they react on each other in a complex manner. A very good family experience can make a child with only average ability look good in school. A very good school can make a child with only average innate ability look good.

Since inborn ability and disability cannot be changed in a person after he is born, we tend to stress the importance of family background and of school training, both of which can be influenced. Some people believe that the family does more for the child's intellectual development than the school, while others stress the role of the school more than that of the family.

At the present time, especially in the big cities, the school people generally feel that they are getting more than their fair share of the blame for unsatisfactory school work by children whose families are mainly to blame. On the other hand, it is natural for parents to blame the schools when they feel that their children are not doing as well as they should or could.

How much may we expect of the schools? It is well known that children of low-income families *on the average* do poorer work in school than children of middle- and high-income families. This might conceivably be due to the low-income parents passing on inferior mental ability biologically to their offspring. But scholars who have studied inheritance of ability doubt this. They doubt that there is any difference in innate potential intelligence in children born in poor families and children born in rich families. They doubt that there is any difference in the innate potential intelligence of Negro children and white children and Chinese and Japanese and Indian children. There is abundant scientific evidence that infants from poverty-stricken parents and even from dull parents develop into adults with average or superior intelligence if they are taken from their true parents and reared by educated people.

There are inborn or biological differences of intelligence, of course, but these are between individuals, not between large social or racial groups. No doubt there are inborn differences of potential intelligence among the children of a family; and every class of 30 children has 30 different levels of inborn intellectual potential.

The schools receive children with a wide variety of inborn intelligence and also with a variety of family experience which helps or hinders school learning. Let us call these factors A and B, respectively. The school provides factor C, a program of teaching. When element A or B is weak, element C may be used as an *opportunity factor* to make up for the weakness. If the school factor is very strong, it may compensate in whole or in part for the weak family factor. Hence we speak sometimes of *compensatory* education for children from poor families. In this report we shall generally speak of *opportunity* education rather than compensatory education, since the school is really providing extra opportunity for children whose families or whose biological handicaps give them less opportunity than the average child receives.

A fourth factor enters into a child's school achievement after about the age of 10. This, factor D, is the self-concept or aspiration of the pupil. He has it in his power to determine how hard he shall work, and toward what goals, and what his attitude toward school will be. Factor D is influenced by the B and C factors. Thus, effective education consists of cooperation of the family and the school and eventually of the child to make the most of his potential.

The schools have taken increasing responsibility, in recent years, for children handicapped in factor A, the biological factor. They provide special education at extra expense for children who are mentally handicapped or are physically handicapped with blindness or deafness, or are crippled. This is opportunity education, or compensatory education.

The schools are just now learning to use special methods with children who are handicapped in the family background factor, B. The public is just now learning to support opportunity education for these children, as it has already done for children with biological handicaps.

We may expect the schools to pay special attention to children with a variety of learning handicaps. At the same time we must expect children to show the effects of these handicaps, and we must not blame the schools for these handicaps. If a child is doing poorly, this is not necessarily a sign that the school is failing with him. It is a sign that the school should give him special help. If large groups of children in certain sections of the city are doing poorly, again this does not necessarily mean that the schools are doing a poor job. It may mean that the schools need more money and creative methods to give these children special help.

To repeat, we should *not* expect the schools to bring children of low socioeconomic groups up to the level of school achievement of children of high socioeconomic groups. Schools cannot compensate completely for handicaps in family training and experience, and low socioeconomic status means on the average that the family factor will be low. However, we should expect the schools to give extra opportunity to children of low socioeconomic status.

In order to understand more clearly what we may expect of the schools in Chicago, we should look at some of the records of school achievement and of learning ability to be found in various Chicago schools.

VARIATIONS
IN EDUCATIONAL ACHIEVEMENT

From our consideration of the factors which enter into educational performance, we should expect a good deal of difference between children of different family backgrounds. We will now look at some of these differences.

Socioeconomic levels and school achievement

The differences among the 21 school districts of Chicago are largely socioeconomic in character, and there are parallel differences in school achievement. The school districts tend to consist of people who are somewhat similar to one another in occupation, education and income. Figure 1 is a map on which the districts are shown. Districts 1, 2, 4, 17, and 18 had the highest median family income in 1960. These districts are on the north, northwest, and south edges of the city. They are closest to the suburbs in style of life. At the other extreme are Districts 9, 11, 13, 19, and 21, all "inner-city" districts.

Another socioeconomic characteristic with data available from the census is median level of education of adults. Districts 2, 14, 16, 17, and 18 are the top five, with 6, 8, 9, 13, and 19 at the bottom. A third characteristic of socioeconomic nature is the occupational level of adults. These three are closely interrelated.

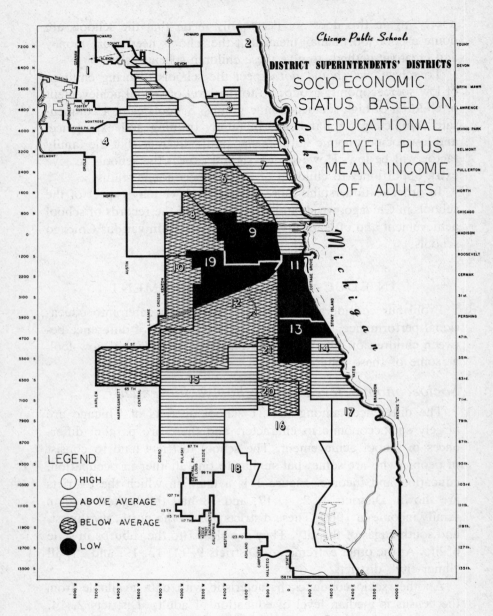

Figure 1
School districts according
to socioeconomic status

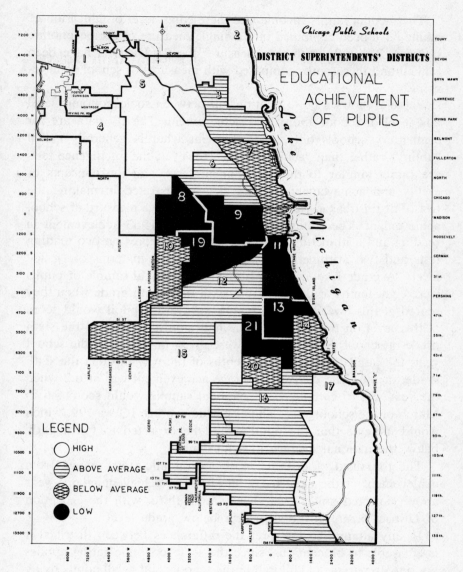

Figure 2
School districts according to achievement
of elementary school pupils.
Sixth-grade reading and arithmetic;
first-grade reading readiness

The median family income and the median level of education of adults have been combined into a single measure of socioeconomic status in Table 2. With this measure[1] the 21 Districts have been ranked and these ranks compared with measures of school achievement.

Table 2 shows a close relationship between socioeconomic level and level of school ability and achievement. The IQ data are for elementary schools only, and represent what is generally called "ability" rather than "achievement." However, the intelligence tests are rather similar to the achievement tests, and the concepts of ability and achievement are not clearly separated in making the tests. For this reason we will treat IQ as largely a measure of school achievement. The column headed "Grade 6, 1963 achievement in reading and arithmetic" is an average of the scores on two reading tests and two arithmetic tests and is reported in terms of "grade level." A grade level of 6.8 means that a national sample of pupils were eight-tenths of the way from sixth to seventh grade when they scored at this level on the tests. Or, an average pupil would score at this level on the tests when he had almost completed the sixth grade of school. Since the tests were given in March of the school year, the pupils were about six-tenths of the way through the sixth grade, or 6.6. The city-wide average achievement was at 6.2 when the year was .6 completed. A national sample would score 6.6 in March of the school year. The city-wide average IQ was 99, which would indicate that the pupils could be expected to fall slightly below the national average in achievement.

The top third of districts in socioeconomic status range from achievement at the expected grade level to achievement one year above expected grade level. The bottom third, with the exception of District 6, are all about a year below grade level.

In any attempt to interpret the differences between districts, it is advisable to be cautious, since the socioeconomic rating applies not only to parents of children in the schools, but to all adults living in the district. If the parents of children attending the public schools differ in some important socioeconomic way from the other adults

---

[1]*Compensatory Education*, Chapter 2. Staff Study Report, Chicago Public Schools, 1964.

Table 2
Socioeconomic status, school achievement, and race by school districts

Rank order in SE status District no.	IQ	Grade 6, 1963 achievement in reading & arith., grade level	Grade 1, 1963 reading readiness, % average or above	October 1963 % of elementary pupils Negro
2	111	7.5	75	0
18	104	6.8	74	37
1	112	7.8	89	0
17	108	7.4	74	7
16	101	6.4	67	77
4	107	7.1	78	1
3	107	6.8	74	0
14[1]	95	5.8	48	85
7[2]	94	5.8	44	48
5	109	7.2	85	0
15	109	7.2	79	16
10	96	6.0	48	67
20	93	5.7	47	100
12	103	6.7	65	1
6	99	6.3	52	69
21	91	5.5	41	92
8	89	5.4	33	81
11	92	5.5	45	96
19	93	5.6	45	61
13	90	5.5	42	100
9	90	5.3	34	81
City wide	99	6.2	55	

[1]District contains University of Chicago, with many children going to the University School (private).
[2]District includes North Side "Gold Coast," with many children in private schools.

in the district, then the district rating is not a good indication of what might be expected of the public school pupils. At present, almost half of the white children of Chicago attend Catholic parochial schools. Catholic population is especially heavy in Districts 4, 5, 12, 15, and 17. In District 17 there is a large Catholic working-class population and also a large Jewish middle-class population. The Jewish children mainly go to public schools while the Catholic children divide between parochial and public schools. Therefore the socioeconomic rating of District 17 may be lower than it would be if parents of public school children alone were counted.

Reading readiness. The ratings for reading readiness also show a close relation to socioeconomic level. This test, given at the beginning of the first grade, helps the teacher to know what to expect of her pupils as they learn to read. Those who score average or above on the test may be expected to learn to read during the first grade, if they are not already reading when they come to the first grade. In September of 1963, 55 percent of Chicago first graders scored average or above. The remaining 45 percent are expected to have difficulty in first-grade work. They should be given a good deal of individualized help. Most of them will fail to pass the first grade, unless they are promoted automatically and taught to read in the second grade.

In District 1, only 11 percent of first graders are in the "difficult" group. They are likely to get a good deal of individualized help, since they are few enough that the teacher can pay attention to them. At the other extreme, Districts 8 and 9 have two-thirds of their first graders in the "difficult" group. Their teachers need extra help if these children are to get much individualized attention.

Emergence of Negro middle-class schools. In the top third of the districts, there are two with substantial numbers of Negroes. District 16 has 77 percent of Negro pupils in the public elementary schools while District 18 has 37 percent. The advantages associated with higher socioeconomic status are seen when the records of Districts 16 and 18 are compared with the districts in the bottom third which have high proportions of Negro pupils. As Negro parents move up the economic ladder, the educational achievement of their children will increase.

Achievement in contrasting high schools

To illustrate further the variations of school achievement and their relation to socioeconomic status, the data in Table 3 have been collected and organized to compare and contrast two very different Chicago high schools. In tests given to 11th graders, these were the top and bottom schools.

School B is in a section of the city with the highest socioeconomic ratings on occupation, income, and education of adults. School A is in the lowest section of the city. Table 3 shows the ages of the students in each of the four high school grades. The underlined figures indicate the age groups which are normal. For instance, a child who entered school at the age of 6 would be between 13 years, 9 months and 14 years, 8 months at the beginning of the ninth grade if he had made average progress, never failing a grade and never "skipping" a grade. School B has more than half of its students just at the "normal" age, and about 25 percent over-age. But School A has 61 percent of its ninth graders over-age, and 55 percent of its 12th graders. School A has only a fourth as many 12th graders as it has ninth graders. At least half of its entering ninth graders drop out of school within the first two years. School B has very few drop-outs. (The ninth grade is larger than it was two or three years ago, and thus the apparent drop-out figures are exaggerated.)

The two schools show a great contrast in the proportion of pupils in the various "tracks" of the program. School A has 4 tracks or ability groupings, called Basic, Essential, Regular, and Honors. School B does not have the lowest, or Basic, track.

The two schools contrast sharply in their offerings of Basic, Essential, and Honors courses. Students with reading or arithmetic scores below a grade level of 5.9 are placed in "basic" courses. These pupils are three years retarded or more, since they are in the ninth grade or above. Furthermore, many of them are over-age, and therefore even further retarded. Those with a reading or arithmetic score between grade level 5.9 and 7.9 are placed in "essential" courses. They are from one to two years retarded if they are in the ninth grade.

School A has 65 percent of its ninth graders in Basic or Essential English, and 75 percent in Basic or Essential Mathematics. By the

Table 3

Comparison of two contrasting high schools
(Schools A and B)

	Grade 9		Grade 10		Grade 11		Grade 12	
	A	B	A	B	A	B	A	B
Age								

Age	A	B	A	B	A	B	A	B
Percentage distribution of ages								
11-9 to 12-8	2	0						
12-9 to 13-8	6	16	0	0				
13-9 to 14-8	31	53	2	10	0	0		
14-9 to 15-8	39	23	25	58	4	14	0	0
15-9 to 16-8	18	7	43	23	35	56	10	14
16-9 to 17-8	3	1	24	7	38	28	35	69
17-9 to 18-8	1	0	5	2	18	2	38	16
18-9 to 19-8			1	0	4	0	15	1
19-9 & over								
Number	2,039	668	1,246	549	676	524	503	443

Percentage enrollments in Basic, Essential, and Honors courses

Basic course	A	B	A	B	A	B	A	B
English	35	0	23	0	—	—	—	—
Mathematics	19	0	0	0	—	—	—	—

Essential course	A	B	A	B	A	B	A	B
English	30	12	36	0	42	0	31	0
Mathematics	56	14	44	0	—	—	—	—

Honors course	A	B	A	B	A	B	A	B
English	1	12	2	5	4	5	7	6
Mathematics	2	12	0	23	0	10	0	18

sophomore year there have been many drop-outs, but Basic and Essential English still enroll 59 percent of the students. An Essential Mathematics course continues with 44 percent of second year students. Essential English is continued throughout the four years, with 31 percent of the seniors in it.

In contrast, School B has nobody in Basic English or Mathematics, but has 12 and 14 percent of ninth graders in Essential English and Mathematics, respectively. After the ninth grade there are no Essential or Basic courses.

Honors courses enroll 12 percent of ninth graders in School B, in English and in mathematics, and they continue through all four years. But School A has only 1 percent of ninth graders in English Honors, and 2 percent in Mathematics Honors. Mathematics Honors does not continue, but English Honors continues, getting up to 7 percent of the senior class.

School A has 15 classes in foreign language, while School B (with a lower enrollment) has 41. School A has a one-semester course in trigonometry for 11th grade students, and nothing beyond that, while School B has honors courses in advanced mathematics, analytical geometry, and calculus for 11th and 12th graders.

There are, in School A, about 4 percent of 11th and 12th graders who are in the top quarter of all students in the city in ability and achievement test scores. In School B, 63 percent are in the top quarter. Such a vast difference in the abilities and achievement of pupils means that the program of School B is probably better and richer for bright students. One might argue that the program of School A can be expected to be better for slow students. At least, it offers that possibility.

Both of these schools have unusually good faculties in terms of experience and interest in their work. The principal of School A has energy and insight and determination. Though this is his first year at this school, he has developed a plan for intensified teaching of Basic English which appears to be working well. He has also established biweekly meetings with new teachers to help them learn to teach in this kind of school.

Young people in Chicago are a very diverse group. By the time they get to high school, their abilities, their scholastic knowledge, and their expectations in life are so widely different that those who go to one school may have to be taught in ways that would not work in another school.

Achievement in contrasting elementary schools

The influence of family background on a child's school performance is seen when we examine closely the test results in relation to the age distribution of children in any two schools of differing family circumstances. This can be done by studying Table 4 on pages 46-49, where the facts are presented for the sixth graders from 12 schools.

This rather complicated set of tables is presented here because careful study of it will explain many of the problems which beset the Chicago schools.

The 12 schools were chosen to represent a wide range of local neighborhoods. For each school a chart was made of the reading levels of the sixth-grade pupils in relation to their ages. In Table 4 one can see at a glance how many pupils are advanced or retarded in reading for the sixth grade, and how many are over-age and under-age. One can also see how many are within the usual age range and reading levels for sixth graders. The usual age range for pupils in the sixth grade is from 11 to 12, in March, when the tests were given. For the "normal" reading level we have taken arbitrarily a two-year range, from 5.5 to 7.4. That means that a child is reading at a level of comprehension which is between the average child halfway through the fifth grade and the average child halfway through the seventh grade.

It is well known to teachers, though not all parents know it, that only a small fraction of pupils are reading at their "normal" grade level for their age. For example, School I has 36 percent, or 13 out of 36 pupils who are reading at the appropriate grade level and at the same time are at the normal age level for sixth graders. This is the highest proportion among the 12 schools. School D and School F have only 10 percent at the appropriate grade and age levels.

Some of the relevant facts about the 12 schools are given in Table 5, page 50. The median IQ ranges from 88 to 120. The percent of pupils under-age ranges from 0 to 28, while the percent who are over-age ranges from 8 to 74.

School A is located in an upper-income area. The vast majority of sixth-grade pupils are reading above the seventh-grade level, and 15 out of 112 pupils are reading at the level of high school seniors. They may be contrasted with School B, which stands only a mile or so from School A but in a neighborhood which has recently filled with white migrants to the city from the rural South. The majority of sixth-grade pupils in School B are reading below the fifth-grade level and are also over-age.

School C is located in a neighborhood of middle-income professional and business people, about half of them white and half Negro. They like the idea of integration, and work well with an outstanding faculty and principal. The achievement pattern of the sixth grade is very similar to that of School A, most children reading above their age level.

Schools F and H are very similar in achievement, though one is all-white and the other all-Negro. Both have a majority of sixth-grade pupils over-age and reading below the sixth-grade level. Both are located in areas of high transiency and low-income level.

The problem of judging quality of teaching. The facts from these 12 schools illustrate graphically the difficulty of making a judgment about the quality of teaching from test data and age data alone. Consider Schools A and D, for example. Both have a high proportion of pupils reading above their expected levels. Both have pupils with high-average intelligence quotients. Both are in economically favored neighborhoods. School D has 28 percent under-age while A has 7 percent under-age. Probably this fact is not related to quality of teaching, but to different policies of the schools worked out in relation to the desires of the parents. School A has only 5 percent reading below normal, whereas School D has 24 percent in this category. But the neighborhood of School D has a few families of low socioeconomic status, while School A has a neighborhood of solid middle-class families.

The three schools with the highest proportion of over-age pupils are all in low socioeconomic neighborhoods, but two are practically all-white and the other is practically all-Negro. School C which is 50 percent Negro is very similar in achievement and age distribution to School K, which is all-white. Both schools are in middle-class neighborhoods.

Table 4
Chronological age and reading level in typical sixth grades

Ages	Below 3.4	3.5–4.4	4.5–5.4	5.5–7.4	7.5–8.4	8.5–9.4	9.5–10.4	10.5–11.4	11.5 +	Total
School A										
Below 10:11				1		1	1	5		8
11:0–11:5				9	4	4	2	3	4	26
11:6–11:11			3	19	9	5	8	14	11	69
12:0–12.5			2	3			1			6
12:6–12:11				1	2					3
13:0–13:5										
13:6 & above										
Total			5	33	15	10	12	22	15	112
School B										
Below 10:11		1			1					2
11:0–11:5		1	2	4	3					10
11:6–11:11	1	8	6	12	2	1	2	3	3	38
12:0–12.5	4	3	6	8	1				1	23
12:6–12:11		9	2	5	2					18
13:0–13:5	1	5	3	2						11
13:6 & above	2	2	1	1						6
Total	8	29	20	32	9	1	2	3	4	108
School C										
Below 10:11							1			1
11:0–11:5				2	3	1	1	3	2	12
11:6–11:11		2	2	5	3	1	1		1	15
12:0–12.5			2			1	1	1		5
12:6–12:11			2							2
13:0–13:5				1						1
13:6 & above										
Total		2	6	8	6	3	4	4	3	36

	Reading level									
	Below 3.4	3.5 4.4	4.5 5.4	5.5 7.4	7.5 8.4	8.5 9.4	9.5 10.4	10.5 11.4	11.5 +	Total
School D Ages										
Below 10:11			1	6	3	4	4	8	2	28
11:0-11:5			2	3	3	3	3	2	2	18
11:6-11:11		3	1	7	2	5	1	5	2	26
12:0-12:5	1	2	1	7	1		2		1	15
12:6-12:11		8		1						9
13:0-13:5	1	1	1							3
13:6 & above	2									2
Total	4	14	6	24	9	12	10	15	7	101
School E Ages										
Below 10:11								1		1
11:0-11:5				4	1	2				7
11:6-11:11		5	2	6	1		1		2	17
12:0-12:5			3	2						5
12:6-12:11		1		1						2
13:0-13:5			1	2		1				4
13:6 & above										
Total		6	6	15	2	3	1	1	2	36
School F Ages										
Below 10:11				1						1
11:0-11:5			4	3		1				8
11:6-11:11		4	3	6		1		1		15
12:0-12:5	1	9	9	8						27
12:6-12:11	4	6	5	4				1		20
13:0-13:5	5	6		2						13
13:6 & above	1	5	2	1						9
Total	11	30	23	25		2		2		93

Table 4 continued
Chronological age and reading level in typical sixth grades

Reading level

	Below 3.4	3.5 4.4	4.5 5.4	5.5 7.4	7.5 8.4	8.5 9.4	9.5 10.4	10.5 11.4	11.5 +	Total
School G Ages										
Below 10:11			1							1
11:0-11:5			1	3		2	1		1	8
11:6-11:11		2	1	14	1			1		19
12:0-12:5	1	2	3	7	2	2	1			18
12:6-12:11	2	2	3	7			2		1	17
13:0-13:5	1	4	3	2						10
13:6 & above		3	2	2						7
Total	4	13	14	35	3	4	4	1	2	80
School H Ages										
Below 10:11										
11:0-11:5				3						3
11:6-11:11				3						3
12:0-12:5			3	5	2					10
12:6-12:11	1	2	2	4	2					11
13:0-13:5	1	5	1	1						8
13:6 & above	1	1		3						5
Total	3	8	6	19	4					40
School I Ages										
Below 10:11					1					1
11:0-11:5		1		6				1		8
11:6-11:11				7	2			1		10
12:0-12:5		2	1	3	1	1	1	1		10
12:6-12:11		1	2	2						5
13:0-13:5		1	1							2
13:6 & above										
Total		5	4	18	4	1	1	3		36

	Reading level									
	Below 3.4	3.5 4.4	4.5 5.4	5.5 7.4	7.5 8.4	8.5 9.4	9.5 10.4	10.5 11.4	11.5 +	Total
School J Ages										
Below 10:11										
11:0-11:5			1	3	1					5
11:6-11:11		3	9	9	1	1				23
12:0-12:5	1	5	4	4						14
12:6-12:11	2	4	4	1						11
13:0-13:5	3	2								5
13:6 & above		1								1
Total	6	15	18	17	2	1				59
School K Ages										
Below 10:11										
11:0-11:5			1	1	1	1	2	1		7
11:6-11:11		2	1	13	4	1	5	1	2	29
12:0-12:5				4	3	1				8
12:6-12:11			1	1			1	1		4
13:0-13:5					1	1				2
13:6 & above				1		1				2
Total		2	3	20	9	5	8	3	2	52
School L Ages										
Below 10:11				2	5	2	1	2		12
11:0-11:5		1	2	2	3	5	2	2	2	19
11:6-11:11		1	1	10	1	4	3	5	2	27
12:0-12:5				6	2	1	1	1		11
12:6-12:11		2	1	1						4
13:0-13:5				1						1
13:6 & above										
Total		4	4	22	11	12	7	10	4	74

Table 5
Characteristics of selected sixth grades

School	Median IQ	% at age & reading level for Grade 6	% under-age	% over-age	% Negro
A	120	25	7	8	0
B	95	15	2	53	0
C	114	20	3	23	50
D	115	10	28	29	50
E	103	23	3	31	100
F	88	10	1	74	99
G	98	23	1	65	2
H	96	15	0	71	2
I	99	36	3	47	100
J	93	20	0	53	80
K	111	28	0	31	0
L	112	16	16	22	40

Schools obviously in need of opportunity or compensatory programs are B, F, G, H, I, and J. They are all in neighborhoods of low income, and low parental education. Three are all-Negro schools, and three are all-white.

Judgments of quality of teaching can be made for these schools, but not on the basis of test results alone. One would have to observe the school; talk with teachers, principal, and parents; look at the teaching materials used. One would have to take account of the family backgrounds of the pupils. One would have to decide whether the school has realistically related itself to what the children bring to school in the way of family training and expectations. One would have to ask whether Schools A, C, and D are providing materials which challenge children from homes of high educational level and aspirations. At the same time one would have to ask whether Schools B, F, G, H, I, and J have systematically supplemented the low levels of family education by working with pupils after school, by helping parents to learn how to encourage the children in their school work, by adapting curriculum materials to the limited experience of these children.

Differences among districts in intelligence quotient

The differences among schools are most closely related to differences of socioeconomic level in the city. These socioeconomic differences are seen when school districts are compared, as has already been noted. Consequently, the school districts show differences of intelligence as measured by intelligence tests.

This is shown clearly in Table 6, where the intelligence quotients of elementary school pupils are collected in three broad groups. An IQ below 90 means that a child will have to work hard to get along in school, and cannot expect to get high grades in competition with average children who are working equally hard. In the country as a whole, about 23 percent of children have IQ's below 90, about 23 percent are above 110, and 54 percent are between 90 and 110. The Chicago elementary schools are slightly below the national average.

An IQ above 110 means that a child can do quite well in school if he exerts himself. He should succeed in college, if he wants to do so. In fact, many students with IQ's of 100 do succeed in an average college if they work hard.

Table 6 shows that about a third of the school districts have between half and a third of their pupils in the superior group, or the group above 110. Another third have between half and a third of their pupils in the slow group, or the group below 90. All districts have between 45 and 55 percent of pupils in the middle or average range of ability.

Districts A and B contrast strikingly with districts R, S, T, and U. The high-level districts have very few pupils in the slow group, while the low-level districts have very few pupils in the superior group. It would seem obvious that the school programs in these contrasting districts should be quite different.

Before commenting on the meanings of the IQ differences, we shall say once more that the IQ cannot be taken as a reliable measure of the learning ability of many of the children in the districts with

Table 6
How the districts differ in IQ

*Percentages of elementary school pupils
at various IQ levels, 1964*

District	Below 90	90-110	Above 110
A	5.9	45.6	48.5
B	8.5	46.5	45.0
C	8.8	49.3	41.9
D	10.7	47.9	41.4
E	11.4	50.0	38.6
F	13.1	50.6	36.3
G	12.7	52.6	34.7
H	17.1	50.0	32.9
I	19.3	54.4	26.3
J	22.8	52.5	24.7
K	29.2	50.1	20.7
L	24.2	57.6	18.2
M	33.2	53.8	13.0
N	32.0	55.4	12.6
O	33.2	56.0	10.8
P	34.5	55.4	10.1
Q	40.8	49.3	9.9
R	36.8	54.9	8.3
S	39.3	52.9	7.8
T	44.5	47.9	7.6
U	42.5	51.1	6.4
Total	26.3	51.6	22.1

Source: *Staff Study Report on Intermediate and Upper Grades of the Elementary Schools.* Chicago Public Schools, 1964, Table 4.

low socioeconomic status. It is more nearly a measure of what the children have learned so far. One of the goals of the schools in the poor areas of the city is to raise the IQ's of children, and that is what compensatory or opportunity education attempts to do. However, it is not an easy matter.

The significance of the IQ in the low-scoring districts

In the low-scoring districts, the family background factor is weak for many children. Parents do not read to their children very often, or set an example of reading. Their conversation uses a limited supply of words, and consequently the children's vocabularies are limited. There is a good deal of useful research which shows that children from many low-income families suffer an intellectual deprivation which puts them at a severe disadvantage when they come to school.

This does not mean that the parents do not love their children as much as do parents with higher income. Also, some low-income parents give their children the same kinds of intellectual stimulation that middle-class parents give. But *on the average* the children of families of low socioeconomic status are handicapped in the family background factor. The low IQ scores simply reflect this fact.

Therefore the schools are called upon to increase the opportunity factor in the districts of low IQ. As they succeed, the IQ will rise.

There is nothing easy about establishing a program of opportunity education for underprivileged children. The facts given in this chapter should help a careful reader to understand the schools' problems better, and also to see why teachers and school administrators often feel that the public expects the impossible from the schools.

SCHOOL ENROLLMENTS AND PROJECTIONS

School enrollments have gone through an interesting history since 1930. In that year the total enrollment of the Chicago Public Schools was 470,000, almost exactly the same as in 1960. In the 30 years between, enrollments were less, due to the low birth rates of the depression decade of the 1930's. It was not until the high

Table 7

School enrollments in the City of Chicago, 1930-63

(Age 5 *through* 18)

	1930	1940	1950	1960	1963
Total Chicago school enrollment[1]	630,000	567,000	512,000†	685,000	740,000*
White and other	596,000	517,000	436,000	497,000	490,000*
Negro	34,000	50,000	77,000	189,000	250,000*
Chicago Public Schools[2]	470,000	420,000	350,000	476,000	536,000
White and other	440,000*	374,000*	276,000*	290,000*	286,000
Negro	30,000*	46,000*	74,000*	186,000*	250,000
Chicago Catholic Schools[3]	157,000	143,000	184,000	232,000	234,000

[1]Data from the United States Census, in the age group 5 through 18.
[2]Data from the Chicago Public Schools.
[3]Data from the Catholic School Board of Chicago.
*Estimated by the author.
†Kindergarten pupils were under-enumerated in 1950.

Note: Other private schools are not included, and should make up the difference between the sum of the public and Catholic school enrollment on the one hand and the total on the other. There are currently about 20,000 pupils in other private schools. When this number is added to the public and Catholic school enrollments, the reported enrollments exceed the census figures. One source of discrepancy is the fact that the enrollments reported by the schools contain some pupils over 18.

birth rates following World War II had been in effect for about 13 years that school enrollments reached the predepression high.

Table 7 shows these facts, as well as the facts about the numbers of Negro pupils in the schools. This number became noticeable after World War I, which brought the first large group of Negro workers to Chicago. It reached 34,000 about 1930 and then rose slowly during the 1930 decade, when there was little Negro in-migration. During and after World War II the number

Table 8
School age population
of Chicago and suburban area

| | City of Chicago | | Suburban Ring | | Grand Total |
	White	Nonwhite	White	Nonwhite	
1950					
5-14 years	389,000	72,000	229,000	6,600	697,000
15-19 years	172,000	31,000	94,000	3,100	300,000
1960					
5-14 years	409,000	175,000	532,000	17,000	1,133,000
15-19 years	172,000	51,000	177,000	5,600	405,000
1965					
5-14 years	398,000	220,000	607,000	25,000	1,250,000
15-19 years	179,000	82,000	252,000	10,000	523,000
1970					
5-14 years	384,000	303,000	744,000	35,000*	1,466,000
15-19 years	175,000	115,000	333,000	14,000*	637,000
1980					
5-14 years	344,000	340,000	828,000	69,000*	1,581,000
15-19 years	164,000	165,000	393,000	29,000*	751,000

*Gross estimates by the author.
Source: U.S. Census and *Population Projections for the Chicago Standard Metropolitan Statistical Area and City of Chicago*. Population Research and Training Center, University of Chicago, 1964. See Supplement G for statement of assumptions on which the projections are based.

of Negro pupils increased, with a gain of 110,000 during the 1950-60 decade. By 1965 the numbers of Negro and white pupils in the public schools will be about equal, and thereafter the number of Negro pupils will increase while the number of white pupils decreases, unless present trends are changed by a determined effort to improve the quality of schools and achieve racial balance to keep and attract white families in the central city who would otherwise live in the suburbs.

Total school enrollments are expected to increase only slightly, as can be seen in Table 8, which is based on the work of population experts. The increase will be about 2 percent a year, from 1964 to 1970, after which enrollments will level off, and even decrease slightly in the elementary schools. Secondary school enrollments will account for much of the increase from now on, due to improved holding power for youth beyond the age of 15. To balance this effect at least partially, the improved school performance which can be hoped for will reduce the amount of failure and grade-repeating, and thus reduce enrollment by means of the more rapid progress of pupils through school.

In general, then, the cost of public schools will not rise very much due to increased school enrollments, as it has during the past 10 years in which the increase in elementary and high school enrollments has been 37 percent, or 150,000 in numbers. More money for schools can be used for improving the *quality* of education, since not so much will be needed for increased *quantity*.

Furthermore, the shortages of elementary school teachers which plagued Chicago and other big cities during the 1950's are now pretty well past. The total number of elementary school teachers will not increase very much, though there will have to be an active program of recruiting and training new teachers to take the places of those who leave the profession.

The greatest need currently is for more high school teachers, due to the recent increases of high school enrollment. This need will continue through the next three or four years.

Moreover, the new "crop" of young adults will suddenly become much greater in 1969 and subsequent years, as the 1947 increase in birth rate takes effect. This will create a larger reservoir of young men and women from which to recruit new teachers.

I V

Education of the Socially Disadvantaged

The most important challenge facing the City of Chicago as it considers the program of public education is the challenge to provide adequately for the education of socially disadvantaged children.

The term "socially disadvantaged" is not altogether satisfactory, but it will serve if we can agree at the beginning that it is being used as a convenient abbreviation to cover a multitude of factors affecting many of the children in our city schools. These factors include low educational level of the parents, low family income, and little or no experience of the wider community outside the rural or city slum environment in which the child has lived. Despite the limitation in varieties of experience, these children have been subjected to much moving from place to place, and the older ones have been in many different schools. Poor housing, poor health conditions, and broken or incomplete families are among the conditions affecting these children to a much greater than average degree. Such socially disadvantaged children may be white or Negro, but if they are Negro they are also affected by the whole complex of problems and attitudes relating to race.

As seen by the teachers, these children come to school pitifully unready for the usual school experiences, even at the kindergarten level. Teachers remark that some don't know their own names and have never held a pencil. Their speech is so different from that of the teachers and the primer that they almost have a new language to learn. They have had little practice in discriminating sounds, colors, or shapes, part of the everyday experience of the middle-class preschool child, whose family supplies educational toys and endless explanations.

As seen by the sociologist, these children and their families have a culture, but it is not attuned to the school nor is the school attuned to it. By the time the child is admitted to school, nearly 6 years old in many cases, he may already have absorbed a climate of low expectations, unfavorable opinions about himself, and a concept of the school as an alien and unfriendly place. The school itself is seldom well prepared to counteract this attitude or to understand the approach of the disadvantaged child to school situations.

Recent research is placing more and more emphasis on the actual learning disadvantages suffered by these children, as compared to middle-class children, because of the differences in home environment. For example, Benjamin Bloom[1] lists four specific factors which handicap children in a deprived environment, compared with children in what he terms an "abundant" environment.

1. Poor speech habits and language patterns in the home discourage language development and restrict the number and variety of words which the child recognizes; this contributes to lower scores on IQ tests and lower school achievement, especially in reading.

2. Families have less time, opportunity, or know-how to take their children on expeditions to zoos, museums, stores, or different neighborhoods; the children also have fewer indirect experiences with the world around them through books, pictures, films, etc. Such experiences not only increase verbal facility, but help in making distinctions, comparing objects, ideas, etc., all important not only for IQ tests but for learning itself.

3. Children in these "disadvantaged" homes have fewer opportunities for solving problems or for thinking about a variety of issues, as compared with children in more abundant environments. Their parents do not have the habit of encouraging children to ask questions or to think things out for themselves.

---

[1]Benjamin S. Bloom, *Stability and Change in Human Characteristics* (New York: John Wiley and Sons, Inc., 1964), p. 77.

4. There is less interaction generally between adults and children. Discipline tends to be authoritarian, and the "good" child is quiet and out of the way. This, too, limits the background of experience and language which the child brings to school.

Basil Bernstein[2] has also studied the differences in language and sentence structure between lower- and middle-class groups and has concluded that these patterns affect the way children think and the ways in which they set about solving problems. All these differences are likely to be seen by teachers as evidences of slowness or even stupidity.

Contrary to popular notions, people who are culturally deprived do place a high value on education, but they lack confidence and know-how in how to go about getting one. In the case of working-class Negro families, the generally wary lower-class attitudes toward school authorities may be further reinforced by resentment and frustration arising from racial problems.

To deal successfully with these children, educating them for economic, social, and civic competence, the school must take these factors into account. The present school program is not adequate to do the job. Although there are shining exceptions, the evidence shows very clearly that, in districts serving deprived children, achievement levels are as much as two or three years below national norms, 30 to 40 percent of the children are over-age for their grade placement,[3] and, when the age of 16 is reached, the number of dropouts is over 50 percent.

It hardly seems necessary to review here the great stake that the city, the state, and the nation have in developing a program that will enable many more of these culturally deprived children to succeed in school. The future of democracy depends on our ability to do this. Even in the narrowest economic sense, we need the human resources that these children represent. Furthermore, if we cannot find ways to educate them for economic and social competence, we will pay several times over in the future in costs of unemployment,

---

[2]Basil Bernstein, "Social Class, Linguistic Codes and Grammatical Elements," *Language and Speech,* October-December, 1962. "Elaborated and Restricted Codes: Their Origins and Some Consequences," *American Anthropologist,* in press, 1964.
[3]Staff Report, *Compensatory Education,* Table 3. Chicago Public Schools, 1964, p. 6.

dependency, delinquency, and crime. Lack of money is accepted too easily, even by those closest to the situation, as a reason for not doing even those things which are already known to bring substantial results. The Chicago Board of Education in 1963 approved a plan for a 1964 saturation program in one district in which the great majority of children are "culturally deprived." But when it came to allocating funds for the 1964 budget, the "regular" expenses of the school program required all available funds and the saturation program was sacrificed. The Board of Education cannot spend monies it does not have. But it can shout from the housetops that such monies must be provided, and that this kind of "economy" is the worst form of waste. Even in the short run, in this district money well beyond the average will go for children repeating grades when they might not have failed if the saturation program had gone into effect.

The responsibility for this situation, of course, does not belong to the Board of Education alone, but to citizens and leadership at every level from which greater resources could come—the local taxpayers, the state legislature, the Congress of the United States, and all those whom they represent. Until all of these are willing to give more than lip service to the idea that education is an investment and that it is better to spend now than pay later for social misfits, we will continue to pay the cost of our failure to educate the majority of our culturally deprived children.

More than a third of the children now enrolled in Chicago elementary and high schools are affected by the factors included in our definition of "socially disadvantaged." Ten of the 21 school districts serve areas of the inner city where incomes are low, educational level of adults is low, and many heads of families are either on relief or in semiskilled or unskilled occupations. These 10 districts in September, 1963, enrolled 40,387 high school pupils and 209,221 elementary pupils, a little less than one-half of the total elementary and high school enrollment of 536,000. (See Chapter III.) In all of these districts there are varying numbers of pupils whose families do not belong in the category of socially disadvantaged. It is important to remember that working class, lower class, and socially disadvantaged are all different concepts, and that some families who are economically deprived give their children good preparation for learning. Some districts (notably District 14) include typical slum areas side by side with areas where families are much better off. In any program designed to help the socially disadvantaged, criteria should be established rather carefully as between schools rather than districts, and two or more levels of need and service might be established.

The administrative staff and many principals and teachers in the Chicago Public Schools are, of course, already aware of the special needs of culturally deprived children. Dr. Willis was a leader in the organization of the Great Cities Program for School Improvement, which undertook as its second major area of study the education of the culturally deprived and which is now working on training teachers for urban schools. In Chicago, a Ford Foundation grant was obtained for a project in District 11 for over-age and culturally deprived children in elementary school, designed to prevent early school-leaving. This project has resulted in the development of a number of worthwhile approaches, some of which have been extended throughout the district and beyond it. In the same district, another Foundation grant sought to develop more democratic procedures in the classroom and to involve parents with pupils and teachers in developing common values and stronger motivation for learning.

One approach that seems to have won general approval by the participants and that may provide a pattern for schools in disadvantaged areas is that of the Experimental Summer Schools, started in 1960. These schools, all but one in areas serving culturally deprived children, differ from the regular elementary schools in having lower class loads (25 per class), more generous auxiliary services, and a time schedule which permits daily, continuous planning by the staff as a whole and in special groups. Other differences lie in the fact that the teachers have been specially selected for excellence and interest in the project, the achievement levels are limited within each group, and teachers eat lunch with their pupils. The pupils come from a number of schools in the area served, and are supposed to include slow, average, and gifted children. Through 1963, approximately 600 pupils were enrolled in each summer school, 100 at each level, Grades 1 through 6. In the summer of 1964 some of the 20 experimental summer schools included the kindergarten groups, and several had also a four-year-old group. In addition to the full-time teacher-nurse, librarian, psychologist, and physical education teacher, the 1964 schools were assigned a parent coordinator to establish contact with the parents, develop classes for them, and in other ways enlist their aid in helping their children to get more out of their education.

These experimental summer schools were designed to show and did show that children taught under these improved conditions made much better than average progress in learning and school adjustment. Tests seem to indicate that the gains have in many cases been retained. It must of course be remembered that, although there was a range of pupils' abilities, a certain amount of selection was involved, in that at least one parent had to agree to attend certain meetings and attendance was voluntary. There can be no question that many teachers found renewed satisfaction in teaching under these special conditions and that most children enjoyed the summer schools, as shown by their good attendance records.

On entering one of these schools, the "different" atmosphere is at once evident. Grade levels are organized around a lively theme, such as travel to foreign lands. A visitor from one of these countries may be talking to several classes of the children, showing slides and interesting artifacts, while the teacher is preparing materials for a later lesson. The teacher-nurse and psychologist have group meetings with pupils in addition to performing their customary services. The parent coordinator is talking to a group of kindergarten mothers about child development and inspiring a lively discussion on encouraging independence in the little ones who cry in kindergarten. Both mothers and older children from the neighborhood are serving as volunteer helpers in various ways; one mother makes calls to find out about absentees. At lunch time, the teacher and his group sit down together with their bag lunches and afterward he teaches them to play chess or to relax through rhythmic dancing or a lively game. The teachers are enthusiastic about the benefits of daily planning together, sharing skills, and the freedom to experiment. Their only complaint is that the summer school period is too short to develop their ideas adequately and carry them out.

Other means designed to help children in areas of cultural deprivation include extra transportation provisions for field trips, after-school libraries, reading clinics, and remedial reading classes, extra book and supply allowances for high-mobility schools, master teachers in some schools, and vocational guidance and education centers for over-age elementary pupils.

At the local school level, many dedicated principals and teachers are using their time, imagination and skills trying to help these culturally deprived children. There is probably not a single suggestion made anywhere in the country for the improvement of the educational program for such children that is not being tried out, *within the limits of available resources,* in some Chicago school. Primary children are being encouraged to take home both primers and supplementary books, and their parents are being shown how to help them at home. There are orientation classes for children from rural areas and special groupings for children affected by high mobility or language difficulties. Through the cooperation of private agencies, a limited number of culturally deprived children are attending preschool classes or nursery schools serving 3- and 4-year-olds, and there are the beginnings of integration of such classes with kindergarten and first grade. Some schools use their special service teachers for home visits and at least two are receiving the benefits of a school-centered social work program through a private agency. A number of schools are taking advantage of volunteer services for programs of cultural enrichment, special tutoring, and study centers. In quite a few cases, the school staff pays for free lunches and even breakfasts beyond what is allowed under the school lunch program, and clothing and shoes are provided in addition to what is secured through the School Children's Aid. Teachers are trying out all kinds of special educational tools, projects, methods, and curriculum materials to find effective ways of motivating and teaching disadvantaged children.

The fact is, however, that the job cannot be done in the framework of the regular school program. It is no criticism of teachers or staff to say that they cannot be expected to devise fresh new methods of reaching and teaching deprived children with the present class loads, staffing, and time schedules. It is simply not enough to see to it, as the present administration has done, that pupil-teacher ratios and auxiliary services are equalized throughout the city. The limited special measures taken so far are quickly swallowed up in the whirlpool of necessity. Master teachers, special service teachers, and even the librarian, adjustment teacher, or gym teacher are too often called upon to take a class when a teacher is absent and no substitute is provided by the downtown substitute center. This means that inexperienced teachers often do not get the help and direction the master teacher is supposed to provide, and teachers with over-size classes do not get the assistance which the special service teachers are supposed to be giving them. If the principal is determined to maintain his library, adjustment, gym, and master teacher programs as scheduled, teacher absences mean doubled-up classes for other teachers, an impossible situation. Actually, there are so many day-to-day problems that have to be taken care of in a school of this kind, that the time of special service teachers and even master teachers is often taken up with hall duties, disciplinary matters, trying to reach parents of sick children, keeping records, etc. Every problem which is a minor irritation in the ordinary school —hall, playground and lunchroom duties, interruptions for money and fund collecting, requests for information, discipline cases, tardiness, and so on—constitutes an excessive burden in the school serving culturally deprived children and makes it hard for even an experienced teacher to concentrate on the professional task of teaching, in the very situation in which every bit of skill and energy is needed.

The situation was clearly reflected in the answers of teachers in such schools, when they were asked in the Teacher Questionnaire what kinds of help would be most welcome in their particular teaching situation. Lower class loads, more clerical help, and special teachers to work with small groups were preferred, in that order, to any other kind of special provision.

What is required first of all is a full and frank acceptance of the fact that the education of culturally deprived children requires a special program and substantially higher per pupil expenditures than are now being spent on a city-wide basis. This acceptance should be embodied in a forthright statement of Board policy. The schools that are affected by high mobility, low educational level of parents, and other indices of low socioeconomic status in the community from which the children come should be identified by a staff committee. This should be done on a school-by-school rather than district basis, since in some areas (such as Uptown and Woodlawn-Hyde Park-Kenwood) the socioeconomic indices for the district as a whole do not reveal the extent of need in certain schools.

Degree of retardation in school and turnover in staff, including the number of substitutes, can also be taken as measures of need for special help. However, this might penalize schools in which good leadership and possibly other factors have reduced staff turnover and superior efforts within present resources have raised achievement levels to some extent. It would seem advisable, therefore, to classify schools in need of help first on the basis of the socioeconomic characteristics of the area from which the pupils come. All schools falling in this class would qualify for the basic compensatory program. Then special additional support, such as extra master teachers and curriculum advisers, would be given to those schools in which the number of substitutes was above average for the group, and/or the achievement levels were below average for the group. Further study should be made to isolate the factors which may be bringing about these differences between schools whose pupil population is very similar. Leadership is an obvious factor, of course. One essential ingredient, vital to the success of any school serving culturally deprived children, is the conviction that the children have the capacity and the desire to learn.

When schools have been identified by the foregoing procedures, a massive effort should be made to put compensatory programs into effect. Resources must be sought through every possible avenue, public and private, including state general and special education aid, federal programs, foundations, local community agencies, and volunteer efforts. Nor should it be assumed that the limit of local tax contributions to education has been reached. The citizens of Chicago must understand that there are only two alternatives: to provide the funds necessary to educate these socially disadvantaged children or to incur the social and financial costs of a growing body of dependent and undereducated adults.

At the outset, it must be clearly recognized that not all compensatory programs will be effective. Principals and teachers in the identified schools should be given opportunities to use their own initiative and creative abilities to try out different approaches; and objective evaluation procedures should be established to learn what works and what doesn't. No stigma should be attached to experimental programs that do not bring results; the facts on such programs should be circulated as part of the process of school improvement. Freedom to fail is an essential part of freedom to grow.

There are strong indications, based both on scientific data and experimental programs, that the earlier the child can be reached, the more effective the program will be. J. McVicker Hunt of the University of Illinois and Martin Deutsch[4] of the New York Medical College are among the scholars who have marshalled impressive evidence for the thesis that the nature and extent of experiences in the years from 1 to 5 have much to do with school achievement. Bloom has published a study[5] supporting the proposition that variations in the environment can produce changes in human characteristics and that such variations have the greatest effect at the period when the particular characteristic is changing most rapidly. This bears out Hunt's thesis (which was also that of Mme. Montessori) that different age levels are crucial for different kinds of learnings, and that children go through various phases of learning, with each phase lending support to those which follow.

Bloom has also assembled the results of research indicating the extent of educational growth experienced by children at various age levels.[6] Results indicate that at least one-third of the learnings which will determine later levels of school achievement have already taken place by age 6, and at least 75 percent by age 13. These findings point to the most important periods for school programs directed to raising achievement levels of children. Based on the estimate that 33 percent of educational growth takes place before age 6, Bloom suggests that "nursery schools and kindergartens could have far-reaching consequences on the child's general learning pattern." The approximately 17 percent of growth which takes place between ages 6 and 9 suggests that elementary Grades 1 to 3 are also crucial. Tending to support this suggestion in another way are the rather

[4]Martin Deutsch, J. McVicker Hunt, *et al.,* "Selected Papers from the Arden House Conference on Pre-School Enrichment of Socially Disadvantaged Children," reprinted from the *Merrill Palmer Quarterly,* July, 1964.
[5]Benjamin Bloom, *op. cit.*
[6]Benjamin Bloom, *op. cit.,* p. 110.

disappointing results now being reported of the Higher Horizons program in New York, which has not attempted to reach any children below the third grade.[7] On the other hand, experimental programs at the prekindergarten level in Baltimore, New York, and elsewhere have already shown gratifying results in better performance on IQ tests and other measures of readiness and achievement.

A final quotation from Bloom sums up the situation:

> A conservative estimate of the effect of extreme environments on intelligence is about 20 I.Q. points. This could mean the difference between a life in an institution for the feeble-minded or a productive life in society. It could mean the difference between a professional career and an occupation which is at the semi-skilled or unskilled level. . . . The implications for public education and social policy are fairly clear. Where significantly lower intelligence can be clearly attributed to the effects of environmental deprivations, steps must be taken to ameliorate these conditions as early in the individual's development as education and other social forces can be utilized.[8]

With these general considerations in mind, a tentative program for socially disadvantaged children in the Chicago Public Schools is outlined below:

1. *Leadership.* The difference between a successful and an unsuccessful school in a culturally deprived neighborhood lies to a very high degree in the kind of leadership exercised by the principal and the morale and attitudes of the teaching staff. Good educational programs in which children were making significant gains in achievement and even in scores on IQ tests were observed in old as well as in new buildings, and in schools where more than half the teachers were substitutes or recently assigned as well as in schools with all experienced teachers. The vital factor in every case seemed to be the leadership given by the principal, his organizational ability, and his ability to convey to his staff an enthusiasm for the task of teaching these children and a conviction that these children could be helped to achieve successfully in school.

---

[7]In New York, however, the Higher Horizons program was an addition to the larger special services provisions already applicable to schools serving disadvantaged pupils.

[8]Benjamin Bloom, *op. cit.,* p. 89.

It follows that special attention should be given to the selection and preparation of principals in these schools. An effort should be made to select principals who have positive and informed attitudes toward the potentialities of lower-class children. Such attitudes can be encouraged by courses in social anthropology, cultural differences, and human relations; and by requiring that candidates for positions of principal and assistant principal have teaching experience in culturally deprived areas. There should be a planned program of visitation or, better, internships in successful programs for candidates for these positions. A principal who does not want to serve in this kind of school should not be forced to do so. Once appointed, if the program is going well, every effort should be made to retain the principal in the school for at least five years. Continuity and knowing what to expect mean a great deal in a culturally deprived neighborhood; and a system which snatches away the successful principal within a year or two is not in the best interests of the children.

In addition to a belief in the ability and desire of the children to learn, principals in these schools should have a willingness to let teachers try out their own ideas, without insisting that every experiment be a success. Teachers are surprisingly conscious and appreciative of an atmosphere that allows them to grow. At the same time they want clearly understood goals, plus direction and support when they feel the need of it.

2. *Classroom teachers.* It has been pointed out in other chapters that the proportion of substitute teachers and teachers with less than five years' experience is substantially higher in low-education areas and in schools in which pupils are all or almost all Negro than in high-education areas and in schools with practically all-white student bodies. This has been confirmed by visits to many schools.

Many of the substitute and newly assigned teachers are doing outstanding work. Nevertheless, it seems unquestionable, as the Hauser report points out, that, by and large, better teaching would be promoted by having a larger proportion of assigned and experienced teachers. This can be done: (*a*) by holding the presently assigned teachers in these schools; and (*b*) by persuading experienced, assigned teachers to transfer to these schools.

It is recommended that a variety of measures be taken to accomplish these twin goals, placing the highest emphasis on measures that will make teaching in culturally deprived areas more satisfying, and the least emphasis on measures that will restrict the freedom of the assigned teacher to apply for transfer after a given period of time. Increased pay for teachers serving in schools designated for compensatory aid is not recommended at this time.

All of the measures hereinafter suggested to improve the educational program in these schools should help in the retention of presently assigned teachers. Both improved teaching conditions and improved pre-service and in-service training will help teachers to feel the sense of accomplishment at the end of the day that is the basic factor in holding teachers in a particular situation. In addition, a program should be started to permit experienced teachers now serving in other areas to volunteer for one or two years or to exchange with another teacher in schools serving culturally deprived children. The arrangement could be prolonged with the consent of the teacher. Many teachers might be interested in the challenge of teaching in these schools if they did not feel they were taking an irrevocable step. Some of our teachers volunteer to cross the ocean to try out a new teaching situation; they would surely be willing to cross the city, if they did not feel permanently committed.

If teacher candidates for principal and assistant principal were required to teach at least one year in schools serving culturally deprived children, as is being done in some large cities, the schools would have the benefit of their talents at the same time that they improved their own preparation for leadership.

Finally, it is suggested that a strenuous effort be made, in consultation with teachers' organizations, to work out a plan whereby some vacancies in schools with a high proportion of experienced, assigned teachers be used as training stations for new substitute and assigned teachers. Assignments for new teachers to such schools might be limited to one year, following which a year in a school serving culturally deprived children would be required.

3. *Preparation and training of teachers.* Present curricula of the teacher institutions should be carefully reviewed and all teachers in training should be required to have at least a minimum requirement in social anthropology, sociology, and human relations. It is surprising how many teachers cite a sociology course as the

one most helpful to them in their teaching in a deprived neighborhood. Such courses should involve actual experience in such neighborhoods, in community agencies, and in the schools themselves, culminating in practice teaching experience in these schools. Good results have been seen in cities where two years of the training program revolved around experience in a particular school.

For the teachers already in these schools, in-service training should be greatly expanded, taking in basic material that will help in understanding and working with the children, visits to successful classrooms, and plenty of time for discussion of problems. Reorganization of the time schedule to make more time for such programs is discussed in a later section.

4. *Staffing.* The immediate goal for class loads in schools serving educationally disadvantaged children should be 30 pupils. Further reduction in class loads should be subordinated to the provision of adequate auxiliary professional staff, as outlined below. At the same time, principals should be given reasonable latitude to vary individual class sizes within the over-all framework, including the authority to establish classes for children with special needs, such as recent inmigrants, children with language difficulties, social adjustment groups, etc.

As far as possible, the school should be staffed so as to take care of its own mentally handicapped and socially maladjusted pupils. For the latter, for his own sake as well as for the sake of his teacher and classmates, prompt referral to a special classroom, providing skilled guidance and individual attention, should be made possible as soon as the problem has been identified by the school's guidance team. All consultants who have visited our schools and classes for socially maladjusted children have recommended that the younger children, at least through sixth grade, should be cared for within their own school or at least in their own district.

5. *Auxiliary professional staff.* Auxiliary services for a school of 1,000 children should include—in addition to the customary gym teacher, librarian, adjustment teacher, and assistant principal—two or three master teachers and a full-time teacher-nurse, psychologist, social worker, and school-community coordinator. Assuming that the present class load in such a school is 33, that it already has one master teacher, as would be likely in a school serving disadvantaged

pupils, and is receiving ⅕ time of a psychologist and ⅖ time of a teacher-nurse, it would be necessary to add 3 regular teachers, one master teacher, ⅘ time of a psychologist, ⅗ time of a teacher-nurse, a social worker, and a school-community coordinator. This would represent a total additional salary cost of $57,000, or $57 per pupil.[9] Space, of course, would be a major problem and would have to be considered in each case, along with such possibilities as mobile units, transportation, or construction. An interim guidance room, for pupils with special problems awaiting diagnosis or special placement, would require additional staff and space, as would the supplementary clerical help mentioned elsewhere.

The social worker would accept cases of children referred for emotional and behavior problems, nonachievement, evidence of economic deprivation (food, clothing), and persistent truancy and tardiness beyond the scope of ordinary attendance officers; would counsel with children, parents, and teachers in an effort to resolve these problems which are impeding the child's learning; would make referrals as necessary to community agencies and follow up on action taken.

The community coordinator would establish lines of communication with community organizations, set up programs for parents, coordinate and direct volunteer activities, and help develop the after-school program.

One, two, or three master teachers should be assigned to the school in proportion to the number of substitutes or first- and second-year teachers. The main responsibilities of the master teachers would relate to working out curriculum plans and the in-service training of teachers.

6. *Nonprofessional staff*. In order to free the teachers to teach, enough clerks or staff aides should be assigned to the school to take care of all clerical work and reporting which could be done by nonprofessional personnel. Part-time teacher-aides, recruited from the community, should be assigned to the school at the request of the principal and given duties agreed upon by teachers and principal. These could be either volunteers or paid personnel. At present, class-

[9]Allowing $8,000 each for the psychologist, master teacher, and social worker, and $7,500 each for the remaining personnel.

room teachers are guarding halls and doors, escorting children
through the halls, serving or supervising in lunchrooms, supervising
indoor and outdoor recess, collecting and handing out milk and
lunch money, and performing many other tasks that could be done
very well by nonprofessionals, lifting a considerable load from the
hard-pressed teacher and leaving more time for planning and reviewing her program. As state and federal anti-poverty programs
seek jobs for those now unemployed, the possibility of setting up
part-time in-school jobs for high school students and mothers in the
community should not be overlooked.

7. *Volunteer programs.* Along with its problems, a great city has
tremendous advantages in the variety of its human and institutional
resources. The willingness of able and talented people to give their
time and effort when channels are provided and the goal is clear
and inspiring has been demonstrated again and again. Yet up to
now much too little has been done by the school system to channel
the enormous reservoirs of good will and talent into specific programs to help the schools meet the needs of culturally deprived
children. A hopeful sign that this attitude is changing was a recent
recommendation by the General Superintendent that a volunteer
program be developed in cooperation with the Chicago Junior
League. This is a good beginning, but such a program must not be
restricted to any one organization. Other groups are ready for expansion and improvement of volunteer services with the proper encouragement and direction.

One of the principal volunteer activities in Chicago is tutoring,
notably by students from colleges and universities in the area. The
pioneer effort in this field was the Northwestern Student Tutoring
Project, begun in 1960. From October, 1962, to May, 1963 (last
report available), this project involved 165 tutors and 400 tutees
in the Lawndale area. Systematic evaluation is lacking, but before
and after reading scores and grades of a number of the tutees showed
marked improvement. Moreover, such programs bring other positive
results in the attitudes and motivation of pupils, better understanding of inner city problems by college students, and involvement of
the community in an educational project. This Northwestern project
brought foundation support and the cooperation of settlement
houses, boys' clubs, the YMCA, and business groups.

An outgrowth of this project was the Junior Tutoring Project, through which high-achieving upper grade and high school students in disadvantaged areas are paid on an hourly basis to tutor other pupils referred by teachers. Such a program holds promise of benefiting both tutor and tutee, making academic excellence a source of immediate profit and prestige in the kind of neighborhood where such values are needed.

Other activities besides tutoring have grown out of these projects, such as cultural and recreational trips, music and art projects, counseling, etc. Other volunteer efforts have focused from the beginning on cultural enrichment. The Urban Gateways Program, sponsored by the Institute for Cultural Development, has not only introduced thousands of culturally deprived children to a wide variety of plays, concerts, and other artistic performances, but has provided interpretation and discussion before and after these events, as well as escorts to the performances. This has led to active participation by the children in choral groups, art classes, and Great Books discussions, under the leadership of volunteers who are often professionals or gifted amateurs in the arts.

There has not been in Chicago, however, the kind of in-school volunteer program which is being successfully carried out in other cities. In Washington, D.C., the schools received a substantial foundation grant to establish a volunteer program which now provides over 100 reading aides working in the school reading clinics, and another group of volunteers serving as counselor's aides. In New York City, over 500 volunteers are working in 22 elementary schools, five junior high schools, and one high school. Each one is performing services which have been identified by the school as appropriate for volunteers; they serve only with teachers who have asked for their services. On March 7, 1963, the New York City Superintendent of Schools in a letter to the Public Education Association School Volunteers said: "I think what you are doing is one of the most important things in the schools system."

What is needed in Chicago is a systematic plan to utilize school volunteers, both in school and out of school, with adequate orientation and supervision. Experience shows that the problem is not recruiting capable volunteers, but providing needed pre-service and in-service training and a proper organizational framework.

To coordinate and assist all the groups wishing to sponsor volunteer programs and to recruit and train other volunteers, a Division of Volunteer Programs, with a director assigned by the Board of Education, should be established. Policies should be outlined and training programs developed to make maximum use of volunteers, so that they will be filling needs recognized by teachers and principals and will be serving where there is a willingness to work with them. District superintendents and principals should be encouraged to experiment with in-school as well as after-school volunteer projects, and to list the jobs in their schools which they believe could be performed by a competent volunteer.

8. *In-school time schedule.* The period between 8:30 and 8:50 is very unsatisfactory for in-service training in any school. It is especially unsatisfactory in a school for culturally deprived children where other demands on the teacher's time and attention are at a maximum. The same applies to the lunch hour. Yet, as has been said, in-service training programs are an absolute essential in these schools. Teacher after teacher who had experience in the special summer schools referred to the daily in-service meetings as one of the finest features of the whole program. At present, principals have various ways of meeting the problem. Some "steal time" by doubling up classes, using student monitors or special service personnel. Some use the 20 morning minutes to take up just one topic, leaving the discussion for another day, but find the time still inadequate. Some use the lunch hour, although they admit that their teachers need the time for relaxation. Some just give up. The moral is clear: More time must be set aside for in-service training. A study should be made of the school day and school calendar to see whether it would not be possible, within state requirements, to allot at least one half day per month for in-service training, with the pupils dismissed. If this proves impossible, alternatives should be found: paying substitutes on a regular schedule, paying teachers for after school in-service classes, lengthening the school day for teachers only, etc. Whatever the plan adopted, more time for in-service programs in schools serving culturally deprived children is a necessity.

9. *Early education.* The strong reasons for the establishment of programs which will reach socially disadvantaged children at the earliest possible age have already been discussed. It is probable that

a well-planned nursery school program beginning at age 3 would do more for the later school achievement of such children than any comparable expenditure applied at a later age. While it is not practicable to suggest that programs be instituted immediately for 3-year-olds in all school communities serving socially disadvantaged children, this should be the ultimate goal. Private agencies and other public agencies such as the Housing Authority, the Park District, and the Welfare Department should all be urged to cooperate in every possible way, including the provision of space.

The curriculum of such programs should be directed to the correction of those factors in the "deprived" environment, already cited, which handicap socially disadvantaged children in learning and school achievement. Thus, speech habits and language patterns should be improved and enriched through much oral practice, recognition of new words and objects emphasized, and all kinds of exercises directed toward verbal facility, word recognition, and speaking in sentences; limited experience of the outer world should be enriched by trips, by bringing various kinds of people and things into the classroom, and by all kinds of films, books, pictures, and other visual aids; opportunities should be given for working out simple puzzles and problems and for planning simple activities; and just plain conversation and interaction with adults and other children should be encouraged. Materials based on children's own experiences should be developed and used. Approaches should also be based on the findings of psychology about crucial periods for various kinds of learning, indicating primarily that children in the early years learn best through motor activities and direct sensory experience with learning materials.

It is unfortunate that in Chicago at the present time, when the need for reaching disadvantaged children at the earliest possible age is being demonstrated, the annual admission program actually delays the admission of pupils to a greater degree than at any previous time. A child whose sixth birthday comes after December 1 of any given year is not admitted to kindergarten until September of that year, when he may be 5 years and 9 months old.

Up to 1933, children in Chicago were generally admitted to the afternoon kindergarten division when they were 4 years old. In 1933, this practice was given up in the interests of economy, and children were admitted to kindergarten from 4 years, 11 months to 5 years, 6 months, according to their birthdays. Since 1960, the annual admission program has delayed kindergarten experience until almost 6 years of age for a considerable number of children.

It is also a fact, recognized by the Chicago school administration, that proportionately fewer families enroll their children in kindergarten in disadvantaged areas than in neighborhoods that are better off. Efforts to correct this situation should be redoubled through every avenue of community cooperation. This would be one of the responsibilities of the school-community coordinator in each school area. As soon as possible, programs should be established for the 3- and 4-year olds. In areas where the repetition of a grade every three years is not unusual for many children, it would be an economy if this could be prevented by adding a year or two at the beginning.

In the meantime, other avenues should be sought for enriching and guiding the preschool experience of culturally deprived children. Teachers could be assigned and other help given to assist private agencies and nursery schools to provide programs for these children. With proper publicity and through groups organized in settlement houses and housing projects, such a program might reach a considerable number of children and at the same time show parents ways to improve the preschool experiences of their children. Many administrators are already distributing leaflets designed to show parents how they can help their children at home. A task of the school-community coordinator would be better distribution of such materials, and the organization of groups of mothers who would discuss the materials.

In addition to extending the kindergarten program downward to 4-year-olds (or ideally to 3-year-olds), the kindergarten program itself should be the subject of special study.

Visits to kindergartens serving culturally deprived children reveal many teachers who are aware of the special learning needs of these children. However, there is need for a thorough re-thinking of the program in the light of all that is known about such children. The approaches, gaps to be filled, goals to be met, etc., should be carefully worked out; teachers of such classes should have the benefit of orientation and in-service programs to clarify purposes and techniques. They should be given a chance to visit other kindergartens and preschool programs. A variety of experimental approaches should be tried, including some Montessori-type classes.

In any re-thinking and extension downward of the kindergarten program, major attention should be given to working with parents. The goal should not be to acculturate the child by dividing him from his parents, but to establish relationships of trust and cooperation with the parents, so that both family and school can work together to see that this child gets an education. Where there are six or eight kindergarten groups (counting morning and afternoon divisions), one extra staff person should be provided to serve the entire group by developing ways to involve the parents. Volunteer helpers are an accepted part of many preschool programs, and participation in such programs would be a valuable way of developing good relationships with the mothers of these culturally deprived children.

The vital importance of the kindergarten program should be re-emphasized throughout the system. Kindergarten teachers need a fresh conviction of the importance of their work demonstrated not only by words but by deeds. This means more and better materials and play equipment, with more informed attention to its selection; fewer interruptions; lower class loads; and an end to such practices as putting two kindergartens in one room, or sending other classes into the kindergarten room when the teacher is absent.

10. *After-school programs.* A school which serves culturally deprived children ought to serve, to the fullest extent possible, the needs of the whole child. To the extent that such schools are now open for after-school recreation and for special library and reading programs, this need has already been recognized. But much more is needed. For example, the after-school reading classes meet only two days a week for part of the semester and for very short sessions. As part of the compensatory program, every effort should be made to expand after-school services and to involve parents as well as children.

All principals and teachers recognize that parental attitudes are vital to the child's success in school, but in too many cases negative attitudes are regarded as facts of life, rather than challenges. A weak PTA, limited to a few faithful souls, is accepted as inevitable. Parents are seen only when there is a problem. ("We send home a note saying that their child will be suspended until they come in with him, and they come fast enough.")

Principals and teachers can hardly be blamed for these attitudes, for they have too much to do already. The usual PTA approach simply does not work with culturally deprived parents. For these reasons, the school-community coordinator and the social worker are necessary to help bring about changes in the attitudes of parents toward the school and to show them how they can help their children succeed. After-school classes and interest groups for parents as well as for children should be encouraged.

For the pupils, in addition to improvements in the remedial classes both in quantity and quality, after-school special interest groups should be fostered with the help of volunteers. The child who develops a deep interest in one subject, and learns to work at it with enjoyment, has been won over to the cause of education for life.

11. *Summer programs.* Summer programs in areas serving culturally deprived children should be as extensive as possible. Ideally, all schools in the compensatory program should be open 12 hours a day 12 months in the year. This would promote more economical use of the many fine new buildings, reduce wasteful repetition of grades, provide constructive summer activities, and permit a variety of special programs to meet special talents and needs. Full-time employment of teachers might cut down on the moonlighting which is too general, among men teachers especially. (See answers to Teacher Questionnaire.) For schools which are not open during the summer, a core staff of principal and key staff members should be employed for several weeks in the summer to plan the program for the coming year, make tests for special placement, follow up problem cases, etc.

V

Gifted and Above-Average Youth

In a big city school system, it is important to pay special attention to gifted children. There is always danger that the necessary stress on work with disadvantaged children will make the school program lopsided, and cause neglect of the abler children.

Chicago schools have not neglected gifted children. The general impression obtained by the consultants in their school visits was favorable. They would rank Chicago with the best of the major cities in providing for students of high ability. But there is much room for improvement.

Who are the gifted?

In the elementary schools, an IQ of 120 is commonly used as an evidence of giftedness. Half of the schools with programs for the gifted use this level or something above it as the basis for assigning children to classes for the gifted. Another half, mostly schools in

* * *

This chapter is based largely on reports by two consultants who have long been identified with school programs for gifted children. They are: Walter Barbe, Professor of Education, Kent State University, Ohio, and Paul Witty, Professor of Education, Northwestern University.

79

poor neighborhoods, go down to 110 or even lower in their search for children to put into a program for the gifted.

The general procedure is to select the top 10 percent in a given school as "gifted." In addition, pupils of outstanding talent in music, art, or writing are receiving some encouragement and special help in many of the schools. The deciding criterion for selection in Chicago schools "is the ability of the pupil to perform successfully at a high level of achievement, whether it be academic, artistic, mechanical or physical."[1]

Three levels of intellectual ability are involved in Chicago's program. They may be called: (1) the highly gifted, (2) the academically able, and (3) the relatively able.

The highly gifted. The highly gifted are those above 130 or 135 in IQ. These children are in the top 2 or 3 percent of the nation's children. Chicago has many of them, though not as many as would be found in a cross-section of the population. There is some evidence that the number of these children has decreased in Chicago in recent years. For example, the percentages of pupils with high IQ's in the elementary schools as measured by the group tests given regularly in the schools were:

	1957	1959	1964
IQ above 130	3.1	2.6	1.2
IQ above 125	5.8	5.0	2.8
IQ above 110	22.5	27.5	22.1

These figures would be modified somewhat by using individually administered tests rather than group tests, but they may be taken as roughly accurate. The reason for the reduction in size of the group above 130 IQ is no doubt migration of high-income people from the central city to the suburbs. Chicago, with its high proportion of socially disadvantaged children, must have a number with high potential which can be developed if these children are identified and assisted.

The program of the schools does not raise or lower the IQ of a child with high ability, though it may affect the IQ of children of

---

[1]Staff Study Report, *Education for the Gifted.* Chicago Public Schools, 1964.

average or low ability. A high IQ is a product of the factors of inborn ability and family background that were discussed in Chapter III.

The task of the school with the highly gifted pupil is to give him a chance to make use of his ability in ways which are good for him and for society. The school should be judged for this, rather than for the number of highly gifted children it contains.

For this reason, one should not credit or blame a school for the number of its pupils who score high on scholarship tests. The National Merit Scholarship Examination, for example, should not be used to measure the quality of a school system. Chicago does not produce its proportionate share of Merit Scholars because it does not contain a proportionate share of highly gifted pupils.

In the production of very high-scoring high school pupils on the National Merit Scholarship examinations, it is clear that the suburbs outweigh the city, although their total high school enrollments are smaller than that of the central city. Thus, in 1964 there were 63 suburban Merit Scholarship winners, against 25 in the city of Chicago, counting public and private schools together.

Another form of comparison can be made between the numbers of National Merit semifinalists in the City of Chicago and in the state as a whole. Those who are semifinalists in the Merit Scholarship examinations are approximately in the top one-half of 1 percent of young people by intellectual ability. In 1964 in Illinois there were 741 semifinalists, with 90 of these coming from Chicago public high schools. This is 12 percent. On the other hand, the proportion of Chicago public high school graduates in the total for the State of Illinois was about 20 percent.

The superiority of the suburbs in the production of Merit Scholars and Merit semifinalists is probably due mainly to the much higher average socioeconomic status of the suburbs. It would be difficult to separate the factor of family socioeconomic status and what this does for the scholastic ability of youth from the factor of the quality of the educational program. Some of the suburban schools spend more per student, have relatively more experienced teachers, and in other ways provide better services than the central city. But there is much doubt that Chicago would increase its output of Merit Scholars very greatly even if it spent another $300 or $400 per student.

There are also great differences in high student achievement within the Chicago school system. Of the 90 semifinalists of 1964, 11 out of 50 schools had 75; three schools had 30, or one-third of the total. Here, too, the difference appears to be largely due to differences in family background.

In order to retain its present proportion of highly gifted pupils and to increase their numbers, the school system must find ways of holding and attracting families who are now migrating with their gifted children to the suburbs, and of discovering and developing more fully the latent ability of the socially disadvantaged.

The academically able. The "academically able" group includes the top 10 to 15 percent in scholastic ability. The term is used rather loosely by various writers on gifted children. For the purpose of studying Chicago schools, it is useful to speak of this group as consisting of those with IQ 115 and above. They will constitute as many as 30 percent of the pupils in some of the favored areas of the city, and as few as 2 or 3 percent in the less-favored areas. Chicago's program for the gifted is planned largely for this group of pupils.

The relatively able. The "relatively able" group are the top 10 or 15 percent in the low-achievement schools, where the family background factor has held down the intellectual level of the majority of pupils. Such schools have only very small numbers of the academically able, and a program for the gifted must either be limited to those small numbers or be expanded to take in the top 10 percent, on the assumption that the children have latent ability which has not yet been developed.

The Chicago schools have included the relatively able in their programs for the gifted, and for that reason some 30 percent of the schools identify as gifted pupils whose IQ's range from 100 to 115. Among the high schools, approximately two-thirds regard all students above IQ 115 as academically able, but 11 schools begin at IQ 110 and five schools begin at IQ 105 for the selection of students in programs for the gifted. At the other extreme, one high school in a favored area uses an IQ standard of 130 as the minimum for a student to enter its honors program.

As might be expected, the work done by the "relatively able" is not altogether satisfactory for a "gifted" group. We shall consider how such programs might be improved.

Programs for the gifted

The Chicago schools employ the basic method of ability grouping in elementary as well as in high schools. This is seen in the following overview of programs in the elementary schools.

In 1964 replies from the elementary schools indicate that 364 elementary schools now maintain a program for gifted or talented pupils. While 320 elementary schools report adoption of ability grouping as a practice, almost one hundred schools state that they have devised a complete full-time organization based upon ability grouping. These schools, for the most part, have large memberships so that their administrators have a certain degree of flexibility in scheduling groups. However, other elementary schools state that they group intermediate and upper grade able or talented students on a part-time basis during the school day.

Scores on intelligence tests and reading tests as well as teacher judgment are the basic criteria used in grouping the academically able. Pupils in 363 schools are grouped primarily on the basis of achievement scores in language arts. Two hundred fifteen schools report that they utilize a combination of intelligence and reading tests for ability grouping. Almost 200 schools have set up ability groups in mathematics. Grouping for foreign language instruction is followed in 164 schools. One hundred sixty schools group able science students in science seminars or special science classes.

Talented students are served in 120 schools by grouping them for special art, music or creative writing. In descending order of frequency, elementary schools provide grouping for special language arts classes, speech, social studies, dramatics and dance groups. Elementary principals write that by sectioning gifted pupils in areas of their proficiency they are able to reduce the range of pupil needs; and that in classes for the gifted, the teacher may work at a higher level of attainment with his pupils while other learners at lower levels are taught more effectively.

There still are many small schools where grouping, of necessity, takes place in the classroom. To provide for the range of abilities in a classroom in a small elementary school, teachers organize small informal groups. Purposely, these groups are kept small and flexible so that an able pupil may have opportunities for exploration and depth in learning. More than half of the elementary principals state that where they have not been able to schedule gifted or academically able pupils by groups, they have provided enrichment materials or activities for them in the regular classroom.[2]

This summary shows that programs for the gifted are generally built upon a broad practice of ability grouping, with the top group regarded as "gifted." Teachers then have the opportunity and the responsibility to enrich the learning experience of the brighter children with such things as individual and group projects, wide use of the library, and field trips. Some schools also have special interest groups in music and the arts.

Ability grouping has spread widely in Chicago schools mainly because the wide range of ability among the pupils made it practically impossible to teach all the pupils of one grade by the same methods and with the same materials. But ability grouping is no panacea. It was popular 30 years ago, and then lost popularity until it was brought back in the big cities in recent years for the reasons stated above.

The consultants who visited high-ability classes were generally pleased with what they saw. Teachers displayed a diversity of approach which was determined largely by their own experience and the local school situation, and was not dictated from the Central Office. In no instance was a substitute teacher observed to be working with a gifted group. No doubt these classes get teachers selected for experience and ability to work with gifted children.

However, the work with the "relatively gifted" was not evaluated so favorably. For instance, the following comments were made by a consultant who visited a school in a low-income area where the average IQ was about 93.

> The school contained a Continuous Development Program for gifted children. This consisted of three classes of their most able children, selected on the basis of teacher judgment and intelligence tests. One of the classes was at first-grade level, one at second, and one at third. The children were selected on the basis of either demonstrated or tested potential high achievement. There were approximately 33 children in each of the classes. There was reason to believe that many of the children in the class, however, were below 100 in IQ. The stated purposes of the program were to produce changes in IQ,

---

[2]*Ibid.*, pp. 20-21.

achievement, pupil attitudes, and attitudes of the parents. It was clear that the goals of the program were not clearly defined. The principal emphasized creativity, and the supervisor saw the program as one not particularly different from the regular program other than the fact that it provided "more materials."

This program was a good one for these particular children, but should not be called a program for the gifted.

There is a remarkable contrast between this school and the following example, where the average IQ is about 115.

_____ is an elementary school having approximately 800 students. The work is departmentalized in grades 7 and 8, while grouping according to ability and attainment is found in the remaining grades. Two outstanding features characterize this school—science under a science coordinator for pupils in grades 4-8; and extensive opportunities for varied forms of enrichment. Instruction in French is provided for pupils in grades 5-8. Unusual library resources are also available. Through the management and production of the school newspaper, students have unusual opportunities in creative writing and related activities. A volunteer algebra class is offered for eighth-grade pupils at 8 a.m. This is a school which is distinguished by high academic achievement. One-third of its pupils, above 125 in IQ, are offered a varied, enriched program.

In these programs, the teaching is aimed at *enrichment*. This is the most widely practiced procedure throughout the country. An alternative is *acceleration*.

Acceleration of the gifted in the elementary school. Acceleration means permitting gifted children to proceed through school at a rate determined by their ability and effort rather than according to chronological age standards. The traditional grade skipping is one form of acceleration, and is being used less in Chicago than formerly. In the current staff study, 156 elementary schools reported skipping, or double promotion, compared with 299 schools in 1957. Probably one reason for this decrease is the change from semiannual to annual promotions. It is easier for a child to skip a half year than a full year.

The most popular form of acceleration at present is the "continuous development" plan, used mainly in the primary grades, and reported by 220 schools. In this plan, pupils progress at their own rate through the two major areas of reading and mathematics in sequential blocks of learning which are termed "levels." Whenever a pupil has mastered the work in one level, he is moved into the next level. There are no arbitrary time limits set for each level.

Although the mastery of reading and mathematics is emphasized in the continuous development plan, pupils also study the curriculum areas of language arts, science, social studies, art, music, and physical education. Each child may complete the primary grade content at his own pace; for the gifted child, the continuous development plan offers the opportunity to complete the basic primary three-year plan in as little as two years.

Twenty-four schools report extension of a form of the continuous development plan to the intermediate levels, and 18 to the upper elementary grades.

The "place-out" procedure has become popular in recent years at the close of the elementary school and in the high school. This means that, on the basis of a high grade in a subject or by means of a special examination, a pupil is permitted to omit a particular required course and to proceed on to the next higher level. This applies especially to mathematics, science, and foreign language. The growth of place-out practices may be attributed to a greater degree of articulation between the high school and its contributing elementary schools, the improvement of instruction in elementary school science and mathematics, and the increased emphasis placed upon the six-year program in foreign language instruction in both elementary and high schools.

In 1963, reports from the schools indicate that 2,180 able elementary school graduates placed out of General Science, by examination, and elected Biology as their freshman laboratory science. Nine high schools report that 310 freshmen placed out of Algebra and were assigned to advanced mathematics classes. Other high schools report that 280 elementary graduates who had been enrolled in elementary foreign language classes were assigned to advanced classes in either French or Spanish. One high school reports a place out class in English. Many high schools will place out individual freshmen of outstanding ability when there are not enough candidates to warrant a full class. These freshmen, in effect, have an individual program especially designed to meet their abilities.

In the mathematics place-out program, several elementary schools report that, by special arrangement, their gifted eighth-grade groups are taught Algebra in early morning classes by high school mathematics teachers in the high school building. Other elementary schools report that some high schools are following this practice in the field of instrumental music and that their gifted seventh and eighth graders report before regular school hours to the high school for this special instruction.

While these forms of acceleration are working well, there is danger that they may be permitted to take the place in a large way of enrichment for gifted pupils. This would be unfortunate. A speed-up which enables bright children to move rapidly through school is not a good substitute for a rich and broad program that challenges their ability and captivates their interest at every stage of the school.

Foreign language in the elementary schools. A valuable form of enrichment for gifted children is the offering of foreign languages. Most of the instruction has been given in Spanish and French, and admission to these classes is generally limited to pupils whose reading and writing abilities are above their grade level. In 1946, there were 2,732 pupils studying foreign language in 45 elementary schools. This number grew to 13,159 in 138 schools in 1963. Actually, a peak was reached in 1961 with 210 schools and 23,124 pupils, at which time a review by a staff committee resulted in a rise of standards for instruction and a drop in the numbers of classes.

During 1963-64, a total of approximately 9,100 pupils in primary and intermediate grades worked with 160 classroom teachers, mainly in Spanish and French, with a few classes in German and Italian. The more systematic work of the seventh and eighth grades involved 3,990 pupils in 144 classes. Much of this teaching is done by "non-quota" specialist teachers who have passed oral proficiency tests showing a considerable mastery of the language they teach. They are assigned to schools "off the quota," that is, without regard to the formal pupil-teacher ratio set for the schools.

The high school program. The high schools have four ways of enriching or accelerating the programs of gifted students. Chicago's "100" program, begun in 1958, deserves first mention.

. . . this program identifies the twenty-five top scholars in the ninth, tenth, eleventh and twelfth grades. The "100" scholars are usually those students who enter high school with place out in science and mathematics. They are the scholars who elect challenging programs in science, mathematics, English and social studies. This means that in their four-year stay in high school they may elect a fifth major, four units of a laboratory science, four or five units in mathematics, English, social studies and foreign language. Most scholars have aspirations of attending college and of entering upon a professional career; hence they are the students who elect advanced placement classes, college classes and independent study in advanced science or mathematics seminars.

The "100" scholars are guided carefully by counselors in making decisions and long-term plans. In order to give them broadened opportunities for leadership and socialization, "100" scholars are not grouped separately by divisions, but are assigned to various homerooms in the high schools where they associate with other students of varied talents and abilities.

Many schools utilize the talents of the "100" scholars in tutorial programs, as leaders in student councils, as editors of school publications, as exhibitors in science fairs, as leaders in honorary societies and as school representatives to various community and civic conferences and luncheons. The intent is to provide a varied, rich and meaningful experience so that the scholars may develop into well rounded citizens.

By grouping the top high school students into the "100" program, it is possible to orient them for the external scholarship examinations such as the American College Test, the National Merit Scholarship Tests and the College Entrance Examination Board tests. All schools report special guidance groups for this purpose.

Each high school keeps a master list of the "100" scholars on file in its office. At periodic intervals, the achievements and marks of the scholars are evaluated by the associate superintendent, district superintendent, the principal, counselors, department chairmen and class teachers. Where scholars are not working up to capacity, conferences are held by counselors with the students, parents and teachers to make needed adjustments. Other honor students may also transfer into the "100" program if they display high potential and are recommended by teachers and counselors.[3]

Honors classes represent a more generally available form of en-

---

[3]*Ibid.*, pp. 23-24.

richment. These are classes open to academically able pupils in nearly all schools and also open to the relatively able in some of the low-achievement schools. The number of Honors classes has grown since 1959 from 603 in 20 high schools to 1,194 in 46 high schools. In order of numbers of classes, the subjects most frequently offered are English, mathematics, science, social studies, foreign language, and business education. There were 27,975 enrollments in Honors classes in 1963-64. There is much duplication in this number, since many students were in two or more classes of this type. The Honors classes represent the highest of four levels of ability grouping in the high schools.

A more restricted offering for academically able students is the "advanced placement" course, which is a college-level course taught by a high school teacher and conforming to a syllabus produced by the national College Entrance Examination Board. Examinations are set for these courses by this Board. A number of colleges give college credit for such courses and therefore admit a student from high school with "advanced standing." There were 48 such classes in 1963-64 with 1,135 pupils.

There are also a number of advanced art and music classes, and much opportunity for creative writing. Student newspapers, yearbooks, and literary magazines are outstanding for the quality of work they contain.

The state program for the gifted

Since 1960, the schools have been doing research on programs for the gifted with assistance from the Illinois Plan for Program Development for Gifted Children. These research projects have opened up some interesting avenues for further research and development. This is an area in which assistance might well be sought from some of the university research specialists in the Chicago region. It requires more research sophistication than has been shown in the projects to date.

The state program has also supplied funds for partial support of five Demonstration Centers located at Kelly High School, and Bell, Bryn Mawr, Carver and Tesla Elementary Schools. Each of these is interesting in its own way. The Bryn Mawr School offers an enrichment program for children of IQ 130 or above. The Bell School offers a program for gifted handicapped as well as gifted normal children, all over 115 IQ. One-third of the group are handicapped; most of them are deaf, but there are six blind children in the group. The Kelly High School project stresses "cultural" enrichment in the humanities and arts for academically able students who come mainly from stable working-class and lower white-collar families. The programs at Carver and Tesla Elementary Schools are designed for the relatively able but culturally disadvantaged pupil. These are important for a better understanding of the problem of enriching the educational experience of socially disadvantaged children.

Evaluation of programs for the gifted

The consultants found a favorable attitude toward special provisions for the gifted, and approved the diversity of approaches which they believe represent the interests of superior teachers interacting with the efforts of the Curriculum Department to provide curriculum guides of value to teachers of the gifted.

As might be expected, the consultants were most critical of the work with the "relatively able" pupils in schools where low parental education and income produces socially disadvantaged children. It is easy for teachers of such pupils to accept intellectual mediocrity and apathy as inevitable, and therefore to fail to give the stimulating encouragement and challenge that these pupils need if they are to move toward the levels of achievement one finds in the more favored schools. What is needed is more creative dissatisfaction among the faculty in these schools, with support by the administration for innovations which will jog the minds of the pupils.

Work with gifted children might be improved if there were a single coordinator for programs for the gifted, located in the Curriculum Department. Working with this person might be three or four consultants or supervisors whose duties were to develop inservice training programs for teachers. They also could work with such demonstration centers as are developed in the future.

VI

The Improvement of Teaching

This is a decade of wide and deep change in the school curriculum. The teaching of arithmetic is changing fundamentally in the elementary school. Science both in the high school and in the elementary school is being taught with new textbooks and in new ways. Foreign language is taught for speaking as well as reading. The 10 years of the 1960's will see more change in the curriculum than the 30 years before 1960.

Because the knowledge that the schools teach to children and youth is growing so rapidly, and because the requirements for a

* * *

Consultants whose reports have been used in the preparation of this chapter are: George A. Beauchamp, Professor of Education, Northwestern University; Emma M. Birkmaier, Professor of Education, University of Minnesota; Wells F. Chamberlin, Associate Professor of Romance Languages, University of Chicago; Dorothy Fraser, Professor of Education, City University of New York; Phillip S. Jones, Professor of Mathematics, University of Michigan; Arthur H. Livermore, Deputy Director of Education, American Association for the Advancement of Science; Charles E. Olmsted, Professor of Botany, University of Chicago; John R. Palmer, Associate Professor of Education, University of Illinois; H. Alan Robinson, Assistant Professor of Education, University of Chicago; Lloyd S. Michael, R. Bruce Allingham, and LeRoy Knoeppel, superintendents of suburban high schools. (See Supplement F.)

competent vocational career now demand more and different preparation, the schools have to work all the time to keep the curriculum up to date.

At the same time that the *what* of teaching is changing, the *how* of teaching is also changing. This is seen in the primary grades, where new methods of grouping children are coming into practice. Also, there is much experimenting with methods of teaching young children from socially disadvantaged homes. Again, the new Vocational Education Act of 1963 will stimulate a revolution in vocational education.

Every large school system must have a procedure for: (1) updating choice of content and methods of teaching; (2) helping teachers now in service to work effectively with new materials and methods; (3) adapting the curriculum to the various types of pupils that make up a big city school population. The purpose of this chapter is to evaluate the Chicago procedure for doing these things.

The Department of Curriculum

The Department of Curriculum is located in the Central Office, and is directed by an Associate Superintendent. The staff of the Department consists mainly of about 24 "curriculum consultants" who work in the areas of English, foreign languages, mathematics, science, and social studies. They are all experienced teachers. Their work consists largely of writing and revising the curriculum guides, preparing bulletins for use by classroom teachers, and conducting in-service workshops to demonstrate new materials and methods to teachers. Since there are three or four persons to a given subject area, these individuals may divide their responsibilities according to areas of the city, or according to grade levels. The curriculum consultants are available for visits to schools and district headquarters on request of principals and district superintendents.

Somewhat similar responsibilities are held by supervisors in the fields of home economics, art, business education, health and physical education, music, industrial arts, guidance, speech correction, and education of the mentally and physically handicapped. These supervisors are under the direct supervision of bureau directors, and have somewhat different working arrangements than the curriculum consultants. They take more initiative in making visits to schools.

They have a more direct relation to the classroom teacher. However, they also prepare curriculum guides. There are an art and a music supervisor assigned to each of the 21 districts. The total number of supervisors with curriculum responsibility is about 75.

These two groups of people would all be called *supervisors* under the traditional terminology of school systems, but the curriculum consultants have less direct influence over classroom teachers than the supervisors have.

Other professional workers in the Department of Curriculum are the evaluation and research staff and the editorial staff.

General curriculum policy is determined by the Curriculum Council. Chairman of the Council is the General Superintendent with the Associate Superintendent in Charge of Curriculum as secretary. Members are: all district superintendents, all directors of bureaus connected with the curriculum, representatives from citizens organizations and from six universities in the Chicago area, representatives for principals and classroom teachers. Most of the work of the Council is done through its study committees which work on the revision of the curriculum.

The responsibility of a study committee is to revise the curriculum in a given subject area and at a given grade level. This process of revision follows a four-year cycle. The cycle is divided into three stages: (1) one year developing the revised course; (2) two years' trial and revision of the new course through use in selected schools; and (3) one year for the final review and publication of the new course.

Several methods are used to evaluate the revised materials at each stage. Questionnaires are sent to teachers for criticism and suggestions about past materials, and university specialists in the area under review check the new materials before they are finally accepted. The final revision is then incorporated in "curriculum guides" intended to serve as major resources for classroom teaching. The guides prescribe a central core of content and activities, but they include a variety of learning experiences designed to encourage varied approaches for differing types of pupils. A guide is intended to be as comprehensive as possible. It contains suggested references for teachers and students, audio-visual aids, and other supplementary materials.

At the end of a four-year cycle, textbooks in each subject area are re-examined and a limited number are included on an approved list from which school faculties select texts. The approved list is drawn up by teachers relieved of their regular duties or employed during the summer for this purpose.

What the curriculum guide should accomplish. The curriculum guide is the central instrument in the Chicago design for curriculum development. It should do two things: (1) serve all teachers as a basis and point of departure for their teaching; (2) present subject matter and methods appropriate to the objectives of the schools.

An essential task of the Survey was to find out how well the Chicago curriculum guides do these things. Survey consultants and staff studied the guides, talked with curriculum staff members, and talked with classroom teachers and with school principals. The Teacher Questionnaire asked all classroom teachers to give their judgments about the guides.

There was substantial agreement among the Survey consultants in their conclusions with respect to the quality of the guides and to the effectiveness of the guides in the schools.

What is the Chicago procedure? The Chicago procedure for curriculum development has evolved over the past 10 years. It has five distinctive characteristics. Most of these characteristics have alternatives which might have been used. In the following description we shall outline the procedure which was actually followed, and also suggest alternatives.

1. Curriculum planning is done for the entire school system through the Central Office. It might have been done separately by districts and even by separate schools. Some·special students of curriculum believe that the individual school building is the best place to do curriculum planning.

2. The work of curriculum planning is done by a specialized curriculum staff with the help of selected classroom teachers working on committees. These are relatively small groups in terms of numbers. The work might, instead, be done by large groups of classroom teachers, or by committees of professional personnel combined with representative lay citizens.

3. The procedure of the curriculum staff is to read the books in the appropriate fields; consult with university professors who are

experts in the subject matter to be taught, such as chemistry or mathematics; secure evaluations of the current curriculum from classroom teachers; and try out new course materials with the aid of a research and evaluation staff.

4. The curriculum is organized around separate subjects, rather than in broad fields or around persistent life problems, as might have been possible. The typical product of the curriculum staff is a published *Guide* which contains suggestions for the content to be taught and also a manual of suggested methods for the teacher.

5. The implementation of the curriculum guides in the classroom is done by the Central Office staff who have been included in the first four phases of the work. The curriculum consultants are expected to work with district superintendents and school principals, to get them to introduce the materials to the classroom teachers, and to guide them in their use.

All big city systems develop their own schemes of curriculum engineering. All fall short of perfection in this very complex work. The Survey consultants believe that the Chicago plan might be improved. If one accepts the first four principles of curriculum development which have just been stated, one must ask how well the curriculum guides are actually working. To what extent are the classroom teachers actually using the guides? It appears that the answer to this question is not satisfactory. The range of use of a given curriculum guide is from no use at all to a very intelligent adaptation of it to the children of a particular school.

The quality of the Chicago curriculum guides

The first main question to answer is about the quality of the curriculum guides, which supposedly carry the curriculum into the classroom. There are two types of answer to this question. One is given by the university professors who studied the guides, observed classes, and talked with teachers. The other answer is given by the classroom teachers who responded to the Teacher Questionnaire concerning their experience with the guides.

It should be remembered that there are guides for a given subject, such as English or mathematics, for various courses and grade levels. Also, some guides are new this year while others are four years old now, and will soon be replaced by new ones. Hence the guides may be expected to be uneven in quality, and no single global judgment will be very useful.

However, the general plan is regarded by the Survey consultants as basically sound. One consultant says, "The guide for the primary grades in language arts is one of the finest of its kind I have ever seen. Its design could well be a model for all types of curriculum planning. Attention has been given to problems of scope and sequence of subject matter throughout the grades; suggested materials of instruction are included; activities for teachers and pupils are suggested. In my judgment a teacher who could not use this guide ought not to be teaching school. I have every confidence that remaining guides for the elementary school will be equally good."

On the other hand, the guide to literature content for high school English is seen as too severely limited to traditional American and English literary works. "While the twelfth grade course is to include novels translated from other languages, all authors listed are western European except for a few Russian authors such as Tolstoi and Turgenev; literature of Asiatic and Latin American cultures is represented only in a few poems. Thus the trend to broaden the pupil's horizon through some attention to world literature does not seem to be reflected in the English curriculum."

In mathematics for the elementary grades, new guides are being prepared with the aid of university professors interested in the "new mathematics." Nineteen elementary schools have tried out experimental programs. The results of these experiments are being studied by the research division of the curriculum department which will make recommendations about the inclusion of elements of modern mathematics in the new guides.

In elementary school science the guides are regarded as sound, though definitely conservative. They do not take adequate account of the modern stress on teaching pupils to inquire and discover things for themselves. The high school guides are outdated, in the opinion of our visiting consultants. More detailed comments on the guides will be given in Chapter X.

Adaptation and application of the curriculum guides

From the interviews with over 300 classroom teachers and about 100 elementary and high school principals it is clear that there is a great range in use of the guides. Some teachers use the guides for the subjects in which they feel the least competent. Some do not use them at all. Some teachers use the guides because they feel they have to; others use them because they feel that the guides are an integral part of making the schools work.

Extremes in the way schools handle the curriculum materials are illustrated in the responses of two elementary school principals to the question, "What do you do with the new curriculum guides when they are sent to you from the central office?" One principal replied that he discussed the material in a faculty meeting and decided with his staff what parts were directly usable and what parts had to be rewritten to fit that school. The other principal replied that he put the guides on a shelf near the door to the office and the teachers could look at them if they wished.

The responses of teachers to the Teacher Questionnaire indicate a similar range in acquaintance with and appreciation of the guides.

There is a widespread opinion that the guides are not useful for teaching pupils who are more than a year below their grade level in reading ability. On the other hand, they might be adapted for such use by teachers or curriculum workers who are familiar with pupils from disadvantaged backgrounds.

It is also clear that the school principal is the key person in the application of the guides. In schools where this person conceives his position as one carrying responsibility for use of the guides, the guides are generally well used. But where the principal takes no such responsibility, a few teachers find the guides a great asset while many others find little or no use for them. In such situations the principal and some of the teachers point out the weaknesses of the guides and blame the "downtown office" for it.

Teacher opinion of the guides

Teachers were asked on an anonymous questionnaire whether their teaching is guided: more by curriculum guides and supplements, more by the approved textbooks, or about equally by both. Responses were rather different for high school teachers than for elementary school teachers. High school teachers made considerably more use of textbooks than did elementary school teachers. Among the latter, 10 percent said their teaching was guided more by textbooks than by guides, whereas 25 percent of secondary school teachers said they were influenced more by textbooks. Still, 27 percent of high school teachers said they used guides more than texts, and 36 percent of elementary school teachers said guides were more important. Thus both groups of teachers were more likely to use guides than textbooks as the main base for their teaching.

Teachers were also asked who familiarizes them with curriculum guides and supplements as they first come out. The majority of both groups of teachers responded, "I do it myself." Fifty-six percent of high school teachers and 64 percent of elementary school teachers gave this response. Among elementary school teachers, 22 percent said their building principal worked with them, while only 5 percent of high school teachers gave this answer. High school teachers credited Curriculum Department consultants (8 percent), supervisors (15 percent), and fellow teachers (11 percent). Much smaller percentages of elementary school teachers gave these answers.

It appears then, in general, that teachers tend to take it on themselves to study the guides without much instigation from above, and that about 30 percent rely more on the guides than on the approved textbooks for the direction of their teaching.

A more definite picture of the teachers' opinion is found in the answers to questions about their use of guides and supplements in specific subjects. Teachers were asked to respond, for each subject which they taught, to the following directions.

Please rate the usefulness of the guides and supplements which are (or were) available by checking:

    1 Excellent   2 Good   3 Fair   4 Unsatisfactory

Please check the degree to which you use (or used) available guides and supplements for daily or weekly planning:

    1 Often   2 Sometimes   3 Never or almost never

Check for each subject the amount of help you now (or did) receive in the use of guides and supplements from principals, supervisors, department chairmen, or consultants:

    1 Much   2 Some   3 None or practically none

Table 1, pages 100-01, shows how the elementary school teachers report on the curriculum guides which are generally available to them. It will be seen that between 50 and 60 percent say they use the guides in the four basic subject areas "often." These same guides were voted by 31 to 41 percent as "excellent." There is a small but steady tendency for the Science guide to be preferred and used more often, while the Social Studies guide is the least popular and the least used of the "Big Four." Among the three special areas for which classroom teachers generally take less responsibility, art, music, and health and physical education guides have about equal use and equal popularity.

Table 1 also confirms the finding earlier stated that a majority of teachers claim they get little or no help in the use of the guides and supplements.

Table 2 shows comparable data for high school teachers, with respect to the guides for courses most frequently taught. Other data on high school teachers' use of curriculum guides are shown in Tables 3 and 4 of Chapter X. From these two tables and Tables 1, 2, and 3 of this chapter the following conclusions may be drawn.

1. High school teachers make less use of the guides than do elementary school teachers.

2. The less experienced teachers find the guides less helpful and make less use of them than the more experienced teachers. This is true for high school and for elementary school teachers.

3. From 50 to 70 percent of classroom teachers say they get no help from principal, supervisor, curriculum consultants, or department chairman in the use of guides. More elementary school teachers say they get help from principals than do high school teachers.

4. There is some variation of attitude toward the various guides, indicating that some guides need more interpretation or more revision than others do. This is noticeable in Table 2A and 2B.

The attitudes of the high school teachers toward the guides for Basic and Essential courses were generally less favorable than their attitudes toward the guides for Regular and Honors courses. A similar attitude was observed among elementary school teachers who worked in low-achievement schools. They found the guides for language arts, science, and social studies less useful than did those who taught in high-achievement schools. This was found by the visiting consultants, by the Survey staff in their interviews with teachers, and in the results from the Teacher Questionnaire.

The problems of preparing curriculum guides for low-achievement classes are not easy to solve. The lack of commercially

Table 1
How elementary school teachers view curriculum guides
(percentages, unless otherwise stated)

A. Evaluation of guides and supplements

Subject area	Excellent	Good	Fair	Unsatis-factory	Not familiar; do not use	Number
Art	9	25	25	16	25	4,512
Health, Physical Education	8	25	23	10	34	4,438
Language arts	41	36	15	4	4	4,632
Mathematics	39	39	12	3	7	4,624
Music	11	22	25	13	29	4,506
Science	42	35	12	4	7	4,603
Social studies	31	37	18	7	7	4,612

B. Degree of use of guides

Subject area	Often	Sometimes	Never or almost never	Don't teach this subject	Number
Art	14	34	39	13	4,381
Health, Physical Education	11	29	31	29	4,410
Language arts	57	31	7	5	4,580
Mathematics	59	27	6	8	4,572
Music	14	29	41	16	4,433
Science	61	24	5	10	4,560
Social studies	54	30	8	8	4,553

C. *Help or direction given by principal, supervisor,*
or consultants in use of guides

	Much	*Some*	*None or practically none*	*Don't teach this subject*	*Number*
Art	10	26	52	12	4,397
Health, Physical Education	5	15	53	27	4,433
Language arts	16	26	52	6	4,558
Mathematics	16	23	52	9	4,551
Music	10	24	52	14	4,485
Science	15	22	52	11	4,545
Social studies	13	21	57	9	4,547

Table 2
How high school teachers
view curriculum guides
(percentages, unless otherwise stated)

A. Evaluation of guides and supplements

Subject area	Excellent	Good	Fair	Unsatis-factory	Number
Art	18	25	37	20	73
Music	19	30	25	25	83
French	35	25	28	12	40
Spanish	23	23	27	27	82
English, Regular and Honors	21	40	26	13	886
English, Basic and Essential	4	14	35	47	104
Math, Regular and Advanced	20	39	28	13	606
Math, Basic and Essential	16	31	24	29	174
General Science	29	33	26	12	189
Biology	18	40	27	15	157
Chemistry	22	28	22	11	83
Physics	24	24	39	13	41
History	18	34	28	20	855
General Business	27	32	21	20	66

B. *Degree of use of guides*

Subject area	Often	Sometimes	Never	Number
Art	24	56	20	72
Music	18	47	35	83
French	36	32	32	41
Spanish	28	41	31	81
English, Regular and Honors	37	45	18	883
English, Basic and Essential	14	42	44	107
Math, Regular and Advanced	24	42	34	615
Math, Basic and Essential	34	31	35	174
General Science	34	47	19	187
Biology	35	42	23	155
Chemistry	21	49	30	82
Physics	20	40	40	42
History	26	45	29	851
General Business	30	40	30	66

Table 2 continued
How high school teachers
view curriculum guides
(percentages, unless otherwise stated)

C. Help or direction given by principal, supervisor, department chairman, or consultants in use of guides

Subject area	Much	Some	None or practically none	Number
Art	10	29	61	72
Music	7	42	51	83
French	24	27	49	41
Spanish	15	33	52	81
English, Regular and Honors	11	30	59	879
English, Basic and Essential	4	26	70	104
Math, Regular and Advanced	9	25	65	608
Math, Basic and Essential	7	25	68	174
General Science	6	26	68	185
Biology	10	24	66	154
Chemistry	7	20	73	81
Physics	5	24	71	41
History	13	28	59	853
General Business	14	23	63	66

Table 3
Degree of use of curriculum guides by elementary school teachers
(percentages, unless otherwise stated)

Subject area	1 - 2 years' experience					3 - 15 years' experience					16 + years' experience					Total			
	O*	S	N	DT	No.	O	S	N	DT	No.	O	S	N	DT	No.	O	S	N	DT
Art	7	25	56	12	719	12	32	44	13	2,395	24	43	22	11	1,242	14	34	39	12
Health and Physical Education	5	20	44	31	728	9	29	32	30	2,414	18	35	20	26	1,242	11	29	31	29
Language arts	43	39	12	6	737	55	33	8	5	2,488	68	25	3	4	1,327	57	31	7	5
Mathematics	53	30	8	9	741	57	28	7	8	2,489	65	24	4	8	1,314	59	27	6	8
Music	6	19	57	19	728	11	28	44	18	2,412	25	37	27	12	1,265	14	29	41	16
Science	58	28	7	7	742	61	25	5	9	2,487	64	21	4	12	1,302	61	24	5	10
Social studies	45	33	14	8	740	52	31	8	8	2,472	62	28	4	7	1,313	54	31	8	8

*O=Often; S=Sometimes; N=Never; DT=Don't teach this subject.

produced textbooks and other published materials for use with slow learners is well known, and committees representing the nation's largest cities are just beginning to seek ways of overcoming this deplorable shortage. This helps explain why the curriculum guides in several subjects indicate only a very small number of readings and activities for the "less academically able students." Perhaps an equally responsible factor, however, follows from the fact that few of the teachers serving on the committees which prepare the guides and few of the Central Office consultants are selected from low-achievement schools. There is a definite tendency, in fact, to choose teachers from the high-achievement schools. Since the teachers with more experience and advanced training are found in the more favored schools, it may seem natural that they should be selected for curriculum work.

The need for in-service training and adaptation of curriculum guides

Two conclusions emerge from consideration of the facts about curriculum guides and their use. One is that the guides need to be adapted to the schools of the low-income areas of the city. The other is that teachers need more help and direction in the use of the guides and supplements.

Some further help is certainly needed to adapt and apply the curriculum guides fully. Some more people must be assigned to this work. Where and under whose auspices should they work?

One answer to this question is that the "downtown office"—the Department of Curriculum—should have its staff of curriculum consultants doubled in number, and the extra consultants should hold more in-service training workshops to show teachers how to adapt and use the guides. They might also work more with principals who in turn could work more effectively with their teachers. Also, some of the curriculum staff could do special assignments on adapting the guides to pupils who are below average in achievement and motivation.

All the Survey consultants recommended that more people be added to the supervisory and consultant positions. However, most of them recommended that these new appointments be *not* added to the staff at the Central Office but rather to district offices. In other words, the recommendation was for *decentralization* of the curriculum development work.

Before discussing the pros and cons of this recommendation, it is necessary to relate the discussion to a well-known problem in the art of administration of complex enterprises. The problem of line and staff organization is involved. The classroom teachers and the school principals and district superintendents are in the *line* organization, with responsibility coming down to them from the General Superintendent. On the other hand, the Department of Curriculum and the curriculum consultants and supervisors are a part of the staff organization. Their job is to prepare curriculum guides and other materials for use by the line members, and to help the line organization whenever they can. When adding new members to an organization, it is wise to consider the relationships that exist between line and staff and to ask where the new members can be most effective.

In educational administration the line versus staff problem was encountered three or four decades ago in the form of a conflict between supervisors and school principals. The supervisor, whether of art, or music, or English, or some other subject, was an expert in his own subject and an enthusiast for it. He worked directly with the classroom teachers and sometimes upset the balance which the principal had established in the teacher's program. An enthusiastic art supervisor might so stimulate a teacher that she would sacrifice other subjects by giving an undue amount of her attention to art. If the principal objected to this, the supervisor might appeal to the superintendent for support.

The problem was more or less successfully resolved several decades ago by making the principal more of a supervisor himself. And the number of supervisors in a big city system decreased. It was expected that the principal would be the person with the most general knowledge about the curriculum and the one best fitted to adapt the curriculum to his own particular school, which he knew better than anyone else.

Although the problem was partially settled by making the school principal more of a supervisor as well as an administrator, it was recognized that in certain special subject areas the principal could not be expected to have anything approaching expert knowledge, and therefore he either should have experts in his own school to work in those special areas, or he would need help from a staff organization. Such areas are music, art, home economics, physical education, industrial arts, and the area of special education. Therefore a big city school system generally maintained a staff of supervisors in these areas, attached to the Central Office. The principal was responsible for supervision in the "regular" curriculum areas of English, mathematics, social studies, and science.

The situation in the Chicago schools at present is as follows: The line of responsibility for instruction goes from the General Superintendent through the associate superintendents for instruction to the district superintendent to the principal to the classroom teacher. However, the principals do not in all cases grasp fully their responsibilities and the accompanying tasks for curriculum implementation. The supervisors in the various Bureaus of the Central Office work with particular schools and districts on request from the principal or the district superintendent. The curriculum consultants in the Department of Curriculum work mainly at the planning and writing of curriculum guides, and what time is left over they give to in-service training of teachers at the request of district superintendents and principals.

It has been pointed out that most of the consultants favor strengthening the curriculum development program by placing more people in district offices to work more directly with district superintendents, school principals, and classroom teachers in terms of the particular needs of the pupils of the district or school. The advantage claimed for this procedure is that of being close to the actual use of curriculum guides, learning where they are inadequate, and revising them to fit local pupil needs.

As part of a plan for better adaptation and application of curriculum guides, the principal would be expected to give more of his time to curriculum supervision and to stay longer in a particular school, so as to get to know the school and the neighborhood better. Also, in the high schools, the department chairmen would be given more responsibility than they now have for curriculum adaptation.

The argument for this arrangement at the high school level is set forth in the report by the Suburban Superintendents' Committee of

Michael, Allingham, and Knoeppel, in Supplement F. They make the following five recommendations:

1 The curriculum in each high school needs greater adaptation and adjustment to the needs of the pupil population it serves.
2 Greater flexibility should be explored in establishing teacher assignment quotas (and classroom facilities) for specific high schools, which have clearly varied needs evident in the character of student bodies and communities served by each.
3 Greater autonomy of districts in the Chicago system could be reflected in more flexible curricular possibilities in the various general high schools, and probably would result in a markedly higher morale among the professional staff.
4 The role of the department chairmen should be enhanced by granting them more time for the performance of their duties.
5 The desirability of continuity of educational leadership in a school would seem to call for a recognition of the high school principalship as a position of increasing importance.

In accordance with the recommendation just cited, the district organization might be reorganized. The present districts might be retained with little or no change, but they might be coordinated for curriculum purposes into four to six regions. The regions might be made up of schools with certain pupil characteristics, and certain family and neighborhood characteristics. However, a particular school with unusual characteristics might be placed in a region different from that of some of its neighbor schools. The nature of such a regional structure will be discussed in Chapter XIX.

One region might consist of high schools with a heavy college-preparatory enrollment, and their feeder schools. Several curriculum workers might be located at the regional office, who were specially selected for their ability to adapt curriculum materials to gifted children. Another region might consist of high schools with the greatest number of low-achieving students, and their feeder schools. The curriculum staff for this region would specialize on adapting curriculum materials to the needs of culturally disadvantaged students. This might be the answer for the inner-city principal, who said, "How are you going to get the curriculum down to our level—down to the grass roots? We need more resources in terms of consultants to bring these down to school level. These people are spending their time writing and planning and when they come out to us they really don't know the situation. Look—these are merely competent teachers who are taken from the classroom and put to work as consultants or curriculum makers. They never had any sociology; they're unfamiliar with the sociology of this area. They can't feel an over-all need. I think it would help to have consultant training along these lines. We need special consultants for special areas or districts who would stay and work in these areas. It would help the consultants to have some work experience in these areas so they would be able to understand our problems."

Three or four other regional districts might be created for other groups of schools with situations and problems which make them similar.

The subject of district organization will be treated more fully in Chapter XIX, after other topics which bear upon the subject have been presented.

Where the Central Office should be strengthened. The argument of the preceding paragraphs would lead to strengthening the curriculum staff in district offices, where curriculum staff can work closely with principals and classroom teachers who have similar school situations. This applies especially in the "regular" curriculum fields—mathematics, English, social studies, and natural science. In other areas the argument loses much of its force.

It would probably be better to strengthen curriculum staff in the Central Office and to give them more authority, if necessary, when they deal: (1) with an area of subject matter which is not regarded as central to the curriculum, and therefore would not be staffed with many supervisors even though it is an important subject—such as physical education; (2) with an area of subject matter which needs a special support from the Central Office—possibly home economics and industrial arts fall in this category; and (3) with an area of subject matter which has a special developmental need that requires attention and authoritative backing from the Central Office in selected schools that are not likely to be in a single district. An example of this might be foreign languages, which are now undergoing a revolution in teaching method and at the same time being introduced in the elementary school. As will be seen in a later chapter, problems of coordination of foreign language instruction between elementary school and high school are serious, and the current changes in methods of teaching foreign language are not understood by the average school principal.

Textbooks and other teaching materials

Another aspect of the curriculum is the choice of textbooks and the provision of library books, films, recordings, etc., for use in teaching. The plan in force is to revise the list of approved textbooks and auxiliary materials at the end of a four-year cycle of curriculum revision, so that the new list coincides with the introduction of a new guide.

The approved list of textbooks is one from which a school or a department of a school may choose their books and place an order. Once an order is placed, the choice must stand until the books wear out, since there is not enough textbook money to change books frequently on a large scale. The effect of this procedure is occasionally to omit a very good book for an accidental reason. For example, a very highly regarded book in high school United States history is not on the current list. Probably this is because, when the list was made out, this book had not been revised recently. Now the book has been revised, but cannot get on the list until the present four-year cycle is over. It is true that, in Chicago, machinery exists through which a school may request permission to purchase a book that is not on the approved list. The views on this arrangement expressed by principals ranged from "No problem—every reasonable request is granted." to "It can happen, but actually it doesn't very often."

Some arrangement should be made for greater flexibility in the procurement of textbooks and other teaching materials. Possibly the list could be revised more frequently. New York City has an "approved list" which is much more inclusive and is updated annually.

In this connection, our consultants suggest that the new policy of allocating textbook money specifically by school grade may be too mechanical. This policy, summarized in a Report from the General Superintendent to the Board of Education on April 8, 1964, sets up a scale of textbook allocations ranging from $0.70 per pupil in kindergarten and $1.50 per pupil in first grade to $7.00 per pupil in high school. The Report says, "Money is to be spent only by grade in relation to amounts allocated by grade." It is not clear how this will work out in practice in a high-achievement elementary school operating on the continuous development plan. In such a school, who is a second-grade pupil and who is a third-grade pupil? Probably such a school should have a good deal of fourth- and fifth-grade textbook material used by children technically in the third grade. Another problem may arise when a particular principal wants to work intensively with his teachers of a certain grade level on the revision of their curriculum in a given year. He may need more money for that grade in that particular year, which will be balanced out by greater expenditures for other grades in other years.

Some procedure should be established to permit a desirable flexibility in using local school textbook allotments.

Promotion policies and standards of grading

The quality of teaching is related in a complex way to the policies of promotion and of marking pupils for success or failure. The complexity is seen when we attempt to answer the following hypothetical questions.

If 95 percent of pupils are promoted, does this mean that the schools are doing a good job of teaching, or does it mean that their standards are too low?

If teachers are informed directly or indirectly that they should not give more than 10 percent failing grades, does this force them to lower their standards and to reduce their teaching effectiveness?

Should pupils be admitted to high school with reading and arithmetic achievement of fifth- to seventh-grade levels?

Should pupils be given honor grades in School A for work which would get them only average grades in School B?

Anyone who thinks these questions should receive simple yes or no answers has not grasped the realities of a modern educational system. How can one apply the same standards of grading and promotion in the high-achievement and low-achievement high schools reported in Table 3 of Chapter III? How can one establish a simple set of standards for sixth grades as diverse as the ones shown in Table 4 of that chapter?

On the Teacher Questionnaire, 55 percent responded "sometimes" and 20 percent responded "often" to the question: Do you ever promote or give a passing grade to students who you feel have not achieved the basic requirements of the grade or course? There was little difference in responses of high school and elementary school teachers. Of those who responded "sometimes" or "often," 44 percent of high school teachers and 32 percent of elementary school teachers said this was due to administration pressure, while 38 percent of high school teachers and 53 percent of elementary school teachers said it was a consequence of a policy of social promotion. These responses probably indicate that high school teachers are less content with standards of grading than are elementary school teachers.

In visits to high schools, the Survey staff found that the teachers generally *perceived* an upper limit on failing grades as being about 10 percent. There were a few schools in which principals had issued or strongly implied such a policy. In the words of a teacher at one of these schools, "If students are alive at the end of a semester, they pass. Our principal comes around and tells teachers with few or no failures, 'You're doing a fine job' "! But other principals had taken pains to make it clear that they would support the judgment of their teachers, and thus tacitly encouraged them to give as many failing marks as they thought were deserved.

There is probably too much emphasis on grades and on grading in some of the high-achievement schools. This is part of a general overemphasis on school grades and test scores of which parents as well as teachers are guilty just now. The period from 1955 to 1970 will probably go down in educational history as a time when competition for grades and for admission to the "best" colleges robbed many children and youth of the joy of learning for its own sake and at their own most comfortable rates.

On the other hand, some of the low-achievement schools are too low in their standards and too lax in their grading schemes for the best interests of their better students. Overpowered by the problem of keeping low-achieving students in school, they necessarily adopt low standards for promotion of those students. Such low standards have an influence on the standards in the Regular and Honors tracks of those high schools. This influence is even greater in elementary schools where the system of ability grouping is not so clearly marked.

The problem is most pressing in the low-achievement schools, and for them we suggest the following procedure.

1. The principals, teachers, and counselors of such schools should confer and formulate a clear policy on standards and grades for the top third of their students. This policy should then become the basis for practices in grading, and it should be interpreted by counselors to pupils and their parents.

2. For the lower two-thirds of the students there should be a heavy emphasis on the pupil's *effort* in grading him, combined with an interpretation to him of his test scores in a way that he knows when he is improving. Test scores should not be presented to the low-achieving pupil in such a way that he becomes discouraged at his retardation, but instead can be used to show him that he can improve and to inform him when he is doing so.

3. There should be careful consideration of the desirability of establishing several high schools in low-achievement areas in which eighth-grade achievement level on standard tests would be a condition for admission. Such quasi-selective schools might produce an environment for learning which would stimulate the better students and give them and their teachers a more realistic basis for judging their educational progress. There are obvious disadvantages to such an arrangement, centered about the problem of the remaining schools which would lose some of their best students. Possibly the better solution would be a stricter set of standards for the Regular and Honors tracks of the present schools.

Finally, for the average and high-achievement schools the two evils of rigid mechanical standards and easy passing marks must both be avoided. The best solution of the problem is the improvement of teaching, so that students become excited and eager to learn for the joy of learning. The current trends in curriculum revision lead in this direction.

Nevertheless, school grades will have a real importance to students who are going to college. The new system of awarding grade points to determine rank in high school class in relation to ability level or track enables students in the higher tracks to get more grade points for a given mark than they would if they were in a class of lower ability level. For example, a mark of A (S on the old system) will earn 6, 5, or 4 grade points in Advanced Placement, Honors, or Regular classes, respectively, and will not be given to pupils in Essential or Basic courses. This will place more weight on the system of ability grouping in the high schools.

Ability grouping is justified only when it results in better instruction for the high- and the low-ability students. The Chicago schools should set up a thorough program of evaluation of the results of the practices of ability grouping.

Conclusions

From the reports of a number of Survey consultants there emerges a picture of a complex organization providing a curriculum for 500 schools with various types of pupils. This organization appears to function rather well up to the point of preparing curriculum guides for the various subject areas. At this point, the next step is to implement the curriculum guides in the classroom, and this part of the process is not as well done. It seems to succeed least in the schools in which the pupils have the greatest need. These schools have teachers with the least training who need the most help from supervisors and principals. However, it should be kept in mind that schools with low-achievement levels are almost certain to be the ones where the curriculum procedures appear to be least efficient. These schools will always show up badly.

Nevertheless, it is necessary to concentrate on the areas of great need. The Survey consultants have made suggestions, which are rather similar to suggestions made by representatives of the State Superintendent of Public Instruction who visited two of the 21 school districts during the period of April 6-17, 1964. In a letter dated July 2, 1964, addressed to the General Superintendent of Schools, the visitation team had the following to say concerning improvement of the educational program. We quote these recommendations with approval.

a. Consideration should be given to the teacher placement policies in order to develop a stabilized staff in those areas of greatest need.

b. Opportunities should be provided to develop additional in-service workshops and teachers' meetings to improve instruction.

c. There appears to be a need at the high school level to develop increased leadership on the part of department chairmen. Perhaps, by assigning additional responsibility for leadership of instruction, the total programming of their specific area could be improved. There is a need for some released time, and perhaps, some additional incentives should be provided.

d. In both the high schools and the elementary schools there is evidence of long-range planning in the development of curriculum guides. The program of curriculum development is good and should be continued. Greater effort should be made to implement this desirable program.

The principal was seen as the key person in the improvement of instruction.

It was evident that the principals were competent and well-trained school administrators. They showed sensitivity to the pupils and their needs, and were making every effort to develop programs within their resources to satisfy these needs. The principals should be given increased responsibilities to develop the school program, and should assume leadership opportunities in their school communities. We suggest consideration be given to the following items relative to the principals:

a. The program providing principals with increased leadership opportunities is to be commended. This provides an atmosphere which encourages individual incentive. However, greater stability is needed in some areas of the city. Perhaps, it would be advantageous to study this problem in light of the need for greater stability in these areas.

b. Supervision must be the major role of the principal if he is to be effective in his school. Supervisory leadership, as it has developed, has enhanced the quality of instruction. It is suggested that continued emphasis be given to principals' workshops and in-service programs to improve the methods and techniques of supervision.

c. Excellent materials are provided by the central office in the area of curriculum and should make possible an improved educational program. It is imperative that these materials be further implemented in every classroom in the City of Chicago. It appears that the only means of accomplishing this task is to provide the principals and the teachers with additional time to study and become acquainted with the curriculum materials. It is suggested that principals be provided with the opportunity of holding additional in-service workshops at more advantageous times. The further implementation of this program should lead to improvement in the educational offering.

VII

Reading, Libraries, and Television

Reading, libraries, and television are grouped in one chapter since they represent media used for instruction. Obviously, learning takes place through the media of visual materials, and the use of television capitalizes on an audio-visual presentation.

READING

Reading is regarded both by teachers and by parents as the corner stone of education. Parents are more aware of and sensitive to their children's reading progress than to any other element of education. Teachers in the primary grades pay more attention to reading than to anything else. Teachers in the intermediate and high school grades find their greatest problem with pupils who are retarded in reading ability.

At the beginning of the first grade, a test of readiness to learn to read is given to all pupils. There are five levels or grades in the test as follows:·

* * *

This chapter is largely based on reports from the following Survey consultants: Leon Carnovsky, Professor in the Graduate Library School, The University of Chicago; H. Alan Robinson, Assistant Professor of Education, The University of Chicago; and Daniel Tanner, Associate Professor of Education, Northwestern University.

A. Superior. Should be given opportunities for enriched work.

B. High normal.

C. Average. Likely to succeed in first-grade work.

D. Low normal. Likely to have difficulty in first-grade work. Should be assigned to slow section and given more individualized help.

E. Poor risk. Chances of failure high under ordinary instructional conditions.

An average first grade of children who are 6 years old or nearly 6 contains about 30 percent who make a grade below the "average expectancy" level (D or E), and consequently can be expected (unless the test was wrong) to have difficulty with reading and to need special help.

As Table 2 in Chapter III shows, 45 percent of Chicago first graders are below the level where they may be expected to learn to read in the first grade without special help. In two of the city's 21 districts, two-thirds of the first graders are in the group of children who are not ready to read. On the other hand, eight of the city's 21 districts have from 74 to 89 percent of first graders ready to learn to read with ordinary amounts and quality of assistance from the teacher.

The result of the present program for the teaching of reading at the sixth-grade level is seen in Table 4, Chapter III, which shows the reading levels of sixth graders for 12 varied schools. In three of these schools, from one-half to two-thirds of the sixth graders are a year or more retarded in reading. In four more of the schools, from one-fourth to one-half are a year or more retarded. On the other hand, in three of the schools, more than half of the sixth graders are a year or more advanced in reading, and some are five years advanced. These 12 schools have reading readiness scores in the first grade from which one could predict the sixth-grade performance of the pupils.

Methods of teaching reading

The method of teaching reading is a balanced one, making use of phonics as far as possible and at the same time teaching children to recognize whole words by sight. This method has arisen out of discussion by the Curriculum Department with a number of outside specialists in reading. It appears to be the only realistic way to teach the reading of English. A pure phonic method might work with Spanish and German, which are phonetic languages; but it could not work with English and French, in which the spelling is not phonetic. The phonic approach falls down on such common words as: write, right; threw, through; two, too; believe, receive; tough, bluff.

There are a number of interesting new approaches to the teaching of reading which deserve experimental trial. One such approach was observed in the Chicago schools, led by a principal who had made a special study of reading and taught the primary grade teachers to use this particular method. Probably other experimental variations are being tried.

Most experts who have studied the problems of reading in the schools would be reasonably satisfied with the basic methods used in the Chicago Public Schools, *except* for the work with the socially disadvantaged or culturally deprived child. For this child a consultant writes:

> Tried and true traditional approaches are not working. In Chicago, in those districts with the largest percentage of culturally disadvantaged families, standardized reading tests indicate one and a half to two years' retardation. A highly visual and tactile approach to words growing from students' experiences should be explored in the early grades. These students should not meet typical basal readers and other books until they have more familiarity with the concepts attached to the printed symbols. This early approach might capitalize on audio-visual approaches, manipulative materials, and very brief booklets.

This analysis and recommendation might be made with equal force in New York City or Philadelphia or Los Angeles. It points to one of the major problems of education in the big city.

Curriculum guides in language arts

> Curriculum guides in the language arts, at least for the primary and intermediate grades, are based on sound pedagogical principles, delineate objectives clearly, contain many sound suggestions for activities and materials to use in carrying out objectives, and show evidence of resulting from continuous evaluation. The six language arts consultants on the central staff plus the other members of the

Department of Curriculum Development responsible for the final production of the guides should be justly proud of their work.

With these words the consultant approves the work of the Curriculum Department in the area of reading and of English language instruction in the elementary schools. He goes on, however, to say that the curriculum guides are not being effectively applied in the classroom, nor are they suitable in total for all situations.

> In practice, however, there seems to be little use of them. Classroom observations and interviews with numerous teachers indicate lack of acquaintance with either the old or the new guides. Many of the teachers who do make some use of the guides as reference tools say that the bulk of activities and materials suggested are not suited to the needs of the children they teach—especially the culturally disadvantaged. The guides are primarily devoted to a basal approach and classroom grouping (three to four groups) rather than to the needs of individuals who must probably use materials closer to their experience backgrounds. Guides are based on a middle-class philosophy and the constructors of the guides undoubtedly feel that the culturally disadvantaged must begin to adhere to such standards.

This consultant's recommendation, like that of consultants in other subjects, is that the curriculum guides should be worked over in several different regional districts, each district being relatively homogeneous in the characteristics of its pupils. The Central Office curriculum staff would produce the more general parts of the curriculum guides, while the regional district staff would produce the parts which show the teacher how to apply the general principles in her own classroom.

This recommendation means that the number of specialists in reading would be substantially increased. There are only six language arts consultants in the Central Office. The recommendation is that there be at least three language arts consultants for elementary schools and one for high schools in each of several regional districts.

Supervision of the teaching of reading

The actual work of the teaching of reading in the individual classroom should depend on the principal, the reading consultant, and the department chairman of English in the high school.

In those few elementary schools where the principal has been well-trained in the teaching of reading and where he has time to devote to supervision, the program may be excellent. But, generally speaking, most of the elementary schools do not have reading and language arts programs understood and carried out by the total faculty. Each teacher carries out his own program to the best of his ability, clinging primarily to the trappings of the basal reading program and spelling lists.

At the high school level there is virtually no supervision of the teaching of reading and the other language arts. The high school principal must be concerned with the numerous facets of school administration and cannot possibly, even if he had the competence, supervise a language arts program which should permeate the total curriculum. The few central staff consultants must be concerned with so many details; reading instruction becomes just one of those details. Department chairmen at the high school level, who could be effective supervisors (if trained, remunerated, and freed of classes), function now as clerks and teachers without supervisory duties.

This reference to the teaching of reading in high school is most important. We saw in Table 3 of Chapter III that 35 percent of the ninth graders of High School A are in Basic Reading courses, which means that they are reading below the sixth-grade level. They are three or more years retarded in reading. And there are a dozen other high schools with a similar problem. Such pupils need a kind of instruction in reading that the ordinary high school English teachers do not know how to give. Teachers of such courses need in-service training in special institutes, and supervision by a department chairman or reading consultant or principal who knows this field.

The reading program in action

In a growing number of elementary schools the *continuous development* program is used. This means that pupils are grouped together at the same level of reading readiness or reading proficiency, regardless of their age, and are promoted from one group to another at any time during the year when their progress justifies it. The continuous development program will be evaluated in Chapter VIII. The Survey consultant in reading sees this type of program to have good possibilities, but observes that too few Chicago teachers are using it effectively. These teachers need systematic training in the continuous development program which is applied to reading.

Continuous development organization of primary grades generally extends only through Grade 3. From the fourth through the eighth grade the teaching of reading is "haphazard and lethargic as it is in many other communities," according to the Survey consultant, who naturally would like to see a closer approach to perfection in his own field. He has a similar criticism of reading instruction in high school. It is not that Chicago is relatively weak, rather it is that all the big city schools are so weak in this field. The consultant urges action in this area:

> In-service training programs in reading and the other language arts at all school levels are essential and needed immediately. Since it is impossible to hire teachers well trained in reading, the obligation belongs to the school system. The in-service program should emphasize "working" workshops where teachers meet in small groups under competent leadership and actually learn by doing. Even if students have to come to school for fewer hours while workshops are held partially during school hours, the result is bound to help the students.

The present after-school reading program is approved in general, but too many teachers are simply treating this as a study period, without making the attempt to diagnose the difficulties of the pupils and to build a remedial program on such a diagnosis. Here, too, in-service training should be helpful. Furthermore, after-school reading comes only two days a week and for only 30 to 40 minutes a period.

The reading clinics which are operated by specialists in the Bureau of Child Study appear to be helping the small numbers of pupils who get to them, but the Survey consultant believes that the persons manning these clinics are so well trained in reading and the language arts that they ought to take part in the in-service training of classroom teachers, perhaps as district-level supervisors with a clinic or clinics under the jurisdiction of each. They ought to use the clinic as a training laboratory for classroom teachers and remedial teachers.

Pre-service training of teachers in reading

The branches of Chicago Teachers College are doing an adequate job of training new teachers for the teaching of reading, as far as pre-service training can go. The West or Crane Branch of Teachers College South appears to be doing an especially good job of training in-service teachers for work with culturally disadvantaged children. It might be well to encourage this or some other branch to specialize in the in-service training of teachers in the low-achievement schools, working with the reading specialists in a regional district office that dealt especially with the adaptation and application of curriculum guides for such schools.

LIBRARIES

The school library has two main purposes: to help boys and girls get into the habit of reading books, and to supplement the single textbook for classroom learning. It is difficult to see how the goal of making the pupil a self-motivated learner can be achieved without major reliance on libraries.

The improvement in the Chicago Public Schools during the past three decades shows very clearly when school libraries of 1964 are compared with those of 1932. The Strayer Survey report indicates that elementary school libraries did not then exist. "Despite the fact that elementary schools have been planned to provide space for school libraries, such space is usually utilized as storage room for sets of textbooks," says the 1932 report. Five of the 25 junior high schools had no libraries, and two of the 24 senior high schools did not have libraries. Only one of the junior high school librarians and 11 of the senior high school librarians were college graduates with library training.

At present, all but five or six schools have libraries. The number of school libraries has grown in the last decade as the number of schools and the school population have increased. From 1953 to 1963 centralized high school libraries increased from 47 to 51; high school branches with central libraries from four to 26; elementary schools with centralized libraries from 320 to 435. (There was a total of 441 elementary schools in September, 1963.) All schools have classroom collections, whether or not a central library is also available. The number of books and personnel has also shown substantial increases in the decade; over half a million volumes are available in the high schools and over a million and a third in the elementary schools. Since library expenditures are keyed to enrollment, appropriations have gone up consistent with increasing enrollment. At present $1.50 per high school pupil per year is allocated for library book acquisition, and $1.00 per pupil in elementary schools. These figures bring the libraries well within the North Central Association standards.

Examples of good library service

The following brief reports on one high school library and one elementary library were selected as examples of good library service available in the Chicago Public Schools.

Library A serves a high school with a racially mixed enrollment (80 percent white) in a middle-income area.

Upon entering this library one senses *quality*: a comprehensive book collection in excellent condition; tables and chairs arranged to get away from the typical somber institutional pattern; a group of librarians on top of their jobs; excellent spirit and fine rapport with the principal and teachers—in brief, a first-rate operation.

Because this school goes back a good many years, its book collection has had a chance to develop, and today it numbers 12,500 volumes. Annual accessions approach 800, and periodical subscriptions number 53. Book selection follows the usual procedures: suggestions from faculty, regular checking of book lists, reviews, bibliographies, etc. Cataloging is done at the library headquarters downtown, as it is for all high school libraries.

The library's book budget is $4,300, based on $1.50 per pupil. In addition there is approximately $100 paid for lost books (this money is spent for more books) and $400-$500 from fines. Interestingly enough, money from fines has been used to buy some library furniture, and this has been done with intelligence and imagination.

There is no limit on the number of books allowed to be taken out, and the circulation is good. About 200 seats are available. The shelves are becoming a bit crowded, and before long something will have to be done to provide additional space. The librarians mentioned the desirability of having running water available, as well as an office. Book losses unfortunately tend to be high.

The 1962-63 figures (latest available) showed a total book collection of 11,733, with additions during the year of 1,044 and withdrawals of 1,456, indicating more than average weeding in process. Pupil enrollment in June, 1963, was 2,415. Annual circulation of books came to 27,960. Library expenditures were $2,619 ($1.08 per pupil), of which $450 was for rebinding.

This library's excellence is due to many factors, but certainly not the least of these are the quality and imagination of its professional library staff.

Library B serves an all-Negro elementary school (K-6) in a culturally deprived area.

Enrollment here is 1,500. The library facilities are good: spacious and light. The collection (4,750 books) is in fine shape, the result of continuous weeding carried on by the young, personable, and apparently very capable librarian. About 500 books a year are added, accompanied by careful weeding so there is no problem of crowded shelves and shabby books. In addition to periodicals—18 professional, 14 for the children—there is the usual collection of good film strips, records, games, and other supplementary teaching materials.

Money is not a serious problem, with an appropriation of $1 per pupil, or $1,500. Procedures in ordering books are satisfactory, and there is no complaint about speed of delivery of the books.

As elsewhere, processing of the books is something of a burden and is certainly time-consuming; even so, there is little complaint. Good use is made of student assistance in filing, checking out books, etc., but the cataloging and classifying must be done by the professionals. Here the Wilson cards—widely used and deservedly so—are a great help.

The librarian, supported by a good man as principal, makes a fine impression. She is firm with the students but no martinet. Since she is the type who can have an excellent influence on the children, it would be good to see her relieved of the technical work. Additional personnel is needed; this school is too large for only one person to handle. The librarian would welcome more clerical assistance, even on a limited basis, such as once or twice a week.

The quarters are adequate, with about 50 seats. However, there is lack of storage space and little chance for privacy. Book losses are not considered serious.

Although not at all in a carping spirit, the librarian did express some concern about occasionally being called out to do other things, for example, to supervise a study room. If this is done frequently, it indicates a failure to appreciate the full-time nature of library duties.

Organization of library services

The elementary and secondary school libraries come under the general supervision of the Division of Libraries, itself under the Bureau of Instructional Materials and the Department of Curriculum. The division, through its annual issuance of the *Approved List of Elementary Library Books* and the *Approved List of Periodicals for Elementary Schools,* exercises some control over elementary school collections, since purchases must be made from the approved lists. Secondary schools, however, have complete freedom of choice, and may select books and periodicals on the basis of faculty recommendations, general lists (for example, the *Standard Catalog for High School Libraries*), book-reviewing media, or personal knowledge of books and authors. In both cases there is a wide latitude of choice, and no attempt is made to dictate acquisitions or to lay down restrictions. In addition, the Division maintains the Board of Education Library, a professional library for the instructional staff.

Professional personnel at the Central Office consists of the Director, five district supervisors, a supervisor of the cataloging section, and two teacher-certified librarians for the Board of Education Library.

Major problems and suggestions

The following comments are indicated for special attention.

1. *Physical facilities.* No library can ever be large enough to accommodate all the books it will ever acquire; with rare exceptions, acquisitions always exceed withdrawals, and the cry goes out for more space.

In older buildings, kindergartens, gymnasiums, or classrooms have been converted into central libraries; the newer buildings have made specific provision for libraries. We need no involved projections to tell us that, with the increase in student enrollment, more and more books will be required, and better planning should be devoted to the library and its growth in any new school construction. It is depressing to see libraries in schools erected within the past half-dozen years already exceeding their book capacity and resorting to all sorts of makeshift arrangements to take care of hundreds of volumes. This is especially true of high schools.

Whatever the virtues of the lunchroom/library combination, they are outweighed by its faults. The library as an institution makes an impact that transcends its immediate utilitarian function, and it should be given the stature commensurate with its importance in continuing education. This basic objection is even more important than those based on obvious inconveniences—interruption of program, unsuitable furniture and physical arrangements, limitation on exhibits, etc.

In many schools there is no office or work space for the library staff. While it is true that the librarian should be in close contact with pupils, numerous responsibilities require some privacy—book selection, ordering and preparing books for the shelves, consultations with teachers, pupils, or associates, etc.—and it would be desirable that some provision be made for sometime seclusion.

2. *Condition of book collections.* One inevitable result of heavy book use is wear and tear, and no one should complain. At the same time, books in torn and ragged bindings or with stained and broken covers are repellent and should not remain in a school library. The librarians are loath to spend part of their funds on rebinding, and they are reluctant to discard a book if it retains any possibility of usefulness. In some libraries such a high proportion of the books are worn and shabby that, if these were discarded, very little would remain.

It is recommended that there be a general directive to the entire school library system—especially pertinent to the older elementary school libraries—advocating a liberal retiring of physically unattractive or deteriorated books, replacing them by the same titles or by others. If this is now going on at all, progress is too slow; too many shabby books remain. Many of the books probably do not deserve rebinding; it would be as cheap in many cases to acquire new copies. It may be objected that such wholesale discarding would endanger the school's status if the remaining titles were so few in number as to fall below NCA standards. If so, let the books be kept, but isolated from the fresh and attractive volumes. The shelves should be genuinely inviting.

Some books, of course, especially in the high schools, deserve rebinding. Since the librarians prefer using their book funds to add new volumes, a periodic allocation should be made to each school library to be used exclusively for rebinding, the grant to be in addition to the $1.00 to $1.50 per pupil appropriation for books. Spread over a five-year period, the annual cost would not be excessive, and the results would be worth it. (For the high schools, say $500 to each school every five years; this would mean about $25,000 over a five-year period, or $5,000 a year.)

Mention was made earlier of the overcrowded shelves in many libraries. Larger quarters is one (expensive) solution; another (inexpensive) solution is periodic weeding, to remove unnecessary duplicates and out-of-date books, those superseded by better ones, and altogether worthless ones. This would lighten the shelves and make room for newer acquisitions. Weeding takes time and judgment, and cannot be entrusted to students or clerks; but it is necessary and some provision must be made for it.

3. *High school library book selection.* Library acquisition should obviously be keyed to curriculum requirements, but there is a good deal more involved than the formal curriculum. School librarians have a real opportunity to introduce pupils, particularly those in the upper grades, to imaginative and seminal literature—not necessarily to avant-garde writers but to those substantial enough to have made a definite impact on literary history, for example, Hemingway, Faulkner, Steinbeck, Salinger, Golding. Yet brief visits to the libraries demonstrate so much conservatism in book selection as almost to rule out such writers. There are, of course, problems that provision of modern fiction introduces: objections by parents, adolescent leering, shock to sensibilities, etc. However, these should not be permitted to dominate to the extent that they apparently do. It is probable that conservatism in book selection extends to poetry, drama, art, and other areas as well. A contributing cause for such conservatism is the dependence on recommended lists, such as the

Standard Catalog for High School Libraries. The titles listed there, unexceptionable as far as they go, result from votes of high school librarians, themselves fairly conservative in their tastes and preferences. It would be good to see the librarians break out of the circle of librarians-prescribing-to-librarians, and range a bit more widely in their selection. After all, it should be part of the educational process to introduce students to literature of quality beyond that studied in the classroom or required for book-review assignments.

Another evidence of the same conservatism is the plethora of anti-Communist literature, infrequently, if at all, balanced by a kind or objective word about the Soviet system.

More courage and greater willingness to tackle the less popular and not completely safe books would be welcome, not only in acquisition of these books but in bringing them to the attention of the student ready for them. Of course, such courage must be supported by principal, superintendent, and school board; if it is not, the librarian cannot be blamed for unwillingness to take chances.

4. *Personnel: recruitment and selected activities.* The qualifications for assignment as high school or elementary school librarian are as follows:

High school: Successful completion of the examination for High School Librarian—which includes among the requirements for admission 32 semester hours in library science and 18 semester hours in education.

Elementary school teacher-librarian: Certification as an elementary school teacher plus 15 semester hours in library science including the following areas: functions or techniques of the library, reading guidance, library materials for elementary academic areas.

The formal course requirements in library science may be completed in any library school or library science department; a great many of the present corps of librarians have taken their work at Chicago Teachers College. There is nothing wrong with this, but a wider casting of the net in recruiting school librarians may result in variant approaches and possibly novel ideas in operating school libraries. This is not to be interpreted as critical of present practice; the heavy demand everywhere for librarians, coupled with the limited number available from any library school, means that CTC is something of a lifesaver to Chicago. If it could not depend on CTC, the Division of Libraries would have an extremely difficult time in finding a sufficient number of competent personnel. Hopefully the increase in number of library schools and in their enrollment may ease the burden somewhat and may permit the Chicago system to look beyond CTC for some of its school librarians.

The Division of Libraries plays an active role in in-service training and in helping the librarians to keep on their toes. It invites the elementary school librarians to take part in evaluating books for the *Approved Lists,* and the librarians themselves are organized into an Elementary School Librarians Club which meets regularly for book reviewing and exchange of ideas. Workshop meetings for high school librarians are conducted to consider such topics as cultural resources in the Chicago area, the role of the library in human relations, developing teacher-librarian cooperation. The high school librarians are also expected to do some book reviewing, these reviews being subsequently distributed to the schools. Special bulletins, bibliographies, and reading lists are regularly compiled, and undoubtedly are helpful in developing book collections and in serving as reading guides to teachers and librarians. Among them, the following may be noted:

Planning a Book Fair
Significant Readings for Teachers in Elementary
    and Secondary Schools
Library Loose Leaves (professional literature)
Mathematics Reference Materials
Books for Negro History Week
Books Dealing with World Wars I and II and the Cold War
Easy to Read Books for Junior and Senior High Schools
Reading for the Partially Seeing

At least in part because of their background, Chicago personnel tend to be geared too exclusively to the Chicago system. It is recommended that all librarians be encouraged to visit periodically such first-rate school libraries as New Trier, Evanston High, and the University of Chicago Laboratory Schools, and to spend enough time there to absorb some of the atmosphere of wider book selection and unusual programs. Granted that such schools enroll students not typical of the average Chicago student and that they may not have all the same problems to contend with; still students everywhere have much in common, and many Chicago high school graduates attend the same universities as do graduates of the non-Chicago schools. One high school librarian reported that an afternoon spent in one of these libraries yielded a host of new ideas; this kind of contact should be experienced by all the elementary and secondary school librarians in the Chicago school system.

5. *Deposit collections from the Chicago Public Library.* The book collections in many of the elementary schools are supplemented by collections supplied by the Chicago Public Library on long-term deposit. Three factors enter into the decision regarding such deposit collections: (1) size of enrollment, (2) size of the collection already available in the school, and (3) proximity of the school to a public library branch. Schools within four blocks of a branch are not approved for loan collections. On the basis of a standard of three books per pupil to be available in the school library, the Chicago Public Library agrees to provide half, or one-and-one-half books per child, up to 900 volumes or the number necessary to bring the collection up to standard.

With increasing emphasis on school libraries and with wider provision of public library branches, the number of CPL books on loan to schools has declined. In 1953 the figure was 110,680; in 1962, 32,358.

Because of the significance of this Board of Education–Chicago Public Library cooperation, it is to be hoped that more schools will avail themselves of the opportunity provided. It is undoubtedly true that losses would be heavy in some schools (not only of CPL books, of course), and these books would have to be paid for. The alternative, however, is *more* book provision and expense by the Board of Education—or a book collection of lesser quantity, variety, and quality.

RECOMMENDATIONS

Physical facilities

1. More careful planning for libraries in relation to future growth should be made in new school construction. Some schools erected within the past six years already have inadequate book capacity.

2. Libraries should have private work space available for the library staff.

3. The lunchroom/library combination should be abandoned. The library as an educational institution deserves a place of its own in the school and in the mind of the student.

Condition of book collections

1. The entire school library system should be encouraged to retire physically unattractive and deteriorated books. If they must be kept for a while to meet NCA requirements, shabby books should be isolated from the fresh and attractive volumes.

2. A periodic allocation should be made to each school library exclusively for rebinding, but care should be exercised not to rebind those not worth keeping.

3. There should be more frequent and thorough weeding to remove unneeded duplicates and out-of-date books.

High school library book selection

More courage in book selection should be fostered. Books which have high artistic or intellectual value, even though they may not meet with everyone's approval, should be available to students who are ready for them.

Recruitment and training

There is danger of in-breeding, due to the necessary reliance on Chicago Teachers College for the great majority of teacher-librarians. To balance this, recruitment of teacher-librarians from other sources should be encouraged; and day-long visits to the libraries of other school systems should be facilitated and promoted.

EDUCATIONAL TELEVISION

Television is the latest of a long series of devices to bring the outside world into the classroom. Others which have come into the schools recently are radio, motion pictures, film strips, recordings, and a variety of devices for projecting pictures, drawings, etc. Traditionally there have been maps, models, pictures, and books. All come under the general name of audio-visual materials and methods.

Twenty-five years ago, radio and motion pictures were being talked about as the educational media of greatest promise. Since that time the motion picture has grown in popularity and usefulness, while radio has remained on the threshold of the school. It is safe to say that educational radio has not fulfilled its early promise, though it has a certain usefulness. One of the reasons for the limited success of educational radio is that television promises to do the same things that radio can do, and to do many other useful things also.

Educational television (ETV) is now about 10 years old. It has been tried out at all grade levels, from kindergarten to college. A good deal of private foundation and federal government money has gone into experimentation with ETV.

There is no longer any serious doubt that pupils learn efficiently from instructional television. The questions to be answered are: At what levels and in what fields is ETV most useful? What combination is best with ETV—explanation, reading, drill, use of students in the picture, viewing at home with the family, repetition of the lesson, etc.? These are questions which badly need answering before the Chicago program can be brought to an adequate level of effectiveness.

The Chicago schools have access to a variety of television modes for systematic instruction: (1) Channel 11 (WTTW), a noncommercial, ground-based, VHF station administered by the Chicago Educational Television Association; (2) airborne television (UHF Channels 72 and 76), administered by the Midwest Program on Airborne Television Instruction at Purdue University; (3) closed-circuit television, now originating at the Byrd Elementary School and linked to four nearby feeder schools. In addition, beginning in 1965, UHF Channel 20 (WXXW) will be operated by the Chicago Educational Television Association on a noncommercial basis. Present plans call for the location of the broadcasting facilities of educational TV Channels 11 and 20 on the campus of Chicago Teachers College North by June of 1965.

The Chicago Board of Education is to be commended for being among the first school systems to support the experimental Midwest Program on Airborne Television Instruction, and for participating in some of the pioneer efforts in utilizing television for systematic instruction at the junior college level.

At present, the principal uses of ETV in Chicago are found in the elementary schools and in the Junior College.

Instructional TV in the elementary schools

Every elementary school has at least one television receiver and can receive programs from Channel 11 (WTTW). A few schools have secured a second TV receiver through PTA or other funds.

Beginning in 1965, the Chicago Educational Television Association will operate ultrahigh-frequency (UHF) Channel 20 (WXXW). Reception will require a specially adapted receiving set.

For several years, about 20 elementary schools have been using lessons from the Midwest Program on Airborne Television Instruction (MPATI). A special kind of receiver adapted to receive UHF telecasts is required. These schools vary from six to 47 in the number of classrooms equipped to receive TV, and from three to 37 in the number of teachers using TV regularly.

Almost all of the active use of ETV is found in these particular schools. Other schools use their sets for occasional programs, and often place their single set in the library or in the teachers' lounge.

The school that makes active use of ETV does so primarily because the principal promotes it. The following two examples illustrate this fact.

School A. Designated as one of the 25 elementary schools to utilize MPATI lessons, this school has been using its television facilities to the utmost. Although 18 classrooms are wired for television, only six TV receivers were provided, four of which are UHF (capable of receiving MPATI telecasts). With four UHF receivers, systematic instruction via television is being provided for over 900 pupils, with 29 teachers participating. The usual class size is from 37 to 40 children. For most telecasts, two classes are combined. This means that, instead of the standard ratio of approximately 25 pupils per TV receiver, there are some 80 children viewing most lessons. Despite the obvious overtaxing of the equipment, the principal and teachers are enthused about the lessons from the Midwest Program on Airborne Television Instruction. At the beginning of the school year, many of the teachers did not have MPATI manuals which outline the various lessons and include reference materials and suggested introductory and follow-up activities. However, a number of the teachers purchased manuals with their own money.

The faculty has been working to adjust the sequence of the units in the Chicago Board of Education Course of Study so that it is compatible with the MPATI lessons, and the results have been generally satisfactory.

While the TV signal is not always optimum or even satisfactory, the principal makes every effort to report reception difficulties and to have the system serviced as promptly as possible.

The faculty and principal want more TV receivers to eliminate the overcrowding of combined classes. They would also like to have the auditorium wired and equipped for television instruction.

School B. Although this school was also designated as one of the 25 elementary schools participating in MPATI, and 12 rooms were equipped with TV receivers, instructional television has not been utilized. The principal reported that, at the beginning of the school year (September, 1963), the antenna was out of adjustment. She said that she was very busy and did not get around to having the antenna adjusted for satisfactory reception until late March or early April (some seven months later). By then, it was "too late to use the TV lessons." (One TV set was being used in the teachers' lounge.) The principal added that she had some difficulty in determining which channels to go through at the Board of Education for reporting reception difficulties and securing proper servicing.

What about plans for utilizing instructional television next year? The principal anticipates "trouble with the antenna" once again. The principal indicated that she was not aware of the arrangements for certain MPATI telecasts to be re-broadcast via Channels 11 and 20 during 1964-65, thereby helping to solve certain reception problems. She added that she would much prefer radio to television.

Closed-circuit television. Five elementary schools are linked by closed-circuit to a television studio at the Byrd School. The present administrator of this project feels that the closed-circuit operation serves the particular needs of these five neighboring schools, provides for more effective instructional planning, and serves as a powerful means of in-service education by extending the influence of master teachers.

However, the instructional mode tends to be conventional. During the 1964 spring semester, 14 teachers from these schools were engaged in teaching via television, but only one teacher was engaged full-time in television production. Virtually all students at the Byrd School receive some instruction via television, and some 200 students in each of the feeder schools are receiving TV lessons. None of these schools is receiving instruction via open-circuit television.

Teachers interviewed at one of the feeder schools indicated that the teaching style via closed-circuit television has been too conventional. There is need for greater visualization in these telecasts. These teachers were also of the opinion that their school should have the benefit of the open-circuit offerings from Channel 11 (and 20) in addition to the closed-circuit programming. They also expressed the need for more preparation and follow-up materials in conjunction with the telecasts. The recent addition of two video-tape recorders presents new opportunities for making more elaborate preparations in producing the television lessons and thereby improving the quality of the telecasts.

During the spring of 1964, systematic TV instruction was offered at various grade levels in a variety of subjects, including science, arithmetic, English language arts, and handwriting.

Instructional TV in the high schools

During 1963-64, only two high schools were designated for systematic television instruction via MPATI. No high schools were identified for utilizing Channel 11 programming for systematic instruction. In actuality, only one high school attempted to use television on a regular basis during 1963-64. In this case, the MPATI programming was received. Although the television signals were most satisfactory at the time of the consultant's visit, it was revealed that the system was permitted to remain out of order over extended periods of time.

Although the MPATI telecasts are programmed for seven classes at this high school, the school schedule was not altered to accommodate the television lessons. Only one of the seven classes was synchronized with the entire 28-minute telecast. For the other six classes, the period either began after the telecast started, or ended before the telecast concluded. Some adjustments in the school schedule would have accommodated all but one of the telecasts.

Because the system is allowed to remain inoperable over extended periods and because of the lack of teachers' manuals for some MPATI courses, the receiving teachers often have no prior idea as to the scope and content of the TV lessons. The receiving teachers gave no evidence of adjusting their curricular units to better fit the sequence of the telecasts.

Cooperation with metropolitan area school systems

In part because of the difficulty of receiving MPATI programs in many parts of the Chicago Metropolitan Area and in part because of schedule problems arising out of different time zones, the Tri-County School Boards Association (serving Cook, Lake, and DuPage) sponsored the in-school programs which were broadcast over WTTW in 1963-64. The Tri-County Educational Television also supplied teachers' manuals for these programs at cost. Beginning in the fall of 1964, under an agreement between MPATI and Tri-County ETV, a new joint organization, Chicago Area School Television, Inc. (CAST), is presenting a full program over WTTW, utilizing both MPATI tapes and lessons purchased from other sources. CAST supplies advance information, teacher workshops, and teachers' manuals. The cost is shared by school districts in the tri-county area on a membership fee basis based on number of schools and enrollment. However, Chicago has been allowed to adjust its own membership fee. Fuller participation by the Chicago Board of Education in CAST would appear to offer possibilities for better service to the Chicago schools in the use of television.

CAST is also striving to develop more high school use of television by encouraging high schools to join CAST on a reduced fee basis and to experiment with a few classes using television.

The Chicago TV College

Organized in 1956 with a grant from the Ford Foundation, the Chicago TV College, with headquarters at Wright Junior College, serves some 3,000 credit students each semester (or between 800-850 students on a full-time equivalent basis of 15 credit hours). In addition, some 3,500 "noncredit" students are enrolled each semester. It is possible for a student to complete all of the requirements for the Associate in Arts degree via television without attending a single conventional class. Some 95 students have already met degree requirements entirely via television, and over 500 graduates completed approximately half of their work via television.

In addition to the home group, a number of the regular Junior College students were enrolled in TV classes on campus. Studies revealed that the attitudes and level of achievement for the on-campus TV students tended to be significantly below that of the home group. However, achievement differences have been eliminated by supplementing the TV lessons with one hour per week of live contact with the instructor.

The budget for instructional television at the junior college level during 1963-64 was in excess of $416,000, as compared with a budget of only $118,000 for the uses of television at the elementary and secondary levels. The TV College serves an "educational automation" function in that it provides recorded lessons at a cost per full-time equivalent student that is significantly below conventional instruction. The cost at the current level of enrollment is $460 per TV student, compared with $573 for the on-campus student.

Students who have experienced direct face-to-face instruction on a campus tend to react negatively to the television lessons. Most of the TV courses are organized around a "talking-face"—an instructor who tells, explains, and lectures. The television receiver is used primarily as a conveyor of verbal information rather than as a means of new visual experience. If a student should happen to miss some telecasts, he would be able to recover much of the material by listening to *audio* tapes of the programs which are available in the Junior College branch libraries.

The course content and methods tend toward convergent styles of thinking. Noted guests rarely appear and the ferment of a panel discussion is also unusual. For the most part, the visual potentialities of television are not realized. One exception is the course, *Principles of Economics,* produced by Learning Resources Institute.

Evaluation

This is a record of accomplishment and also one of relative failure. Clearly, something should be done to improve the use of ETV in the elementary schools and to extend its use. Furthermore, the high schools should not give up on television without a greater effort to explore and profit from its values.

A clue to what might be done can be found in the report just issued of the research conducted jointly by the Denver Public Schools and Stanford University.[1] Preparing to introduce Spanish into the fifth and sixth grades, Denver school administrators decided to build the course around television. They spent three years in a set of experiments aimed at finding out how ETV could best be used together with the classroom teacher, language recordings, teaching machines, programmed textbooks, and parent participation. There were classes involved in 90 different schools, with 12,000 pupils and 320 teachers. One-fourth of these teachers had no language study at all in their college and high school courses, and over half had never studied Spanish. Practically none of the teachers had any previous experience with the modern audio-lingual method of teaching foreign language.

In-service training was provided for the teachers through summer workshops and through in-service courses for teachers during the school year. Many of the teachers learned Spanish from the television lessons, together with their pupils. After the 15-minute lesson was over, they practiced and drilled their pupils. Some of the inexperienced teachers used the drill period to watch the TV again, until they had learned enough from the expert teacher to take charge of class drill.

The importance of the teacher is indicated in the following conclusion from the study.

> The kind of instruction that worked best in Denver's elementary school Spanish depended heavily on *involvement* on the part of the pupils, interest on the part of the teachers. One of the most revealing passages in this report describes what happened when a few classes were given a program to study in a poorly built, unreliable teaching machine that kept breaking down. The pupils kept repairing the machine, in fact became highly ingenious at doing so. The teachers fumed at the amount of time that was being wasted, but when the scores were in, the classes with the balky teaching machine did better

---

[1]*The Context of Instructional Television.* Stanford University, Institute for Communication Research, 1964.

than any other groups. Why? Apparently because the pupils became involved: it was *their* machine, they had kept it going, they wanted to justify it. Ingenious school systems will, let us hope, devise something better than a balky and inefficient teaching machine to arouse the same degree of involvement.

Even more significant is the part that teacher interest seems to play. In fact, the whole study—which was expected by some to downgrade the classroom teacher in favor of television, programmed instruction, parent help, and so forth—actually made the classroom teacher seem more important than ever. The great difference in pupil performance related to teacher preparation and experience, for example, and the fact that teacher preparation and experience were reflected fully as much in pupils' individual practice as in their classroom practice— these are far from suggesting that the teacher is unimportant in a team activity like the one at Denver. But the real surprise was the apparent importance of teacher interest. If teacher interest is low, then even high preparation and experience will not make for very high levels of pupil performance. It is the combination of high interest and high proficiency that makes the difference.[2]

RECOMMENDATIONS

1. A systematic program of continuous evaluation should be initiated as soon as possible. There is evidence that the Central Office has not been adequately informed as to which schools actually have been utilizing instructional television on a systematic basis and which schools have not been making use of their equipment. Evaluation should also be made of the context in which television is used (that is, for large-group instruction, team teaching, conventional size classes, etc.). A long-range study should be made of the uses of television for *(a)* systematic instruction, and *(b)* enrichment. Special attention should be given to integrating effectively the television lessons with the curriculum of the Chicago schools.

2. Supervisory services should be provided to assist principals and teachers in making effective use of instructional television.

3. Principals must insist on immediate service and repair of malfunctioning equipment. To allow the system to go unused for days or weeks at a time is damaging to the instructional program of the

---

[2]*Ibid.*, pp.158-9.

school. (Here the lapse does not appear to reside as much with the TV repair agency as with the failure of the principal to insist on proper and immediate servicing.)

4. Only all-channel receivers should be installed in the schools, inasmuch as instructional television programming in the Chicago area, beginning with the 1964-65 academic year, will be transmitted via both VHF and UHF. These TV receivers should conform to specifications for school use, including a front speaker and heavy duty wiring.

5. Principals and teachers should be fully informed about the programming on Channels 11 and 26 (also Channel 20, when it supersedes Channel 26 for instructional broadcasting). There is evidence that principals and teachers are not, at present, adequately informed.

6. The budget for instructional television in the schools should be increased substantially. Whereas the TV budget for instruction at the junior college level was in excess of $416,000 for 1963-64, the TV budget for all of the elementary and high schools was only $118,000. NDEA funds are available for TV equipment.

7. At least one or two of the schools served by closed-circuit television should be participating simultaneously in selected offerings via open-circuit television (Channels 11 and 20). This would not only provide greater flexibility in utilizing a variety of offerings, but would present a unique opportunity to assess the complementary roles of closed- and open-circuit television.

8. Greater effort should be made to utilize television as a means of providing learning experiences which are beyond the scope of a conventional classroom. The "talking-face" via television is not much different from the physically present talking teacher. (The acquisition of two video-tape recorders should provide opportunities for more effective preparation of lessons in connection with the closed-circuit system emanating from the Byrd School.)

9. Inasmuch as many of the children served by this closed-circuit system may be termed "culturally deprived," the need to utilize television as a means of social and cultural enrichment is of particular importance. Here, television presents enormous possibilities of bringing to the school a fuller measure of community life, including

concerts, plays, men at work in various occupations, and meaningful lessons on hygiene and nutrition.

10. Attempts at enrolling selected high school students in college-level TV courses should be continued and expanded for purposes of advanced placement and enrichment. This program should be carefully and continuously evaluated.

11. The financial savings accrued from instructional television in the Junior College present an opportunity for improving the quality of the TV courses. Certain courses should be selected for reassessment and revision, with the aim of capitalizing on the unique attributes of television. Consideration should be given to providing more visualized teaching-learning experiences via television. Some courses may lend themselves to cognitive-inquiry styles, rather than being limited to didactic, narrative modes. Noted authorities might be enlisted as guest teachers and as panel discussants. Such approaches should improve the attitudes of the on-campus students toward television, as well as improve the kind of learning taking place.

VIII

The Elementary Schools of Chicago

There are 433 public elementary schools in Chicago, with an enrollment in 1963-64 of 333,000 plus 55,000 children in half-day kindergarten. In addition there were 10,000 pupils in special schools and classes operating at the elementary level.

The most common size for elementary schools lay between 600 and 900, though there were seven with more than 2,100 membership and eleven below 300. The median size was 836. Average number of pupils per classroom teacher was 32.8, a substantial reduction from about 38 ten years ago. Of the 433 schools, 404 were regular elementary schools, 23 were upper-grade centers for Grades 7 and 8, nine were special schools, and seven were educational and vocational guidance centers. Some of the schools house pupils from kindergarten through Grade 4. An increasing number operate from kindergarten through Grade 6, their graduates going on to an upper-grade center.

In the course of the Survey, visits were made to 119 different elementary schools. Visiting consultants made 92 visits to 70 different schools, while several members of the Survey staff made 116 visits to 75 schools. Two staff members concentrated on kindergarten and primary grades. They generally observed and talked with every kindergarten and first- or second-grade teacher in the course of their visit to a school. A third staff member concentrated on Grades 4 and above. He talked with the principal and then selected pretty much at random from the faculty list four or five teachers to be interviewed. Principals were always cordial and gave their time liberally. They also made it as easy as possible for the staff member to interview the selected teachers, by asking a librarian or adjustment teacher to take their classes, freeing them from recess duty, etc. In only one instance did a principal attempt to override the interviewer's choice of a teacher to be visited and urge him to see someone else. The number of teachers interviewed by this staff member was 185 in 40 schools.

The visit to a school consumed a full day and often an extra day was added. In general the staff member made the following: 1) interviews averaging 45 minutes with each teacher; 2) interviews and discussions throughout the day with the principal; 3) short observations of the children in the classroom; 4) observations of the children at recess, moving in and out of the building at lunch time and after school; 5) observations of teachers at their lunch time, at sign-out time, and at their break times; 6) observations of principals handling cases sent to the office or of parents coming to the school; 7) observation of the inside and the outside of the school building.

The interview with teachers was treated as confidential, and in almost every instance the interviewer and the respondent were placed in private quarters. Questions were asked concerning: 1) the ability of the teacher to use the curriculum guides and supplements, given the social composition of the school (the interviewer had already gained some idea of what the respondent thought the social composition of the school was); 2) the ability of the teacher to function as a teacher, again, given the social situation; 3) what the biggest problems were in the classroom; 4) what assistance was given, by whom, and how worthwhile was this assistance; 5) what were factors which assist the teacher in the classroom; 6) what type of cooperation from the community did the teacher receive; 7) what was the background of the pupils.

TYPES OF SCHOOLS

In Chapters III, IV, and V we have seen facts about children in the schools as well as facts about the variety of school programs to foreshadow the following basic propositions about the elementary schools of Chicago.

1. There are enormous differences of pupil achievement between different schools.

2. These differences are related to the family backgrounds of the children.

3. These differences demand different teaching materials and methods for different types of schools.

Before going on to recommend different ways of working in the various types of schools, we shall present another kind of information, obtained from the interviews and observations mentioned previously. This information led us to describe four types of elementary school, which are loosely related to socioeconomic factors. A description of these types and their variations will constitute the first half of this chapter.

The four types or groups of schools were given descriptive names as follows: high-status schools, main-line schools, common-man schools, and inner-city schools. Although there were a number of exceptions to any rule of geographical location, the schools generally were located in the areas marked on the map of Figure 1.

High-status schools

From a teacher in a high-status school—"We're so conscious of the gifted here. We've based our whole course of study on the gifted. It is the same with the curriculum guides. As for discipline problems, well, they are practically non-existent."

These are schools with a high degree of most desirable characteristics. The children are extremely well prepared for what the school demands, and parents are willing and able to supply equipment needs over and above what is needed, and are taking an active part in school life. The children have high academic scores and provide only a small number of discipline problems and, in the majority of cases, no active discipline problems at all. The

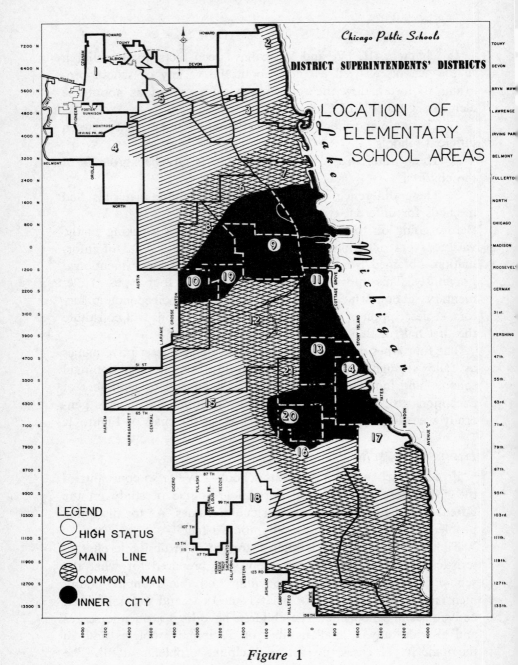

Figure 1

disturbed children are few and for the most part can be handled in the school setting.

One teacher's description of a high-status school area is as follows: "The school community is an old established residential area made up of middle-class families who are economically comfortable. They are proud of their community. The parents are well educated and interested in the educational opportunities provided for their children and often compare these to neighboring schools in suburban areas. The majority of students are academically motivated. The PTA is a cooperative active group. On the whole the parents are eager to work with the school to ensure the success of their children in the educational program."

Teaching is most rewarding in this type of setting and once a teacher enters such a situation, it is very seldom that he leaves. In one such school the length of total teaching experience was as follows: a range of from one year to 32 years with the teacher of one year's experience having had a total of 10 years of teaching experience in other situations. The total faculty median was 15 years. As one principal stated, "My teachers only leave to retire, or if they are married, when they become pregnant." There are also few sick days used by the teachers. "It's always a pleasant place here. We really do not have many teachers who take too many days off. In fact, they only take a day off when they are very sick."

With respect to discipline problems, an eighth-grade teacher said, "Oh, yes, we have discipline problems here, but what would be considered discipline here would be considered heaven in other schools. On second thought, we really don't have discipline problems. We have little things happen in the classroom, but this is normal. No, we have no discipline problems."

A principal in a far North Side school said, "Our so-called discipline problems—why, I can count them on one hand. Our children are so accustomed to consideration, quiet passing, and this type of thing that it does not have to be taught in the school. It's taught in the home. We can simply concentrate on classwork here. There is not much absenteeism, tardiness, or truancy."

Because of the high ability level of the children, the curriculum guides and supplements not only may be used to their fullest, but must even be supplemented. One teacher said, "The guides and supplements suit our students well. I think they're constructed in an excellent fashion. They are realistically attuned to my class, but nevertheless, I have to provide some degree of variety, no matter how good the supplement and guide are. This is because the majority of my children do reference work in the library."

The backgrounds of the students aid the teacher in the presentation of the curriculum and undoubtedly offer the necessary information and skills for success in school—which success again provides the teachers with a rewarding experience. As one teacher stated, "Given a good curriculum, you can really teach in this type of situation. Culturally, these kids have an advantage. I would say about 99 percent of my kids have an encyclopaedia at home, 75 percent have traveled to interesting places, and at least 60 percent have been to the city and have visited all the museums—the Museum of Science and Industry, the Museum of Natural History—and these children take advantage of the school library and the public library. Culturally, they rate high."

The schools are greatly assisted by parental cooperation, not only indirectly by the parents providing background and incentive to the child, but directly through such organizations as the PTA and by attendance at assemblies. A principal stated, "We have a fine PTA with very good relations between the school and the PTA. When we have evening meetings, there is just a magnificent turnout. Usually most schools have about one or two evening meetings a year. We know that we can have four PTA evening meetings a year. When there's an open house, well, the place is just packed!"

Despite this positive situation, there are some areas of dissatisfaction. One teacher summed up such an area when he said, "Many of our problems are caused by pushy parents who want their kids to go faster then they can. We can't change that too much because we can't influence their decision about academics or offer too much advice about their children, at least not as much as I was able to in the lower economic area where I taught before. Here, the teacher is taken for granted. Ninety-nine percent of the time the parents will come in and cooperate, in their fashion, but the attitudes are different. They think more for themselves."

One of the biggest problems centers on the slow child, or slow average, and the need for a program designed for him. As contrasted to other situations, the concern is not that the child is or may become a discipline problem, but that he may become a dropout despite a positive attitude on his part. One teacher said, "We need some shop or home economics courses in this type of school, but they took these out of the schools here. We have high standards, but they are so high that the 90 IQ child has to suffer. Are they to be frustrated and left by the wayside? Last year I sent about 10 children to vocational school and I know they are going to be drop-outs. I just feel frustrated."

Another area of dissatisfaction is the lack of time by teachers for adequate preparation and presentation of material. But this is viewed by the teacher *not* as hindering *him* functionally. Rather it is seen as hindering the *child*. More will be said of this later.

Main-line schools

From a main-line school teacher—"This is just a nice typical school situation with nice typical kids."

Main-line schools are those which have a majority of academically oriented children, but they also have a greater number of discipline problems and parental problems than have the high-status schools. However, these are not enough to interfere with the academic program. This type of school has a majority of children with a strong background of family experience preparing them for school work. However, such a school will have a visible minority of children with poor reading and below-average school achievement. While there are discipline problems, the majority of them can be handled between the teacher, the parent, and the principal. This is a school which is psychologically *in the city,* whereas the high-status school is more suburban in nature. The children and parents of the main-line school exhibit behavior and achievement patterns associated with the mainstream of American culture and society.

The areas in which main-line schools are found show a great diversity in socioeconomic status and social composition. Since conditions within the school are the ranking criteria rather than only socioeconomic factors, one may find main-line schools in a cluster of common-man and inner-city schools. In general, though, clusters of main-line schools are found in stable areas geographically removed from the inner-city, in areas with young families, in areas of new housing developments, or in other areas in which parents are experiencing upward mobility.

In the areas of little population change, the situation is close to that of a high-status school. A principal in a stable main-line school said, "The neighborhood cooperation here is good. This is because 40 to 50 percent of the parents have gone to the school themselves. Where the parents are honestly willing to support the school, there is no difficulty with the children. There is a high relationship between the amount of cooperation from the home and the ability of the child to do well in school. There is a small group not willing to support the school. These will give lip service, listen and not pay attention once they get outside. You also get a belligerent parent now and then."

In the newly settled areas, the parents are not quite sure what their role is in relation to the school, and some either withdraw or become somewhat critical, more so than in the stable main-line schools. One teacher said, in a newly settled Negro main-line area, "Oh, I get some parents up here who don't understand what we are attempting to do. They want to know what the school is doing for their child, and they think the school can do a better job. I tell them that we have to concentrate on the academics, and if they want their children to be taken to museums, to be taken to these extra events, it is up to them to take them. Eventually, they see our point and realize that they cannot expect us to turn out a good academic product and yet spend all our time in these acculturating activities." And as one principal in a similar area stated, "We attempt to explain the program to the parents, and many become involved on their own; but as concerns community outreach, I think at some point we reach a point of diminishing returns because a lot of these parents just won't be drawn into the framework of the school, and consequently one expends one's energy in areas that are not fruitful."

A teacher in a newly settled main-line area commented, "The fact of the two-salary family affects the school, I think. This leaves the children more on their own. Parents don't have the time to assist them like they should. It's difficult to remedy this, too, because it's difficult to get a proper line of communication from school to home. A lot of parents come up and are not too interested in using their own influence on the child. They say, 'Well, whatever you say we should do, we'll do'."

In general, in this type of school, the majority of parents and the community support the schools and the teachers. In one newly settled area, the principal reported, "I gathered together many of the important people of the community and told them the importance of our preparing the children to go to college. I outlined for them what the school was attempting to do and I told them what they could do to help the school. They loved it. I realize that this can't be done in all places and communities, but here, the parents respect the principal's word."

A teacher contrasted this attitude with a high-status school in which she once taught: "My children's attitude in this school, I think, is a little better than the _____ area. The attitude there on the part of the students and their parents was a superior one. It was one which considered the teacher *only* a teacher and one which said, 'My mother knows more than you do'."

The parent organizations are supported, and shows and assemblies are attended, but not to the degree in which they are in the high-status areas. There is also less ability to supply materials needed by the children without the assistance of the school.

In a stable main-line school, a curriculum extra was started in the form of a school band. It is significant in that a boosters' club was organized to serve as a fund-raising committee for the students who could not afford to buy their own instruments. Also, the band director himself must give semi-individual lessons to the children. One can be fairly certain that in a high-status area there would be private lessons with less reliance on the school, and there would be no need for a club to help purchase instruments and music.

With respect to curriculum guides, a teacher in a stable area said, "I think they fit our children well, at least those with good backgrounds; but I wouldn't try to exceed the guides as they do in the schools north of us. We're just right now because our children are very eager to learn and we don't have to pull it out of them."

Main-line schools' discipline problems are not very severe. Those problems which they have may be handled in the school situation.

As in the high-status schools, there is seldom if ever any overt hostility on the part of the student and very little verbal hostility directed towards the teacher. In very rare instances is there any physical hostility. The discipline problems consist of cases of the classroom being upset by behavioral antics or inattentiveness on the part of the children. A stable main-line principal says, "The crisis in this school is: 'Johnny pushed me going home' or else, 'Mary stuck her tongue out at me.' Our discipline problems are not really discipline problems, but they are more or less just little misunderstandings among children. I am usually able to handle them if the teachers send them down to me. But in most cases, the teachers are able to handle them themselves. We've got the kind of a kid where if a note is sent home, that's the end of it for a while. Except for the emotionally disturbed children, we have no problems; and with these children, you sometimes have to have the parent in."

There is a more active recognition of problems in the main-line schools than there is in the high-status schools; one of the reasons for this being the greater number of nonachievers in the main-line schools as compared to the high-status, and the fact that discipline problems are so closely related to nonachievers. As one young fourth-grade teacher stated, "They're all asking the question, 'Why can't Johnny read?' I'll tell you why Johnny can't read. It's because Johnny doesn't pay attention. I'm so tired of going around pointing at the book, trying to get the children to pay attention. At the same time, those who are paying attention get cheated out of what I can offer them. I have some children in here who cry if their homework is not done. And these are the good children who are conscientious. The others just don't care. I think, though, that the majority are conscientious."

Teachers in main-line schools feel the pressure of lack of time, as preventing *them* from teaching effectively. A teacher with eight years of experience, who had a relatively slow group in a new main-line area, said, "Most of the children in my slow group have trouble using the text. This means I have to do most of my presentation orally or with worksheets, and these I have to mimeograph myself. I simply do not have enough time for this preparation. There are always forms and reports to be made out for the district office or for downtown. This takes up the time for grading papers and other time I could be using in preparation. Since my children can't use the text sŏ much, I have to find time somewhere for this mimeographing. As well as the fact that I have a husband to look after. If I could only have some time each week, or a free period, to get this stuff in order! My biggest problem is time."

Another principal, in a stable main-line area, commented, "The extra record work and the duty puts a strain on the teacher and lowers her effectiveness. It's unfair that a teacher has to stand guard like a policeman during her lunch hour. They're making more and more demands on the teachers without taking away any of the extra burdens and the extra duties. There's more and more being demanded on the academic side, but there's less help coming to them regarding this petty part of teaching. Time taken away shows up very strongly in the primary grades. That's when you need most of your time for preparation."

Common-man schools

From a teacher in a common-man school—"They sure play rough, and they can get rough in fights, but they're not bad kids when you really get to know them."

As in main-line schools, common-man schools show a great diversity in student body, parental cooperation, home background, and ability to use the curriculum. The student population tends to be less academically oriented, more independent when dealing with the school and the teachers, and less inclined to identify with the school and its personnel than in the main-line schools. The mass media set the behavioral patterns for many of the students. Parents, for the most part, desire an education for their children and push verbally in this direction, but are not quite certain what educational goals should be achieved, nor how one goes about achieving them. Being good in school behaviorally is equated with doing "good" in school academically.

The schools may or may not be close to the center of the city geographically but they are definitely city oriented. They are attended by a large percentage of second generation foreign-born and/or Spanish-speaking and Negro children.

The common-man clusters are usually found between main-line

and inner-city schools, and they form a kind of buffer zone. We can expect to find great variation in this situation, and we do. We can define three subtypes: stable common-man schools, changing common-man schools, and rough common-man schools.

Stable common-man schools bear a resemblance to main-line schools in parental cooperation and children's behavior. However, there is a crucial difference in the experience and background of the children and in knowledge of what is needed for success in things academic. A child expressing aspirations for a typical middle-class occupation is the exception rather than the rule. As one teacher said, "Children are well mannered on the whole, but there's not too much encouragement for higher education from the home. It seems that the ideas and aspirations come more from TV than from the school."

One principal, with many years of experience in a stable common-man school, remarked, "The parents could keep closer watch on their children and on their activities. They shouldn't let them roam the streets as they do. There's also too much TV. Some parents seem rather messy, and surprisingly enough, come up to the school in slacks and the like. Many do not wear the proper street attire."

Parental interest does not extend to active participation in school affairs or school organization, although there is a core of parents who attempt to awaken interest. In rough common-man schools, this parental cooperation is even less, and the core smaller. This is not necessarily because the parents are at odds with the school, but they either are ill at ease or are busy with other, more pressing matters.

One stable common-man school teacher notices differences between his own students and the nearby main-line students. He commented, "Those from the [main-line] school are better academically and better in behavior. The kids in our school, although they're not problems, nevertheless are slower and don't reach as high a level of achievement, but they're good kids. We are very heavy with foreign-born and foreign-speaking homes, and this may be one reason for the low achievement."

In common-man schools receiving newcomers, discipline problems vary. They may begin to resemble rough common-man situations or, they may resemble inner-city schools. If the influx is gradual, if there is not too great a difference in culture and outlook between receiving and entering groups, the problems are reduced. In one stable common-man school receiving an influx of Puerto Rican and Mexican children, the principal stated, "Our area is experiencing some influx of new students, but they seem to be fitting in all right. This has raised some behavior problems, but we're able to cope with them. And since they're not coming in very fast, we have a stable student body as well as a stable faculty. If we didn't have this stability, I don't think we'd be able to do as good a job of easing the new students in."

However, in the common-man area experiencing quick transition, the situation becomes more serious. In a once heavily Russian and Italian immigrant area which is now receiving a Puerto Rican and working-class Negro influx, one assistant principal with many years of experience remarked, "The job is getting harder, because of the constant conflict in the school between the Puerto Rican and the Negro students. They carry their problems into the school and it has adverse effects. Thank goodness none of the teachers is leaving yet because of it. We have a tradition of keeping teachers for a long time at this school, even if this is what can be called a poor area. But if the situation ever gets to the point where the discipline problems mount, and impertinence to the teachers increases, they will leave."

But despite the problems, the teachers in the rough common-man schools see themselves in a better situation than in an inner-city school, and seem to be, in the main, as positively oriented to the majority of these schools as those in the main-line schools. A teacher who had been in an inner-city school stated, "I feel like a different person here. I really do. I'm enjoying my teaching now and I feel like I'm getting some kind of a reward. A problem that is considered a great problem here just didn't count at the _____. Oh, we have problems at recess. We do have some pretty bad problem kids, but at the _____ we really had our problems. When I was going to transfer, the principal of this school visited me and told me that this school wouldn't be any different than the _____. But it is as different as night and day. And the strange thing is, these kids don't come from any worse backgrounds than the kids at the _____ do. At the _____, discipline was terrible. In the morning there would be kids left over from the previous day and lined up outside the office. One day I just went down and put my name on the transfer list and I came to this school. And it is different."

Probably the greatest difference felt by teachers who have taught at inner-city schools between the problems of the inner-city schools and these schools is in the degree, consistency, and direction of hostility which the teacher experiences. This hostility seems to be more direct, more frequent, and more overt in the innner-city schools of Chicago.

The ability to handle the curriculum varies drastically from one type of common-man school to the other. In the main, the curriculum must be altered downward in all schools of this type, but more so in the rough common-man schools. Again, this adds more to the teacher's burden, for the teacher does not only have to teach, but also must construct a curriculum. One principal said, "When you have reading problems, you have problems in curriculum. I don't care how good the curriculum is. We can't find things to use in the eighth grade. What are you going to do with a kid that is reading at the fifth-grade level and is in eighth grade? To a great extent, it is vocabulary that is a problem. But the difficulty, and I say it again, is mainly in reading. The teachers have to prepare most of the work outside of the textbook, and this is killing."

The problems of using the curriculum are compounded in transient common-man schools. In a school experiencing an influx of Southern whites, a teacher remarked, "Many units in the science guide are rough. Unless the person is oriented to science teaching, it is very difficult. A lot of this is too deep for my children. This is because of the lack of adequate background on their part. Much of what I teach goes over their heads." This teacher went on, "I lose half of my class and get as many new ones during the year. I'm not going to achieve any of the curriculum goals if the transiency continues."

For teachers in common-man schools the problem of time is a problem of getting enough of the child's time to accomplish something with and within him. The school time is especially valuable for learning because neither the child nor his family can be counted on to see that he studies at home or uses his out-of-school time in ways that improve his school work. The teacher must adapt curriculum material and prepare work sheets in any time she can find, outside of class. She must do an active job of teaching, in class. One teacher said, "There is one consolation. We know that the school does all. Anything positive that happens to these kids, we know we did it."

While some schools in main-line areas feel the effects of the parochial schools, these effects are felt mainly in the common-man school areas. One of the reasons for this may be the fact that the public school main-line child is not very different in experience and parental interest from the parochial school main-line child, while in a common-man area, parochial school parents probably take a greater interest in education because of the monetary factor involved in sending their child to a parochial school. Further, there is more pressure on the part of the parent to conform to the expectations of the school and to take part in school life, as well as to do follow-up work at home with the child. This is so because the school is part of a larger institution, the church, which has a more direct influence on the family and on the parents' life. One principal estimated, "Of about 55 kids in our kindergarten, I would say that a little less than half will be drawn off by the parochial schools. For some reason it seems that these are the kids with the better potential. They seem to be those that we would like to keep."

Inner-city schools

A teacher in an inner-city school—"Each day I'd enter the school, each day the problems would begin, and each day I'd say, 'Dear God, what can I do?' "

Inner-city schools face the gravest problems of any schools in the system. They also face the greatest challenge in any attempt to remedy the problems. For these schools, the problems are rooted mainly in the subculture and subsociety beyond easy reach of the schools and, indeed, beyond the effective reach of many agencies designed especially to deal with these subsocieties.

What we are calling the *inner-city school* is not necessarily a school located in the inner-city in a physical sense. There are actually a number of common-man schools and even some main-line schools located in areas where inner-city schools predominate. The inner-city school is a psychological as well as a sociological phenomenon. Whether a given school will have inner-city or common-man characteristics depends partly on the principal and his faculty and their relations with the parents and children.

The inner-city school suffers from a syndrome of problems. Covert and overt hostility to the teacher; lack of self control on the part of pupils; lack of experience and background needed for success in school; an outer society which hardens, alienates, and produces a negative type of maturation; and intellectual apathy in the student all combine to produce in many instances an unrewarding and impossible teaching climate. It is a situation in which the teacher's hardiness and physical stamina count as much as teaching ability. It is a situation in which the young experienced teacher survives better than the young inexperienced or older experienced teacher. It is a difficult situation.

Yet the inner-city schools must work under almost the same operating formulas as a high-status or a main-line school, with the same formula relating numbers of pupils to adjustment teachers, assistant principals, psychologists, and other extra assistance. These schools need help over and above services they now receive. They are not receiving this help. The inner-city respondents felt to an overwhelming degree that they were cut off and abandoned. In most cases, the curriculum guides cannot be used, and it was felt that the curriculum planners were drifting even further away from an understanding of what is needed. With a feeling that their problems are not understood by the downtown office; that those who are to offer assistance, such as psychologists and consultants, are either too few in number or out of contact with their problems; that these problems are covered up by those in authority or that no one in authority or in the public really cares—buffeted by all those forces they feel are out of their control, the inner-city school teachers often give up in frustration after entering with dedication. As one assistant principal contemplating transferring said, "If I was a teacher instead of the assistant principal, I would have been out of here long ago. In fact, I never would have come if I had known what the school situation was. There are dangers that I face all the time that I shouldn't have to. Why do I have to pin boys to the floor? This has happened. Why do I have to take away knives? Why do I have to break up fights? I always thought that I was a teacher, but I'm no teacher. I'm a bouncer and a policeman with the assignment of dangerous duty."

Another young inner-city teacher in a school which had undergone transition from an extremely good main-line school remarked, "Yes, I have my name on the transfer list. I have stayed for five years and I have had it. My parents tell me I'm becoming impossible to live with. I think it has reached the point where I am becoming emotionally disturbed. I want to do a good job but I can't teach. The constant tension in the classroom drains my energy. I am not able to have fun with my children or have anything special for a lesson because with any permissiveness, they go all to pieces."

Another teacher in the same school who thought that she was not prepared adequately for an inner-city school stated, "There's no help for the new teacher. There were older teachers here when I came and they could have helped us through but they left. And why not? Why should you stay here when you go home exhausted every day with the rewards practically nil? In schools like this, the work and the preparation are five times greater than you'll find in your middle-class schools. We have to handle these problems right on the spot."

The lack of rewards causes many teachers to leave. Stated one teacher whose name was on the transfer list: "One thing about this situation that really depresses you is that you can't get any tangible evidence of what you're doing. You don't get any rewards from the children. You can motivate your head off and only see tiny results. Oh, these may be adequate for the situation, but they're just not enough to keep a person in this type of situation. It's the everyday things that wear you out as well. Oh, the big things bother you, too, but it's the constant daily battle in the classroom, out on the playground, out in the halls; this saps all the strength in you as a teacher. A teacher is able to put up with this type of thing for a certain length of time, but not forever. Many teachers here put their names on the transfer list because, to be truthful, they just don't know how long they'll last."

After teaching in a main-line suburban school, a teacher returned to an inner-city school he had attended when it was a stable, common-man school. He said, "I came into this system to help these children. I wanted to help them. I felt I could make a contribution—but I don't know. I had to make such an adjustment when I came here, you'll never know. What would take me a week to teach in other schools takes me a month here. And the discipline is entirely different as well. You know, with a middle-class child you only have to say something and that's that. Or, if the situation is bad, then a parent comes in and it's taken care of and teaching can be resumed. Here—it's just day-in and day-out discipline. I want to be a teacher but I can't."

The Survey staff member reported the following observation:

> I stood with the principal on the playground during the upper-grade recess. Across the street stood five or six older boys who, according to the principal, were drop-outs. He stated that many times these boys enter the school, annoy the teachers, stand outside the windows and shout, or come around during recess time and set their sights on the older girls. Two other boys joined the group and a group of seven or eight girls drifted over to the unfenced sidewalk and moved across the street to join the boys. One of the four teachers on recess duty saw the girls leave the yard and went to tell them to return. From across the street insults were shouted at the teacher by the boys, while the girls engaged in a form of catch-me-if-you-can, dashing back and forth in front of the teacher, taunting her. They moved slowly back into the playground in this fashion.
>
> When teachers attempt yard control, the children completely ignore them, running out of the playground onto the street and into the lot next door. When I independently moved among the children, there were hostile glances and taunts directed toward me. Apparently I was taken for a substitute or a new teacher. When the bell rang, the children completely ignored it and continued to play despite the entreaties of the teacher to line up and pass inside the school. I timed the movement in and it took eighteen minutes from the time the bell rang to the time the last boy and girl reluctantly and belligerently crossed the door into the school.

A sixth-grade teacher with four years' experience in an inner-city school remarked, "My biggest problem is not teaching. My biggest problem is keeping some semblance of an academic environment in my room. Some of these children are so nervous that they just can't handle the school materials. I have five or six in my group that just cannot be reached. These poor kids are just starving for individual attention. But what can I do? These are the same ones that go through school with their problems; these are the same ones that will end up with problems when they reach the upper grades."

A newly assigned teacher who is having some degree of success in an inner-city school commented, "My class is not too bad. In fact, without bragging, I would say it's one of the better ones in the school. I'm very authoritarian and I have a booming voice, and this may be why I've got my class under control. But I don't see why this should be necessary in a school system. I don't know why I should be a warden. I don't know why I should have to spend most of my time just keeping the kids under control. Why, oh why can't I be a teacher?"

A mature woman had this to say: "Academics take second place. I wasn't aware of this, I just was not aware. I heard stories from other teachers, but you just never know. You never realize until you're exposed to it. I've worked since I was thirteen years old and I've never worked so hard in my life as I have in teaching. I never heard worse cuss words come from people than I have from these children. I don't know, I simply don't know how the others stand it. I try to use the theories that I was taught in school; I try to use the methods, but I just can't. And I have an advantage on a lot of these young teachers because I entered teaching late. I saw a lot of those young teachers at CTC North. Many of them were genteel and soft spoken. My heart just bleeds for them because I know what's going to happen. And again I ask, why does it have to be like this?"

In most instances, the teachers are at a loss to explain the motivation behind the hostility. Even teachers with many years' experience in these situations feel at a loss at times. One teacher with 12 years' experience, and described by her principal as a superior teacher, stated, "They are hard to handle. They think little of talking back, even to me. They know me. To some extent, this hurts. They can be extremely rude without any type of provocation whatsoever. I realize what causes this. They bring a lot of problems to the school. You know, I'm no stranger here. They know me and I know them. But I had to fill in with a fifth-grade class and because of the fact that I wasn't their regular teacher, I had a hard time. Now, this is hard to take, this is hard to understand. You know, I come to the school lots of times prepared for a good day. I have things planned. I know I'm going to teach and I can get slapped down in just five minutes, and I wonder why, why this happened. All you have to do is just make such a simple statement as 'Please hang up your coat.' Then you get snapped back to you, 'I won't,' or 'I don't have to,' or 'Nobody's going to make me hang up my coat and *you* can't make me hang up my coat.' Then, with this greeting you in the morning, how *can* you really teach? It just seems to be that the whole class picks it up, like some type of a signal. Then *you* try to control it."

Tardiness and a slow start in September also hinder the teaching situation. Out of 2,000 enrollment in a particular school, there may be as many as 200 children tardy in a single day, some arriving as late as 15 to 20 minutes after the bell. In the fall, children are still entering the school at the end of September and as late as October. The principal said, "When they come in in September, they trickle in. We really don't start school until October. The truant officer this year had 300 names he had to round up to get to school."

A man who had taught for four years at a large inner-city school commented, "I'm not saying that the case is hopeless. I am saying that something is going to have to be done on the home level before you can do anything in the school. Look, you get kids coming in with no paper. They can't even get up a dime to buy a pad of paper. So, what do you do? You make it up to them, you supply the paper. What do you do in the situation in which there's five, six, or seven kids sleeping in one room, and even more than one kid in one bed? Many of these people don't have any medical aid, as well as the fact that there's no challenge in their society for school. I had a kid in my room who was walking around with an excruciating toothache for three days. The parents had to wait a long time to get him into the County Hospital to the dentist. So what do you do? It's not that I'm making a fortune. I hate to see the kid in pain, so I took him to the dentist. The tooth had to be pulled. Here's a poor kid walking around really suffering. Can you study with a toothache?"

The principal of the same school as the last respondent stated, "Oh, there's a definite relationship between high IQ and stability, and the same relationship holds as regards achievement. This is shown by the fact that most of the kids who are in our advanced classes have good home situations. You show me a child with a stable home situation, and I'll show you a child achieving at or above his grade level."

The realization on the part of the teachers that many of the children's problems, which in turn cause *their* problems, are beyond the control of the children themselves, awakens a feeling akin to compassion and some amount of sympathy. The young teacher stated, "You can't come in and teach and not really feel something for these children. You feel as if you want to give them something. I really think for the good of the city, for the good of society, we have to give them something. But I must admit, I just don't know how."

In some of the relatively high-ability classes of inner-city schools the teachers have common-man or main-line school situations. In a school which was considered extremely difficult by the other classroom teachers, a teacher with 20 years' experience, 14 at the school, and with a classroom load of 28 students with a median IQ and reading score of 110 and 8.3 respectively, stated, "I don't mind staying here, and I think to a great extent teaching in these types of schools depends on one's attitude. I've never felt the need for discipline too much at this school, and I've never thought that it was particularly hard. There has, however, been a change in the last three years. The kids have become much rougher and harder to handle. There are times when I get an uneasy feeling when I'm on duty in the boys' playground. A bunch of these very old boys get together and they kind of gang up in a group and they stare at you. And I'm beginning to feel a little bit uneasy, more so than I was before. I think part of the attitude that I had for the past four years was because of this enriched opportunity room. It is just a pleasure to teach in here. Come to think of it, though, I don't know if I would find the regular eighth grade that easy. In fact, I don't think I would find the rest of the rooms as good to teach as they were before."

The difficulty of teaching in classes other than the accelerated was due, according to the teachers, in great part to a hard core of students who are in active rebellion, not only against the formal structure of the school situation, but against the whole of society. An eighth-grade teacher said, "The emotional problems that these kids have are beyond the scope of the schools. For example, I had problem reports on about 10 pupils in my room, and I can't get them out of the room. They use profanity; they're antagonistic. Each moment I have to spend just sitting on them. To tell you the truth, they get to the seventh and eighth grade and the teachers just can't handle them. It's not that we don't understand the reasons for their behavior. Sure, we understand the reasons for their behavior. Even though we have all the understanding in the world, the behavior in the classroom hinders the teacher and this is the most important part."

One teacher, commenting on recent suggestions from university planners on the use of inquiry in teaching said, "I'm not sure that I'm thoroughly familiar with the theory of inquiry in science teaching, but I do know this. In order to state the problems and in order to handle the problems once they're stated, one has to have at least some type of background. These eighth graders can't even read. How are they to get the background to deal with the concepts? And I found—I know this sounds terrible—but I found that these eighth graders cannot think abstractly. At least, they cannot think abstractly about school materials. I'll have to take that back, because some of the accelerated group can think and handle abstract concepts very well. I think some of the accelerated group would be able to handle the inquiry part very well, but for the rest of them, well, I'd say they're out in left field. Look, you people come in and talk about inquiry and talk about the new ideas in curriculum and new ideas in teaching—what you're talking about are the things that work in other situations than these."

A departmental seventh-grade mathematics teacher commented, "I have five classes, and the curriculum guides and supplements as they stand are adequate for only about two of them. These two classes are in a higher socioeconomic status and they seem to have a better background. For the other three classes, there is no background on which to build and I have to go back to a lower level in the guide and supplement. I can't start at the seventh-grade level. Much of what is in these books these children can't relate to. It deals with homes, gives a picture of a man pushing a lawn-mower in front of his nice suburban home. It also deals with such problems as, 'If you had $1,000 in the bank, etc.' Well, many of these are so farfetched the children can't relate to them. There should be supplements put out that will help teachers, and they should be geared to schools like this. I'm in the seventh grade and yet I can't get past percentage. I still have a class that's in common fractions. I'm using a sixth-grade book for many of my classes, and if I ever went down to a fourth-grade book—which some of these children need—they'd think I was crazy. Some of these levels in reading almost demand that I go down, though. My highest here is 6.8 and the median is about 4.0.

"However, I should say that this neighborhood has made tremendous strides lately. It used to be I would hardly ever see the parents. Now I see three or four parents a year without even having to send for them. Many of the parents come in and ask how their children are doing in school and how their behavior is. But, as usual, these are the children who are doing well and you don't have to see their parents anyway."

There are inner-city schools populated entirely by white children, but the majority are largely filled with Negro children. A number of principals and teachers feel that the civil rights movement has taken a form which makes it harder for them to work in such a school. One principal commented, "The problem in this type of school is to build up a school spirit—an esprit de corps. We have to have the child identify with the school in a positive way. But then you get people coming around, tearing down the schools, making these blanket accusations of inferior schools and inferior teachers. I'm damn proud of my faculty. I think they're working their heads off and they're doing a good job. It lowers their morale and it lowers the effectiveness of the school when the parents and kids cannot realize what kind of a job the teachers are doing because they've heard nothing but the fact that the schools and the teachers are inferior. Why, I'd like some of those civil rights people to spend ten minutes in this office and handle the problems that I've handled."

Table 1

Experience in and attitudes toward teaching
in difficult schools
(percentages of teachers)

	Yes		No	
	Elem.	*H.S.*	*Elem.*	*H.S.*
Have experience in such a school?	83	66	17	34
If yes, do you like working in such a school?	53	52	47	48
If no experience, willing to accept such assignment?	28	31	72	69

In giving this picture of inner-city schools it is important to bear in mind the fact that the reports all came from Grades 4 and above. Other staff members visited primary grades, and found little pupil hostility or discipline problems. While many of the children are apathetic, and many show signs of severe intellectual deprivation, they are generally lovable children who reward a conscientious teacher with their affection.

Data on attitudes related to types of schools

These four types of schools have been described as they are seen by teachers and by principals. Perhaps the disagreeable aspects of inner-city schools are overemphasized when teachers are asked to speak about their problems. Perhaps it is a relief to "unload" one's frustrations on an interviewer. In any case, when teachers were asked on the anonymous Teacher Questionnaire whether they had ever taught in a school in a high transiency and low income area, and, if so, whether they liked working in such a school, their responses were not so broadly negative as the interviews indicate. Table 1 shows that 83 percent of elementary school teachers do now or have previously worked in such a school, and 53 percent of this group said they liked working in this kind of school. Among the minority who have not worked in such a school, only 28 percent say they would be willing to accept such an assignment, indicating that there is an attitude against working in the inner-city school.

It seems clear that dissatisfaction is not universal with teaching in difficult schools. It seems reasonable to suppose that measures taken to make the teaching job more satisfactory would improve the teachers' attitudes enough to induce many good and experienced teachers to choose deliberately to work in the inner-city type of school.

In order to find out what improvements in the teaching situation would be most welcomed by teachers, the Teacher Questionnaire asked the following question: "Assuming that the Board of Education should try to make teaching in such schools more attractive to you, how do you think it should proceed? Number *three* of the following 1, 2, 3 in the order of your preference." Then followed two groups of possible changes, one consisting of six and the other of seven choices. The choices of the respondents were scored 3, 2, and 1 for first and second and third choices respectively and added together to give a "weighted score" for each of the 13 possible procedures. The results are shown in Table 2.

It will be noted that the three most popular procedures are:

1. Reduce class size substantially.

2. Group children with more attention to learning ability and/or social maturity.

3. Adjust the curriculum to fit in with pupils' needs and experiences.

Fourth choice among elementary school teachers was: provide the teacher with assistants to work with individual children.

The three procedures involving extra pay for teachers in "difficult" schools were not especially popular, except that male teachers tended to favor the payment of a $500 bonus to teachers in such schools.

It is interesting to note the relative unpopularity of the three choices in Group B which involved the teacher getting into closer contact with the parents and with social agencies and having help

Table 2
How to make teaching more attractive
in difficult schools
(attitudes of teachers)

	Elementary School		High School	
Group A	*Rank*	*Weighted Score*	*Rank*	*Weighted Score*
Reduce class size	1	15,326	1	6,949
Assistants to work with individual children	2	6,765	5	2,848
Pay extra salary for specially trained teachers	3	4,871	3	2,992
Pay $500 bonus to teacher	4	4,866	2	3,113
Assistant for clerical work	5	4,123	4	2,870
Pay teacher for extra hour of work per day	6	3,048	6	2,039
Group B				
Group children by learning ability and social maturity	1	10,531	2	5,105
Adjust curriculum	2	10,124	1	5,922
Provide more textbooks and other material	3	5,523	4	2,774
Make it easy to refer discipline cases to principal	4	5,110	3	3,084
Closer liaison between school and social agencies	5	2,780	5	1,480
Aid teacher to know parents better	6	2,661	6	1,415
Provide half of social worker's time per school	7	2,615	7	1,259

Note: Weighted score gives values of 3, 2, 1 for first, second, and third choices respectively.

from a social worker. It is also interesting that the younger teachers, and especially the younger men, were more in favor of these procedures than the older teachers.

Since the teachers have generally had experience with variable class size, with ability grouping, and with curriculum materials, they appear to have voted for things they know about, and against innovations which were strange to them. This suggests that any changes introduced in order to make teaching in the difficult schools more attractive should be discussed with the teachers beforehand, and that the results should be studied and evaluated by a research staff.

In this connection it is useful to note the aspects of the job of teaching about which elementary school teachers are most dissatisfied. The five items which drew the highest vote of dissatisfaction were, in descending order:

1. Provision for treatment of maladjusted, retarded, and disturbed pupils.

2. The amount of time I spend on record keeping and other clerical duties.

3. Behavior of pupils.

4. The way problems of racial integration and segregation are being handled in the schools.

5. Size of my classes.

Facts about teachers in relation to types of schools. Further information on the attitudes of teachers toward the "difficult" schools is given in Table 3. This table shows that teachers with maturity and seniority show a strong preference for teaching in high-status or main-line schools. To organize the data for this table it was necessary to determine the type of every elementary school in the city. This was not done with complete accuracy, since the staff member who did the elementary school visits could not visit more than a small fraction of the schools. He secured information about schools which he did not visit by asking teachers and principals of a school he did visit which schools in that general area were similar to and what ones were different from their own school, and what these differences were. He then made a "spot check" with a quick observation of the neighboring schools, observing the neighborhoods, children at recess or lunch time, going from and coming to

Table 3
Facts about the various types of schools

	High-status	Main-line	Common-man	Inner-city	Totals
Number of pupils	26,500	60,400	68,600	176,000	331,500
Percent of total enrollment	8	18	21	53	100
Percent of regularly assigned teachers	94	91	86	64	
Percent of substitute teachers	6	9	14	36	
Percent distribution of reg. assigned teachers	11	23	22	44	100
Percent distribution of substitute teachers	1	6	11	82	100
Median years' experience of reg. assigned teachers	19	15	9	4	
Percent of attacks on teachers, 1962-64	0.6	3	12	84	100

school, books taken home, etc. This enabled him to make a rough classification of all schools into the four types. The classification is good enough to show the broad general differences between types of schools.

It is clear that the more mature of regularly assigned teachers have clustered in the high-status and main-line schools, which have 26 percent of the elementary school enrollment. On the other hand, 93 percent of the substitute teachers are in common-man and inner-city schools, and overwhelmingly in the latter type of school. What is called in this table a substitute is a teacher who has a state teacher's license but has not yet met the Chicago requirements and taken the Chicago examination for a certification. Substitutes are often very good teachers, but a large number of them are young and inexperienced. The ones referred to in this table are all working full-time in a single school. Even though the great majority of substitutes are working at inner-city schools, there still are 64 percent regularly assigned teachers in such schools. They tend to be the younger teachers, with a median of only four years of teaching experience.

The general impression of hostility toward teachers in the inner-city type school is supported by the fact that 84 percent of the officially reported attacks on teachers in the period 1962-64 were committed in this type school, which enrolls 53 percent of the children.

FACTORS WITHIN THE SCHOOL

In the foregoing analysis of the four types of schools, the emphasis has been upon the home and family backgrounds of the children and the related abilities and attitudes the children bring into the school. We now turn to factors operating within the school to make the situation better or worse from the point of view of the education of children. It is such factors that make a school in a poor area into a common-man type of school, or that make a school in what looks like a common-man area into an inner-city type school. These factors also influence the attitudes of the teachers toward teaching in one or another type of school.

Every school has both an academic orientation and a behavioral orientation. This means that the teachers are working both to *teach children the curriculum* and to *control their behavior*. Teachers naturally give priority to the academic orientation, if they can do so. This they can do in a high-status school and in a main-line school. They do not have to spend much time controlling the behavior of their pupils. In the common-man and inner-city types of school the control of behavior becomes more of a problem. The school tends to adopt a behavioral orientation, with the academic orientation subordinated to it. Many of the quotations from interviews with teachers of inner-city schools showed their preoccupation with the control of behavior. Teachers say they cannot teach, because they are so busy trying to control their pupils' behavior.

There are three factors within the school that appear to determine whether it succeeds well enough with its behavioral function to be able to work effectively at its academic function.

Grade structure. The typical elementary school in Chicago has been K-8, kindergarten through Grade 8. But this appears to be difficult to handle in the inner-city and common-man types of school. The older pupils are difficult to control, and their behavior disrupts the school for all pupils. Tentatively, we can say that the schools of inner-city geographical areas which resemble the common-man type are all or nearly all K-6. In no case did a K-6 school have the number of discipline problems and the degree of pupil hostility mentioned by faculties of K-8 schools.

The location of upper-grade centers in Chicago probably reflects this experience, though there may also be other reasons for concentrating these schools in the districts of inner-city characteristics.

A master teacher with many years' experience in an inner-city school remarked, "There was a definite change for the better when the seventh and eighth grades were removed. We used to have some really tough characters over here, and many of them were over-age. How do you get a 16-year-old boy to use a fourth-grade reader? Before they took out the seventh and eighth grades, I would say that this was a container institution. We were able to keep control in the classrooms to some extent and there was some teaching going on, but not very much."

System of grouping pupils for instruction. The nature of the grouping of pupils also has an influence on the behavioral climate, which shows especially in the upper grades. Although the trend in recent years has been toward departmentalization of the instruction in Grades 5-8, and especially in Grades 7 and 8, this has not worked very well in inner-city schools. The change to specialized teachers for English and mathematics, and possibly for social studies and science, is generally regarded as good from the academic point of view, but it may create behavioral problems in a school where the behavioral orientation predominates.

A number of rough common-man and inner-city schools have changed recently from a departmental organization to self-contained classrooms. This has been regarded as successful in the common-man and inner-city type schools. Said one teacher of an inner-city school, "Changing classes was bedlam here. The upper grades would disturb the lower grades, which didn't change. And then there was the problem of calming the upper-grade classes down, which wasted at least seven or eight minutes." A principal in a rough common-man school said, "We changed last semester from departmental to self-contained and it's made all the difference in the world. It has cut down on our fights and on kids ducking classes."

On the other hand, an eighth-grade science teacher in a departmentalized inner-city school said, "When that passing bell rings, I have to get out in the hall to supervise the kids. Then my leaving class can't be supervised. When something is happening in the hall and I'm out there, my entering class raises cain. Then, when I come in to calm them down, there's racket in the hall. After that, I have to come back into the classroom again and calm the class down. Of course, with all this going on, with my being a policeman and everything, I'm supposed to change into a teacher calmly instructing my pupils."

From the point of view of the teacher, having only one class of 30 or 35 to control all day is easier than having to meet several different classes of children whose habits and personalities she does not know so well. The teacher tends to feel more secure with a smaller number of pupils and perhaps because of this the pupils feel more secure, too.

The principal

In every type of school certain qualities in the principal appear to be essential to making the school operate effectively. In the inner-city and common-man types, the principal seems to make almost the whole difference between a school that holds teachers and gets a fair amount of teaching done, on the one hand, and a school where teachers and pupils are demoralized, on the other hand.

Wherever the school is successful, the principal has the following characteristics:

1. A willingness to move independently and decisively in matters affecting the faculty or school. This involves matters of discipline, in-service training of teachers, recruiting of teachers, and providing classroom teaching materials. A principal who waits for the initiative to come from above him in the hierarchy, or even some-

times for permission to make a change, does not keep up with the swift-moving events that push the school this way and that.

2. A genuine empathy for the teaching staff and for the people in the area served by the school. This is crucial in the inner-city area.

3. A perspective of the principal's role as one with a primary task of assisting the teacher to teach. This includes a willingness to handle discipline problems so as to protect the teacher from interruption by a few problem children in her class. It also includes work as a leader of in-service training, especially with young and inexperienced teachers.

Illustrating the importance of the principal in the eyes of teachers are the following comments. A beginning teacher in a rough common-man school remarked of the principal, "You probably found that the morale in the school is very high. This is because of Mrs. _____. She really backs up the teachers if they have a problem with a pupil or a parent. I can't speak highly enough of her. If you're wrong, she lets you know, and if you're right, she compliments you. We have very few transfers here and that's because the teachers like her so much. I am beginning to realize more and more the important part that a principal plays. When I was in my undergraduate work, I didn't think that they played that important a part."

The attitude of this principal toward her faculty becomes clear in the following: "I run my school on the assumption that the teacher is the most important part of the school system and that everyone and everything in the system exists only to help that person in the classroom. Downtown, myself, the district superintendent, all of us exist for only one reason, and that's to facilitate the work of the teacher. All these concepts that they come up with are nonsense unless we help the teacher in the classroom. It's important that they feel that the administration is democratic. They have to be able to feel they can make mistakes; be part of a profession; be free to experiment; to have time to know the children's parents and neighborhood; and to learn to talk up in a group of other teachers without fear. Those people are the ones that count."

In a large inner-city K-6 school which resembles a stable common-man school, a male teacher remarked: "I look around here and I've never seen better teachers in all the different schools that

I've been at. This is a fine faculty. It all boils down to the guy who can get people to stay here and we have this kind of guy. I came to this school because he was here [speaking of the principal]. People said I was off my rocker coming to a school in this area, but I like it here. I really do. I think that many of the accomplishments that we see or that you see around here are largely due to his methods. I also feel to a great degree that it is not necessarily the area, it is how well a man can keep a nucleus around him."

A timid and unenterprising principal was described as follows: "He operates everything by the book, without realizing that you have to adapt the book to the situation. He's afraid to operate on his own because he's afraid of how it will look downtown if someone questions him."

A contrasting statement came from another teacher in a different school. "He goes out of his way to get things for us. I imagine they consider him a nuisance, but it helps the teaching. I know he even makes things himself to brighten the school and pays for them out of his own money."

The relatively high transiency of principals is seen by many teachers and by some principals as an obstacle to the maintenance of good schools. One principal who had a successful inner-city school said, "Many of the inferior principals could improve if they stayed longer and really worked on the problems of a particular school. But they don't stay long enough to make a beginning on the job. What is the longest a principal stays? It's usually about three years, isn't it? What can be done in three years? You can't get to know the neighborhood, you can't get to know the faculty, and the only thing you have on your mind is moving out to another situation."

Between September, 1960, and June, 1964, transfers of 125 principals from one elementary school to another were announced. This does not include new principals appointed for the first time. During this period, 53 new schools were opened. The degree of movement is not as great as it has been recently among high school principals, but it is high enough to deserve some study of ways to increase the stability of the position while at the same time providing opportunity for promotion both in salary and in responsibility. This problem will be discussed in Chapter XIX.

Substitute teachers

There are two kinds of substitute teachers, those who fill a position in a single school for months or even years, and those who are "on call" to fill in for a day or a week at a particular school and then wait for another call. This latter group are called "day-to-day substitutes."

The number of substitutes in the first category is more than 4,000 and constitutes about 25 percent of the teaching staff. Many of them become certificated teachers during the course of a year and are regularly assigned.

The common-man and inner-city schools have 93 percent of the full-time substitutes, and also have a great and continuing need for day-to-day substitutes, which is not filled very well.

In 1963-64 there were 75,980 requests for elementary school substitutes and 28,933 requests for high school substitutes. A request is made by a principal who finds that one or more of his teachers will be absent on a particular day and telephones the Central Office to ask for a substitute. In the year 1963-64, 49,245 of the requests from elementary schools were filled, and 26,223 of the high school requests were filled. This means that 26,735 or about one-third of the requests for elementary school teachers were not filled, while one-tenth of the high school requests were not filled. The situation with respect to day-to-day substitutes is reported to be improving.

The inability to get substitutes when needed works a hardship on the whole school. The adjustment teacher, librarian, or gym teacher must take over a class. Sometimes even more substitutes are needed but not supplied, leaving classes unprovided for, and the extra classes must be divided up and parcelled out to other rooms, thus disrupting the work of the teacher with his own familiar class. The inner-city and common-man schools seem to have more trouble with this problem than do the other types of schools.

Time for preparation

Some major sources of dissatisfaction expressed by teachers on the Teacher Questionnaire are, in order of importance as seen by the teachers:

1. The amount of time I spend on record keeping and other clerical duties.
2. The amount of time I spend outside of school hours on my job.
3. My work load.

While teachers expect to do some homework, they prefer to use this time for planning and preparation of materials for the class. But they are often required to spend time on marking papers, filling out records and reports, and other chores they would like to accomplish during the school day. One teacher said, "I use a lot of my lunch period to mark my papers, but whenever I have a week of lunch duty I have to take the papers home and this means two hours' work at home. Consequently, I can't plan adequately for the next day's work. Unfortunately, this also takes away from my time with the family. Then we have records to keep. There are spot maps, lists of children, where they live, what their achievement levels are. There are also a lot of forms sent out by the state that we have to send home. For example, we have to send home one which asks where the children live, if their fathers have been in jail or not, how many brothers and sisters, and so on. This also takes time. You have to ask every day for these children to get the sheets back and this takes up class time. There are also many bulletins, notes, and other classroom interruptions."

There is a clear case for making some reduction in the load of clerical work for the teacher, either by adding clerical aides to the school staff or by reducing the amount of clerical work that is done in the school.

Work on the curriculum

In Chapter VI there was a discussion of the need for adaptation of the curriculum guides to the abilities and experience of children in various types of schools. It was noted that this work should be led in a particular school by the principal, aided by consultants and supervisors. The part to be taken by the classroom teachers is clearly a major one. The teacher must prepare the lesson plans and the lesson sheets after the curriculum design has been laid out.

The principal needs time to work with his teachers, and they need time free from the classroom to work with this material. It is clear that the crowded daily schedule does not allow for this time. The few minutes in the morning before school starts do not permit the teacher or the principal even to get started on serious curriculum work.

One principal commented: "What we should have is one free week after school which would be without children, but paid. In this way, in a relaxed situation we could sit down together and discuss what we did during the year and we could make some evaluation. Also, with a week at the beginning of the year, we could really get the school prepared. We could get the books out, we could really be waiting for the children to come in. And during the year, once or even twice a month we should dismiss the kids early so we could sit down and wrestle with the problems of curriculum and instruction. There is nothing sacrosanct about keeping them in school all the time. The suburbs do it this way and we can too."

A newly assigned teacher saw her teaching being hampered not only by the manifest problems but by the latent chores often overlooked. "I'm sorry to say it, but I think I bit off more than I can chew. I get down here very early to prepare, sometimes I stay late. I want very much to do a good job of teaching, but I really feel as if I'm being drained. You know, it is very hard to stay constantly in a classroom with the kids and have all of this stuff at night, and then come here early in the morning. With the textbook situation, I have to mimeograph papers which means preparing them at night. It also means then that I have to mark the papers at night as well. Once I do have the things mimeographed I have to use class time to explain, whereas the textbook would have explained already. You know I'm not going out nights and my weekends have to be spent doing planning. I just dread Sunday, I just dread it, because I spend all Sunday drawing up some mimeograph sheets and working over the plans I made on Saturday. All this work I think is affecting my attitude in the classroom."

The continuous development program

The single most important change in the elementary schools during the past decade is the introduction of the *continuous development* plan of organization for Grades 1-3. This plan is being tried out in many cities under various names, such as the *nongraded plan,* and the *ungraded primary.*

Essentially, this plan allows each child to progress at his own best speed during the primary grades, by giving him work to do at his own level of achievement and passing him on to the next level when he can pass the tests indicating that he is ready to move on. Thus the usual system of chronological age grades is replaced by a system of achievement grades. Instead of three age grades there are eight achievement grades in the Chicago program. A child may go slowly at first, and then more rapidly later, or vice versa. He is "promoted" whenever he is ready to move on. While most children take three years to move from first to fourth grade, some do it in two years, and some in four years. There is no failure during the first four years of primary school. In practice, children are not kept at the primary level more than one extra year, since their size and social maturity would make this a problem.

There are separate levels for reading and for arithmetic. A child can be at one level or in one block of work in reading, and another level in arithmetic. Within each school room, there may be children in two or three reading levels and two or three mathematics levels. The work in science and social studies is related more or less closely to the child's progress in the two basic subjects.

Started in 1957 and 1958 in a few schools, the plan was further developed and evaluated by Dr. Jerome H. Gilbert, principal of the Tesla School during the period from 1961 to 1963. It spread rapidly to about 200 schools in 1963-64, and more than 300 schools have indicated their intention of using it in 1964-65. At the same time, a few schools are trying the plan in Grades 4, 5, and 6.*

As would be expected, such a rapid expansion has resulted in uneven development of the program. In some of the larger schools the plan is indistinguishable from a system of ability grouping within classes defined by chronological age. A fast group then does three years of work in two, while a slow group takes four years before the children are passed into the fourth grade.

---

*Staff Study Report, *Education in the Kindergarten and Primary Grades.* Chicago Public Schools, 1964.

In some schools there is a highly flexible program, with some children moving from one level or block of work to the next every month or so, and with reading and arithmetic levels clearly separated.

Parents are generally approving of the program, as far as they understand it. The following comments were written by parents of a school in a disadvantaged area when they were asked their opinions by the school principal. The parents' notes have not been edited.

I think you are doing a wonderful job. I like this program.

I'm pleased with the progress so far. On the lever he is placed does is make his grade 2A or 3B?

Perhaps you could send homework for my child every day or perhaps let him bring his reader or work book home every day.

I do hope Selma continues to progress. I yet haven't been familiar with the progress plan. But I am sure that she is benefiting by it. She is yet in the 3rd grade. Isn't she?

I think the whole system is pretty lousy, it makes no sense whatsoever. I don't know what my child is doing and he doesn't know what he is doing. At this rate he can stay in the same grade level forever and think he is progressing. Who thought this one up?

Make Him Stand in the Corner. Earl Jr. Thank you.

I am very glad to know that Linda is making satisfactory progress. I do hope that she will continue and be able to make better progress. I will do all I can.

It is too soon to tell whether the continuous development program is successful. No doubt it has worked well in some schools, while in others it has meant only a nominal change without any real change in curriculum and teaching methods. One principal reported that he was meeting resistance in moving his faculty onto the continuous development program until he arranged for them to visit another school which had the program in action. They came back convinced and enthusiastic because "we don't have to do anything differently than we are doing now." In this case, the teachers of this school probably saw no more than a program of ability grouping quite similar to what they had when they were on the semester rather than the annual promotion plan.

It is recommended that the Research Department start soon with an evaluation of the continuous development program, first defining criteria for such a program and applying these criteria to schools which have the program in action, and then studying the achievement of the children and other aspects of their adjustment to school.

RECOMMENDATIONS

The major recommendations that arise from the study of elementary schools are:

1. *Study the needs of various types of schools.* Schools can usefully be classified into three or four categories, with different characteristics and different needs. The categories or types defined and described in this chapter may not be the best ones for further analysis and planning of programs, but the staff of the school system should work out a set of categories and determine where each school fits. These categories should then be used for a major program of improvement of instruction.

2. *Organize schools of a given type or category into a cooperative curriculum development and in-service training program.* Bring principals, supervisors, curriculum consultants, and classroom teachers together in this organization. Develop a set of parallel programs, one for each type of school.

3. *Support teaching in the "difficult" schools by an added expenditure of $100 to $200 per pupil.* Use this money for three general purposes.

    a. To improve the situation in the regular classroom by reducing class size to 30, supplying assistance for clerical work, and providing more of social workers', psychologists', and remedial specialists' time per school.

    b. To develop more new programs, such as Educational and Vocational Guidance Centers, IMPACT classes, summer schools, pre-school programs, and Guidance Resource Rooms for temporary work with problem children who are disrupting the regular classroom.

c. To provide time and leadership for a program of in-service training and curriculum development.

4. *Develop a strong school improvement program in the more "favored" types of schools.* While spending more money on the "difficult" schools, it is also essential to establish and pay for superior educational programs in the schools of the areas of the city with above-average income and level of education of adults. A program of curriculum improvement should be set up to parallel the one for "difficult" schools. In particular, this program should concentrate on foreign language teaching in the elementary school, science teaching, and the development of a new program in the social studies.

IX

Education of Handicapped Children in the Chicago Public Schools

Public education in the United States today is based on the concept that the schools shall accept all children who can benefit from any sort of educational training, and shall provide for each one of these an educational program designed to help him reach his maximum potential.

A logical development of this concept is that special educational facilities must be provided for children who, for one reason or another, cannot progress satisfactorily in the regular schools and classes. The nature of the handicap determines at what ages provision of special facilities should begin, and how long they should

* * *

Findings and conclusions in this chapter are based largely on the reports submitted by the following consultants: Dr. Robert Henderson, Chairman of the Department of Special Education, University of Illinois; Dr. Eli M. Bower, Staff Member, Research Utilization Branch, National Institute of Mental Health, U.S. Department of Health, Education, and Welfare; Dr. William Desmond Phillips, Associate Professor, Division of Deaf Education and Mental Retardation, Institute of Rehabilitation, DePaul University; Mrs. Dorothy B. Carr, Supervisor, Special Education Branch, Los Angeles City Schools; Dr. Jeanne L. Noble, Associate Professor, School of Education, New York University.

continue. Generally speaking, children should continue in these classes until (1) they are able to function adequately in regular schools and classes; (2) they are ready to progress to some form of higher education; or (3) they are prepared to function in the adult world as well as their handicap will permit. For this reason, children are often permitted to enter special classes earlier than the usual kindergarten age and to continue in special classes beyond the usual age for graduation from high school.

Chicago was a pioneer in recognizing the need for special facilities for exceptional children. About the turn of the century, Chicago initiated public school programs for the deaf, and soon after for the blind and mentally handicapped. In the 1910's, programs for the physically handicapped began; and in the following decades, speech therapy and schools for the socially maladjusted were added. In June, 1953, following the passage of state enabling legislation, the first classes for the trainable mentally handicapped were established in Chicago.

The special education program in the Chicago Public Schools today serves approximately 22,430 pupils, or about 4.5 percent of the elementary and secondary enrollment, in the following categories: physically handicapped; acoustically handicapped; visually handicapped; educable mentally handicapped; trainable mentally handicapped; socially and emotionally maladjusted, and speech handicapped. The total annual cost of operating special education programs in the Chicago Public Schools today approaches $10 million.

While Chicago can take justifiable pride in its record of service to handicapped children and in the many excellent features of its present special education programs, there is a great need at the present time to take a hard look at each of these programs in the light of the special needs of the various types of pupils and the ultimate objectives for them. If the objective for the great majority is to help them become economically and socially independent, is the program in fact effectively geared to these ends? Is false economy being practiced by conducting this $10 million program without adequate evaluation, supervision, or supporting services? Answers to these questions form the basis for the most important recommendations that follow.

Background information

The State of Illinois has accepted the responsibility for helping local school districts pay the extra costs of providing educational facilities for handicapped children, and these programs now cover each of the types of handicapped children listed on page 184.

"Educational facilities," as defined in the state legislation, are broadly understood to include special schools, classes, transportation, professional services other than teachers, and other approved services and equipment "required by the child because of his disability." Thus, reimbursement can be provided for special teachers, social workers, psychologists, or other personnel serving children who are not in special classes, on the ground that the services are needed to help the children succeed in school. This is an important concept because it opens the way for preventive or supportive services supplied when the child's handicap is not severe enough to require special class placement, and for supportive services after he returns from a special school or class.

Article 14 of the School Code sets up definitions of eligible children in each classification, with the age range within which children are eligible. For example, physically handicapped children are defined as "children, other than those with a speech defect, between the ages of 3 and 21 years, who suffer from any physical disability making it impracticable or impossible for them to benefit from or participate in the normal classroom program . . . and whose educational development is such that they are capable of being educated through a modified class program."

In the case of mentally handicapped children, the law adds to its definition a reference to the objective of the program. "Educable Mentally Handicapped" means "children between the ages of 5 and 21 years who may be expected to benefit from special educational facilities designed to make them economically useful and socially adjusted." "Trainable Mentally Handicapped" means children from 5 to 18 "who may be expected to benefit from training in a group setting designed to further their social adjustment and economic usefulness in their homes or in a sheltered environment."

In general, reimbursement is provided through payment by the state of $3,000 annually per teacher or other approved professional worker devoting full time to the program. Psychologists, social workers, and physical therapists are included. For "qualified psychological examiners" (who must have at least a master's degree and one year's experience in examining children), reimbursement is $5,000. Readers for visually handicapped children are reimbursed up to $300 per child. The 1963 legislature added reimbursement of $1,500 a year for teacher-aids in physically handicapped and trainable classes, raised the amount for teachers of preschool deaf to $5,000, and provided $5,000 toward the salary of the "qualified director" of a special education program.

The state also pays transportation costs up to $400 annually for each handicapped child "who the Superintendent of Public Instruction determines in advance requires such service in order to take advantage of special educational facilities."

Under these reimbursement provisions, Chicago collected from the state in 1963 $3,930,149 for staff salaries and other reimbursable expenses, and $475,000 for transportation. Bus service is provided for most physically handicapped children; carfare is provided for educable mentally handicapped and socially maladjusted pupils who have to travel more than one mile to their classes, but no transportation is provided for the trainable mentally handicapped.

The 1964 Annual Report of the Chicago Public Schools says that the state meets 50 percent of the costs of special education.

Overview of the Chicago program

Tables 1-3 show, as of April, 1964, the numbers of special classes and pupils served; the numbers of assigned and temporarily certificated teachers, and the numbers and percentages of identified exceptional children. For comparative purposes, Table 4 on page 190 shows estimates of prevalence of exceptional children in the nation as a whole, in Illinois, and in Chicago. These figures are derived from the Staff Study Report of the Chicago Public Schools, *Handicapped and Socially Maladjusted Children,* 1964.

In spite of commendable efforts to keep pace with growing needs, special education enrollment in the past decade has increased only 27.3 percent while the regular enrollment was increasing 39.6 percent and the average socioeconomic level of pupils was decreasing, with attendant problems.

Table 1
*Numbers of pupils and teachers in special
education, April* 1964

	Pupils	Assigned teachers	Temporarily certificated teachers	Total
Physically handicapped				
In school classes	1,398	131.5	42	173.5[1]
Hospital and home instruction	656	52	13	65[2]
Deaf and hard of hearing	826	68.5	32	100.5
Visually handicapped	706	60	13	73
Educable mentally handicapped	6,737	248	224	472
Trainable mentally handicapped	289	15	18	33
Socially and emotionally maladjusted	2,626	139	60.5	199.5
Speech defective	8,873	74	17.8[3]	91.8[4]

[1]Includes 26 physical therapists.
[2]Teachers meet pupils singly or in groups of two to four.
[3]Fully qualified speech therapists but have not passed certificate examination.
[4]Teachers meet pupils singly or in small groups.

To give some concrete illustrations of the work of individual teachers, the following reports are taken from classroom visits made by Survey staff members.

Social adjustment. Mr. C. has been teaching a *social adjustment class* for many years. He has had some training courses but mostly relies on his long experience. Like many other social adjustment teachers, he feels the advantages of the program are: a quiet sheltered atmosphere; elimination of opportunities for fighting and friction; free lunch with the teacher; recognition of the boys' need to blow off steam and rebellious feelings, with variation of the program according to moods and needs. Woodshop activities are

Table 2
Authorized class sizes

Programs	Class size
Physically Handicapped (in school)	8-14
Deaf Elementary	6-8
Hard of Hearing Elementary	8-12
Impaired Hearing Secondary	10-16
Blind Elementary	5-9
Blind Secondary	8-12
Partially Seeing Elementary	8-14
Partially Seeing Secondary	10-16
Educable Mentally Handicapped Elementary	10-15
Educable Mentally Handicapped Secondary	15-18
Trainable Mentally Handicapped	8-10
Socially Maladjusted Elementary	10-15
Socially Maladjusted Secondary	12-18

available. Mr. C. obtains cooperation by requests and praise rather than by orders. The boys are given some school responsibilities if possible. As elsewhere, most of these are tough boys who swear, fight, and flout authority. However, the class includes one boy from a good home with a very high IQ who is too restless for regular school. He is under care of the Institute for Juvenile Research. He bursts into torrents of speech occasionally; will not eat in school or use the washroom; will not put on his own gym shoes. At first the other boys were inclined to laugh at him, but now they more or less protect him, put on his shoes for him, etc. Mr. C. thinks that adolescence will either give him a chance to "catch up with his mind," or will send him off altogether. "We just have to go along with him until then. He's better off here than at home."

Mr. C. did not feel the need for any changes in the program or for any help for him. He would be glad to help others in a teacher training or visitation program. Greatest need is for more such classes (a statement echoed by the principal).

Table 3
Identified exceptional children in Chicago schools[1]

	Pupils receiving special education, April 1964[2]		Estimate of pupils served during year, not in current special membership		Pupils identified and under study; now served in regular grades		Total identified exceptional children	
	Number	%[3]	Number	%	Number	%	Number	%
ually idicapped aring	671[4]	.14	68	.01	241	.05	980	.20
idicapped sically	805	.16	80	.02	110	.02	995	.20
idicapped ntally	2,032	.41	4,216	.86	—	—	6,248	1.27
idicapped	6,977	1.42	506	.10	3,221	.65	10,714	2.17
adjusted	2,562	.52	4,438	.90	653	.13	7,653	1.56
als	13,047	2.65	9,308	1.89	4,225	.85	26,520	5.40

[1]This table does not include the following handicapped pupils served by the Chicago Public Schools:

24,987 pupils who failed vision screening tests in 1963

10,460 pupils who failed hearing screening tests in 1963, all of whom are receiving teacher-nurse, clinical, and medical consultant follow-up

82 pupils who are being currently served and 250 more pupils being staffed in IMPACT programs (the Improvement of Attendance and Curtailment of Truancy project)

1,307 pupils recommended to be excused for mental immaturity or psychiatric reasons who received psychological assessment, parent guidance, and other follow-up services in 1963

350 TMH pupils whose parents have received guidance

18,042 pupils with major health problems who were served by the teacher-nurse program

[2]Speech handicapped children have been omitted from the table. In April, 1964, 9,383 children or 1.90 percent were receiving services from a speech correction teacher; 12,027 more had been identified as needing speech help; and it was estimated that an additional 4,216 had been served during the year.

[3]Percent of school enrollment, ages 5-17, September, 1963: 492,985.

[4]Figures differ slightly from Table 1 due to accounting procedure.

Table 4

Estimates of prevalence of exceptional children

	Percentage school-age children		
	U.S. Office of Education[1] 1963	*Illinois census*[2] 1958	*Chicago census*[3] 1958
Visually handicapped	.093	1.00	.25
Hearing handicapped	.575	.46	.18
Physically handicapped	1.0	.67	.71
Mentally handicapped	2.3	1.88	2.86
Maladjusted	2.0	2.42	1.79
Totals[4]	5.97	6.43	6.19

[1]Romaine Mackie, *Statistics of Special Education for Exceptional Children and Youth*, U.S. Department of Health, Education, and Welfare, Office of Education (Washington, D.C.: U.S. Government Printing Office, 1963), p. 119. Percentage is exclusive of 1.0 designated as special health problems.
[2]*The Prevalence of Exceptional Children in Illinois in 1958*, 1958 Illinois Census of Exceptional Children, Circular Census-1A (Springfield, Illinois: Superintendent of Public Instruction, 1959), p. 8.
[3]*Ibid.* An additional .99 percent were grouped under multiple and miscellaneous categories.
[4]It is estimated that an additional 3-3.5 percent of school-age children are speech handicapped, but they have been omitted from the table because the great majority are retained in regular classes, and their inclusion tends to distort the estimates.

Advanced EMH. This room is taught by Mrs. D., a graduate of Chicago Teachers College, trained for EMH in the old course for ungraded classes at CTC. She has had an EMH class at _____ for 16 years. Of this class of 15, five are scheduled to "graduate" in June. Mrs. D., the principal, and the adjustment teacher expressed satisfaction at the test scores received by these pupils. Four will go on to _____ High School where there is an EMH program. One, who is reading at a fifth-grade level, quite a bit above his supposed expectancy, may be able to succeed in the basic program at the high school. The fifth pupil, a very nice-appearing

16-year-old girl with a recorded IQ of 56, will go to continuation school and hopes to get a job in a supermarket in the area. When visited, the pupils were reviewing the parts of speech and there seemed to be excellent participation and rapport. Place nouns led to a discussion of department stores, and all the pupils seemed to have considerable knowledge of department stores and their functions. All but one had visited the Loop, and the teacher said she would come for her one Saturday and take her on a trip to the Loop. This teacher and the other assigned EMH teacher both complained of restrictions which made it very difficult to take pupils on trips or even visits around the neighborhood. Because of the time necessary to comply with all regulations, advance bus arrangements, etc., it was impossible to take advantage of a classroom situation or to capitalize on interest generated in some place or topic at the right moment. (This seems to be a general complaint—that many fewer such expeditions are possible than formerly, and that trips are discouraged.)

These pupils attend gym with other pupils, and participate in assemblies. They share in monitor duties and some other school responsibilities. All in all, this was an encouraging class. The teacher felt they would eventually be able to hold jobs and give a good account of themselves.

Primary EMH. Mr. M. is a substitute whose previous teaching experience was as a gym teacher, so this is his first classroom teaching experience of any kind. The children in his room are aged 7 to 9 and look younger. He is a personable young man, and the little girls vie with each other in running up to cling to him and stand close to him when he comes into the room. He is proud of the fact that none of the children has given him any trouble, although at least two were supposed to be incorrigible when he received them. He says that he has been given a lot of help by the other EMH teachers and the primary teachers in the school. The EMH supervisor has visited him two or three times and has also been helpful. He felt the children were making progress in their reading and arithmetic. He was particularly pleased that on the morning of the visit, when he had been a little late due to a storm, he found the children had already said the pledge of allegiance and had begun their regular morning routine, which begins with a "morning story" about the day's weather, which is put on the board and copied by the children. During the visit, these children also played a game with number cards, involving both physical activity and speaking in a complete sentence: "I am number three. I come after number two. Who comes after me?" etc. Mr. M. says he likes working with the EMH class and plans to take the prerequisite courses for permanent assignment.

Waiting lists

The Department of Special Education states that there are no waiting lists for the physically, acoustically, or visually handicapped, other than those of children in process of study and placement; and that the number on waiting lists for classes for the socially and emotionally maladjusted is impossible to state accurately as it fluctuates with the time of year. This apparently means that principals do not refer children who are behavior problems for special class placement toward the end of the school year; it also reflects the fact that the social adjustment schools are already overcrowded, and many principals consider it useless to make referrals when they know no more pupils will be accepted. The waiting list for the educable mentally handicapped is given as 2,800. This is a staggering figure in light of the fact that the IQ used as a point of reference for discrimination between regular and special placement was lowered in 1962 from 80 to 75; and that many schools have a number of children suspected of being eligible for EMH placement who are not counted on the waiting list because the psychologists have not yet had time to examine them. It must be acknowledged at the same time that the number of EMH classes has been increased from 277 in May, 1963, to the present 474, and that the shortage of trained teachers as well as space necessarily limits the establishment of new classes.

A look at the districts in which the EMH classes are concentrated demonstrates that social and cultural deprivation bear some kind of relation to mental retardation. Although there are typically fewer than 10 such classes in the outlying districts, the districts that are located in areas of low income and low education have found it necessary to establish 30 or more classes, and still have long waiting lists. Various research projects in different parts of the country are beginning to examine this relationship. All that need be said here is that any attack on the educational problems of the culturally deprived should provide an opportunity to see whether the number of children who test at 75 or below can be reduced by reaching these children earlier and with better programs. In the meantime, the number of children needing special educational provisions because of mental handicaps or social maladjustment can be expected to grow if the average socioeconomic status of the urban population continues to decline.

The waiting list for the trainable mentally handicapped is given as 400. Undoubtedly, these children are either in private classes or not attending school.

Administrative organization of special education

In recent years the administration of special education programs was changed from a centralized plan in which authority rested in an assistant superintendent who directed the work of the special education classes, to a decentralized plan in which the major authority rests with the principal and district superintendent, who in turn reports directly to the central administration. The Assistant Superintendent now has a staff with advisory responsibility only. They advise the principals and teachers, but cannot direct the program, appoint or transfer teachers, or determine where classes should be located. Under the Assistant Superintendent, there is a Director of the Bureau of Mentally Handicapped Pupils, with five supervisors; a Director of the Bureau of Physically Handicapped with one supervisor each in the areas of the blind, the deaf, and the orthopedically handicapped; a Director of the Bureau of Socially and Emotionally Maladjusted Pupils, with no supervisors; and a supervisor of speech correction services.

In theory, the present plan presents an economical organization consistent with the general program for elementary and secondary children. It adds emphasis to the concept that special education is a part of regular education and should be integrated with it as closely as possible. In fact, however, not all programs of special education lend themselves to this type of organization. The program for the orthopedically handicapped, for example, is divided into four, not 21, attendance areas. Similarly, programs for children with hearing or vision handicaps are found in some districts but not in others.

The only programs which exist in every district are those for speech correction and for the educable mentally handicapped; and even in the latter, nine of the 21 districts have no programs for the EMH at the secondary level. Thus, in many cases, districts are not serving their own handicapped children exclusively, but are either providing programs which include children from beyond their boundaries, or are sending their handicapped children to special education programs in other districts. The variety of patterns of programs between districts requires considerable evaluation and coordination at the central level, and in part negates the advantages of decentralized organization.

Another weakness is the reliance placed by the current system on the district superintendent's commitment to the development of programs for handicapped children and the priorities he establishes for his own and his staff's activities. For example, every district has a sufficient need in terms of number of handicapped children to establish a resource room for the partially seeing, a high school program for the educable handicapped, and some special classes for the trainable mentally handicapped. The fact that all districts do not have such programs is a rather clear indication that the factor of different value systems is operating to limit development of programs.

After a year-long study, Los Angeles placed those special education programs which are of sufficient size to exist in every district under the line authority of the district superintendent, with advisory responsibilities in the Division of Special Education. Special schools and classes for the more severely handicapped whose attendance areas cut across district boundaries were placed under the line control of the Director of Special Education. Such a plan seems most applicable for Chicago's special schools for the maladjusted, the physically handicapped, and the centers for the deaf and trainable mentally handicapped. Specific comments from several of the consultants indicate that more authority needs to be vested in staff with professional competence in those specific areas of special education.

Supervision. Whether or not the line responsibility is vested in the Department of Special Education, the present staff of supervisory personnel in this department is too small: a director and five supervisors for 507 classes of mentally handicapped pupils; one supervisor for 151 classes for physically handicapped; one for 104 classes of deaf and hard of hearing; one for 75 classes of visually handicapped; and none for 244 classes of socially and emotionally maladjusted. In this connection, it should be noted that one-third of the teachers of the deaf and hard of hearing do not meet the Board's certification requirements for teachers of the deaf (see Table 1). In the case of the educable and trainable mentally handicapped, many of the teachers not only do not meet the special certification requirements but are substitutes with limited experience in the Chicago Public Schools. The same is true of a number of those who are teaching classes for the socially maladjusted; moreover, many of these teachers are working in a building which has no other class of the same kind and under a principal who has had no specific training in the area. In June, 1964, 91 schools had one EMH class in the building; 12 schools had one social adjustment class; eight schools had one class for the deaf; and four schools had one class for the blind. A recent staff study showed that only 18 percent of 236 principals responsible for special education programs had been qualified in any phase of special education. When the principal has little or no experience with a particular kind of special education, and when the teacher is often inadequately trained, it is essential to have supervisors who have some authority to direct the work of the teachers and to plan the programs in cooperation with the principal and the district superintendent.

Relations with parents and community groups. There is an urgent need for a more active and positive relationship with parent and other community groups. Almost every contact made with such groups by the consultants elicited comments ranging from neutral to extremely negative feelings. In addition, dozens of letters, telephone calls, and interviews were received by the consultants from parents who had heard of the Survey and volunteered information or complaints concerning the special education program. In most cases, the complaints seemed to stem from lack of concern on the part of the local principal and subsequent "passing the buck" to the Central Office, or lack of staff time to investigate problems and take positive steps to remedy them.

Research and evaluation

Another serious deficiency resulting from insufficient personnel at the central level is the lack of research and evaluation activities in all phases of the special education program. In the area of the socially maladjusted, the consultant commented: "It almost seems as though nobody wanted to find out what happened to these children" after they left the special class or school. Yet how can the program be improved or evaluated if nobody knows the results?

For another example, nobody has the time or assigned responsibility to search out new furniture or equipment and, most important, to conduct carefully controlled evaluations of their utility. Although several excellent innovations were observed in specific classrooms, the needed action research to validate the procedure and, if desirable, to broadcast the results was missing. On the other hand, it was obvious that some new equipment had been purchased without adequate trial, and the teachers reported that it was so unsatisfactory as to be almost useless.

Recruitment and training

With additional staff, special education personnel could undertake more personnel recruiting, desperately needed in these critically short areas. They would have time to provide prospective teachers with accurate answers to questions about the professional aspects of particular programs, and to cut through the red tape which seems to drive some qualified teachers to other nearby school systems. Active efforts should be made to recruit people who are being trained to teach exceptional children in institutions throughout the country and to develop practice-teaching programs with local colleges and universities.

An effective program of in-service training is a necessity for teachers who are attempting, often with very incomplete preparation, to meet the needs of children with special disabilities. The time schedule should be modified to give these isolated teachers more time to visit other classes, schools, and school systems, to meet with other teachers working in the same area, and to attend in-service training programs.

An encouraging effort is now being made by the Chicago Teachers

College to develop improved in-service and pre-service training programs for teachers of the mentally handicapped and of the socially
and emotionally maladjusted.

Psychologists

A focus of concern in connection with all special education programs is the question: How many children who need these special
educational facilities are in regular classes where they are not getting the help they need and may be hindering the progress of others?
It has already been stated that there is a waiting list of 2,800 educable mentally handicapped and 400 trainable mentally handicapped. These are children who have already been examined by a
psychologist and have been recommended for special class placement when there is a place for them. But, in addition to these
children, there are many others who may need special class placement who have not yet been examined. In May, 1964, there was a
backlog of 14,000 referrals for psychological examination. Of
these, the majority were probably referred as candidates for EMH
placement, although some were undoubtedly referred because of
symptoms of social and emotional maladjustment, special learning
problems, or unusual abilities.

The backlog highlights the problem of an adequate psychological staff. State law requires that candidates for EMH, TMH, or
special classes for the gifted must be examined by a "qualified
psychological examiner" before they can be approved for special
class placement. Such examination is also required[1] for children
referred to special programs for the maladjusted. Unfortunately,
some children are placed in Chicago's special programs without
such examination. Beyond the basic question of eligibility, psychological findings are important to planning for these and other exceptional children. Yet of the 113 authorized positions for school
psychologists in the Chicago Public Schools, only 85 are actually
filled. This gives a ratio of one psychologist to more than 6,000
pupils, and fully explains the size of the backlog.

The apparent reasons for the difficulty in filling positions for psychologists lie in the salary scale, the lack of progressive career

---

[1] Rule 7.12 Regulations Governing Special Education Programs, State of Illinois.

opportunities, and the personnel requirements. The Chicago Board of Education requires that psychologists have a teacher's certificate, while the state requires that they have at least an MA in psychology and a year's experience examining children. They are placed on the salary scale along with teachers in general and get no credit for outside, nonteaching experience. As in the case of social workers, this system handicaps Chicago severely in competing for personnel with other school systems and agencies. The psychologists know that $5,000 is paid toward their salaries by the state, and they do not understand why a way cannot be found to reimburse them at least for the extra time required for preparation in their specialized field. They also feel the lack, in the Board's present plan of organization, of opportunities to advance to positions of greater responsibility and reward. An approved field work program for psychologists in training might at the same time ease staffing problems and involve supervisory positions as part of a career program.

Social workers

A physical or mental handicap creates special problems for a child and his family. The manner in which these problems are met and handled determines in large part whether the child will succeed in any educational program. Thus, the skilled counseling which social workers are especially trained to give is a necessity in programs for handicapped children. This necessary supporting service is totally absent in Chicago Public School programs for the mentally and physically handicapped.

In the case of socially and emotionally maladjusted children, any educational program must begin with skilled inquiry into personal and family backgrounds and depends for its success on continued counseling and planning with parents, teachers, and the child himself. This has been recognized in a small way in the Chicago Public Schools by the assignment of two social workers to IMPACT[2] programs in three districts, to work with boys who are problems in the local schools because of truancy. There are also field workers assigned to the social adjustment schools and the Parental School,

---

[2]Letters stand for Improvement of Attendance and Curtailment of Truancy. The program is more fully described elsewhere.

who, although not fully trained in social work, perform some of the duties usually assigned to social workers. A real commitment to an effective social work program not only holds promise for much greater success in identifying and helping maladjusted children, but it should more than pay for itself by reaching children before they become so disorganized that they have to be placed in expensive special schools and classes. The social adjustment classes and schools become progressively more expensive as they deal with children for whom the promise of rehabilitation becomes less and less.

Problems of diagnosis and referral. A general concern with the problem presented by children who remain in regular classes although they obviously present problems which need some kind of expert diagnosis and treatment has led to suggestions of resource rooms staffed by a psychologist, social worker, teacher-nurse, and master teacher trained in group guidance procedures. In such rooms, careful diagnosis, short-term treatment, and proper referral could be made of children who are obviously not profiting from the regular classroom or are interfering with the learning process for others. Large schools might have such a room serving one school; or it might be possible to establish diagnostic and referral centers at the district level. Funds might be sought to make it possible to experiment with both types.

Curriculum

Curriculum goals for handicapped children are of course much the same as for children who are not handicapped. But the nature of the handicap determines to a greater or lesser extent the way in which subject matter is presented, the educational techniques, the materials, and the level of achievement that can be expected. Specific comments must necessarily be reserved for the sections on specific areas, but many visits to special education classes of all kinds seem to warrant two general observations:

1. Most special education programs in the Chicago Public Schools do not seem to be sufficiently geared to what the child will be doing after he leaves school. In the field of the mentally handicapped, the children are not even accepted in high school programs unless they can read at a fourth-grade level; and even these latter classes have no planned work experience programs through which

the transition to adult life can be eased. Yet such vocationally oriented secondary programs for EMH pupils are working successfully in many communities, including our near neighbor, Evanston. Work experience programs are also recommended for pupils with other types of handicaps: the deaf, blind, and physically handicapped. In the case of older socially maladjusted pupils, it seems clear that their chances of rehabilitation will be greatly increased by a successful transition to a paying job. It also appears that more could be done in making vocationally or practically oriented courses vehicles for teaching basic subjects to pupils who need extra motivation. One consultant observed a cooking class for socially maladjusted girls from which the girls who did not know fractions were excluded. Why couldn't the cooking class be used to teach the fractions?

2. Because of the smaller classes and the wide range of pupils' achievement and ability, it is natural that much of the work in special education classes is individually assigned, and the teacher works with the pupils one at a time. Much of this is good. However, these are pupils who also have a great need to experience the satisfaction and stimulation of working with others on common projects. Examples in Chicago and elsewhere show that this can be done with handicapped pupils; but inexperienced teachers especially need help in developing class projects that will give each child a chance to contribute while learning and working at his own level.

Coordination with other bureaus

The level of cooperation and understanding between the various bureaus and the special education staff seems excellent. Generally the flow of information is direct and immediate.

In only one case did it appear that another bureau was active in an area which logically belongs to special education: the Bureau of Child Study's reading clinics. While nobody will challenge the need for the clinics, or their worthwhile efforts, their activities are clearly within the teaching field and not child study. In fact, from the written descriptions supplied it is believed that this program comes within the new regulations for maladjusted children (learning disability) and if properly organized and supervised would be eligible for the $3,000 per professional worker state reimbursement.

Conclusion

The recommendations and criticisms summarized here represent the views of the several expert consultants who compared Chicago with the best they have seen in other school systems. In general, the special education program of the Chicago Public Schools can be rated as good, with some programs much stronger than others. While emphasis has been placed on those areas needing further study or change, the reader is reminded of the solid base of a well-established educational program for handicapped children existing in the schools.

All of the consultants, as well as members of the staff, expressed concern about the deeper, long-range problems which affect the need for special education. The quality of medical care for mothers and children affects the number and severity of physical handicaps. As far as numbers are concerned, the problem of the mentally handicapped and socially maladjusted is even more serious. Any fundamental approach to these problems requires an attack not only on physiological causes but also on the social ills which produce social maladjustments, educational disadvantages, and cultural deprivation.

RECOMMENDATIONS

1 Line authority should be returned to the Division of Special Education for the administration of:
   a) Special schools for the socially maladjusted
   b) Schools for the physically handicapped
   c) Centers for the deaf and the trainable mentally handicapped
2 A study should be undertaken of the effectiveness of district control for other kinds of special education programs.
3 More supervisory personnel should be assigned in each of the special education programs, especially to help the teachers with limited experience and insufficient preparation; time should be provided during the school day for in-service training programs, and for interclass and interschool visitations by teachers.
4 Special education personnel should develop more active and positive relationships with parents and other community groups. When responsibility is vested in other than special education

personnel, steps should be taken to see that such persons accept the responsibility for interpretation of the program to parents and community groups.

5 At least 1 percent ($100,000) of the annual cost of special education should be spent on research and evaluation; and the department should be staffed so as to make this possible.

6 An immediate inquiry should be made into the factors which are making it impossible to fill budgeted positions for psychologists; and steps should be taken to remedy the situation.

7 Social workers should be provided to work with pupils who have special handicaps, with their teachers, and with their families.

8 An immediate effort should be made to improve the vocational aspects of all special education programs, and to include work experience programs wherever possible.

9 Studies should be undertaken to find better ways of meeting the educational needs of multiply-handicapped pupils.

X

The High Schools of Chicago

Chicago has 52 general and vocational high schools with a current enrollment of approximately 145,000. This is the largest enrollment to date, and it will probably increase rather slowly, no more than 2 or 3 percent a year, during the rest of this decade.

* * *

In the preparation of this chapter we have relied on reports by the following consultants.

Foreign languages: Emma M. Birkmaier, Professor of Education, University of Minnesota; Wells F. Chamberlin, Associate Professor of Romance Languages, University of Chicago.

Mathematics: Phillip S. Jones, Professor of Mathematics, University of Michigan.

Natural sciences: Arthur H. Livermore, Deputy Director of Education, American Association for the Advancement of Science; Charles E. Olmsted, Professor of Botany, University of Chicago.

Social studies: John R. Palmer, Associate Professor of Education, University of Illinois.

Curriculum: Dorothy M. Fraser, Professor of Education, City University of New York.

Secondary school superintendents' team (complete report in Supplement F): Lloyd S. Michael, Evanston Township High School; R. Bruce Allingham, York and Willowbrook Community High Schools; LeRoy Knoeppel, Proviso Township High Schools.

The four-year high school is standard in Chicago and most other Illinois cities. Chicago had a number of junior high schools in the 1920's and early 1930's, but they were eliminated at that time and have not been considered seriously since then. However, the growing number of upper-grade centers suggests that this form of seventh- and eighth-grade institution is useful in Chicago and may provide some of the benefits that come from a system of junior high schools. In two instances, at least, a ninth-grade branch of an overcrowded high school has been placed in an upper-grade center, to give a three-year continuous program.

Most of Chicago's youth enter high school, though a few drop out of school before reaching this point. A 1963 study of the age distribution of pupils showed that there were about 4,400 eighth-grade pupils who would be 16 years old or almost 16 by the time they could graduate from elementary school. Possibly one-fourth of this group, or about 3 percent of all youth reaching high school age, will drop out at this point.

The total drop-out rate for Chicago is currently about 36 percent, which is close to the national average. This means that 36 percent of youth in Chicago do not graduate from high school. They may drop out of school while still in elementary school or during high school. They may drop out of private or parochial schools. It seems probable that the drop-out rate has been reduced slightly during recent years, when school systems have been making a special effort to keep youth in school and the difficulty of getting steady employment has been highlighted in messages to young people.

Thus, the public and private high schools of Chicago receive nearly all the boys and girls, and graduate not quite two-thirds of them. Those who do not graduate are mainly found in the poorer sections of the city, and a large proportion of them have suffered from disadvantages due to the family factor described in Chapter III. In the schools of the inner city between half and two-thirds of the entering pupils drop out, leaving a graduating class that is relatively small, while the ninth and tenth grades have large proportions of pupils taking Basic or Essential courses which are not of high school level.

The Chicago multi-track scheme of ability grouping was created to meet this problem of wide diversity of ability and achievement among high school students. There are normally four "tracks" or ability levels. The lowest, or *Basic* track, is for pupils whose reading or arithmetic achievement is below sixth-grade level. The *Essential* track is for those with achievement between sixth- and the beginning eighth-grade level. The *Regular* track is for those with achievement at their grade level or just below. The *Honors* track is for students who are a year or more above their grade level in achievement and have an IQ of 110 or more. The dividing line between Regular and Honors tracks varies among the high schools, depending on the proportions of high-achieving students. Above the Honors track is an *Advanced Placement* level of senior courses which are pitched at the college level and are accepted for college credit by some colleges if the student passes an examination in the course set by the College Entrance Examination Board.

A student may take courses of different tracks, if his achievement warrants a higher track in one subject than in another. Thus, he may be in Basic Mathematics and in Regular English. His placement in science, social studies, and foreign langauge is often based on his achievement test scores in English and mathematics, but after he has had one or more high school courses in a field he is placed at a level which fits his achievement in that field.

Thus, the general practice is to place students at a level appropriate to their performance, and to change them when their achievement appears to justify it.

The high school students

The school achievement of students is, on the average, related to the socioeconomic level of their families. This is seen in Table 1. The socioeconomic rating of the adults in each school attendance area is compared with the average achievement of ninth- and eleventh-grade students on a standardized test of reading. For example, in the four high schools 1, 2, 3, and 4, approximately 50 percent of the students score among the top 23 percent of the city as a whole. These four schools are highest in socioeconomic status. The four lowest schools, 36, 37, 38, and 39, have from 4 to 8 percent of their ninth and eleventh graders among the top 23 percent in the city. In the four low-achievement schools, between 36 and 42 percent of the English classes operate at the Basic level, or three years or more below the grade in which they are taught. On the other hand, there are no Basic English courses in the top four schools. The data in Chapter III on high schools A and B illustrate these differences between high- and low-achievement schools.

The problems teachers encounter at the different types of schools are of course very different. At Schools 3 and 4, teachers who were interviewed complained of being inundated by extra work contributed voluntarily by students. Even the most erudite teachers are frequently embarrassed by students whose knowledge of a topic surpasses that of the instructor. At School 33, on the other hand, teachers spend a great deal of time badgering students to return homework long after it is due. When teachers are embarrassed, it is most often by the blunt language of the students. It is not unusual at School 33 for misbehaving students to create three or four daily contacts between school officials and police officials. Law enforcement officials are a common sight in and around the school. The students react by seeing their school as a prison.

Programs of the schools

In order to look more carefully at the differences among schools and the reasons for greater differentiation of school programs, we shall divide the high schools into three types on the basis of data such as those in Table 1. The three types are analogous to the types of elementary schools, but we shall speak of three rather than four.

High-status schools. There are 10 to 12 such schools in Chicago, the first 10 or 12 in Table 1, and possibly Schools 13 and 20. They are all high in achievement and all located in middle-class neighborhoods. From 50 to 94 percent of their seniors plan to enter college. They are relatively successful with a general college preparatory program.

Common-man schools. Twelve to 15 schools in the middle range of Table 1 belong in this category. Their achievement scores are close to the average for the city. Their pupils come mainly from stable blue-collar families. From 40 to 55 percent of their graduates will enter college, while an equal-sized group will go to work immediately after graduation. They need a curriculum with substantial alternatives to college preparatory courses.

Inner-city schools. About one-third of the schools belong in this category, the ones at the bottom of Table 1. They are all well below average in achievement test scores. They have very high drop-out rates. They need a program which has constructive possibilities for drop-outs, as well as a college preparatory curriculum to guarantee opportunity for higher education to the minority who graduate.

Some of the differences as well as some similarities among these three types can be seen in Table 2, which presents data on some of the conditions that affect learning in high schools. There are no substantial differences in numbers of pupils per English teacher. Schools 36, 33, 30, 23, 18, 16, 3, and 1 all have less than 120 pupils per English teacher. A teacher with five classes will average 24 pupils to a class. It is probably a favorable thing to have small English classes, and this favor seems to be shared about equally by all three types of schools. The same thing can be said for the amount of money spent on textbooks. But there are striking differences in the percentage of fully certificated teachers and the median years of teaching experience, which are related to each other. Among the high-status schools all but one have 90 percent or more teachers with a Chicago certificate, and all but one have a median of eight years or more teaching experience. (The one exception is a school which lost many faculty members recently to a new school nearby.) In contrast, the inner-city schools range from 75 down to 49 percent for certificated teachers, and from one to nine years as a median for teaching experience. There is no deliberate discrimination against the inner-city schools in the assignment of teachers, but the more experienced teachers generally prefer to teach in high-status or in common-man schools.

The consultants remarked that among such different schools there was a striking uniformity of curriculum. A standard approach to curriculum with only minor variations is offered both at the school where half the students are classified as slow learners because they need remedial work in reading, and the school where two-thirds of the students are turning out work which would be acceptable in many colleges. The effort that has been made to equalize educational opportunity by offering the college preparatory curriculum and practical-arts alternatives in every general high school has been commendable. But this standard program is proving unsuccessful with appreciable numbers of students, and substantial modifications

Table 1
*Socioeconomic area and pupil achievement
in high schools*

School number	SER[1]	Achieve-ment[2]	Low read-ing level[3]	Say will enter college[4]	% Negro
1	290	52	0	94	0
2	229	49	0	88	0
3	199	54	0	91	0
4	180	54	0	81	2
5	123	40	12	71	26
6	109	47	0	67	0
7	97	36	0	74	0
8	83	32	0	57	0
9	82	29	22	55	21
10	82	29	12	55	0
11	79	36	5	74	0
12	75	27	5	57	0
13	74	41	0	49	0
14	69	32	0	52	0
15	68	33	14	52	0
16	68	25	23	73	87
17	66	28	4	48	0
18	61	32	8	46	3
19	54	11	16	46	28
20	54	43	0	70	3
21	53	21	15	76	88
22	53	26	0	39	11
23	53	25	12	42	19
24	52	17	15	78	98
25	50	23	0	41	0

School number	SER[1]	Achieve-ment[2]	Low read-ing level[3]	Say will enter college[4]	% Negro
26	49	23	0	44	0
27	39	22	4	38	1
28	34	16	13	35	1
29	27	27	0	44	0
30	24	8	29	53	100
31	23	11	16	36	9
32	22	10	41	65	100
33	22	4	56	53	94
34	20	10	46	65	80
35	20	14	29	39	44
36	19	8	36	61	99
37	17	4	37	51	91
38	14	4	42	53	100
39	11	6	41	53	100

[1]Socioeconomic ratio of adults in attendance area in 1960. See Appendix 1 for details. Certain schools are not representative of adults in area because there is a selective factor in school attendance. This is true of School 20, for example, where the school represents a higher socioeconomic group than the average for the attendance area.
[2]Percent of ninth and eleventh graders in top three stanines on standard tests of reading. For city as a whole, 23 percent are in the top three stanines.
[3]Percent of ninth-grade English classes in Basic English. Pupils are below sixth-grade level in such classes. In some high schools there are too few such pupils to form a class, though almost every high school has at least a handful of such pupils.
[4]Students who will graduate in June are asked in the spring whether they expect to go to college. Composite of data from 1962, 1963, and 1964.

Table 2
Socioeconomic area and conditions
affecting learning in high schools

School number	SER	Pupils per English teacher[1]	% fully certified teachers[2]	Median years teaching experience[3]	Budget for textbooks[4]
1	290	117	93	11	$4.33
2	229	141	82	4	4.29
3	199	119	89	12	4.29
4	180	129	94	8	8.60
5	123	123	92	8	4.29
6	109	121	91	12	4.29
7	97	133	91	16	8.69
8	83	131	92	24	4.29
9	82	134	89	19	4.30
10	82	126	90	9	4.30
11	79	123	93	8	4.29
12	75	127	91	22	4.32
13	74	127	87	12	4.02
14	69	138	95	15	8.30
15	68	130	91	9	8.16
16	68	118	73	4	4.37
17	66	123	87	6	4.35
18	61	119	83	11	4.43
19	54	135	64	2	4.29
20	54	127	79	7	4.26
21	53	126	70	4	3.56
22	53	131	85	6	4.29
23	53	118	82	6	4.30
24	52	121	63	2	4.30

School number	SER	Pupils per English teacher[1]	% fully certified teachers[2]	Median years teaching experience[3]	Budget for textbooks[4]
25	50	137	89	12	$3.30
26	49	131	83	5	4.30
27	39	133	74	4	3.84
28	34	120	75	5	4.38
29	27	134	76	5	3.69
30	24	110	66	5	8.91
31	23	128	83	8	4.67
32	22	129	56	1	4.49
33	22	117	49	1	4.30
34	20	124	60	3	4.87
35	20	135	56	3	4.38
36	19	111	58	5	4.30
37	17	123	53	1	7.54
38	14	169	74	3	4.30
39	11	131	77	9	2.48

[1]This is a more useful figure than the numbers of pupils per full-time equivalent teacher, which varies from 24 to 28 in no regular manner.
[2]This is for Spring, 1963. These teachers are fully certificated in the Chicago schools. All teachers have state teachers' certificates.
[3]A small part of the variation is due to movement of teachers into totally new schools. This accounts for relatively low figure in School 2.
[4]These are dollars per pupil in 1964 budget. The extreme figures are due to under- or over-expenditures in previous year or two as a means of adjusting to sharp changes of enrollment.

have been too few and far apart to make the curriculum relevant to the situations in which many students find themselves. The courses offered and the instructional settings in which they are taught need to be differentiated more thoroughly in accordance with the particular problems students bring to different types of schools.

The programs for students with average or above-average achievement are generally adequate; they need to be supplemented and broadened rather than overhauled. They particularly need more emphasis on foreign languages.

The major thrust in improving the high school program needs to be directed at the thousands of students working below grade level who are not now getting much that is useful to them or appropriate to their abilities. The consultant's observations in the social studies are valid for other areas of the curriculum as well. He found:

> It is distressing to observe classes of tenth graders who read at the fifth- or sixth-grade level stumbling line by line through a history textbook appropriate for the average tenth grader. It is impossible at this time to point out one significant system-wide endeavor in the social studies clearly designed for the purpose of assisting the social studies teacher working with the below-average student. There have been some attempts, but the impact of these on classroom teachers has been nil. Courses, textbooks, and materials are appropriate primarily for students working at grade level or above. Courses specifically designed for the poor reader are urgently needed. Content judged to have particular significance for urban life and for minority groups should be given special attention in these courses. Most teachers working with well-prepared students provide a stimulating atmosphere and fine instruction. But many working with poorer students seem to have little knowledge of how to proceed. Many merely read the textbook through line by line with the students and give only short-answer quizzes. Some do nothing at all; their students can be seen dozing or staring into space.

The most systematic efforts to find appropriate curriculum provisions for students who need remedial and other extra help have been in English and, to a lesser extent, in mathematics. The Chicago schools deserve praise for establishing more special courses at the high school level in these two areas than most other cities and for avoiding a common mistake by holding fairly well to the policy of programming a pupil for remedial work only in the subjects in which his achievement is deficient. On the whole, however, a consultant reports that,

> The provision for students at the low end of the achievement scale, including the great numbers of disadvantaged, is apparently achieving results for a relatively small proportion of the young people who are involved. An important measure of the effectiveness of these courses should be the extent to which they enable pupils to recoup earlier losses in learning and move into regular or even advanced classes. Unless this occurs with some considerable proportion of the pupils, the homogeneous remedial courses may contribute to the creation— or perpetuation—of the academic ghetto that the courses are intended to destroy. The courses cannot be evaluated and, consequently, improved unless records are kept showing movement between levels. Incredibly, it appears that most of the high schools do not even gather this information. Teachers of remedial classes usually estimate a movement from remedial to regular classes in English and mathematics of 10 percent to 30 percent. On the other hand, figures in one school which did keep records showed that only 2.7 percent of the students in Essential Mathematics were advanced to regular courses.

Despite the special efforts in English, the picture is far from encouraging even here. The required materials in English are reasonably appropriate for college preparatory pupils who read at or above grade level, but they do not seem likely to obtain the desired results in interest and performance when used with pupils from underprivileged backgrounds, even including those reading at or near grade level. Teachers need more freedom to choose literature and other materials in terms of the backgrounds and interests of their pupils.

Another area in which the options provided for below-average youngsters are seriously deficient is the practical arts. The need for expansion is clear and immediate. In the small number of schools which send the great majority of their students to college, the problem is minimal because few students elect nonacademic subjects. But in the low-achievement schools and many of the middle-level achievement schools, the facilities and opportunities in these subjects fall far short of accommodating the large number of students who want to elect them and should have them as one part of their programs. Educators everywhere recognize that the opportunity for slow and average students to have successful experiences in a non-academic subject is even more important as a motivating device than as a means of providing practical knowledge which itself is highly serviceable. Yet at one high school with an enrollment of 4,000 students, mostly from low-income families, 200 girls who applied for home economics were denied it due to the lack of space. The consultant recognized that there is a shortage of trained teachers in home economics and recruitment is difficult even when positions and facilities are available. However, this consultant writes,

. . . this fact should not prevent efforts on the part of the school administration to strengthen and expand the program in a study which can contribute so much and so directly to better use of family resources and improved living conditions for underprivileged youth who do not receive this kind of training in their homes. Its vocational aspects for young men and women who may not pursue advanced formal education are also extremely important. Industrial education, business education, work-study programs, and advanced study of art and music have similar value and are similarly limited in the Chicago high schools. At one high school, for example, there are fifteen classes in the three available shops and student requests would fill at least five more classes, but shop space for the additional section is not available. Work-study programs in distributive education and diversified office occupations are offered, but typically many more students apply than can be served. Instructors in these classes state that often three or four times as many students request these programs as can be accommodated in them.

These critical statements about the curriculum for low-achievement students could be made with equal justification in practically every big city in the country. The program for such pupils is bound to appear less successful than the programs for other groups.

In the search for ways of working more effectively with low-achievement pupils, several curriculum guides have been produced by the Curriculum Department to help teachers in the basic and remedial-level courses.

The curriculum guides

It was noted in Chapter VI that the curriculum guides are not as widely used or as useful in the eyes of teachers as would be desired.

Tables 3 and 4 show more data on the usefulness of curriculum guides, including some on the guides for Basic and Essential English and Basic and Essential Mathematics. These tables indicate three things of importance for this discussion.

First, Table 3 shows that between 18 and 44 percent of teachers claim that they never use the guides in one or another field, and the guides for Basic and Essential English are the least used.

Second, Tables 3 and 4 show that teachers with only one or two years of experience find the guides less useful than those of greater experience.

Third, there are substantial differences between the guides as they are perceived and used by the teachers. Thus, the guides for Basic and Essential Mathematics are found to be more useful than those for regular mathematics, while the reverse is true for the English guides. This may point to the desirability of working intensively to improve the guides for Basic and Essential English.

Once more, as in Chapter VI, we observe that the problem of implementing and adapting the curriculum guides is a major one.

Quality of the curriculum

The general high schools of Chicago all have the same basic curriculum, with adaptations for students of different ability levels that have been described. Our consultants felt that the curriculum should be adapted to the needs of different types of students more than it is at present. This conclusion is summarized by the three superintendents of suburban high school districts as follows:

> The curriculum in each high school needs greater adaptation and adjustment to the needs of the pupil population it serves.
>
> Course offerings among most of the high schools show striking similarity regardless of levels of pupil ability, and future educational and vocational plans. More extensive curriculum development, particularly in industrial arts, home economics, business education, art, and music, is urged. The recent efforts to develop work experience programs in a number of high schools are to be commended. The policies and procedures in ability grouping have been other efforts to adapt course offerings and content to pupil needs and abilities.

The curriculum of the general high schools in Chicago is a standard one. Requisites for graduation consist of four years of English;

Table 3

Degree of use of curriculum guides by high school teachers
(percentages, unless otherwise stated)

Subject area	1-2 years' experience				3-15 years' experience				16+ years' experience				Totals			
	O*	S	N	Number	O	S	N	Number	O	S	N	Number	O	S	N	Number
English, Regular and Honors	34	46	20	182	35	47	18	526	46	40	14	175	37	45	18	883
English, Basic and Essential	11	40	49	45	15	38	46	52	20	70	10	10	14	42	44	107
Mathematics, Regular and Advanced	11	41	48	108	27	36	38	356	28	58	14	151	24	42	34	615
Mathematics, Basic and Essential	27	31	42	62	36	28	35	88	42	42	16	24	34	31	35	174
History	18	51	31	142	24	45	31	571	44	36	20	138	26	45	29	851
General Science and Biology	37	37	26	35	33	45	22	209	39	45	16	98	35	44	21	342

*O = Often; S = Sometimes; N = Never.

Table 4
Evaluation of curriculum guides by high school teachers
(percentages, unless otherwise stated)

Subject area	1-2 years' experience					3-15 years' experience					16+ years' experience				
	E*	G	F	U	Number	E	G	F	U	Number	E	G	F	U	Number
French and Spanish	18	14	36	32	22	32	27	19	22	59	24	24	34	18	41
English, Regular and Honors	12	47	29	12	181	20	38	27	15	529	33	39	20	8	176
English, Basic and Essential	0	12	26	62	42	2	14	43	41	51	27	27	27	18	11
Mathematics, Regular and Advanced	8	43	29	20	108	19	36	32	13	350	30	45	21	4	148
Mathematics, Basic and Essential	8	37	22	23	63	17	28	26	29	86	33	25	25	20	25
History	12	32	33	23	146	16	36	28	20	571	36	23	24	17	138
All sciences	18	36	34	12	50	20	35	29	16	274	34	34	23	9	146

*E = Excellent; G = Good; F = Fair; U = Unsatisfactory.

three years of social studies; three years of science and mathematics (two years of either and one year of the other); two years of one of the following—foreign language, business education, home economics, or industrial arts; a year's course in music and in art, and four years of physical education and health.

The effort to provide for various levels of ability among students by offering courses in a subject at two or more levels of complexity has been described. At this point we shall draw on the reports of the various consultants for their evaluations of the standard curriculum for the average and for the college preparatory student.

The present is an especially good time for revision of the curriculum. Scholarly groups in mathematics, physics, chemistry, biology, geography, foreign languages, political science, anthropology, and English have turned their attention to the high school curriculum. They have been aided by funds from private foundations and from the federal government. Many in-service training institutes are provided each summer with fellowships for high school teachers who want to get better acquainted with the new methods and materials. We are in the midst of a curriculum revolution in the secondary schools.

On the whole, the Chicago schools have been conservative with respect to curriculum changes. They have made some changes, as we shall see, but they are not nearly as active in developing and trying out new courses and course material as are the schools in many big city suburbs.

Science. The visiting consultants found the science teaching to be competent in a traditional way. They felt that the curriculum guides supported a conservative procedure, but did not allow teachers to keep up with the rapid changes now going on in the field of science teaching. For example, a consultant writes, "Biology has been moving so rapidly, especially in some of the areas which are least stressed in some of the books on the approved lists, that even the best planned curriculum guide, four years old, can result in a steady decline." The suggested activities do not reflect the current thought that students should learn to investigate in the classroom and the laboratory.

The Survey consultants were dismayed to find that none of the text materials that have come out of the several major national science study projects was on the list of approved textbooks for science, which has just been published and is to remain in force through 1967. This illustrates the inertia of the big city school system in making changes. The physical science course of the Physical Sciences Study Committee has been used in some high schools elsewhere for six years. The National Science Foundation has provided summer training fellowships for approximately one-fourth of the high school physics teachers of the country, to enable them to get acquainted with this new course. A medium-sized city with one or two high schools which was alive to current developments in science teaching could remake its science courses within the space of a couple of years. But a big city like Chicago does not move so rapidly.

There are four major school science programs being supported by the National Science Foundation, one in physics, one in biology, and two in chemistry. All have produced teaching materials, none of which is on the approved list just mentioned. However, a Chicago teacher who has been trained for one of the experimental programs may request special permission to teach this course and to order the textbooks. By the autumn of 1964, about 40 teachers in 21 different high schools were teaching such courses. Of this number, 27 teachers are teaching the "Yellow" version of the Biological Sciences Curriculum Study, which is similar to the Curriculum Guide Supplement for biology. This leaves 13 teachers who are actively experimenting with science courses which depart considerably from the curriculum guides.

The Curriculum Department has been trying to arrange summer and other institutes for science teachers, through an arrangement with one or more local universities and with the aid of National Science Foundation or NDEA funds. This is good, and should be supplemented with an attempt on the part of high school teachers through their own professional groups to organize for improvement of the science curriculum. Possibly a city-wide Science Council should be formed, with one or more representatives from each high school and including several specialists in elementary school science.

Foreign Languages. Modern language instruction within the last decade has undergone drastic changes. The field has moved rapidly from the usual two-year high school grammar-translation approach with a single textbook to what is now called the audio-lingual approach to language learning and teaching with its emphasis on introducing the student to language first through listening-speaking, often starting as early as Grade 3, followed by reading-writing. This approach includes coordinated systems of learning materials (tapes, take-home discs, text, workbook, tests, visuals, and teacher's manual) followed by evaluation and testing techniques alien to the average foreign language teacher, and the use of technological equipment, such as tape recorder, laboratory, film projector, etc., to aid the learning and teaching process.

The foreign language program must be described as a single program, rather than one for the high school and one for the elementary school.

The Chicago school system has recognized these changes in its *Policy Statement on Foreign Languages,* February, 1962, prepared by a committee of elementary and high school teachers. The statement commits the schools to a program which emphasizes *oral communication* as the primary approach to language teaching. To do this job effectively the schools must:

1. Provide for longer sequences of study, especially with emphasis on the six-year sequence starting at the seventh-grade level.

2. Emphasize the listening and speaking objectives.

3. Insist on the student's attaining mastery in one language before he starts a second.

4. Plan carefully articulated language programs between grades and between elementary and senior high schools.

5. Provide for two tracks in the high school, one for those who come with foreign language training in the elementary school and one for those who are beginning their language study in the high school, further differences being taken care of within the class organization itself.

6. Employ teachers with near native ability in the skills and training in methods appropriate to the audio-lingual approach.

7. Employ a core of skilled consultants to assist in the development of the language program.

With changes of such a revolutionary nature as have taken place in the foreign language field there is no doubt that foreign language programs throughout the nation are in a state of confusion. The Chicago schools find themselves in the same dilemma. Objectives now have been clearly defined and directions have been indicated. There is now an obligation on the part of the language teachers and the administration to develop lines of strategy which could make the school system a leader in the field.

In 1963-64 approximately 28 percent (33,000) of high school students studied foreign language, and about 4 percent (13,000) of elementary school pupils were in language classes. Eight languages were taught in the high schools—Spanish, French, German, Latin, Russian, Italian, Polish, and Hebrew—with the largest enrollment in Spanish followed by French. Five of these were also being taught in elementary schools.

The foreign language courses are open only to the student who is in the Regular or a higher track in high school, and in elementary school to pupils who qualify as "gifted." One of the visiting consultants believes that this is too restrictive. More students should be electing a modern language than the number who intend to go to college. Many students of average ability and without college aspirations will find a foreign language useful in later life. At least such students should be given an opportunity to try a foreign language for six months to a year.

In view of the growing program of foreign language in the seventh and eighth grades, the high schools need to make provision for pupils who can enter a second semester or a second-year course in the ninth grade, and who may want to continue through high school with a six-year sequence. At present some high schools are doing this very well and others are not. The consultants saw four high schools in which the articulation had been made very well. These schools are now in process of adding a course above the present senior or fourth-year high school course.

On the other hand, some high schools do not provide for articulation with elementary schools in foreign language. Often their teaching methods are more like the old grammar-reading type than the modern audio-lingual approach. The pupils coming from elementary schools into these courses may lose interest and drop out.

The visiting consultants found the teaching at the elementary school to be superior and more inspiring than what they saw in the high school. Most of the elementary school teachers have been trained for the audio-lingual methods, while many of the high school teachers still rely heavily on the older methods. Only 3 out of 12 teachers observed by one of the consultants had attended an NDEA language institute.

Qualifications of the teachers are quite good, as the following quotation from a consultant indicates.

> Every staff member with whom I visited and whom I observed in the classroom spoke the foreign language he was teaching with confidence and skill. Some had a slight English accent and intonation but not to such a degree that it would be incomprehensible to the native speaker of the language. Some have had study and travel experience abroad. One of the teachers (Spanish) and the cadet teacher observed (Russian) were native speakers of the foreign language. The others would have ratings from good to superior in the four skills—listening comprehension, speaking, reading, and writing—on the Modern Language Association's qualifications sheet for rating modern language teachers.
>
> The teachers were acquainted with the Audio-Lingual Materials developed by the Modern Language Materials Development Center, the pilot materials created for the audio-lingual approach to teaching language. Some approved of these materials, others did not. How well teachers, using these materials, worked with them from day to day I had not the time to observe. What I did see in some cases was good. However, several teachers treated these materials as they would a regular grammar-translation text and had the students write out exercises intended only for oral drill. With the limited in-service programs offered the teachers in the system one cannot expect teachers who have been trained in the grammar-translation-reading approaches to revolutionize their methods.
>
> The five curriculum consultants are excellently trained subject matter specialists, all of them dedicated to the new approaches to language teaching. They have attended NDEA language institutes and a few have also served in the capacity of demonstration teachers. However, there are only *five* of them, three for the elementary program with over 13,000 students, 138 schools, and 186 teachers participating in the program and two for the high school with 33,266 students, 44 high schools, and some 225 teachers involved. This is an utterly ridiculous situation. To top it all, their responsibilities are city-wide, they are to work out guidelines with the teachers for the modern

language programs, they are to demonstrate the new materials, to prepare materials for circulation to the classroom teachers, to conduct in-service training and workshops, implement the NDEA programs under Title III, help coordinate and articulate the long sequences in the language program and help the individual teachers when requested to do so! Most of their time has been spent in editing and writing curriculum guides and doing clerical work in the office. There are not enough of them to really get on with the work that needs to be done when a subject matter field is undergoing the revolutionary changes in its whole approach to the teaching and learning acts. They play no formal part in evaluating the teachers and yet who is there in the school system who could do this better than they? At least, they should be consulted.

Physical equipment is essential for the audio-lingual method. At a minimum there should be a tape recorder and a phonograph. These are not found in many high school classrooms, but several elementary schools are well equipped, with tape recorders and in-dividual listening posts for pupils to work individually on hearing the language, understanding it, and repeating orally. At present the rooms in a number of high schools are being equipped with language laboratories. A visiting consultant says, "in all of the schools visited the acoustics of the rooms, even in the language laboratories, were so bad that a real audio-lingual method with a great amount of listening and speaking going on among the students was out of the question."

In order to give some of the flavor of the teaching in elementary schools, we quote the following from a consultant's report.

There are now 27 full-time FLES [Foreign Language in the Ele-mentary School] teachers in the system. To work as a FLES teacher, certified elementary school teachers must pass a taped test made up by the Board of Education and spoken by a native speaker of the language concerned. There are no fixed requirements in terms of course hours and degrees in foreign language; however, many of these teachers have an undergraduate major in a foreign language, some have M.A.'s, and there is one Ph.D. CTC North is providing some new FL teachers for the system, and it is hoped that other new teachers will come from the Midwest College Group, which sends its FL majors into the Chicago schools for practice teaching assignments.

Only those pupils who are up to grade level or above in English reading ability are admitted. The FLES program is clearly audio-lingual and makes use of the most modern methods and equipment. Full-time programs, starting in the seventh and eighth grades, include four or five forty-minute sessions per week.

A class of 18 eighth-grade boys began their lesson with a warm-up on the date, followed by a snappy structure drill on the pattern *du pain—je n'ai pas de pain,* the teacher giving the cue word, and the student furnishing the answer in the negative. The drill took the class through many vocabulary items already used in other patterns. There were only a few incorrect responses. (This shift from *du* to *de* is a point of French usage which many college students never master.) The drill pattern was changed to *plus de—je n'ai plus de pain,* etc. The class was then led through the first part of AML Level I, unit 8, with individuals answering *Comment trouves tu notre école?* and so on.

Giving all instructions in French, Miss _____ now sent half the class to the listening table to use the headsets and tape recorder on the same material. The other half was drilled, always in complete sentences, on the verbs *aller* and *faire.* The other half of the class came back to their seats for the same drill, while the first half used the headsets.

The class was combined for the final activity of the period, a two-part test. For the first part, the teacher wrote parts of the dialogue on the board, with some elements missing; pupils were asked to write only the missing elements. For the second part, they were asked to write brief but correct answers to five questions based on the dialogue. They corrected their own work as she put the answers on the board.

Miss _____ is so good a teacher of foreign language that it is difficult to find words to describe her work and her skills adequately. To begin with, her French is beautiful—clear, precise, musical, idiomatic, completely natural. In addition to her linguistic skill, she is a master teacher; not a single minute of class time is wasted; not a single mispronunciation or mistake goes uncorrected; and at the end of the class, the one or two who were having trouble are asked to come in for extra help. She conducts her class with effervescent good humor and her students love it. At the same time, she is always in complete control. Her lesson is planned almost to the last second, things move at an extremely rapid pace, and at the end of the period one remains at a loss to explain how so much excellent learning and perfect practice can have taken place in a class period which has gone by so quickly.

An example of good teaching in the high school with a ninth-grade class of 42 who have not had elementary school foreign language follows:

> This class has only just commenced its year's work. They started three weeks ago with Level I of ALM (Audio-Lingual Materials), and are now in dialogue 2. During the initial warm-up, the teacher showed pictures suggesting different kinds of weather, and asked questions suggesting possible answers (example: picture shows sun and flowers—question: *fait-il beau? fait-il mauvais?* etc.). Most individuals called on could answer correctly. The class counted to ten in chorus and did a few simple arithmetic problems. The teacher explained the content of the next dialogue in English, went through it twice in French with gestures, and a third time with chorus repetition of short elements, paying particular attention to pronunciation of difficult parts. The class then heard the native speaker on the record, and gave chorus responses. During the playing of the record, the teacher repeated his gestures but remained silent.
>
> As review, the class was asked to do dialogue 1, already learned, in chorus, and without prompting. There was almost full participation, and what is just as important, there was evident enjoyment in the realization that this learning had been accomplished. A conversational close-out ended the French part of the class (directed questions and answers based on the materials of the first dialogue: *demandez à Jeanne comment elle s'appelle,* etc.). The last few minutes were opened to the students to ask questions in English about details which had been troubling them. When Mr. _____ asked how many would like to borrow recordings of the second dialogue for home listening, about 40 out of 42 put up their hands. Unfortunately, there were only two discs available.
>
> These students are learning, and are quite happy with their teacher and with the method. Mr. _____ is an ideal teacher for this level. He speaks French fluently and correctly, likes and understands his pupils, has great enthusiasm and energy, and knows how to control without stifling. He has no problems of discipline. His willingness to use the methods promoted by the Curriculum Department and his interest in articulation are norms to be worked toward for other teachers.

Social studies. The courses in social studies emphasize history, with some geography. Some of the high schools with many able students offer one or more elective courses, such as Economics,

International Relations, or Comparative Government. These courses are rather limited in number and variety. Students who wish to elect a fourth-year course in social studies often take Contemporary American History, which could be taught with much attention to current foreign relations, domestic political and economic problems, and the structure of American society. However, there seems to be rather little flexibility in this course.

It is significant, when considered along with the course offerings in the social studies, that virtually all social studies teachers in Grades 9 through 12 have secured their certificates by passing the history examination. Although many students who remain in the system through Grade 10 take at least a year of geography, less than a dozen teachers have qualified themselves to teach geography by passing the geography examination. The expectation is that social studies teachers are history teachers. The assumption is made and frankly stated by principals that if someone can pass the history examination, which is restricted to standard historical material emphasizing political developments, he can teach any social studies offering. This policy tends to restrict the social studies curriculum to one of the study of history. Some teachers are obviously very well prepared in one or more of the social sciences in addition to history, and they introduce material from these areas into their courses. But this is the exception rather than the rule, and it is not encouraged by the system. Some high school teachers handling social studies courses other than history are very well prepared for their assignments. Many are not but must attempt to teach geography or economics, for example, because no one in the building is qualified. This is unfortunate but not surprising in view of the certification procedures.

A few schools and teachers are participating in the early stages of experimental programs in anthropology, political science, and geography sponsored by university teachers in these areas who are interested in the current ferment in the high school curriculum. This new approach in the high school social studies curriculum may imply the recruiting of teachers with a broad base of scholarship in the social sciences as well as in history.

The restriction of teachers to textbooks and supporting materials which are on the approved lists works a hardship on teachers of social studies and of literature who are trying to keep up with contemporary events in their courses. The approved lists are revised every four years, but in the meantime a teacher who wants to use new materials must go through a long and cumbersome procedure to get special permission.

Closely related to the question of the approved lists are problems of teaching about controversial issues. The guided study of controversial issues and of current events is standard practice in the more favored communities. Yet Chicago teachers are uncertain about their responsibilities and their rights in this respect. There are instances in which the principal acts as censor. In one school an English teacher was forbidden to assign Upton Sinclair's *The Jungle* for outside reading despite the fact that it is a fundamental source of information in high school history classes throughout the nation. In another case, the same restriction was placed on the novel *Exodus*. In a third instance, social studies teachers were instructed that they must obtain the principal's permission before using anything in the Contemporary American History class that was not on the approved list. Since this is a problems-type course, dealing with topics where materials change constantly, restriction to a list that may be four years old is an insurmountable handicap.

The consultant on social studies asked a number of principals and curriculum consultants whether there was a written or explicit policy on teaching about controversial issues. He could find nothing on this question. A forthright policy regarding the teaching about controversial issues should be drawn up by the administration and made clear to teachers and principals.

Mathematics. These are days of rapid and urgent developments in the teaching of mathematics, which started in the secondary schools and have now reached the lower schools. The "new mathematics" or "modern mathematics" in the elementary schools represents an approach to the teaching of mathematics which stresses understanding of what mathematics is about as well as drill in arithmetic. If it succeeds reasonably well, it will make high school and college instruction in the natural and social sciences much more effective by supplying students with a firmer grasp of the quantitative thinking that underlies all science.

The Chicago schools are experimenting with the new mathematics at the elementary level. They are also teaching algebra to able pupils in the eighth grade, thus leaving room in the high school for more advanced courses. Thus high school mathematics is influenced by changes in the elementary schools as well as by developments in the teaching of intermediate level mathematics, such as algebra, geometry, and trigonometry.

The visiting consultant summarizes his conclusions as follows:

> The most general problem in mathematics education in Chicago seemed to be a dilemma inherent in the size of the system and probably common to all areas of instruction. This dilemma is the need to preserve local adaptability, local "option," with respect to the mathematics curriculum, while still providing the valuable services that should be possible in a large city with a central staff and while providing a stimulus in any locality where it may be lacking to vigorous teaching and planning in the context provided by the student population of that school.

> It seems to me that the greater danger lies in the lack of stimulus to and support for local planning. There seem to be four possible directions for improvement under this heading. First, it seems that a city such as Chicago should be able to supply much more extensive supervisory assistance than is now within the time and energy capabilities of the six persons presently employed. In my conference with five of these six people, I was impressed by their sincerity and their thoughtful planning for their jobs. Although they can and do take some initiative in setting up "workshops," they largely must wait for invitations and emergency calls. I expect that with a staff of only six they could keep very busy merely replying to these requests. Further, although it is true that elementary school teachers are likely to be lacking in both background and confidence when it comes to suggesting or even accepting new and extended mathematics programs, nevertheless secondary school teachers need help and direction, also.

> A second suggestion follows directly from the preceding comments. More recognition of, more careful selection of, more responsibility for department heads including some released time and perhaps some pay differential might help significantly in stimulating vigorous professional activity in mathematics education which is appropriate for the peculiar situation in which each school will find itself.

> Thirdly, the seeking out and explicit recognition of good programs and teachers might very well stimulate added activity on the part of

those schools and teachers who are in the doldrums. A good example and a little implicit friendly competition, together with some explicit reward for virtue can, I would think, do a great deal to stimulate teachers who may have declined in their professional vigor.

One additional device for this is to provide for increased teacher participation in all aspects and at all levels of curriculum development in mathematics. More decisions and recommendations called for from the staff of each school rather than unilateral action by department chairmen or principals with respect to choice of textbooks and curriculum, accompanied by further extension of the use of teachers in workshops and in the preparation of experimental materials as well as on the routine curriculum committees and committees for the preparation of guides would not only provide additional help with all of these matters, but would have the additional incidental value of stimulating professional interest and activity.

These last two suggestions grow out of a conviction which I acquired during the course of the survey, but which is consistent with my experience and observation in other large metropolitan centers. This is that the teachers in the large cities tend to become less professionally interested and active than their colleagues in the suburbs and smaller communities. I would like to make it clear and emphatic that I saw some excellent teaching being done in Chicago Public Schools classrooms. I interviewed at least one teaching department head who with the encouragement and support of her principal was developing a new and partially experimental program for her school using newly developed materials. This testified to both her awareness of professional literature and trends and her initiative and leadership in her own school. Many interested and professional teachers will do these things without any expectation of commendation or recognition in time or money, and I'm sure that others in Chicago are doing so. However, not only do many administrative practices and administrators not encourage this in the ways suggested above, but some even directly if not intentionally discourage it. Limitations upon work in the school before and after the opening and close of the school day, arbitrary assignment of classes without consultation as to preferences, appropriateness, continuity of assignments where desirable are examples of such practices.

However, there are three other items providing some evidence for the feeling that, as a whole, the professional spirit and quality could be improved and pointing toward ways for securing this improvement. I made a survey of the membership of Chicago teachers in the major organization for professional mathematics teachers in the secondary school. Whereas approximately 35 percent of the population of Illinois is in Chicago, only 13 percent of Illinois' membership in the National Council of Teachers of Mathematics is to be found in the Chicago area. The Chicago area does have one of the oldest and best known of the local mathematics teachers organizations. I refer to the Men's Mathematics Club. Although I do not have any precise data, it seems very clear that of the total mathematics staff in the Chicago metropolitan area by far the greater share would be found in the Chicago Public Schools. However, the records of the Men's Mathematics Club of Chicago and Metropolitan Area show that only 25 percent of the persons who attended at least one meeting in 1962-63 were teaching in Chicago schools, and that only 25 percent of the paid-up members of the Club were teaching in Chicago schools.

I asked for data with reference to the continuing professional activity of teachers in the Chicago schools, and also with reference to the frequency and recentness with which Chicago teachers had attended National Science Foundation Institutes, summer session programs, professional meetings, workshops, etc. No such data seemed to be available in the records of the Chicago schools. The fact that no such records are kept and that there is practically no provision for support of Chicago teachers for either travel to professional meetings or leaves for study show that these activities of a professional teacher are neither recognized nor encouraged as they should be.

Other subjects. Among the other subjects of the high school curriculum, English and literature have been discussed at several places and will not be considered here. There are, however, the important subjects of art, music, home economics, industrial arts, and business education, as well as health and physical education. Some exposure to art, music, and health and physical education is required of all students. In addition they may elect advanced art or music and they may choose elective courses in the other areas.

The tendency in the most recent years has been to reduce emphasis on these electives, and to push as many students as possible into a standard college preparatory program, whether or not they are going to college. This tendency has been promoted by the wide reading and widespread acceptance of the recommendations of Dr. James B. Conant in his book, *The American High School Today*. The Chicago curriculum and curriculum practices follow this line.

However, a number of educators disagree with this position. They feel that more electives would better meet the needs of the variety of students in the American high school. Especially, they favor more work in art and music, and more work in home economics and industrial arts. They believe that, even for pupils who will go on to college, it would be better in high school to have a variety of courses in various fields than to concentrate on the "solid" subjects to the extent of getting college-level courses in science and mathematics and history while still in high school.

Enrollments in the Chicago high schools show the influence of the restrictive policy outlined above. A number of high schools have at the most one section of advanced art (beyond the required Art 1 and 2), and one or two sections of music beyond the first-year course. The school principals and the supervisors claim that many more students would enroll for these courses if there was space for them and if teachers were supplied.

The proportion of high school girls taking home economics has decreased since 1953 from 41 percent to 31 percent. This is largely due to the increased number of prescribed courses for graduation, which reduces the opportunity for a girl to elect home economics. A new set of four home economics courses has been outlined during the summer of 1964, including study of child development and of family life.

The time has come for a serious analysis of the effectiveness of the standard college-oriented curriculum, particularly as it bears on the lives of the 40 to 50 percent of Chicago high school graduates who do not go to college. The claims of the so-called supplementary subjects should be weighed against the results of the courses in prescribed subjects.

Textbooks, audio-visual aids, and other teaching materials

Expenditures per pupil on textbooks averaged about $4.30. Students must be furnished texts in three or four majors and one or two minor subjects. This rate of expenditure means that a given book must be in use for six or more semesters. Eighty-one percent of the high school teachers reported on the Teacher Questionnaire that they had sufficient *numbers* of textbooks, but only 58 percent said that they received a satisfactory *variety*. The reasons noted for these lacks were inadequate funds, student damage or theft, and inefficient administration, in that order.

The Board of Education provides emergency appropriations to correct the most glaring deficiencies, and the bulk of these funds go to schools in the lowest-income and most disorganized communities. The problem in these schools is partly due to careless and even malicious mishandling of books, and partly due to transiency of teachers. A teacher who is on a substitute basis and does not expect to return to a particular school next year is more likely to be careless in accounting for books than one who is going to have to use the same books next year.

In recent years the National Defense Act has made grants of half the cost of a variety of school equipment for laboratories, for general science classes, and the like, and consequently the situation is vastly improved in this area. The three-man team of superintendents reported that equipment was inadequate in business education, industrial arts, and home economics. Many schools face severe shortages in consumable classroom and office supplies (especially paper used in duplicating materials for classroom use).

The present arrangements for audio-visual services in the high school could be substantially improved. The consultant reports:

> In many schools the equipment is inconveniently stored, and films ordered through the regular Board of Education facilities too often do not arrive on schedule or arrive in such poor condition that they cannot be shown effectively. The situation seems to be better in cases where time in the schedule is provided for a teacher (or more than one teacher, with each serving certain departments) to do the work of ordering films and supervising the distribution of equipment and films. At Taft High School and at Crane, for example, considerable use seems to be made of the audio-visual equipment which is stored, together with the school's collection of filmstrips and records, in the school library and is checked out through the librarian. At Crane, where I was shown the materials and records in some detail, a teacher has time assigned to serve as audio-visual coordinator and works with the librarian, who also takes an active part in the audio-visual program. As a result, considerable use is made of filmstrips, films, records, and the overhead projector. For example, the library records show

that in the month of April, 174 filmstrips were used among the departments of social studies, English, science, mathematics, art, music, and health education.

These examples suggest that all schools could make more effective use of audio-visual materials if sufficient teacher time were allotted to a coordinator for the ordering of materials and coordination of the program, and if at least a partial collection of materials could be housed in the school. It is not economically feasible to build a film collection in each school, of course, but in a school with 2,500 to 4,000 students it certainly seems feasible to develop a school collection of filmstrips, slides, records, and materials for use with the overhead projector. It is generally recognized that sensory materials are especially needed for improving the learning of pupils of low verbal facility and impoverished cultural backgrounds. The Chicago schools, with a rising number of such pupils, can ill afford to neglect these kinds of learning materials. With regard to the distribution of films from the Board of Education, I suggest that consideration be given to examining the plan to see whether or not regional arrangements would be feasible. It is my impression that some large cities are handling it through such regional offices, and that this system works better in actually getting materials to the schools on time and in good condition than the completely centralized operation.

Administration of the school for effective teaching

The key to effective teaching in a complex and changing school system is the continual involvement of the teachers in some kind of in-service training which keeps them studying their tasks as teachers and improving their ability to teach. Responding to the Teacher Questionnaire, 58 percent of high school teachers say that they have participated in some kind of in-service training project during the past five years. These may be special institutes, workshops, research projects, or university classes of a practical nature. Thirty-two percent took part in projects sponsored by the Chicago Public Schools. These teachers tend to be the older and more experienced ones.

Faculty meetings are held infrequently in most schools. Twenty-three percent said that they had general or departmental faculty meetings once a month or more often. Such meetings could serve for training purposes only if they occurred as often as once a month. The team of suburban superintendents notes that:

General faculty and departmental meetings are not the end-all of professional growth and school improvement. However, they may be the means of generating concern about educational needs and problems and an opportunity to plan, organize, and evaluate programs aimed at staff growth and school improvement. Means should be found to schedule such professional meetings. The staggered sessions in most high schools should afford time during the first and last periods for monthly meetings with the two groups of staff members. In addition, faculty committees concerned with curriculum, instruction, student activities, in-service education, lay participation, and the like could also work at the task of school and community betterment.

Time for in-service training may be found on Saturdays or during the summer if the Board can secure the money to pay teachers for this extra work. Otherwise it may be desirable to set aside certain regular school days or half-days for each training, excusing the pupils from attendance at those times.

The principal as the key person. The report of the suburban superintendents stresses the importance of the school principal as an educational leader. This person, if effectively supported by assistant principals in a big school, should be responsible for a program of in-service training and experimental innovation in his own school. This person should stay long enough in one school to establish himself in community and school as the educational leader.

There is some reason to believe that the current system of promotion within the principals' group based on size of school encourages such frequent moves as to reduce the effectiveness of principals. Of 38 general high schools enrolling freshmen through seniors between September, 1960, and June, 1964, only nine had one officially-appointed principal throughout the entire period. Nine high schools had three different principals during this time. The total number of reassignments in high school principalships was 40 in four years. Twenty-four of the 40 appointments represented persons who were moved from elementary school principalships or from the Central Office to a high school. The remaining 16 appointments represent principals who were transferred from one high school to another.

Each time a new principal is appointed, the faculty and students must adjust their expectations and the principal must make a new start in identifying the underlying forces and problems in the school. Few educators believe that a high school principal can even begin to initiate improvements in much less than one or two years. The difficulties are compounded in schools as large as most Chicago high schools; several have faculties of 150 or 200 and it may take months just to learn the names of the teachers.

There are now nine salary lanes for principals, related to size of school. The committee of suburban superintendents suggested that a smaller number of salary steps could be combined with the allocation of larger numbers of assistant principals and other supervisors to the larger schools, to make service in the larger schools more attractive without the need for so many salary steps.

The department chairman. The department chairmen are seen by nearly all the outside consultants as people who could contribute a great deal if their jobs were so defined and they were given time to do the work. The suburban superintendents recommend that "Department chairmen, selected for classroom competence and leadership qualities and reassigned annually on performance only should teach a maximum of four classes daily so that they might assume greater responsibility for orientation of new teachers, classroom supervision of all teachers, requisitioning of and accounting for supplies and equipment, assisting the principal in the selection of new teachers, chairing all curriculum work in the department, and assisting the principal in teacher assignments."

Under present conditions, most department chairmen have a full load of five classes which makes it very difficult for them to perform even their currently limited functions. Only the chairmen of the English and physical education departments are commonly freed from one class. It is especially important to have the chairman work with young and inexperienced teachers, and these teachers are found mainly in the low-achievement schools. For instance, the five schools showing the lowest achievement in Table 2 have an average of 40 percent of their teachers not yet certificated for Chicago schools.

Faculty participation in making decisions. "Basically, high schools grow and improve in direct relation to the opportunities provided for school staff to become more professional and to work cooperatively at the task of all-school improvement." With this statement of the suburban superintendents we are in thorough agreement. There is no formally defined procedure that gives classroom teachers a part in making decisions about what should be taught and how the school should be organized. On the initiative of the principal several schools have faculty councils which are encouraged to play an important part in the life of the school; but at most schools how the teachers are treated depends entirely on the understanding and good will of the principal. On the Teacher Questionnaire, 32 percent of high school teachers said they were dissatisfied with the leadership given by their principal, while 38 percent said they were satisfied. Some further effort is recommended to bring classroom teachers into more of a give-and-take relationship with the principal. In particular, the teachers might have more of a say with regard to their teaching assignments. Forty-five percent of high school teachers said on the Teacher Questionnaire that they were dissatisfied with the extent to which they were consulted in the making of their teaching program, while 29 percent said they were satisfied. There is evidence that the most difficult and unwanted courses are often assigned to new, inexperienced teachers.

Organizing the school term. One problem that concerns most high school teachers is the confusion that often reigns at the beginning of the school term. Out of the 54 aspects of the job on which teachers were asked to express satisfaction or dissatisfaction, the item "process of getting school started at the beginning of the school year" was fifth in the order of dissatisfaction.

It requires, on the average, nearly two weeks of fall semester before classes are stabilized, books are distributed, and continual interruptions have died down. Yet at one school an assistant principal worked without compensation during his vacation and succeeded in stabilizing classes on the second day of the semester. At the other extreme, there were schools at which students' and teachers' programs were still being overturned in the eighth week. It was proposed by the committee of suburban superintendents that the high school administration office should be staffed during the summer, with some of the counselors and clerical staff available. If the money is not available for this, classes might be delayed one week in September while students are called in by appointment, books are distributed, classes are scheduled, and classroom teachers hold in-service training periods.

Clerical services. Few citizens who have not taught in the public schools realize the vital importance of clerical services in the operation of a school. Several research studies, in fact, have offered evidence to justify the conclusion that the ratio between students and clerks is more closely associated with the quality of a high school program than any other single measure of excellence. The number of students per clerk varies from 248 at School 29 in Table 2 to 710 at School 23, with a median at 575. The committee of suburban superintendents noted, "A clear need for more extensive secretarial and clerical services" in Chicago high schools, and added the following suggestions to illustrate the potential utility of an increase in such services:

> Such supportive services would not only release teachers from many non-teaching responsibilities so that they might give greater attention to classroom preparation and development of their essential teaching competencies; such services would also assure more efficient office operation and broader measures of assistance to the teaching staff in preparation of materials for class work. For instance, there should be clerical service for counselors to permit them to give undivided attention to working with student problems. . . . Also, most attendance matters should be handled by clerical personnel.

Buildings and facilities

There are two levels for discussion of buildings, facilities, and classroom space—the essential level and the desirable level. Chicago high schools are below the essential level. The shortage of classroom space is already critical, and is rapidly growing into a major problem.

A "regular" schedule may be defined as one consisting of nine periods. This means starting school at about 8 A.M. and closing about 4 P.M. However, there are very few schools now operating on this schedule. It is regarded as "normal" to have 10 periods, and a number of schools have had to stagger student and teacher programs within 11, 12, and even 13 or 14 period schedules.

Such expedients make it difficult to hold faculty meetings; they destroy cohesion among student bodies, and they create inequities in the schedules of students and teachers. To alleviate pressure on building space, 20 of the 39 schools listed in Table 2 were attempting in 1963-64 to educate some or all of their ninth-grade pupils in one or more branches located in elementary schools and upper-grade centers. But students in branches have fewer opportunities to study biology and foreign languages than those in the main buildings, and their libraries are inferior.

Mobile classrooms are being added to a number of high school buildings, but these can only be regarded as temporary makeshifts.

Many schools are much too large. It is generally accepted that the best range of enrollment for a high school is between 1,000 and 2,000. The number might go to 2,500 with good facilities, gaining the advantage of supporting more specialized and elective courses. But 15 of 40 general high schools had more than 3,000 students in 1963-64.

The high school enrollment will increase by 20 to 25 percent in the next 10 years. This means an increase of about 30,000 students, enough to fill a dozen large schools, and still leave things in their present critical state.

A major building program should be planned at once, and construction begun on at least 10 new buildings without further delay.

We have been discussing needs that exist at the critical level. To move to the level of what is desirable, and urgently desirable, there is need for more industrial arts and homemaking facilities. Many science laboratories are still obsolete, though substantial progress is being made with the aid of federal NDEA funds to bring them up to date. Office space for classroom teachers and especially for department chairmen simply does not exist in many schools. Teachers must have places for individual study and preparation. Counselors in some schools have only makeshift cubicles in which they can talk with students. There is almost a total absence of the individual study spaces for students that are so attractive in the new schools in favored communities.

CONCLUSIONS AND RECOMMENDATIONS

The most general recommendation to be made concerning the high schools of Chicago is that the school programs should be related more realistically to the abilities and motives of the students.

This requires study of the local community from which the school draws its students.

The school principal should be the instructional leader and his department chairmen and classroom teachers should form a team for study and action on the problems of their school.

Schools with similar student bodies should be grouped together under an administrative arrangement which provides curriculum consultants in district offices who have specialized in the adaptation of the curriculum to those particular kinds of students. This administrative arrangement will be discussed more fully in Chapter XIX.

The schools can be grouped loosely into three categories, each of which has its own peculiar needs.

The low-achievement or inner-city schools need a great deal of experimentation with methods and materials for low-achieving students. Improvement of these schools cannot be bought at bargain prices. The experimentation already under way in Chicago schools with such students should be continued and subjected to careful evaluation. More money must be spent on these schools, but we do not yet know what forms of added expense are most worthwhile.

One of the principal problems is that of "standards" for these schools. What standard should a pupil who is three years retarded in mathematics be required to achieve in order to get a passing grade in Basic Mathematics? What standards should be expected of the relatively small numbers of students in the Honors track? These pupils are likely to be substantially below the Honors track of a high-achievement school. If they are graded high, they may form false notions of their scholastic ability which will lead them to difficulty if they go to a selective college. If they are graded low, they may become discouraged and fall back into the Regular track, where they do not have to work so hard for grades. There is no simple solution to this problem. The goal is clearly to encourage these relatively able pupils to work hard and become ready to compete with others of high ability from the high-achievement schools.

The common-man or medium-achievement schools need a broadening of the curriculum with perhaps less emphasis on college preparation. They have their own peculiar needs which are apt to be lost to sight in the face of the more visible needs of the other two groups. A group of teachers and administrators who became really interested in this type of school could produce some valuable and interesting work. Here, among other things, the problem of standards is also a pressing one. Many students in this kind of school are apt to get along by putting out minimum effort, since they are not motivated by scholastic ambition.

The high-status or suburban type school needs a great deal of work in a big city. Parents whose children are in such a school want the best schools that money can produce and are willing to pay for them. The following report of the General Superintendent for September 9, 1964, tells of a meeting with a representative committee from the Taft High School community who came to talk about requirements for improving education not only at Taft but throughout the school system.

Because of its proximity to the suburban community the Taft High School group is conscious of the advantages which are provided by suburban schools because class size is small and physical facilities are spacious. The representatives of the Taft community expressed their belief that providing these requisites for quality education within the Chicago Public Schools must be given priority.

The members of this group pledged on behalf of their community a willingness to support vigorously any building bond issue or referendum to increase the school tax rate which is necessary to give assurance to each and every community that the teaching-learning conditions for quality education would be improved through lowering class size, providing adequate physical facilities, increasing the funds for instructional materials, and staffing the schools with highly qualified teachers.

At the present time Taft has one annex in an elementary school building which provides facilities for a portion of its ninth-grade students. The main building is crowded to the point where vital services such as counseling, laboratory sciences, and programs for gifted students may have to be curtailed. The community fears that this curtailment of services for the high percentage of potential college students at Taft may serve to motivate responsible families to leave the city in their quest for quality education. As a temporary measure, representatives of this high school would welcome the placement of additional mobile classrooms at the branch school to provide added facilities for ninth-grade pupils, thus providing the release of much needed classroom space in the main building for 10th-, 11th- and 12th-grade students.

Although Taft is in a favored community, the school needs more money, to be used for its particular needs.

SUMMARY OF MAJOR RECOMMENDATIONS

The demands made by a complex city and by the twentieth-century knowledge explosion upon the American high school make this a fascinating as well as a frustrating place to work. Like the teachers and administrators in other big cities, those in Chicago should be congratulated and also be assisted with better conditions for their work.

The visiting consultants who studied the high schools were in substantial agreement on the following major recommendations.

1. A major program of school construction should start immediately. The situation is already critical, and will grow worse with the inevitable increase of enrollment.

2. The curriculum should be broadened in directions that allow more room for experimentation, introduce modern concepts and methods more widely in all the subject fields, and encourage more meaningful and stimulating classroom experiences.

3. More attention and proportionately greater resources should be given to differentiating programs, providing special materials, and improving the supporting services for students whose achievement is low.

4. The work of district offices should be strengthened for the kinds of services that will improve instruction. More consultants should be assigned to district offices. Districts with similar types of schools should work together under some kind of cooperative arrangement which permits a consultant to specialize in the improvement of instruction for a certain type of school.

5. More attention should be given to the in-service training of teachers, and especially of young teachers who are working in inner-city schools. This means an expansion of the services of supervisors and consultants and their assignment to types of schools and districts for which they are especially fitted.

6. The position of department chairman should be strengthened so that persons who serve in this capacity can get time and recognition for working with less experienced teachers, for developing instructional materials, and generally for exercising educational leadership.

7. Arrangements for promotion and salary increases for principals should be made so as to encourage them to stay longer in schools where their experience and abilities make them especially valuable.

XI

Vocational Education

The Division of Vocational and Practical Arts Education has responsibility for the nine vocational high schools, the two technical high schools, Washburne Trade School, and industrial arts education in the general high schools. Each is seen as serving a separate purpose. The vocational high schools provide occupational training in a variety of skills for those students whose education may be terminal and who need employment upon completion of high school. Some of the vocational high schools provide programs at a sufficiently advanced level to enable graduating students either to enter apprenticeship in one of the trades or to seek additional higher education at a technical institute or liberal arts college. The two technical high schools, Lane on the North Side and Tilden on

* * *

The conclusions and recommendations of this chapter on vocational education are based in part upon the visits and work of the following consultants to the Survey: George Philips, Vice President and General Manager, Corplan Associates; Robert I. Shackford, Field Director, Office of Manpower Automation and Training, U.S. Department of Labor; Thomas Van Sant, Assistant Superintendent, New York Public Schools; Dr. Edward W. Brice, Director, Adult Education Branch, Office of Education, U.S. Department of Health, Education, and Welfare.

the South Side (the latter now in the process of being transferred to Lindblom), provide a heavier concentration in mathematics, science, and shop work in technical fields to prepare students for admission to engineering, scientific, and technical studies at institutions of higher education.

The Washburne Trade School has been operated as an apprenticeship school by the Board of Education since 1919. It accepts students over 16 who are employed and whose employers have entered into an indenture contract with them. The Board of Education provides not less than 144 hours per year of classroom instruction related to a particular trade and supplementary to on-the-job training. In the past and at the present time, students who attend Washburne are not selected by the Board of Education. By agreement between employers and trade unions, apprentices are selected and sent to Washburne as part of their apprenticeship training. The Board of Education merely provides one day per week of schooling for these students and takes no responsibility for who enrolls.

The industrial arts program in the general high schools, although a shop program, is differentiated from the program of vocational education in the vocational high schools. Whereas vocational education theoretically equips a student with sufficient occupational skill and competence to secure a job upon completion of the course, industrial arts provides general shop work and an introduction to a specialized shop for boys and home economics for girls. Industrial arts generally is a one- or two-year program, depending upon the student's interests, although some students remain in it beyond two years.

For many years, vocational education in special high schools has been regarded as especially useful for students not interested in a straight academic program and not intending to continue their education beyond high school. Both the vocational high schools' program and the industrial arts programs in the general high schools are considered by many to be the chief means of holding in school those students with little or no interest in the academic curriculum. In part, the educational program in the vocational high schools does serve this purpose by training students for a particular occupation and by holding out the hope of employment upon graduation. It is open to doubt whether the industrial arts program serves the same purpose of inducing many students to remain in school after age 16 since this program is not designed to provide extensive occupational training.

Vocational education is constantly faced with the problem of keeping the shop curriculum and equipment current with changes in technology and industry, and with labor force requirements. In Chicago, during the postwar decades this problem has become acute as the composition of Chicago-based industry has changed and as the population sending children to Chicago schools has changed. Many types of industry now operate with such complicated technology that the Board of Education finds it impossible to duplicate the equipment or the processes even in one school, let alone several. Moreover, many firms want to conduct their own technical or vocational training for new employees. But they are increasingly requiring that new employees possess basic intellectual tools and a high degree of personal maturity, which are commonly understood to result from a sound high school education.

Thus the vocational high schools today must prepare students in academic subjects at a level comparable to that of the good general high school and at the same time offer training in a variety of occupations, some of which are far more complex (jet aircraft engine repair or architectural drafting) than others (shoe repair or upholstery).

Vocational schools, if they are to justify their existence as separate institutions, must keep pace with changing technology and changing labor force requirements by providing—in addition to a good general education—sound, basic, vocational training in those areas or skills in which industry wants to do much of the training itself (for example, electronics) and for those occupations which are growing in size and importance (for example, food service, home maintenance, or repair of household appliances). Vocational schools must also progressively reduce shop training in those occupations which do not require a large number of new workers (cabinetmaking and carpentry) or in those industries in which the older technology and equipment are being replaced by automated equipment (printing). It is wasteful both for shops in the vocational high schools and shops in the industrial arts program in the general high schools to train students on outmoded equipment such as that existing in most of the print shops or to train students for occupations with limited employment possibilities. In short, the vocational education program must be made increasingly flexible to cope with rapid technological change. This will require changes in the program and elimination of certain present rigidities that are discussed later in this chapter.

Gross changes which have occurred in Illinois in recent decades, such as the shift in population from rural areas to urban centers, the in-migration of Spanish-speaking people from Puerto Rico and Mexico and of Negroes from southern states to Chicago, and the shift in types of jobs performed by the labor force, have had important effects upon the composition of the school-age population and upon the Chicago labor market. While socially and intellectually disadvantaged children have increased in numbers in the Chicago schools, the kinds of unskilled and semiskilled jobs in industry which such students could formerly obtain upon leaving school (whether drop-outs or high school graduates) have decreased markedly.

In the Chicago metropolitan area during the period 1958-63, nonagricultural wage and salaried workers have increased about 5 percent, from 2,384,000 to 2,495,700. Of this increase of 111,700, only 9,000 have been in manufacturing.[1] The increase in nonmanufacturing employment has occurred in wholesale and retail trade, finance, insurance and real estate, service, and government. At the same time, all other nonagricultural workers have decreased almost 5 percent, from 264,000 to 252,600; and agricultural employment has decreased over 11 percent, from 18,500 to 16,600.

Changes in the families of jobs and types of work available in Chicago which have already occurred may be expected to continue. Technological advances have automated many unskilled and semiskilled jobs out of existence. Computers are making steady encroachments upon some skilled and many clerical jobs. But as jobs decline at lower levels of skill, they increase at higher levels.

---

[1] *Chicago Standard Metropolitan Statistical Area Employment, Hours and Earnings. Number IV, Revised Employment Data 1962-63.* Division of Unemployment Compensation, State of Illinois Department of Labor, Chicago, 1964.

The field of research and development needs, and will need at an increasing rate, scientists, engineers, and technicians. The new machines of the future must be built, operated, and maintained by skilled workers and craftsmen. Trade and service occupations of all kinds may be expected to increase. Public and professional service will grow to keep abreast of a growing population and a population increasingly able to afford services. All of these changes have profound implications for the kind of education which the Chicago Public Schools must provide its students to fit them for the new jobs. In particular, the vocational education program must be more responsive both to the kinds of students who attend the vocational high schools and to the labor force requirements of the metropolitan Chicago area.

Present program

Vocational high schools in Chicago have a mixed reputation. Several of them are very well regarded in their communities and by industries which accept their better students for employment. Several of them are not so regarded. Within the public school system itself, in the minds of too many administrators and teachers vocational education is remedial in nature. To the academically oriented teacher or parent, the general high school is for bright and average students while the vocational high school is for the slow student who is not expected to do well with academic subjects or to continue into post high school education. Too often, the vocational high school is placed in a buffer position between the general high school and "undesirable" students. This general attitude is not only unfortunate for the future of the vocational high schools and the progress of the students in these schools but erroneous as a judgment upon the quality of education offered by several of the vocational schools.

While every vocational high school is to some extent a neighborhood school, except Jones Commercial which is city-wide, most of them attract students from a wider attendance area. The educational programs of Chicago Vocational, Dunbar, Prosser, and Flower are organized to accommodate students whose achievement and ability indicate a capacity for work at a level comparable to that of the good general high school. Chicago Vocational, Dunbar, Prosser, and Jones have admission requirements beyond the elementary school diploma which serve to screen out students of below average ability, although in the case of Dunbar these requirements are often waived. (They are occasionally waived in the other schools as well.)

Many administrators and shop teachers in vocational schools take the position that the advancement of technology has removed today's shop training from the grasp of the student with less than normal ability. As a result, there is a tug-of-war for the better students between the general and the vocational high school, with the elementary school organization usually siding with the general high school.

The more some vocational schools are able to resist accepting below average students for enrollment, the more college-preparatory conscious these institutions become. This kind of upgrading of vocational training by the prestige schools eliminates some students with high interest and motivations who could profit from vocational training and admits others whose aspirations could more effectively and directly be realized in a general high school.

Nearly every high school (including the vocational high schools) has some variation of the multi-path system, usually called levels:

	Level	*Criteria*
A	Advanced placement (college credit)	Teacher recommendation
B	Honors	Achievement 9.6 and up in a subject area
C	Near honors	9.0-9.5
D	Regular	7.5-8.9
E	Essential	7.4-6.0
F	Basic	below 6.0
G	EMH	IQ 55-75 (generally)

The above criteria are generally used, but variations occur according to local determinations by the administrator and his guidance staff. The differences among the nine vocational high schools are indicated in Tables 1 and 2 which compare their student bodies, racial composition, pattern of organization, entrance criteria, and the number of vocational offerings claimed.

Table 1
Student body and racial composition

	CVS	Cooley	Cregier	Dunbar	Flower	Jones	Prosser	Richards	Westcott
Student body composition[1]									
Boys	3,129	528	928	1,399	0	11	920	0	451
Girls	1,309	371	0	1,079	1,848	594	0	612	450
Total	4,438	899	928	2,478	1,848	605	920	612	901
Racial composition[2]									
Negro	1,057	574	794	2,285	1,338	36	0	53	717
White	3,261	217	44	1	350	546	878	543	107
Other	15	26	0	1	73	0	0	2	15
Total	4,333	817	838	2,287	1,761	582	878	598	839
Racial composition in percent[2]									
Negro	24.4	70.3	94.7	99.8	76.0	6.2	0	8.9	85.4
White	75.2	26.5	5.3	.1	19.9	93.8	100	90.8	12.8
Other	.4	3.2		.1	4.1			.3	1.8

[1]*High School Membership By Grades and Sex, Average Daily Attendance and Percent of Attendance on September 27, 1963.* A report prepared by the Bureau of Research, Development and Special Projects (Chicago: Board of Education, 1963).

[2]*Data on Attendance and Drop-Outs: Attendance on October 13, 1963.* A report prepared by the Bureau of Research, Development and Special Projects (Chicago: Board of Education, 1963).

Table 2
Number of vocational offerings, entrance criteria, and pattern of organization

	CVS	Cooley	Cregier	Dunbar	Flower	Jones	Prosser	Richards	Westcott
Number of vocational offerings claimed	40	10[1]	8	32	5[2]	4	14	4	9
Number of vocational categories indicated by classification of graduates (Aug. 1958-June 1963)	26	14	11	27	3	4	7	7	13
Entrance criteria									
Elementary school diploma only		*	*						*
Achievement	*			*	*	*	*	*	
Capacity	*			*	*	*	*	*	
Aptitude				*[3]		*			
Interest	*			*		*	*		
Interview	*			*		*	*	*	
Pattern of organization									
Advanced placement	*					*	*		
Honors	*			*	*	*	*	*	
Near honors		*							
Regular	*	*	*	*	*	*	*	*	*
Essential	*	*	*	*	*			*	*
Basic		*	*	*	*				*
EMH		*							

[1]Commercial Cooking (Baking) moving to Washburne, September, 1964.
[2]Expects to add Beauty Culture in September, 1964.
[3]Claimed but not evaluated.

In Chicago, every high school student is required to complete successfully 18 units of work in order to graduate. Each unit is equivalent to two credits or majors, and four minors. (These terms are used interchangeably.) The basic requirement for graduation— 18 units—consists of 12 units of stipulated subjects or sequences in English, mathematics, social studies, science, and music and art, leaving six units to be elected. In the vocational high school the 12 basic units are the same as those for the general high school, except that mechanical drawing is substituted for music and art in programming boys. For girls the basic units are identical with those required in the general high school.

In the vocational high school, the remaining six units are composed of exploratory and vocational shop, selected by the student with guidance and counseling, theoretically in accordance with his interests, abilities, aspirations, and the offerings of the particular school. There is considerable variation in the vocational curricula among the vocational high schools, with Chicago Vocational, Prosser, and Dunbar offering far more extensive work than Cooley, Cregier, and Westcott.

Male vocational high school students are required to take mechanical drawing for two years as a minor (one unit, or two credits —one-half credit each semester). During the first two years or first four semesters every boy takes a different exploratory shop in each semester or one-half year, for which he receives one-half unit (one-half credit or minor shop). The exploratory shops meet daily for a double period of 80 minutes.

At the beginning of the third year every boy begins vocational shop, that is, a shop specializing in a specific trade or skill. This shop meets daily for four consecutive periods (160 minutes) and entitles the student to a full unit or major credit. The vocational or major shop is chosen from one of the four shops in the student's exploratory experience.

The vocational high school program for girls substitutes a year (two semesters) of clothing and a year or two semesters of foods for the exploratory shops which the boys take. The vocational offerings for girls are limited primarily to home economics and business education; however, a few girls are found in mechanical drawing classes, and a few girls pursue vocational drafting.

On parent-interview day a counselor from the intended high school comes to the elementary school to confer with the prospective elementary school graduate and his parent concerning the student's freshman program. The counselor knows his school's organizational pattern and before him are the pupil's scores from the California Test of Mental Maturity and the Metropolitan Achievement Test. Programming becomes a matter of placing the child in the school's organization. However, a reading score is more persuasive than any other MAT score. Often children with reading scores between 6.0 and 7.5, regardless of higher science, arithmetic and/or social studies scores, are placed in *all* Essential classes. Such a program for a boy might include: Essential English I, Essential Mathematics I, Community Civics, and an exploratory shop. The same program would hold for a girl, except that instead of a shop she would receive a home economics course, that is, Food, Clothing, Home Management, etc.

Because of the organization of courses and the requirements for graduation, counselors have very little leeway in planning a student's high school program. His program is charted on parent-interview day and it is very difficult to change it, despite changes in his motivation, interests, or performance. Historically, the placement of freshmen depended almost entirely upon the student's IQ; today, stress is placed on the eighth-grade achievement battery with extra emphasis on the reading score. Today's theory of counseling and placement too often clings to the antiquated concept that the school trains either brain or brawn—not both—and therefore students with below-average academic ability should be placed either in vocational high schools or in the industrial arts course in general high schools.

During the five school years from August, 1958, to June, 1963, 9,228 students graduated from the nine vocational high schools in Chicago. This figure does not include 119 students who finished in the area of Distributive Education (this program is not unique to the vocational area and is not restricted to these schools). On the average, 1,845 students (roughly 20 percent of the total) graduated every year from all the vocational schools of Chicago.

The number of students graduating from each of the nine vocational high schools in the five-year period considered is shown in

Figure 1
*Vocational high school graduates
in five years by vocational schools*

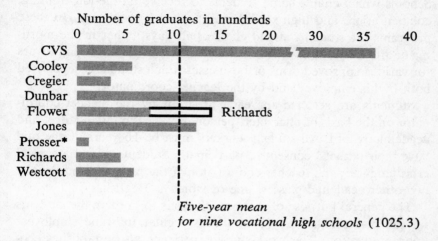

Number of graduates in hundreds

Five-year mean
for nine vocational high schools (1025.3)

*Graduates last three years only.
Source: Data compiled by the Chicago School Survey from the *Official Report
of the Proceedings of the Board of Education of the City of Chicago,* July 1,
1958-June 26, 1963.

Figure 1. The average number of students graduating from
each school during this five-year period is 1,025 (approximately
11 percent). Three schools exceed this average—CVS, Dunbar,
and Jones. If Flower's Richards Branch is added to Flower, then
it also exceeds the average, and there remain four schools which
are below the average—Cooley, Cregier, Prosser, and Westcott.

Because means are affected by extremes and CVS's gigantic
physical plant sustains a large enrollment, it seems reasonable to
compare the other schools, exclusive of CVS. The mean for this
grouping drops to 700, and four schools remain below this average
—Cooley, Cregier, Prosser, and Westcott.

Prosser's small number of graduates can be explained by its
recent establishment as a vocational school. At the time of this
study, it had had only seven graduating classes, compared to 15
for the other eight schools. Prosser opened in 1959 and had its
first graduating class of 23 in June, 1962.

Work-study programs

There are three work-study programs in the Chicago Public High Schools which enable some students to receive on-the-job training, compensation, and high school credit toward graduation. In these programs the students attend classes half-days, either in the morning or afternoon, and work two to four hours as part-time employees for various approved firms or businesses. Each student is supervised both by his employer and by the teacher-coordinator.

Students are selected for each program by the teacher-coordinator on the basis of character, personality, health, attendance, and academic record. All student workers must be 16 years of age and have their parents' consent to participate. Students attend a special class taught by the teacher-coordinator of the program and usually two other academic classes, one of which is English.

The general purpose of these programs is to prepare the students for job placement. Many continue as regular full-time employees upon graduation. The work-study experience also establishes economic competence which provides the student with useful skill and information regardless of whether he is going to remain in employment or continue in some form of higher education.

All jobs are obtained through the combined efforts of the teacher-coordinator and the local school administration. Considerable effort is made to secure positions convenient to the school and to the student's home.

Although these work-study programs provide students with vocational training, they are not restricted to vocational high schools; many general high schools have them and some vocational schools do not.

The Cooperative Distributive Education Training Program operates through the combined efforts of the Chicago Board of Education and the retailing, wholesaling, and service concerns of the area. The merchant-trainer agrees to provide the student-trainee with acceptable working conditions, the standard wage of other beginning employees, a minimum of 15 hours per week of employment, varied work experience in the operation of the business, capable supervision, counseling and guidance, and periodic evaluations of the student's performance.

Distributive Education is restricted to high school seniors, 16 and over, with satisfactory academic records, who "demonstrate an interest in and an aptitude for retailing." The student must obtain parental consent and agree to work at least 15 hours per week. He is also required to observe rules and regulations governing other employees pertaining to appropriate dress, conduct, and accuracy in the performance of his assignments.

The number of students who desire to work exceeds the number of positions that a teacher-coordinator is able to secure. More students are turned away than are selected for participation.

The Coordinated Office Occupations Work Experience Program is for high school seniors, 16 and over, in career office occupations: stenography, dictation, transcription, office machines—adding, listing, posting, calculators, duplicators, typing, and filing. This program originated at Jones Commercial High School in 1951 and was instituted at Dunbar Vocational High School in 1961. Since then, eight other general high schools and Flower Vocational have begun Office Occupations programs.

Jobs are secured by the teacher-coordinator. Again, the number of students who want to work is greater than the number of jobs a coordinator can manage to secure and supervise. The employer-trainer agrees to participate in the supervision of these student-employees and to maintain standards of safety.

Office Occupations students receive the same compensation as other beginning workers and conform to the same standards of performance and demeanor as other employees. As a student, the worker carries three subjects: Office Occupations, English, and an elective. He receives two credits for Office Occupations and one credit for each of his other majors; all credits apply toward graduation.

The third work-study program is Diversified Occupations, which provides on-the-job training in areas other than those covered by Distributive Education or Office Occupations. This program was designed to take advantage of the job opportunities which exist in both the school and the community. It is available to both juniors and seniors, who must be 16 years of age. The work load for these students is a minimum of 15 hours per week. The academic load includes a class in Diversified Occupations and two other classes.

The Diversified Occupations class provides the technical subject matter for the occupational areas in which the students are working and tends to be individualized instruction to meet specific needs of each job. Student workers receive the same compensation as other beginning employees.

Findings of the Survey with respect to the vocational education program

1. For better than average students who have the opportunity of attending certain vocational high schools—Chicago Vocational, Prosser, and Dunbar—and for juniors and seniors who attend Jones Commercial, the present vocational program succeeds very well. Usually, graduates of these vocational high schools are able to secure employment in the fields for which they were prepared or can enroll in institutions of higher education if they so choose. In CVS, Prosser, and Dunbar, honors courses are available in academic subjects and some of the more technically complex or advanced vocational courses provide the student with excellent training. A variety of extracurricular and physical education activities are available for students in these schools.

2. For the student of average ability and for some students of below average ability *who are motivated to remain in school throughout the four years and who graduate,* the vocational education program succeeds reasonably well. Such students who may take, for example, programs of auto repair, foundry, baking, or beauty culture are usually able to find employment, although not necessarily in the fields for which they were trained.

3. For most students of below-average ability in the vocational high schools, neither the academic nor the shop program succeeds well. Unfortunately, many of these students attend the vocational schools with the least impressive physical facilities—Cooley, Cregier, and Westcott. Because of the informal counseling pattern which prevails among eighth-grade and adjustment teachers in the elementary schools, many students of below-average ability are recommended to attend a vocational high school, although they are effectively screened out by CVS and Prosser because of admission requirements. Despite the earnest and sincere efforts made by the teachers in these schools, and indeed in all the vocational high

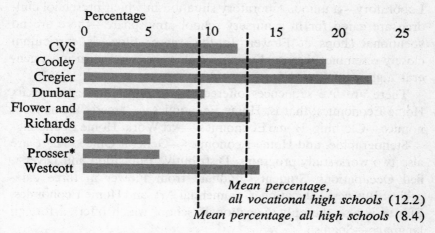

Figure 2
Mean percent of voluntary withdrawals
for nine vocational high schools
for five years (1958-1963)

Mean percentage,
all vocational high schools (12.2)
Mean percentage, all high schools (8.4)

*School was four years old at the time of this study.
Source: *Comparative Annual Voluntary Drop-Outs by High Schools; From 1954-55 to 1962-63 (nine years).* A report prepared by the Bureau of Research, Development and Special Projects (Chicago: Board of Education, 1963).

schools, it is apparent from the drop-out figures that the school program is not able to hold a large number of these students. Figure 2 shows the percentage of drop-outs for the vocational schools and compares it with the mean percentage for all high schools in the public school system.

4. There is a wide variation among the vocational high schools with respect to adequacy of facilities and equipment. CVS, Prosser, and Dunbar have excellent facilities and equipment. Three of the four schools serving a predominantly Negro student body are grossly insufficient: Cooley, Cregier, and Westcott. The inadequacies of Jones Commercial High School will be remedied by the construction of the new building now being planned.

Libraries in several of the vocational schools are inadequate in respect to size of the library room, quantity of books and periodicals, and range of technical subjects covered.

5. Flower was a girls' technical high school until 1956, at which

time its name was changed to Flower Vocational High School. Today, Flower appears to occupy a hybrid position somewhere between a technical high school and a general high school. With the exception of its very fine and unusual Child Development Laboratory—a unique laboratory situation in which preschool children are cared for in a nursery school atmosphere—there are no vocational shops at Flower. In this sense, Flower's curriculum closely resembles the usual commercial courses found in most general high schools.

There are five sequences offered, all of which have the prefix Home Economics; that is, Home Economics—Careers, Home Economics—Clothing, Home Economics—Art Work, Home Economics—Stenographic, and Home Economics—General Office. There are also two work-study programs, Distributive Education and Diversified Occupations. Students graduate from Flower in three categories: Business Education, Commercial Art, and Home Economics. Flower is also the only "vocational" school which offers a foreign language—Spanish.

The Richards Branch of Flower has one vocational shop, Beauty Culture. It offers both a certificate program in Beauty Culture Science for those girls who are not working toward high school graduation and a diploma program in Cosmetology for those girls who are carrying academic sequences in order to meet graduation requirements.

6. There appears to be a pattern of exclusion of Negroes from Prosser. No Negro student has ever attended Prosser in the regular daytime program (through June, 1963), although Negroes do enroll in the special Tool and Die Institute program in the evening. Attendance areas for Cregier, Cooley, and Prosser appear to have been drawn in a way such as to establish Cregier and Cooley as schools in almost wholly Negro neighborhoods and Prosser in an almost wholly white neighborhood. Because of counseling patterns referred to earlier, all the vocational high schools and particularly those located in predominantly Negro areas are to a considerable extent neighborhood high schools.

7. The academic curriculum in those vocational high schools with admission requirements is comparable to that in the good general high schools. The academic curriculum in those vocational high

schools with a large number of basic and essential classes does not appear to be meeting very well the needs of students in those classes. Many of these students need remedial work in reading and language arts, and in mathematics, but the academic high school teachers do not regard the teaching of remedial subjects as their responsibility. Programming for these students appears to be rigid. In general, students who are placed in Basic or Essential English are also programmed for Basic or Essential classes in other academic subjects almost automatically. Insufficient attention appears to be given to students' differential abilities. Guidance counseling for many students in the vocational high schools is based almost completely upon eighth-grade test results and does not include testing for vocational aptitude. Under the present arrangement, neither student nor counselor nor teacher knows what the student's vocational abilities may be. In some of the schools, students are not infrequently placed in a particular exploratory shop in order to fill the class. All boys must take mechanical drawing irrespective of their interest and aptitude. In several of the vocational high schools a limited opportunity exists for students to participate in music and art.

8. In the vocational curriculum, the two-year period of exploratory shop is too long for all those students who know what skill they wish to acquire and impedes them from faster personal development. For those students of below-average academic ability who may have considerable vocational ability, two years in exploratory shop delays their entrance into a vocational shop where they can learn a specific occupational skill. Unable to enter a vocational shop until their junior year, and uninterested in academic subjects, many students find the first two years of vocational high school only a waiting period until school-leaving age is reached.

9. The administrative practice requiring a minimum number of students per class, strictly enforced in most schools, results in a large number of academic and shop classes containing students at different grade levels. These composite classes work a hardship on teachers who are expected to present several different levels of subject matter involving different kinds of materials simultaneously to students at different stages of progress. Such division of the teachers' time and attention is a disservice to both teachers and students.

10. Although industry advisory councils are in existence, they do not seem to function meaningfully with respect to curriculum revision based on technical developments within industry. Conversations with the staff both in the vocational high schools and at the Board of Education leave the impression that very little curriculum revision actually occurs in the vocational shop program despite the preparation of curriculum guides. In some cases, curriculum revision must wait on new technical equipment which the Board of Education has been unable to acquire.

11. Individual shop teachers often have personal connections with firms or businesses in their particular trade and are able to recommend successfully the best of their students for employment in these firms. This is a highly informal process, with obvious weaknesses and inequities. If the vocational schools are going to take responsibility for placing their students in industry, a formal placement service should be developed, available to all students. At present there appear to be no industry advisory councils for each separate vocational high school. Were such councils to be developed, improvements could be expected with respect to curriculum revision for individual vocational shops and with respect to employment of all qualified graduates.

12. Students in vocational high schools do not appear to receive much personal guidance concerning the kinds of jobs available to them upon completion of their course. Many students do not seem to understand that they can prepare for work within a family of skills or that acquiring a particular skill may fit them for employment in a related or adjacent field. Their vision of the kinds of work they may be able to perform is narrow. The present curriculum does not include a unit on occupational information which would be especially useful to students who have not decided upon a specific trade or skill.

13. Despite the best efforts of many teachers and administrators in the vocational high schools, there does exist within the school system as a whole a certain unfortunate negative attitude toward vocational education. To many academic teachers and guidance personnel, vocational schools are remedial in nature and exist to clear the way in the general high schools for academically talented students. This attitude has several results: first, some students of

average academic ability or above who might benefit greatly from the vocational are counseled into the general high school; second, some students of below-average ability are advised to enter the vocational program when they might be better suited for a program in a general high school; third, in order to compensate for the negative attitudes shown toward vocational education, staffs of the vocational schools frequently concentrate on the better students in their classes, leaving the academically below-average students to drift or to work at repetitive jobs; fourth, feelings of mistrust and hostility between the academic and shop teachers within the vocational high schools affect the morale in these schools.

RECOMMENDATIONS

1. All vocational high schools should be open to students on a city-wide basis. Existing selection standards should be maintained at Chicago Vocational, Prosser, Dunbar, and Jones Commercial.

2. Cooley and Westcott Vocational High Schools, because of their inadequacy as schools for high school youth, should be transformed into Adult Education Centers, operating day and evening. The student body should include adult men and women and high school drop-outs.

The present student body at Cooley and Westcott should be transferred to other vocational high schools in the city, under the city-wide open enrollment policy, and to neighborhood high schools. (It is anticipated that those boys now at Cooley who want a vocational program can attend either Cregier, Prosser, or Dunbar and the girls, Flower, Richards, or Dunbar. Boys at Westcott can attend CVS, Dunbar, or Cregier and the girls, CVS, Dunbar, or Richards. Those students who want an academic program can attend neighborhood high schools.)

3. Although Flower and Richards are described as vocational high schools, their educational programs are indistinguishable from those in most general high schools. If they are to be regarded truly as vocational high schools, facilities and shops for vocational and technical courses, in addition to the present commercial art, home economics, and business education, should be established.

Many occupations and skills are now open to women for which vocational and technical training of a specialized nature is necessary.

Girls in the Chicago public school system could and should be offered these opportunities in special high schools; both Flower and Richards can be made suitable for this purpose.

4. Increases in enrollment in the vocational education program may be expected in the future because of the improved holding power of the school system as a whole and because vocational education, as it becomes more adaptive to Chicago industry, will become more attractive to students whose primary school interests are not academic but preparation for employment.

Students who are now in the Vocational Guidance and Education Centers should have the opportunity of staying in these Centers through the ninth grade and then continuing to vocational high school in a course which is articulated and coordinated with the work of the Centers. Such a plan would in all probability also result in increased enrollment at the high school level.

In order to provide more opportunity for a vocational program to those students who would be attracted by it and could benefit from it, the present seven Vocational Guidance and Education Centers should be extended to include the ninth grade and there should be a substantial increase in the number of such centers, beginning as early as possible in 1965. A goal of five additional centers does not seem unreasonable in 1965. In order to replace Cooley and Westcott, which are inadequate, and to accommodate the anticipated increase in enrollment at the high school level, the Board of Education should consider building or establishing two new vocational high schools with modern equipment and facilities and with programs for both boys and girls.

5. Vocational aptitude tests should be given to all students entering a vocational program. The use of such tests would help counselors and students in the selection of students' programs.

6. Because there appears to be a considerable amount of unprofitable time spent in the present two-year exploratory shop period, we recommend the reduction of this period to one year. The first half-year might consist of a general shop program, such as now exists in the industrial arts sequence in the general high school; the second half-year might consist of exploratory shop to include four separate shop experiences. The time gained will permit earlier entrance into the vocational shop program, which is desir-

able for all students. The experience of the Milwaukee vocational schools' program in reducing and compressing exploratory shop is relevant here.

7. For those students of average or above-average ability who have decided upon their vocation when they reach ninth grade or during it, the exploratory shop period should be waived. Thus, students with well-defined interests and the ability to progress should be offered an accelerated shop program that will provide them an extra year of advanced technical and related shop work within the regular four-year high school period. Indeed, an accelerated shop program should be available for all students who show ability to progress at a rapid rate in their own vocational shop, irrespective of their interest and success in the academic program.

8. For those students who are likely to leave school before graduation, either because of disinterest or failure in the academic program or for reasons of economic pressure, a three-year certificate program should be offered. In communities such as Milwaukee, the certificate program appears to keep in school some students who might otherwise leave. Such a certificate program in Chicago would require completion of two years of vocational shop (which could be accomplished under the revised and compressed time schedule suggested in Recommendation 6) and would serve to hold some students in school for a third year. Thus they would obtain greater competence in a trade or skill than they would otherwise have achieved, leaving school at age 16.

9. All students in the vocational high schools, age 16 and over, boys and girls, should be given the opportunity to participate in one or another of the work-study programs. These programs, with trained staff to operate them, should be greatly expanded in order to accommodate the large numbers of students who would be attracted by this chance to stay in school, earn needed income, and work in a field related to their vocational courses.

10. A unit of study entitled Occupational Information should be included as part of the first-year program for all students. This unit would expose students to the variety of work and jobs which are available in the metropolitan Chicago job market. It should include field trips to factories, plants, laboratories, department stores, and governmental agencies.

11. Advisory councils with membership from local industry and trade unions should be formed for each vocational high school. These councils should meet regularly for the purpose of advising the schools on curriculum revision and relating the schools to the surrounding community. In addition, specialists should be added to the Division of Vocational Education who would keep in close touch with the needs and shifts in the Chicago labor market. The vocational education program could then be more closely related to the changing requirements in the Chicago labor force.

12. Each vocational high school should have an employment counselor whose special function would be to advise graduates and also students leaving school before graduation of employment opportunities in the Chicago area.

13. Unless the Board of Education can establish policies governing the admission of all qualified students to all trades presently taught at Washburne Trade School, those apprenticeship programs which discriminate against Negroes and others should be withdrawn from the school.

14. The resources of the federal government made available to the field of vocational education through Public Law 88-210, passed in December, 1963, should be utilized to the utmost in strengthening vocational education in Chicago. The Board of Education should submit at the earliest practical time to the Board of Vocational Education and Rehabilitation in the Office of the Superintendent of Public Instruction in Illinois, through which requests to the federal government must pass, a plan for the further development and expansion of its own vocational education program for regular high school students, for drop-outs, and for adults.

The Vocational Education Act of 1963 authorizes federal grants to states, and to public education systems within states, for the purpose of assisting them:

> to maintain, extend, and improve existing programs of vocational education, to develop new programs of vocational education, and to provide part-time employment for youths who need the earnings from such employment to continue their vocational training on a full-time basis, so that persons of all ages in all communities of the State— those in high school, those who have completed or discontinued their

formal education and are preparing to enter the labor market, those who have already entered the labor market but need to upgrade their skills or learn new ones, and those with special educational handicaps—will have ready access to vocational training or retraining which is of high quality, which is realistic in the light of actual or anticipated opportunities for gainful employment, and which is suited to their needs, interests, and ability to benefit from such training.

Funds may be used, in accordance with an approved state plan, for purposes in addition to those outlined, including:

a. Vocational education for persons who have academic, socioeconomic, or other handicaps that prevent them from succeeding in the regular vocational education program.

b. Construction of area vocational education school facilities.

c. Ancillary services and activities to assure quality in all vocational education programs such as teacher training and supervision, program evaluation, special demonstration and experimental programs, and development of instructional materials.

Industrial arts

There is some ambiguity in the term "industrial arts" as perceived by the general public and used by high school faculties. It is most frequently confused with vocational education and sometimes with technical education. As stated earlier, if vocational education is terminal in nature, its purpose is to train students in employable skills. Technical education in the Chicago schools is generally thought of as a program preparing students who are college bound in the fields of science or engineering. The Curriculum Guide for industrial arts states:

> Industrial arts helps prepare students for effective living and intelligent citizenship in our industrial society by providing educational shop experiences which deal with the materials, processes, products, occupations, and problems of our industrial world.
>
> Industrial arts, in the curriculum of the modern high school, teaches the principles, techniques, and appreciations of selected trades and crafts as they are encountered in our present industrial society. In order to provide the students with a sound experiential background upon which to base interpretation of the general principles

and broader theoretical aspects of the subject matter, the instructional method in industrial arts is primarily manipulative. These manual activities, involving the tools, processes, and materials of industry, are carried out in specially equipped shops or laboratories in accordance with the area involved. The emphasis in the total program may be technical or vocational. For the student who is college bound, anticipating a career in engineering, more attention is accorded to technical and theoretical aspects. Where high school is terminal education, more concern is given to practical aspects and saleable skills. The industrial arts program, administered according to purpose, provides for a range of abilities, needs, and goals.

Industrial arts courses are not officially designed to be vocational training, as are shop courses in vocational high schools. The stated purpose of industrial arts in the general high school is to familiarize students with basic tools and processes. The general shop work taken in an industrial arts course may serve as an introduction or exploratory experience leading to a specialized shop in a vocational school at a later time. Actually, some of the industrial arts courses in some schools are vocational and even technical.

The industrial arts or industrial education program, as it is sometimes referred to, consists of 18 subjects. These subjects and the maximum number of units a general high school makes available to its students are as follows: Architectural Drafting, Automotive, Aviation, Cabinet Making, Carpentry, Drafting, Electricity, Electronics, Foundry, General Shop, Linotype, Machine Drafting, Patternmaking, Plastics, Print Shop, Sheet Metal Shop, Welding, Wood Shop. Theoretically, the industrial arts student may take as many as four units or as few as two units in this area. This leaves him free to select from two to four other electives to earn the six units, beyond the basic or required 12 units, necessary for high school graduation. No general high school has all of the foregoing offerings but most have at least three or four.

For reasons stated earlier, many freshmen students of below-average academic ability are often counseled or persuaded to attend vocational high school by counselors' statements on parent-interview day that a certain minimum attainment must be achieved before successful matriculation in the general high school is possible. If "counseling away" fails, the general high school has the responsibility of admitting and educating these students, as it does for all students. It must make available to them facilities, teachers, and instructional materials which appeal to and suit their interests and abilities. The industrial arts program, whatever its original purpose and design as part of the general curriculum of a general high school, has largely become a program attended by students at the Basic, Essential, or EMH levels.

The Curriculum Guide for industrial arts is carefully prepared and comprehensive. But it does not appear to answer the needs of those industrial arts courses which accept students for more than the prescribed number of units. For example, the guide stipulates that the general high school may offer one unit of carpentry, one of electricity, two of printing, etc. Yet many classes were observed with students in their fourth, fifth, or sixth semester of wood shop or print shop. Neither the curriculum nor the equipment or materials are adequate to provide students with these additional units. Teachers and administrators attribute the necessity of extending these shop courses to the caliber of students who are programmed into the industrial arts sequence and to the necessity of keeping them in that sequence in order to keep them in school. If the industrial arts sequence is to be a good answer to the problem of providing education for general high school students of below-average academic ability, then it must make provision for a carefully prepared and full program for students in their second, third, and even fourth year. This will mean changing the present program into a vocational education course for second and third year students, after an initial year of general shop.

Since equipping every general high school with truly vocational shops in each of the basic vocational skills would be very costly, it is suggested that individual high schools specialize in different shop programs. Under an open enrollment policy, or a cluster policy, students could transfer to the school that offered the particular vocational shop they wanted. With respect to the cost of changing the industrial arts program into a vocational program in any particular school, the Board of Education should keep in mind the resources available for this purpose from the Vocational Education Act of 1963, previously noted.

Consideration should be given to the establishment of a three-year certificate program for students in the industrial arts sequence in the general high school, as suggested in Recommendation 11 of this chapter for students in vocational high schools.

Students in the industrial arts sequence in the general high schools should have an opportunity to participate in one of the work-study programs on an equal basis with other students.

Adult vocational and remedial education

Among the matters which the Advisory Committee on Adult Education to the Survey undertook to investigate was the status of vocational education for adults. The Committee's findings and conclusions are reported in greater detail in Supplement C. Here it is important to note that the Committee calculated there were about 21,600 adults in Chicago presently engaged in some form of institutional vocational education (figures as of January, 1964). Of these, 6,663 adults were enrolled full- or part-time in the public schools and 531 adult trainees were enrolled in courses organized by the public schools under the Manpower Development and Training Act, a total of 7,194 adults in public school vocational programs.

In 1964, there were 8,265 adult students in the literacy program, a cooperative program of the Board of Education and the Cook County Department of Public Aid. Of these, 6,262 were in elementary classes and 2,003 in high school, women comprising the great majority.[2] About 7,500 students were enrolled in the Americanization program (December, 1963).[3] The Urban Youth Program has been treated elsewhere in this report, but it should be noted that insofar as some of the participants in this program are counseled to enter the Manpower Development and Training programs, they may properly be considered as part of the potential student body for adult vocational education.

While there may be some discrepancies among the figures for students in adult vocational programs between this report and the report of the staff Committee on Adult Education, due to the dif-

[2]Committee on Adult Education. *Adult Education of the Chicago Public Schools, 1964* (Chicago: Board of Education, 1964), p. 31.
[3]*Ibid.*, p. 35.

ferent dates and the number of sources from which the data were collected, the striking conclusion emerges that only a small number of the potential adult students in Chicago are engaged in Board of Education vocational courses.

The total number of unemployed in the Chicago Standard Metropolitan Statistical Area was 118,000 as of July, 1964. Most of these people are in Chicago. All of them could profit from some form of vocational training. Many of them are also functionally illiterate and thus candidates for the literacy program. The Cook County Department of Public Aid estimates there are between 20,000 and 25,000 adult persons on its records who are not otherwise disabled who could benefit from this program, again, most of them in Chicago. In all probability, there are many tens of thousands of adults in Chicago, including young adults out of school and unemployed, persons receiving some form of public assistance, unemployed and underemployed, who should be given the opportunity to participate in a literacy training program, followed by a vocational training program.

The Advisory Committee on Adult Education to the Survey recommends a 10-fold increase in the vocational training capability of the Board of Education and a greatly expanded remedial education program, including literacy training and other basic education courses, in order to meet more fully the city's responsibility for these matters.

This Committee and the staff Committee on Adult Education of the Board of Education both recommended the establishment at the earliest opportunity of full-time adult education centers with day and evening classes, full-time staff and supervision, and a range of vocational, basic, literacy, and citizenship education courses. The concurrence of these two committees, one a committee of concerned adult citizens of the Chicago metropolitan area and the other a committee of Board of Education staff, provides a strong basis for Recommendation 2 in this chapter.

XII

Marginal Youth and the Schools

In the decade of the 1960's, society has become increasingly aware of the problem of young men and women, aged 16 to 20, who are both out of school and unemployed. The schools, churches, welfare organizations, and other institutions have developed a variety of means for reaching these young people whom we may call "marginal youth." We shall discuss in this chapter the present and projected size of the marginal youth group in Chicago, the programs which the schools and other agencies have created to assist them, and programs which must be expanded and developed in the future if these young men and women are to become constructive and productive members of society.

Young people in the United States can be classified into three broad, roughly equal groups with respect to their education. One-third enter college, and move from college to a job or to marriage. One-third stop their formal education with high school graduation and then get a job or get married. One-third do not complete high school. They drop out of school somewhere along the line and seek work, while some of the girls get married.

We can say that the drop-outs are *marginal to the school system*. However, at least half the boys in this group get jobs fairly quickly

270

and hold steady jobs. Also, a number of girls get jobs, while others get married as early as age 15 and thus make what is regarded by society as a legitimate but early start on the career of wife and mother.

A considerable fraction of drop-outs do not get steady work or contract a steady marriage. These we shall designate *marginal to the labor force* or *marginal to the adult role*. It is this group who are marginal both to the school and to the labor force (or to the adult role, in the case of girls) with which we are particularly concerned in this chapter.

Young people, 16 to 20, who are both marginal to the school and marginal to the labor force, have become objects of increasing concern to society because they comprise a group larger than that in previous decades and because they are more visible. In an earlier time, out-of-school youth could often find work on farms, and indeed a greater number of them lived in rural or semirural areas than is the case today. Marginal youth today live mostly in cities and when they are idle or perhaps involved in delinquent acts, the effects of their behavior are more widely advertised.

By the mid 1950's, two forces or phenomena were becoming visible which were to have drastic effects upon the position and numbers of marginal youth: first, the large population increase of children and young people due to the "baby boom" of immediate postwar years; second, the revolution in manufacturing technology caused by automation and computers. Children born in the postwar period are now entering the 16 through 20 age group. In 1960 there were 12.6 million (born 1940-44); in 1965 there will be 16.1 million (born 1945-49); and in 1970 there will be 18.1 million (born 1950-54). Or putting the problem another way, 26 million young people under the age of 25 will enter the labor force during the decade of the 1960's. Of these, it is estimated that 6 million, or 23 percent, will have some college and another 12 million, or 46 percent, will complete high school. Eight million or 31 percent will not complete high school. This is a larger number of drop-outs than was produced during the 1950's. There is every reason to believe that the social problem of marginal youth will be even greater during the next 10 years than it has been in the past decade.

Table 1
Numbers of youth in City of Chicago, 1960

Age in 1960	Males	Females	Total
6	31,985	31,411	63,396
7	31,524	30,974	62,498
8	30,673	29,953	60,626
9	28,861	28,572	57,433
10	28,630	28,381	57,011
11	28,568	27,883	56,451
12	28,871	28,526	57,397
13	27,986	27,911	55,897
14	22,377	21,950	44,327
15	21,562	21,833	43,395
16	22,741	23,495	46,236
17	24,177	25,626	49,803
18	20,063	23,302	43,365
19	17,401	22,340	39,741
20	17,749	23,658	41,407

MARGINAL YOUTH IN CHICAGO

The numbers of marginal youth in the City of Chicago will now be estimated, to serve as a basis for a realistic discussion of what is being done and what might be done through schools and other agencies to help this group become competent and self-supporting young adults.

First, it is necessary to determine the numbers of youth in Chicago in the age group 16 through 20. For this we turn to the 1960 census. Table 1 shows the numbers of youth in the City of Chicago by single-year age groups in 1960. This shows graphically the increasing size of the youth population as a result of the "baby boom" of the postwar years which shows first in the 13-year-olds of 1960. Table 1 also shows that the number of young women aged 16-20 exceeds the number of young men. This is characteristic of big city populations. Young men leave the city for military service and other reasons, whereas young women tend to come to the big city from smaller communities to get employment. This sex difference in population has been considered in data presented later.

The numbers of youth aged 16-20 can be estimated with reasonable accuracy from Table 1 for any year from 1965 to 1970, if we assume that the in-migration equals the out-migration since 1960. On this basis we find that the 16-20 group grows from 221,-000 in 1960 to 257,000 in 1965 and to 301,000 in 1970.

Estimating the number of drop-outs

Three methods have been used to ascertain the drop-out rate for the City of Chicago.

The first method for estimating the drop-out rate of *all high school students* in Chicago uses the relationship between the number of high school graduates, in public and private schools, in a given year and the number of 17-year-olds in the city. For the school year ending June, 1963, this formula indicates a graduation rate of 62.6 percent and thus a drop-out rate of 37.4 percent.

The second formula is based on the percent of 20-year-old youth who are "enrolled in school" and "not enrolled in school," and the percent of those not enrolled who are "not graduated from high school." These figures are derived from the 1960 Decennial Census and show that approximately 36 percent of the males and 33 percent of the females, age 20, were drop-outs in the City of Chicago in 1960.

The third formula is based on the proportion of students enrolled in ninth grade of public schools in a given year to the number of students who graduated in the same class in the 12th grade. From this ratio we find about 65 percent of the number enrolled in ninth grade in 1959 graduating in 1963, or a drop-out rate of 35 percent.*

Facts and Figures. Chicago Public Schools, 1962-63, p. 32. See also: School Staff Study Report, *Programs for Potential Dropouts.* Chicago Public Schools, 1964, p. 43.

The drop-out rate reported in the School Staff Study Report varies from 9.0 to 6.9 percent during the past 10 years, but this is an "annual rate" or the percentage of drop-outs in one year. For the four years of high school, these numbers should be multiplied by four (approximately), giving a drop-out rate from the four-year high school of 36 to 27.6 percent. This does not include an estimated 3 percent who drop out before reaching high school. Thus, this estimate agrees with the three estimates made by other methods.

This applies to public high schools. Probably the drop-out rate of Catholic parochial high schools was similar.

From these analyses, it seems reasonable to assume that the current drop-out rate for the City of Chicago is about 35 percent, and it is decreasing slowly. Since more boys than girls leave school, a good estimate is a 37 percent drop-out rate for boys and 33 percent for girls. By using data from the 1960 Decennial Census one can calculate the drop-out rate for the United States as a whole; these data also show that approximately 60 percent of 20-year-old youth were high school graduates in 1960 and therefore the drop-out rate for the country was about 40 percent shortly before 1960.

Specific numbers of drop-outs can now be determined, using the population data of Table 1. In 1965 the number of 16-year-olds will be approximately 56,000 (this is the number of 11-year-olds in 1960). If 35 percent of this number leave school without graduating, the number of drop-outs from the single-year age group will be 19,600. Applying the same drop-out rate to the numbers of youth aged 16-20 between 1965 and 1970, we estimate a total of 35 percent of 280,000 or 98,000 boys and girls who have dropped out before finishing high school and are in the age group 16-20. The number will be somewhat smaller in 1965 and larger in 1970, because the total number aged 16-20 will grow during that period.

As was noted earlier, roughly half of these young people either get stable work or get married and therefore are not marginal to the labor force or to an adult female role, though they are marginal to the school system. This leaves approximately half of the group out of school, not working, and not married (if they are girls). These are marginal to society.

The number of marginal youth can be calculated more accurately by another method, using the 1960 census for the metropolitan area of Chicago. The census indicates that 9.8 percent of males aged 16-20 were not in school and not at work or not working more than 15 hours a week in 1960. These we shall call marginal. This proportion is for the entire metropolitan area, and it would be greater for the central city than for the suburbs, with their higher proportion of young people in school and college. Assuming that the proportion of marginal youth is twice as great in

Table 2
Projected number of 16- through 20-year-old
marginal youth in the City of Chicago,
1965 through 1970

Year	Male	Female	Total
1965	16,800	25,600	42,400
1966	17,700	26,900	44,600
1967	18,600	28,200	46,800
1968	18,900	28,700	47,600
1969	19,300	29,100	48,400
1970	19,600	29,900	49,500

the City of Chicago as it is in the suburbs, we estimate that 13 percent of Chicago males aged 16-20 were marginal in 1960, in the sense we use the term. In the same way we estimate that 20 percent of Chicago females aged 16-20 were marginal in the sense that they were not in school, not employed as much as 15 hours a week, and not married. Combining the figures for males and females we get a percentage of 16.5 for marginal youth in the City of Chicago, which is close to the 17.5 we obtained by the other method.

Applying these estimates to the numbers of youth aged 16-20 during the five years after 1965 we get Table 2, the numbers of marginal young men and women in the City of Chicago between 1965 and 1970.

Programs for marginal youth over 16

The Chicago schools, as in other large cities, have recognized the problem of drop-outs and potential drop-outs and have attempted to develop educational programs and services to meet the problem. Despite the excellence of the individual programs, the scope of the programs and the energy and resources which have gone into them have not been commensurate with the size of the problem.

Information and descriptions concerning the Chicago schools' programs for drop-outs and potential drop-outs have been presented in some detail in two reports issued by the General Superintendent: *Programs for Potential Dropouts,* Study Report No. 3, 1964 series, and *Compensatory Education,* Study Report No. 4, 1964 series. Reference should be made to these reports by the reader for information concerning the extent of the schools' programs in this area.

For youth who have left school before graduating from high school, the major programs designed specifically to meet their needs are: the *Urban Youth Program* of the Chicago schools; the *Jobs for Youth Program* of the Sears YMCA, which is assisted by the Chicago schools; the *Job Opportunities Through Better Skills* (JOBS) project, financed by the federal government through the Manpower Development and Training Act, and conducted jointly by the Chicago YMCA, Chicago Boys' Clubs, and Chicago Youth Centers; the Illinois State Employment Service; the Cook County Department of Public Aid; and a number of agencies with smaller job placement programs, such as the Back-of-the-Yards Neighborhood Council, the Chicago Commission on Youth Welfare, and the Northtown Vocational Council.

How well is the need being met?

The number of job placements per year of drop-outs now being made by the agencies working with drop-outs can be estimated in Table 3 for the marginal youth in the age group 16-20. Even though these are crude estimates, they are useful if we take seriously the task of evaluating the results of the present program of job training and placement of marginal youth.

Since we know the number of marginal youth, we can calculate the extent to which the existing programs meet the need. First, however, we must make some reasonable assumptions about the age distribution of marginal youth within the age range 16-20. We know the total numbers of youth at each age, the numbers in school, the numbers at work, and the numbers of girls who are married. At 16, 17, and 18, the numbers of marginal youth are

Table 3
*Estimated numbers of job
placements per year
among marginal youth aged* 16-20

	Minimum	Maximum
Urban Youth Program of the Chicago Public Schools	250	300
Jobs for Youth, Sears YMCA and Public Schools	60	100
Job Opportunities Through Better Skills (JOBS) (Federal Government MDTA)	600	700
Illinois State Employment Service*	200	300
Other Agencies (private youth-serving agencies)	500	550
Cook County Department of Public Aid	500	550
Total	2,110	2,500

*Does not include high school graduates who are placed in jobs as a part of the normal operation of the ISES.

Table 4
*Results of job training and placement
programs over four years*

Age	Initial no. in marginal group	No. being placed in jobs	% being placed in jobs	No. in marginal group after four years
16	7,000	200	3	7,000
17	10,000	400	4	9,800
18	10,000	400	4	9,000
19	10,000	700	7	9,000
20	8,000	700	9	6,300
Total	45,000	2,400	5.3	41,100

Note: The numbers in the last column are based on the assumption that this program has operated for four years in the face of unchanging conditions productive of new marginal youth. The only factor which operates to change the numbers is assumed to be the job-training and placement program for marginal youth.

increasing, due to dropping out of school. At 18, 19, and 20 the numbers are decreasing, due to marriage of girls, entry into the armed services for boys, and successful search for jobs by youth who have been marginal for some time.

On the basis of reasonable assumptions based on this knowledge, we estimate the numbers which appear in Table 4. It seems that present programs for drop-outs meet about 5 percent of the need for jobs by marginal youth. If these programs are continued at this present level of job placement, after four years the number of marginal youth will have been reduced from 45,000 to 41,500, and will stay at that level unless other factors come into play— such as a more successful program in the schools for working with disadvantaged children which will hold them in school longer and teach them more effectively, or a change in employment conditions for youth which will make it easier or more difficult for them to get jobs.

It is clear that the existing programs for helping out-of-school youth get training and find jobs fall far short of dealing with the numbers who need help. There is also a good deal of evidence that these programs are helping the ones who are most nearly able to help themselves. That is, many of the existing programs help marginal youth who seem to have the most to offer, and exclude the poorer risks.

If the present programs were to be expanded even as much as five-fold, they might encounter two types of difficulty. One is the difficulty of finding jobs for the young people in the programs. Competition for jobs is keen and will probably grow keener among young people for the semiskilled jobs which this group seeks. The other difficulty is that of finding young people in the marginal group with attitudes toward work which make them good risks for employment.

Yet we are convinced that the attempt to help these young people through work training and job placement is a sound one. Turning them back into the schools for another compulsory year or two would not have as much maturation value for them as helping them to try themselves out in the adult work role.

Federal work experience programs. The new work experience programs to be supported by the federal government under the recent anti-poverty law seem to offer the best available chance to help the majority of marginal youth. Under this program the schools can secure federal government support for programs of work experience for youth aged 16-21. These pay a subsistence allowance (not a real wage) to the young people for work or projects of social value which would not be done by private enterprise. Some of the work projects will be organized on a residential basis, similar to the Civilian Conservation Corps of the 1930's. Most of them, however, will be for youth who live at home, and can be operated with very little extra trouble by local public school systems. For example, the Urban Youth Program can be much expanded, and it should include a well-defined vocational or on-the-job training component.

While this kind of work experience is probably not as useful for a young man or woman as a "regular" job, there seems to be no real prospect of their finding regular jobs until they are a few years older. Consequently, a year or two of work experience in this kind of project, with related school work, may prove to be a very good investment both for the individual youth and for society.

It is important to have work programs for girls as well as for boys. A variety of experimental projects should be established to find out how marginal girls can best use a combination of work experience and related schooling.

Programs for youth below age 16

Most boys and girls who will become marginal after age 16 are rather clearly visible by the time they are 13 or 14 years old. They are already maladjusted to school and often are behavior problems in school. They are apathetic about school work, and generally have dropped out of school in the psychological sense long before they can drop out physically.

It would seem desirable to identify and work with these young people just as early as their maladjustment to the ordinary school program becomes evident. The Chicago schools have made a start in this direction with the seven Educational and Vocational Guidance Centers. The first of these was established in the Drake School in February, 1962. This came after an age-grade study revealed that some 8,000 elementary school pupils were 15 years of age or older, and most of them were doing poorly in school work. Soon seven centers were in operation, in seven districts with relatively high numbers of over-age pupils.

The functions of such a center are: (1) completion of elementary education as rapidly as possible; (2) vocational guidance, education, and supervised work experience to help the pupil get a job; (3) guidance into high school for those capable of high school work.

Class size was limited to 20, and school size to 350. Pupils are admitted to a center generally from a seventh or eighth grade, but occasionally from a fifth or sixth grade. They are graduated to high school at the end of any semester when their reading scores and teachers' recommendations indicate that they can succeed in high school.

As the program has developed since 1962, the emphasis has shifted from the development of vocational skills to improvement in reading and arithmetic and consequent preparation for high school. Special remedial reading materials have been used. As of February, 1964, there were 335 graduates from the first center, and 90 percent went on to high school. This is an excellent record, and the gains reported in reading achievement were remarkable.

If this kind of result can be achieved with the ordinary over-age pupils of inner-city schools, it is a discovery of the first magnitude. Similar remedial work has been tried in a number of other large cities with poor results. It is recommended that a controlled experiment be set up with one group of over-age pupils working in a center while a matched group is left in regular seventh- and eighth-grade classes. If the gains just indicated are repeated in such an experiment, the numbers of centers should be expanded as rapidly as possible to provide for over-age and under-achieving pupils.

At the same time, it is recommended that the work experience and vocational training aspects of the original center program be continued in at least some of the centers. There is evidence from other cities that a program of work experience and specially organized academic training has value for boys, especially, who have not done well in school and appear to be probable drop-outs.

The Educational and Vocational Guidance Centers might include the beginning of true vocational training as early as the

seventh grade, and continuing to the ninth, with provision for entrance to a vocational high school for pupils who meet certain
requirements.

It is recommended, also, that a three-year experimental program be developed in some centers to serve boys and girls who
are probable drop-outs from the seventh through the ninth grades.
For pupils with low achievement this might be far better than entering from an eighth-grade class in an elementary school to the
Basic track of a general high school, where most of them will remain no more than one year before dropping out.

Possible objections to such a three-year institution are obvious.
First of all, there is danger that such institutions would become
known as places for low-achieving students, all of whom will drop
out as soon as they reach school-leaving age. This might have the
effect of reducing the motivation of pupils who would like to go to
high school and succeed there in spite of a poor elementary school
record. But this danger could be avoided if there was a positive
program of promoting pupils from eighth grade to a general or
vocational high school if they could meet certain reasonable standards. The reports from existing centers of high morale and of success of graduates in high school indicate that it is possible to avoid
the stigma of a "dummy" school.

The most serious behavior and discipline problems exist in the
seventh and eighth grades of inner-city elementary schools, as do
the most serious problems of low achievement. Here is where the
majority of marginal youth are recruited. The proposed experimental school should have a strong work-study program, a strong
program of remedial teaching of reading and arithmetic, and a
flexible system of transfers to general and vocational high schools.

At the same time, the general high schools in low-achievement
areas should have substantial assistance in the form of more counselors and remedial teaching designed especially for marginal youth.

XIII

Chicago Teachers College and Chicago City Junior College

This chapter is concentrated on higher education programs under the Chicago Board of Education. These comprise the Chicago Teachers College with its branches and the Chicago City Junior College with its present eight branches.

* * *

This part of the Survey was planned by Professor Alonzo G. Grace. The team which studied the Teachers College consisted of George W. Denemark, Dean, School of Education, University of Wisconsin—Milwaukee; Warren C. Lovinger, President, Central Missouri State College, Warrensburg; Walter J. Moore, Professor of Elementary Education, University of Illinois, Urbana; Gordon M. A. Mork, Director of Student Teaching, University of Minnesota, Minneapolis; Charles M. Allen, Coordinator of Teacher Education, University of Illinois, Urbana (Chairman). The Junior College was studied by Professor Lee Medsker, Associate Director of the Center for the Study of Higher Education at the University of California at Berkeley.

This chapter consists largely of material drawn from the reports and recommendations made by these consultants to the Survey Committee. In addition, the attitudes and opinions of faculty members are reported as they appeared on a questionnaire study which was sent to all faculty members, and filled out anonymously by 73 percent of Teachers College and 85 percent of Junior College faculty.

Since 1953 in Illinois, the enrollments of colleges and universities have increased every year, and the 1964 enrollment is twice that of 1953. This will probably double again during the next 10 years. The need for public-supported colleges in Chicago is beyond question. The question is: What forms should public higher education take and how should the cost be met?

For Chicago the need is especially great because the metropolitan area is growing so rapidly. Sixty-two percent of the Illinois population live within 40 miles of the Chicago City and County Building. Public-supported higher education must be planned for the metropolitan area in close relation to what is planned for the City of Chicago. The college-age population (18 through 21 years) in the City of Chicago in 1960 was 180,000 while in the Chicago suburban area it was 108,000. By 1970 these numbers will have grown to 234,000 and 240,000, respectively. That is, there will be more college-age youths in the Chicago Metropolitan Area outside the City of Chicago than in the city itself.

College enrollments of the metropolitan area are estimated conservatively to go from 155,000 in 1964 to 215,000 in 1970, an increase of 60,000 which must be cared for mainly by public-supported institutions—the University of Illinois, the Chicago Teachers College, the Chicago City Junior College, and the other public junior colleges in the area.

Since the state has generally been responsible for public-supported higher education and since there is a major problem of expense during this decade, it is natural that a number of states have made state-wide plans for the support and development of higher education. The new state plans of California and New York are especially noteworthy. These plans generally include provision for increasing state support and decreasing local support. At the same time, public-supported colleges are coming more and more under the administration of state boards. There are only three municipally administered teachers colleges remaining in the United States—Chicago, Washington, and St. Louis.

The Illinois Master Plan

The Illinois Legislature in 1961 established a Board of Higher Education and asked it to prepare a "Master Plan" for the state, taking into account the public and private colleges and universities and two-year colleges. This Board has created three advisory committees and 10 study committees to aid it in drawing up a provisional Master Plan, now being studied and discussed by the public. The State Board will present its plan in final form to the legislature in 1965.

For Chicago, the final Master Plan recommends that:

1. The state acquire the Chicago Teachers College and place it under the governance of the Board of Governors of State Teachers Colleges. Provision is made for a new campus for Teachers College South.

2. A state Junior College Board be established to coordinate planning, programs, services, and state aid for public junior colleges.

3. A separate Junior College District be established for the City of Chicago, with its own governing board. The Chicago City Junior College would be transferred to a new local Junior College Board, its members to be named by the Mayor.

If the state legislature approves the Master Plan in 1965, it is proposed that existing junior colleges maintained by school districts, such as the Chicago Junior College, be changed over as follows:

a. The board of education controlling the present common school district, by a two-thirds vote should divest itself of all governing and control powers over the junior college or colleges under its jurisdiction.

b. A new seven-member governing board for the junior college district should be named by the mayor.

c. No member of a board of education controlling a common school district could also be a member of a junior college district board.

d. The board of education controlling the present common school district should agree to continue to govern and administer the junior college until the new junior college district board has been duly elected and sworn in.

e. If the existing district has not authorized a tax for junior college support, such a tax should be approved for the junior college district under current law.

4. State support be provided for 75 percent of the cost of new

Junior College buildings during the first five years, and for approximately 50 percent of the operating costs of the Junior College. No tuition charges are to be made against any Illinois resident.

The Survey Committee recommends that the Chicago Board of Education approve the new Master Plan, for three reasons:

1. It would transfer some of the cost of higher education from the city to the state.

2. It would increase the quality of public higher education in Chicago.

3. It would meet better the educational needs of the Chicago Metropolitan Area.

The financial savings to the Chicago Board of Education under the Master Plan would be as follows:

There would be an immediate saving of $5 million per year, which is the approximate cost of the Chicago City Junior College over and above what is received from the state. This amount will increase during the next few years as junior college enrollment grows. The $5 million or more would have to be raised by the new Junior College Board through local taxes separate from the tax levied by the Chicago Board of Education, or through increased aid from the state.

Under the Master Plan the Chicago Board of Education would be relieved of the responsibility for providing money for new buildings for the Teachers College and the Junior College. A conservative estimate of the money needed immediately for new buildings is $25 million, with an equal sum needed within the next five years. The Chicago Board of Education would have to get approval through a referendum for a bond issue of some $50 million, in addition to what it will need for new high schools and elementary schools, if it undertakes to build the needed buildings at its own expense.

It may be supposed that some federal government funds will become available for college buildings, but such funds will probably not be more than one-tenth of what is needed. They would come through the State Board of Higher Education, together with state funds. The Chicago Board of Education will have to work out some kind of financial arrangements with the State Board of Higher Education if it decides to remain in this field.

ADMINISTRATION AND FACULTIES
OF THE COLLEGES

Some major changes are recommended by the Survey Committee for the Teachers College and the Junior College. These changes could take place with relative ease under the state Master Plan. However, they should be made as soon as possible, and the committee urges the Board to start them, no matter what decision is made concerning the Master Plan.

Certain recommendations apply equally to the Teachers College and the Junior College, while others apply particularly to one or the other. The more general recommendations will be given first, followed by those dealing with the separate institutions. Before presenting any recommendations we shall describe the colleges.

Chicago Teachers College

In 1869, with state authorization, the Cook County Board of Supervisors established its normal school in the village of Englewood. Englewood was later annexed to Chicago, and after 1896 Chicago controlled the school. But in 1951 the General Assembly of Illinois provided for state support of Chicago Teachers College, as it is now known, in the form of reimbursement to the Board of Education for the operating expenses (but not capital costs) of the institution.

To relieve the overcrowding of the main Chicago Teachers College campus, one or more branches have been maintained since 1949. Their success and increasing enrollment pressures led to the decision in 1957 to establish a permanent North campus, which was opened in 1961. The old campus was named Chicago Teachers College South.

The primary purpose of both Chicago Teachers College South and North is to prepare teachers for kindergarten through eighth grade for the public schools of Chicago and its area. In addition, Chicago Teachers College South prepares teachers for Grades 7 through 12 in a number of fields, and both colleges provide extensive in-service training, as well as graduate work leading to the master's degree in a number of specialties.

Organization and administration. Chicago Teachers College South and North are under the jurisdiction of the Chicago Board

Table 1
Where Chicago teachers went to college

| | Percentages of classroom teachers who studied in each type of institution | |
	Elementary	High school
Normal school	10	8
Chicago Teachers College	53	29
Other teachers college	10	9
Liberal arts college or university	57	75
Teacher education courses after gaining a bachelor's degree	28	29
Industry	2	9
Number of teachers	6,954	3,729

Note: Many teachers have studied in more than one institution, as graduates or undergraduates. Consequently the percentages total more than 100.

of Education with the General Superintendent of Schools exercising administrative control through his Associate Superintendent in Charge of Higher Education.

No formal relationships exist between Chicago Teachers College North and South except through the Associate Superintendent in Charge of Higher Education, although there are a number of informal contacts.

In order to comply with a provision in the School Code of Illinois, a single Chicago Teachers College exists for certain fiscal and other report purposes. Teachers College South has two campuses, one being the Crane Campus on the west side of the city, whose chief administrative officer is responsible to the Dean of CTC South.

The Teachers College has provided basic teacher training for approximately half of the elementary school classroom teachers, as can be seen in Table 1. This table comes from the Study of Teachers, in which they were asked where they had secured their preparation for teaching. Many teachers have attended more than one higher institution as undergraduates or graduate students, and consequently the percentages in Table 1 total more than 100. It appears that about half of the present classroom teachers attended Chicago Teachers College while an equal number prepared for teaching in a liberal arts college or a university. About one-fourth of high school teachers also have studied in Chicago Teachers College. Many of these started as elementary school teachers, took courses to prepare for high school subjects, such as history, science, and English, and eventually transferred to high school teaching.

Finance. The basic operating costs of the Teachers College program are reimbursed by the state. In addition, the colleges charge modest student fees of $20 a trimester. Funds for capital expenditures for equipment and physical plant are provided by the Board of Education. Construction funds for the new Chicago Teachers College North campus were obtained through a bond issue of approximately $7,000,000. Additional amounts for urgently needed space and to remodel or rebuild the South campus and to expand the Crane campus seem unlikely of attainment under the existing tax structure for the city. A substantial increase in the budget for maintenance would seem essential, however. The inadequacy of proper maintenance of the South campus plant, especially at Crane, reduces teaching effectiveness and is readily apparent to the visitor.

Certain discrepancies seem to exist between the budgetary allotments to the two campuses. In 1962–63, for example, the semester-hour credits at the South campus were 67 percent greater than those at the North campus. The instructional budget for South, however, was only 7 percent more. In 1961–62, South had 120 percent more semester-hour credits but only 23 percent more dollars. While the differences in the budgetary allocations for the two campuses may reflect North's emphasis upon innovation and experimentation, it must be pointed out that the South campus offerings include a substantial graduate program (the most expensive per student) which this past year saw 198 students complete their course requirements for the master's degree. For the year ending with the winter trimester of 1963–64, the number of students enrolled in extended day classes for master's degree credit was:

South (including Crane)   1,996

North   498

Because it has more space per student and better equipment, the North campus costs more to operate. Also, the North campus has needed substantial funds to build up a new library. Any equalization of funds should increase the allocation to the South campus without reducing the money for the North campus; neither institution is supported to the point of opulence.

The Chicago City Junior College

The Chicago Board of Education has provided tuition-free junior college education since 1911. Junior college courses were given at first in Crane Technical and Lane Technical High Schools and Senn High School. Crane Junior College, which reached an enrollment of 3,616 students in 1929, was closed as an economy measure in 1933; however, the next year a Junior College was opened with three branches: South Side Junior College, later renamed Woodrow Wilson; Wright Junior College on the North Side; and Medill Junior College, later renamed Herzl Junior College. This West Side branch was transferred to Crane Technical High School in 1954 and renamed Crane Junior College.

Enrollments rose to more than 6,000 by 1940, and increased rapidly after the war. The peak enrollment was 29,700 in 1963, and there is a large anticipated increase in 1964 due to the sharp rise in the number of 18-year-olds. The Junior College became more and more a "community college," adapting to the needs of the city and local community areas. Five additional branches were opened: the Amundsen Branch serving the northeast section of the city (1956); Southeast Branch in the Chicago Vocational High School building (1957); Fenger Branch in the Fenger High School building on the far South Side (1958); Bogan Branch serving the southwest area in the Bogan High School building (1960). The recognized need for a centrally located branch led to the purchase of a high-rise building in the center of the city, and the Loop Branch opened in September, 1962.

In 1956, a grant of $500,000 from the Ford Foundation enabled the Chicago City Junior College to study the feasibility of offering by television an accredited junior college program leading to an Associate in Arts Degree. Chicago was also the first city to use open circuit television for mass college education.

A considerable number of students attend on a part-time basis. If one counts the number of semester hours or credits for which students are registered and considers 15 semester hours as full-time, the number of "full-time" units is about 55 percent of the number of persons registered. The number of first-year students is more than double that of second-year students, indicating that many students drop out after a semester or two, some going to four-year colleges, but many simply stopping their formal education.

Functions of the Junior College. As seen and defined by the administration of the Junior College:

> The Chicago City Junior College is a community institution organized to meet the *total* life needs of all its students: local, national, and world citizenship in a democratic society, family living, use of leisure time, appreciation of our cultural heritage, effective communication, and vocational preparation. In other words, the college should teach the students *how to live and how to make a living.*
>
> The junior college is organized (1) to educate the great majority of the junior college population for effective participation in a dynamic society into which these students will immediately go after one or two years of study, and (2) to provide the first two years of specialized or pre-professional study for such students who expect to transfer to higher institutions of learning, and (3) to offer an extension of the college facilities to the adult members of the community.
>
> As a community institution, the city junior college must maintain close ties with the high school. It must adapt standards and curriculum content to students with varying levels of ability and interests, so that all students may "grow" in understanding of our dynamic society and may achieve desirable changes in their behavior patterns.

To serve these functions, the Junior College offers the following curricula.

The liberal arts curriculum. This may lead to further study in a four-year college or university, or it may complete the student's college education.

Curricula leading to professional schools in a university. Agriculture; Architecture; Art; Business; Dentistry; Engineering; Chemical

Engineering; Food Service Administration, Home Economics, Dietetics; Industrial Relations; Journalism; Law; Medicine; Veterinary Medicine; Music; Nursing; Pharmacy; Physical Education; Social Service; Speech and Drama; Teaching in Elementary and High School; Industrial Vocational Training.

The largest single group of students consciously aims for transfer to a four-year college. In a questionnaire study made in 1963, 46 percent of the students said they were expecting to transfer to a four-year college, while 41 percent were expecting to get a job based on the two-year curriculum. Another 13 percent said they had special interests which did not fit either a four-year college or an occupational program.

Curricula leading to positions in business or industry. General Business; Merchandising; Secretarial; Medical Secretarial; Engineering Technical; Home Economics.

Of special interest in this connection is the growing enrollment in business courses, from 6,150 in 1955 to 12,460 in 1963.

Technical and semitechnical education. Technical education is a primary function of junior colleges; it is characterized by the application of knowledge from basic fields of science and mathematics with emphasis upon practical aspects. Semitechnical education involves less emphasis on cognitive skills and more on manipulative skills; it includes training of repairmen for office machines and other complex machinery.

Estimates made in 1960 indicated that Illinois would need 20,000 new technical and semitechnical workers each year in the 1960's. Yet the Master Plan committee reported that in 1962 Illinois produced fewer than 3,000 graduates from post-high school technical and semitechnical programs of one or two years.

Services to gifted high school students. The Junior College offers a number of college-level courses in which the gifted high school student can get college credit for some of his work. In 1963 there were 1,372 students from 35 high schools who took such courses. Some courses were given in high school buildings, some in junior college buildings, and some by TV.

TV College. The TV College is an integral part of Chicago City Junior College and offers courses leading to an Associate in Arts Degree. Courses are offered to regular college students and to students who are unable to attend classes or who find the schedule inconvenient, such as housewives and handicapped and institutionalized persons.

TV College has served almost 70,000 individuals in over 100,-000 course registrations. In the autumn of 1963, 2,846 individuals enrolled in the TV program for credit, equivalent to a full-time registration of 838. There were 3,940 noncredit enrollments. Television students are predominantly women, mature and highly motivated.

One out of six June, 1963, graduates had credit for television courses. There were six graduates in Stateville Reformatory. Since 1956, 900 graduates have taken some work by television; of these, 95 had all of their work by television.

Services to adults continuing their education. The continuing education of adults through regular college-credit courses offered in the evenings has been a major service of the Chicago City Junior College. The TV College has extended this service to thousands of adults who might not otherwise have been able to attend.

Services to students with academic deficiencies. A Basic Program of precollege courses has been developed for students who need additional preparation before attempting the regular junior college programs. Two branches, Wright and Wilson, now offer this program. One-third of the entering first-year students at Wilson are placed in the basic studies, while about 10 percent of applicants at Wright are so scheduled.

Although some success has been achieved, only 4 percent of the students in the Basic Program at Wilson completed four semesters of college-level work. It was concluded that the emphasis should be shifted away from college preparation and toward a terminal job-training program.

Other developments. Recently, with the aid of National Defense Education Act funds and grants from the Kellogg Foundation, the Junior College has been developing a variety of two-year technical programs and two-year business internship curricula. A Nurse Training Program is one example.

Administrative organization and finance. The City Junior College is legally one institution consisting of eight branches. Administrative responsibility is exercised by the General Superintendent of

Table 2
Comparative costs per pupil
by kind of school,
1961–62

	Cost per pupil
Junior College	$ 578
Teachers College	1,055
Regular high school	581
Trade, vocational, commercial high school	701
Regular elementary	442

Schools and through his office by the Associate Superintendent in Charge of Higher Education. Authority is delegated from the central administration to the Executive Dean of the Chicago City Junior College. Each of the branches is administered by a dean, who is assisted by an administrative staff.

The Chicago City Junior College was completely financed through local taxation until 1955 when the Illinois State Legislature provided $100 state aid for each full-time student. This was increased to $200 in 1957. Since 1959, the state has provided a flat grant of $7.60 per credit hour (about $225 for a full-time student for two trimesters).

Cost per student. The cost per student (full-time equivalent) has increased from $488 in 1956–57 to $578 in 1961–62. The cost per credit hour was $18.60 for 1962–63. Table 2 shows the costs per student were higher in the regular and vocational high schools than in the Junior College, although the costs in the latter have risen to $595 in 1962–63, and will probably be $610 in 1963–64.

Student charges. Although there are no tuition charges for Chicago residents, there is a general service fee of $5 per trimester for those taking eight trimester hours or less and $10 per trimester for those taking more than eight trimester hours. There are also fees for laboratory courses. Under the proposed state Master Plan, junior college education will continue to be free.

Nonresidents of Chicago may be admitted but are required to pay tuition in addition to the regular fees, based on the cost of instruction. For 1963–64 tuition for nonresidents of Illinois was $19.10 per trimester hour; residents of Illinois, but not of Chicago, paid $11.50.

Relation to the State Master Plan

The Teachers College and the Junior College should be developed in accordance with the State Master Plan for higher education. This means that the Teachers College would be placed under the governance of the Board of Governors of State Teachers Colleges, and the Junior College would be transferred to a new local Junior College Board which would deal with the state through a state Junior College Board.

The chief reason for this recommendation is that the colleges should be directed and supported by an agency which focuses its full attention on higher education. The Chicago Board of Education must give its major attention to elementary and secondary schools, and thus either overlook the problems of the colleges or apply solutions appropriate only to the lower schools. It would not be necessary to sacrifice the close relationships of the colleges to the problems of the local area if this change in governance were carried out.

If the above recommendation is not accomplished at the next session of the Illinois General Assembly, the following improvements should be given immediate attention by the General Superintendent of Schools and the Board of Education.

Administrative responsibility
for the Teachers College and
the Junior College

Major responsibility for the administration of the Teachers College and of the Junior College should be assigned to its immediate head administrator—at present the Dean. The responsibilities of this official should be commensurate with those of the president of an institution of higher education elsewhere, subject to limitations which are necessary in order to deal with the Board of Education through the General Superintendent of Schools. As part of this increased responsibility, the Dean should have charge of the physical plant of his institution.

Faculty—certification and personnel policy

There is some difficulty in recruiting faculty for the colleges in spite of relatively satisfactory salary levels. According to faculty members and administrators, this difficulty centers around the examination and related procedures necessary to secure a permanent position.

No person may be employed as a teacher or administrator at any grade level (including college) in the Chicago Public Schools without a certificate issued under the authority of the Board of Education. The Board of Examiners, composed of the General Superintendent and two additional members appointed by him, is authorized by law to issue certificates under policies established by the Board of Education.

There are three major steps in the process of securing a permanent position. The first is to secure a temporary certificate, which results from the Dean's recommendation and request to the Board of Examiners that they review the candidate's credentials, primarily transcripts of college and university work completed. If the candidate has met the requirements, the Dean submits a recommendation to employ the candidate to the Associate Superintendent for Higher Education. This then goes to the General Superintendent, and if he concurs, to the Board of Education.

The second step is to place the candidate on "trial period." This may or may not be done at the time of initial employment. The Dean's recommendation must have the approval of the Associate Superintendent for Higher Education, the Board of Examiners, the General Superintendent, and the Board of Education. The recommendation may be disapproved at any of these points.

The trial period status, though not a legal status, must be held for at least two trimesters before the candidate can take the examination for the permanent certificate. The examination for the final certificate consists of three parts: (*a*) a written examination dealing largely with the philosophy, curriculum, and methods of teaching in a teachers college or a community college; (*b*) the Dean's evaluation of the applicant during the trial period; and (*c*) an oral examination to evaluate the applicant's record and provide an opportunity for a committee, selected by the Board of Examiners, to confer with the candidate. The written examination does not include questions in the applicant's major field of scholarship but does include questions on how to teach his field.

After the certificate is granted, the appointee is on probation for three years, including the time spent teaching on the temporary certificate.

The Survey group asked the Board of Examiners whether this kind of examination was necessary, and received the following explanation:

1. The law requires that "the Board of Examiners . . . shall prepare all necessary eligible lists. . . ."

2. Eligible lists can be prepared only upon the basis of scores received on written and oral examinations.

An alternative to the examination, consisting of scrutiny of the applicant's credentials along with an evaluation of his teaching by the Dean and letters concerning him from scholars in his own field, was regarded as unacceptable by the Board of Examiners. However, the Survey group believes this alternative to be legally acceptable.

In any case, this procedure would not be required if the colleges were to pass to other governing bodies as is proposed in the state Master Plan.

The attitudes of faculty members are indicated in the returns on the Teacher Questionnaire given in Table 3.

In answer to the question: What is your attitude in general about your present position? the responses were as follows, in percentages:

	Junior College	Teachers College
Very favorable	28	36
Favorable	46	46
Neutral	12	9
Unfavorable	10	6
Very unfavorable	3	2

Table 3
*Selected data from Junior College
and Teachers College questionnaire*

		% satis- fied	% neutral	% dissat- isfied
Salary	Junior College	49	28	24
	Teachers College	58	26	16
Examination procedure for securing a certificate	Junior College	13	26	62
	Teachers College	15	22	64
Experience with process of obtaining tenure	Junior College	28	37	35
	Teachers College	29	31	40
Faculty participation in selection and promotion of staff members	Junior College	15	34	51
	Teachers College	29	47	24
Chance to work on challeng- ing projects and experiments	Junior College	28	38	33
	Teachers College	38	31	30
Size of classes	Junior College	29	34	37
	Teachers College	45	32	21
My work load	Junior College	34	21	45
	Teachers College	53	24	23

Conditions affecting staff morale. In general, the opportunities for attendance at professional conferences and meetings away from the campus and out of state seem quite satisfactory, and funds are available for out-of-state travel. Provisions of faculty rank and a special salary schedule are other examples of desirable differential treatment. These policies were found to have had a beneficial effect on the *esprit de corps.*

The Survey team found, however, that attempts to force the colleges into the mold established for the elementary and secondary schools were reducing *esprit de corps* in the colleges, and working unnecessary hardships on faculty and administration. The following examples were reported:

1. Required procedures for employing faculty members create problems as described in a presentation by representatives of the Chicago Teachers College Chapter of the American Association of University Professors at a hearing of the State Board for Higher Education in May, 1964. Following is a quotation:

> Certification procedures for College faculty are controlled by the Board of Examiners of the Chicago Public Schools. In order to be permanently appointed to the staff of the College, faculty members must submit to a written and an oral examination conducted by that body. There have been cases of teachers found qualified in their fields of specialization by professors in their graduate schools, found qualified by their colleagues on the faculty of the Teachers College, recommended for appointment by the Dean of the College, then deemed uncertifiable by the Board of Examiners on the basis of a written examination consisting of broad, general questions, typically not related to the candidate's field of specialization, and a brief oral examination. In the last two months, there have been two instances known by this speaker in which extremely promising prospects for faculty positions at the College have broken off negotiations for hiring when informed of the cumbersome and somewhat humiliating certification procedure which they would have to undergo.

Although the specific cases mentioned above have not been verified, the Survey team is convinced that the procedure does prevent the College from recruiting a number of the most able faculty members. This was also reported for the Junior College by the "College Committee" chaired by Dean Peter Masiko, in a memorandum of May 17, 1962, in which he recommended:

> The recruitment, certification and evaluation of college teachers is the responsibility of the college administrative staff. This is the standard practice in American colleges and universities, and this, in general, was the intent of the changes in practices which the accrediting agencies prescribed as a condition of accreditation in 1941.

2. Board of Education rules specify that all teachers must sign time sheets for a certain number of hours each day. Such a ruling

interferes with maintenance of the scholarship of faculty members and causes scholars to reject appointments in Chicago Teachers College.

3. Board of Education rules require that an applicant for sabbatical leave file either a travel plan, or a plan for organized study which must involve taking classes at an institution of higher learning. A distinguished professor of linguistics in one of the Teachers Colleges wished to pursue independent research but could not because he was required to attend classes.

4. Members of the professional faculty do not have keys and thus cannot get into the building on Saturdays and Sundays, or in the evening when the building is not opened for classes. The library is open only while classes are in session. Access to buildings is also limited by the numerous single holidays required of the elementary and high schools.

5. The budget makes no regular provision for released time for research, professional writing, or other similar activities. The effect is to discourage these activities which are in need of encouragement in all colleges.

Faculty participation in policy making

In the Teachers College and the Junior College there has been dissatisfaction with the role of the faculty in making educational policy. This is seen in Table 4, page 300.

The power of the college faculties in policy making is difficult to define since it is not formally defined in writing. There is an elected faculty council at each branch of the Teachers College and the Junior College. The Junior College Faculty Council was established in April, 1964, when the combined college faculty approved a constitution for the Council, indicating its expectation that the Council will represent and act for the faculty in "all matters of general policy affecting the welfare of the Chicago City Junior College, and shall act in an advisory, consultative, and planning capacity to the Executive Dean."

The faculty of the Teachers College has had more responsibility through its councils on the North and South campuses. Both faculties seem to be substantially involved in such matters as selection and admission of students, development and adoption of curricula, and

Table 4
*Selected data from Junior College
and Teachers College questionnaire*

		% satis- fied	% neutral	% dissat- isfied
Faculty participation in	Junior College	14	27	59
educational policy making	Teachers College	32	29	39
Channels for discussion and	Junior College	17	36	47
settlement of grievances	Teachers College	22	39	39
Faculty participation in	Junior College	15	34	51
selection and promotion of	Teachers College	29	47	24
staff members				
Relations with administrators	Junior College	58	22	19
in my college	Teachers College	74	16	10

establishment of standards for retention and graduation. One has
the impression that such faculty involvement exists because the
deans permit and encourage it rather than because it is established
by legislation or written policy.

In course and curricular matters, decisions are normally the
province of the individual college faculty. When North campus was
initiated, however, details of its curriculum were approved specifically by the Board of Education, leaving the faculty with little control over the curriculum. The action by the Board appears to be
contrary to sound delineation of responsibilities between the faculty,
the administration, and the Board.

In both Teachers College North and South, and in the Crane
branch, there seems to be strong support of the administration by
the faculty and a feeling that the Deans, and the Assistant Dean of
the Crane branch, are doing everything possible to improve condi-

tions and build better programs. The central office is viewed as frequently standing between these officials and their goals. One of the most apparent deterrents to good faculty morale is a reflection of public school philosophy and practice in policies governing the colleges.

It seems likely that, when the faculty councils become more active, the level of faculty satisfaction will rise.

Faculty rank

A system of faculty rank with differential salary schedules was introduced in the Teachers College in 1958 and in the Junior College in 1962. Promotions are made on the recommendation of the Dean and the General Superintendent of Schools. Faculty committees on promotion are consulted. Promotions are based on teaching performance, research and professional activity, educational preparation, experience and length of service, and college service.

Academic calendar

The colleges introduced the trimester system in September, 1962. Under the trimester system the academic year is divided into three basic units of 16 weeks each. Beginning in September, 1963, the calendar consisted of a 16-16-8-8-week year with a 12-week term superimposed on the second trimester to accommodate midyear high school graduates. Difficulties of scheduling and record keeping were greatly increased; it was estimated that the work of the registrar's office was increased by almost 50 percent.

Nevertheless, the plan allows a student to cover three years' work in two, with all-year attendance. It keeps the buildings in use the year round and will help to reduce overcrowding in the critical years ahead.

The Junior College faculty in general opposes the trimester plan at present, as is seen in the following responses to questions on the Teacher Questionnaire.

In your judgment, does the trimester system in your college:

Work to the advantage of most students?	20 percent
Work to the detriment of most students?	66 percent
No opinion	14 percent

In your judgment, does the trimester system in your college:
Facilitate good program planning and course scheduling?   8 percent
Complicate planning, scheduling, and preparation?   84 percent
No opinion   6 percent

The Teachers College faculty was not asked these questions.

It is recommended that the new Faculty Council study the trimester plan, together with other possible plans for maximal use of the buildings.

TEACHERS COLLEGE FACILITIES AND PROGRAM

The North campus is an extremely attractive and functional facility. In addition to provision for various new media of instruction, the facilities include attractive study carrels for students and attractive open-type architecture. A major air-conditioning program is begun, and should carry on to include the entire plant.

In contrast, the South campus is discouragingly drab, inadequate, and ill-kept. The return of a major building from recent use by Wilson Junior College makes space more nearly adequate on the campus. But lighting is poor in many of the classrooms; there are no laboratories for certain sciences; the auditorium and stage are inadequate; and library stack space is so grossly insufficient that the library is forced to discard a book each time it adds a new one.

The libraries on both campuses are inadequate in current holdings, as well as in the annual budget for acquisitions. It was reported on both campuses that there are difficulties in getting other than current books. Such problems limit the development of adequate library holdings for a college-level program, especially one which includes graduate work.

The Crane Branch of Teachers College South was started in 1956 to help meet the need for new teachers in the West Side schools. In 1963-64 it has an enrollment of 254 day students and 1,264 in the extended-day program. Crane now has a cadre of 16 full-time instructors, as well as 57 part-time lecturers. A large growth is expected for 1964-65.

Occupying four classrooms of a building used for other purposes, Crane offers 36 classes in 16 different locations in the city. Its housing is entirely inadequate for anything other than a small, temporary operation. Yet it is doing a remarkable job of recruiting people who go on to teach on the West Side. Of a group of over 200 graduates, some 70 percent are now teaching in West Side schools. It has specialized in the problems of teaching in the inner city.

None of the campuses, including North, makes adequate provision for faculty study and research through libraries or laboratories and by having buildings available many hours each day.

Instructional program

Chicago Teachers College South and North educate teachers for grades kindergarten through 8; but only the South campus prepares teachers for the secondary grades in a number of fields. A similar program is needed for Chicago Teachers College North.

Chicago Teachers College North is different both in its original conception and in its present emphases. The curriculum at North is considered new and experimental, with emphasis on the liberal arts. More credit hours are required for graduation—144, as compared with 128 at South.

Both college programs are officially designed to produce graduates who have: (1) broad liberal arts background, that is, familiarity with the humanities; with the natural, social, and behavioral sciences, and with mathematics; (2) professional knowledge: courses in educational philosophy, educational psychology, and history of education; (3) professional skills: managing a classroom, working with children, supervising learning; (4) knowledge and understanding of the subject matter or areas to be taught.

To reach these objectives, Teachers College South and North proceed somewhat differently. The number of general liberal education semester (trimester) hours at CTCS ranges from 74 to 80; at CTCN from 84 to 96. At CTCS the number of required professional education hours ranges from 20 to 36, including seven semester hours in practice teaching. The number of professional course hours at CTCN is 21, of which three, in psychology, are counted as part of the general education requirement.

Student teaching. Student teaching, required in the senior year, carries normally six (North) or seven (South) trimester hours of credit. Participating students must first complete certain prerequisite professional courses.

The student teaches half-days, five days a week, for an entire trimester. In addition, two seminars are held each week during the trimester. Student teachers in kindergarten-primary, intermediate grades, and general elementary curricula teach at each of two grade levels; those with an upper-grade major field do all of their teaching in their field in the upper grades. Students preparing to teach at the high school level in business education and industrial education take teaching courses similar to those for upper-grade teachers.

Admission to student teaching at both colleges is by application, completed by the student but checked by the responsible college officer. The application includes a list of professional courses taken, and vital statistics. The procedure could be materially strengthened by making admission to student teaching a specific clearance point, formally requiring a recommendation from appropriate faculty members. This would also permit students with problems to be given special attention and counseling well in advance of the student teaching experience. Pre-student teaching laboratory experiences, mentioned on page 305, could also be an aid in screening students for student teaching.

Placement of student teachers is made through the Chairman of Student Teaching at South, and the Chairman of Education at North. The placement is made to a school, with recommendation for the experiences at two grade levels. The principal of the school has the final authority for placement, however, and student teachers are sometimes shifted without the authorization or prior knowledge of the college.

Student teacher placement with a cooperating (supervising) teacher should be determined jointly by representatives of the college and the school and only with the approval of the cooperating teacher.

The supervising counselors (college supervisors) of the Chicago Teachers College impressed the Survey team with their quality. The directors of student teaching are highly competent people, well qualified and experienced, and genuinely concerned about the students, the supervisors, and the total program. The typical supervising counselor is reported as having a load of 22 student teachers at North, 27 at South. The latter load should be reduced.

College supervisors attempt to visit their student teachers five or six times each trimester. In case of serious problems, there are more frequent visits. North reported that, if all goes well, there may be as few as three visits each trimester. After each visit, the counselor confers with the student teacher and, when possible, with the cooperating teacher.

A notably excellent feature of the CTC student teaching programs is the seminar, at which each college supervisor confers with all his student teachers. The seminars meet for two periods weekly, and are devoted to informal discussion of problems encountered by student teachers, as well as to highly structured presentations by students or faculty.

Student teaching grades are given by the college supervisor, but conferences with cooperating teacher and principal encourage cooperative decisions on marking. When student teachers are not succeeding, South's approach appears to favor an "incomplete" with repetition of student teaching, while North uses "withdrawal" as well as the "incomplete."

Pre-student teaching laboratory experiences. It would appear to be particularly necessary in preparing teachers for the Chicago area to require a pre-student teaching experience with children or youth in a community agency. The Urban Ecology and Urban Community courses seem to be especially well adapted to providing for such community observation and participation.

Field experiences. The Field Experience course at North, now an elective, should be given consideration as a required course. Individual differences in college student readiness and characteristics could be met by variation in the assignments. Excellent work of an individual nature is being done at Crane in preparing teachers for the highly challenging needs of that area.

Graduate study. Both CTCN and CTCS offer the master of arts degree in classroom teaching of English, mathematics, natural science, and social science. CTCN also offers the master of arts in special education. CTCS offers the master of education degree in school librarianship, the teaching of industrial education, the teaching of mentally handicapped (both educable and trainable), and school guidance. Now being phased out at CTCS are the master of education programs in the teaching of deaf and hard-of-hearing children, blind children, and partially seeing children. CTCS offers graduate courses (but no degree sequences) in art, music, and speech.

To be admitted to graduate work (at North or South) for the purpose of pursuing a master's degree, for keeping up professionally, or for working toward the third lane of the Chicago salary schedule (master's plus 36 hours), a student must hold a bachelor's degree from an accredited institution, be a United States citizen (or possess a State Department study permit), certify his intent to teach in Illinois, and have at least a B-minus undergraduate grade average.

In-service offerings. Both of the Teachers Colleges have extensive programs of late afternoon, evening, and summer classes and workshops for practicing teachers. The offerings for the last two winter trimesters and the eight-week summer sessions totaled 500 courses with 15,000 enrollments. Although the workshops and institutes are quite limited for a teacher population the size of Chicago's, both the number of classes and the enrollment in them are substantial.

In-service offerings may be initiated in several ways:

1. Informal requests from teachers, principals, district superintendents, or the Central Office staff lead to the trial of a new course or workshop. If there is enough interest, more sections are added.

2. Official requests come from the Central Office, particularly from the Department of Curriculum. For example, it has recently requested courses which will acquaint elementary school teachers with the "new mathematics," and has requested courses or workshops which will familiarize teachers with a new curriculum guide for the social studies.

3. Occasionally, a department of one of the colleges will propose courses that are designed to acquaint elementary or secondary school teachers with new developments related to the fields they are teaching.

In-service courses are reported to be not at all difficult to introduce. The faculty of each Teachers College guards its undergraduate and graduate programs rigorously but regards in-service workshops and institutes subject to less scrutiny. Thus, such offerings may be instituted by the Dean without approval by the faculty, although approval of the department concerned is required. Credit earned in a number of in-service courses cannot be counted toward degrees.

Requests for workshops appear to originate largely from the central administrative offices, whereas proposals for courses come from departments of the Colleges. Improvement might result from more joint planning involving college faculty members and officers of the central administration.

Emphasis on preparation of elementary school teachers?

A major question for which an answer must soon be provided has to do with the range of purposes of the Teachers College. Shall it restrict itself as far as possible to the preparation of elementary school teachers, or shall it extend further its preparation of high school teachers and its program of graduate work?

The argument for concentration on the preparation of elementary school teachers is based on (1) the difficulty of getting college students in a multipurpose institution to choose elementary school teaching among the various alternatives; and (2) the need for a substantial source of elementary school teachers to meet future needs of the Chicago schools.

The arguments for extending the program of the Teachers College to make it more of a multipurpose institution are (1) that the trend throughout the country is toward the preparation of elementary and high school teachers in the same institution, and (2) that Chicago's needs for school teachers will be better met by a Teachers College that prepares teachers for all levels in the schools and also offers graduate work for teachers.

At present, Teachers College South, in addition to preparing elementary school teachers, offers curricula for Business Education, Industrial Arts, Home Economics, and Physical Education which prepare teachers for high school work. Furthermore, a number of CTCS students follow a curriculum that prepares them for teaching departmentalized subjects in Grades 7 and 8, such as History, Mathematics, Natural Science, and Language Arts. These people customarily take and pass the examination for a high school certificate in these subjects, and thus are effectively, though not officially, prepared for high school teaching. No doubt these arrangements for preparing high school teachers are mainly responsible for the fact that CTCS has a woman to man ratio of 2:1 among students, while CTCN has a 5:1 ratio. Teachers College North would like to be allowed to offer a wider range of curricula.

The Survey Committee favors a continuing *main* emphasis on the preparation of teachers for elementary schools, combined with a *growing* emphasis on the preparation of high school teachers. The actual program of Teachers College should be a response to supply and demand factors during the coming years, which will be different from those of the past decade.

The demand for elementary school teachers will not be so strong as it was in the 1950's when the postwar increase of births flooded the elementary schools. During the next 10 years, however, the high schools will grow more rapidly than the elementary schools, and there will probably be a greater need in Chicago for new high school teachers.

In any case, the municipal teachers college that is limited to the preparation of elementary school teachers will soon be a thing of the past. State colleges and public universities which are located in or near big cities are taking most of the load of teacher preparation, and they are all preparing high school and elementary school teachers in a single institution, generally with a parallel offering in liberal arts.

Service to the metropolitan area

Whether or not the Chicago Teachers College becomes a state college, it seems wise to plan for serving the Chicago Metropolitan Area. School enrollments in the suburbs are growing rapidly, while enrollments in the city will soon level off and become relatively stable. The need of suburban school systems for teachers will be met largely by Chicago institutions. At present, 10 percent of day students at CTCS and 20 percent at CTCN are residents of the suburbs.

The proportion of suburban students is bound to increase if Chicago Teachers College serves them well. If it does not do so, there will be a pressure for the establishment of new state colleges in the southern and the northwestern suburbs. Such a development would probably reduce the level of state support for CTC, and also reduce its attractiveness to good students.

It seems desirable for public teacher-preparation institutions to serve the entire metropolitan area, as they do in almost all of the big cities.

JUNIOR COLLEGE FACILITIES
AND PROGRAM

The First and Second Reports of the Chicago City Junior College, presented in 1956 and 1958 by Superintendent Willis to the Board of Education, laid out plans for expansion of the College to its present eight branches. This expansion has been accomplished by using existing high school buildings on a part-time basis, by purchasing and remodeling a building at 71st Street and Stewart Avenue, and by securing a downtown building to house the Loop Branch.

The reports of 1956 and 1958 both regarded this expansion as a preliminary phase to a period of new building construction. The 1958 report speaks of 1960 to 1965 as a "period of building construction." It says:

> The first phase, however, is an interim one, looking forward to the period of building construction starting after 1960. A high quality college program is made possible within proper building facilities. Adequate classrooms, laboratories, and library facilities must be available. In addition, the branches should have sufficient private office space for counseling with students and for study. To provide these necessary facilities will require new building construction as well as conversion of some existing buildings for junior college use.

This period is almost over, but there has been no new building construction. Meanwhile, the Junior College is growing rapidly and needs more than ever the new quarters which it has so long been denied. At its meeting on July 10, 1963, the Board of Education took steps to authorize some new construction, but none has been started.

If the recommendation of the state Master Plan is adopted, the state will pay 75 percent of the cost of new buildings constructed by the Junior College Board. This Board will want to share certain buildings with the present Board of Education—buildings which can be used for late afternoon and evening classes. Close cooperation will be needed between the two boards.

If this plan is not adopted, the Chicago Board of Education should place a high priority on the early construction of new Junior College buildings. The survey of building facilities in Supplement B will give some idea of the inadequacy of the present situation. Classrooms are overused; office space is scarce or nonexistent; library and

Table 5
*Selected data from Junior College
and Teachers College questionnaire*

		% satis- fied	% neutral	% dissat- isfied
Physical facilities of the buildings in which I work	Junior College	17	22	61
	Teachers College	33	9	58
Materials and equipment with which to work	Junior College	38	29	33
	Teachers College	42	26	32
The library in my college	Junior College	53	22	26
	Teachers College	44	25	31
Availability of professional materials and journals	Junior College	52	27	20
	Teachers College	56	22	23

laboratory facilities are grossly inadequate; parking space for students and faculty is badly needed.

The administrators of the Junior College and the Teachers College feel that the inadequacy of physical facilities is the largest single factor contributing to faculty dissatisfaction. Attitudes concerning facilities are shown in Table 5.

Libraries. Each branch of Chicago City Junior College has been provided with a library. In addition to a 3,000 volume reference and reserve library in the Wilson building, the Wilson Branch shares the maintenance and use of the Joint Library at Chicago Teachers College South. Library facilities at the Crane Branch are shared with the West campus of Chicago Teachers College South.

The libraries are in general adequately staffed, meeting American Library Association standards of at least two professional librarians and one full-time nonprofessional staff member for any junior college with an enrollment up to 500 students (full-time equivalent).

Generally, a professional librarian is on duty during all library hours.

The critical shortage of space and the inadequacy of funds are evident in the book collections. The ALA recommendation is 20,000 volumes, exclusive of duplicates and textbooks, for a two-year institution of up to 1,000 students (full-time equivalent), and roughly 5,000 volumes in addition for every 500 students beyond 1,000. It is also suggested that seats should be provided for at least 25 percent of the student body, equated to full-time. Only Wright, Wilson, and Crane Branches reach the minimum of total volumes. Seats are available for less than 10 percent of the students.

The shortage of space in most branches prohibits expansion. Additional shelving can be provided only if seats are removed at Fenger, Bogan, Crane, Southeast, Wright, and the Joint Library at Chicago Teachers College South. At Chicago Teachers College South, at Wright, and at Crane each book added requires the discarding of a book. It is estimated that the installation of the shelving needed in 1964-65 will eliminate a minimum of 24 seats in the library of Southeast Branch.

The Junior College program

The effectiveness of the Junior College will be greatest and its influence in the area served will be more profound if it is organized as a community college. This essentially is the basic philosophy underlying the Chicago Junior College and its branches. The procedure for organizing a junior college on this basis is provided for in the report of the State Board of Higher Education—the final Master Plan.

Throughout the United States, junior colleges are not only developing rapidly, but are also being housed on separate campuses in adequate buildings amid aesthetic surroundings. Since Chicago has long maintained a junior college, it would seem now to have the golden opportunity of providing a junior college program that compares favorably with the rest of the nation. But drastic action must be taken immediately to develop a bold and imaginative plan for housing the college program.

Pending formation of a Junior College District, the College would remain under the jurisdiction of the Chicago Board of Education. During this period steps should be taken immediately to develop a five-year Master Plan, aimed at providing the educational and non-instructional program necessary to fulfill general institutional objectives. A major part of the plan should relate to the acquisition of new facilities and the modernization of existing ones.

Counseling, vocational guidance, and job placement. A junior college program in a big city must offer different things to a wide variety of students. A considerable proportion of the student body has disadvantages—in academic potential, in past academic achievement, in level of educational background, in attitudes and values. Some students lack an understanding of what it means to be a college student. They expect to work full-time while following a college-level curriculum. Counseling is essential for these students.

Individual counseling is limited to full-time day students (39 percent of the students) and academic counseling is emphasized almost exclusively. There were seven full-time counselors in the Chicago City Junior College in 1963-64. The 1964 annual budget provides for the equivalent of 19.3 full-time counselors. These counseling positions are usually distributed as part-time assignments among academically oriented teachers, as released time from teaching to be used for a counseling class or for counseling students individually.

Three branches (Bogan, Fenger, and Crane) have no full-time counselors. Three branches (Amundsen-Mayfair, Loop, and Southeast) have one full-time counselor. The registrar acts as the main academic counselor in branches which have no full-time counselors. In those branches with one full-time counselor, the counselor, in addition to being director of academic counseling and programming, usually acts as director of student activities, vocational guidance and placement counselor, director of placement testing, supervisor of advanced placement, veterans' counselor, foreign student advisor, Selective Service counselor, college representative to high schools, and is a member of the admissions committee, the probation and exclusion committee, and others. Counselors are often tied up during registration in administering examinations, although this is the time many students have the greatest need for counseling.

Personal counseling by clinical psychologists is available at Wright Branch. The others refer students with serious personal problems to agencies in the community.

The need for academic and personal counseling on the part of the older, part-time students is probably not as great as that of day students, but a great many evening students could probably make good use of counseling services.

Group counseling is offered for approximately one-half of the entering freshmen in some branches in the form of courses. Orientation to college, library use, selecting a college program, choosing a career, etc., are among the topics discussed in these courses. Vocational interest inventories and other tests are generally given.

The counseling courses are taught by trained counselors or by regular teachers, some of whom have no background for formal counseling. It is not unusual to find a counseling course with 40 to 50 students registered. Students who are likely to take courses leading directly to a job need especially some aptitude testing and some help in selecting vocational courses at the time they enter college. Job placement services are available in most of the branches. The registrar or counseling office either keeps a file or posts part-time or full-time employment opportunities on the bulletin board.

Institutional research. For as wide a range of college offerings as a community college with such a diversified student body must provide, it is essential to have a competent staff, with time and money for research and development. This is needed and has been provided for a major innovation, such as the TV College. It is also needed for less ambitious undertakings.

The Division of Institutional Research and Evaluation of the Chicago City Junior College conducts many activities aimed at institutional improvement. Supervision of examinations used in required general education courses, consultation service in the development of valid and reliable examination materials or research projects, and collection of data each term in the testing program are examples of the areas in which this Division is engaged. It has also assisted in major research projects, including a three-year analysis of open-circuit television instruction.

The Wright Branch established a Committee on Research Projects to coordinate and assess projects submitted by the faculty for which released time from teaching duties is requested. A faculty committee of Wilson Branch conducted an analysis of students which preceded the establishment of the precollege basic program. The registrars at Crane and Bogan conducted follow-up studies of graduates.

The Junior College administration has shown substantial interest, but resources of the College have been primarily channeled into instruction, and the result has been minimum funds, time, and personnel for research activity.

RECOMMENDATIONS

General

1 The Teachers College and the Junior College should be developed in accordance with the state Master Plan for higher education.
2 Major responsibility for the administration of the Teachers College and of the Junior College should be assigned to its immediate head administrator.
3 Procedures for employing faculty should be simplified, and the present practice of examinations for certification should be discontinued.
4 Faculty should participate more fully in the making of educational policy.
5 Further development of the scholarly activity of the faculty should be encouraged.
6 Libraries should be substantially enlarged, with more efficient provision for the prompt acquisition of books.

Teachers College

1 Teachers College South should have a new campus, and planning and construction should commence very soon. Study should be given to the need for a West campus to replace the present inadequate facilities of Crane Branch of CTC South.
2 The instructional program should be extended
   a) by additional emphasis on the training of high school teachers,
   b) by additional emphasis on graduate work,
   c) by improved coordination of the in-service activities provided for teachers.
3 The instructional program should be strengthened
   a) by provision of laboratory sciences at Teachers College South,

b) by provision of pre-student teaching laboratory experience,

c) by making the assignment of student teachers a joint responsibility of college and school personnel. No assignment by unilateral action of the principal of a school or the supervisor of student teaching should be possible.

4 Procedures for student admission and promotion should be studied thoroughly by the faculty councils.

a) A time for admission to advanced standing in each teacher education curriculum should be set. Among requirements for such admission should be average marks, recommendation of the major subject matter department (if the student is in a curriculum which requires a major), and evaluations of the student's physical well-being, his speech, and his personality.

b) Admission requirements should be studied with a view to making them somewhat more stringent. At present, both colleges are accepting students from the lowest quarter of their graduating classes.

c) Consideration should be given to providing alternatives to teacher education curricula, so that students will not be required to leave the institution if they are found unsuited for teaching.

Junior College

1 There should be immediate and major action to get new buildings for the Junior College. This should be the major concern of the governing board and administration of the College.

2 The College should recruit more faculty members from outside the Chicago area. Although the quality of the faculty is good, it is desirable to have wider variation in past experience.

3 Admission policies and standards and a tuition-free policy should be continued according to the present regulations.

4 There should be continued development of terminal vocational courses related to the employment needs of the Chicago area.

5 The professionally trained counseling staff should be doubled, at least, and should contain specialists in vocational counseling and placement. New freshmen should be counseled before registration.

XIV

Adult Education in Chicago

The major reason why the Board of Education should sponsor a strong program of adult education is that it can in no other way so powerfully, positively, and immediately influence the quality of life in Chicago. The adult who increases his occupational skills adds at once to his and his city's economic capital. The adult who learns more about painting, music, drama, or the other arts becomes part of the participating audience needed to create a great cultural center. The adult who studies social and civic affairs becomes a more responsible citizen, helping to shape and carry out the policies not only of government but also of all those smaller public and private associations whose operation builds the texture of community life. The adult who raises the level of his general education opens doors for himself onto larger vistas of opportunity, and thereby refines and increases the human resources of Chicago.

* * *

This chapter was written by Professor Cyril O. Houle of the University of Chicago. It is based on his own familiarity with education in Chicago, and on the report of the Advisory Committee on Adult Education headed by Mr. George Overton. This report is summarized in Supplement C. The Survey also had the assistance of Dr. J. Richard Smith, Assistant Superintendent for Adult Education in the Los Angeles City Schools.

In these and other ways, adult education is vital to modern society. The adult can learn most things better than can the child, and his knowledge is put more directly to use. If the Board of Education hopes to elevate the quality of life in Chicago, it cannot depend solely on the delayed effect of the education of children, particularly because the children will be constantly conditioned as they come to maturity by a social order controlled by their elders.

Even if the Board of Education were to define its central task as the education of children, there would be urgent reason for it to sponsor strong adult educational activities. The 1963 Annual Report of the General Superintendent of Schools provides an illustration of this point:

> The effect of the educational level of parents on the educational needs of their children may be seen, perhaps most clearly, in the results of the tests for reading readiness administered to children when they enter first grade. In those school districts where, according to the 1960 U.S. Census data, the median number of years of education of adults 25 years of age and over is high, the percentage of children ready to read also is high; where the median adult level of education is low, the children's readiness-to-read scores also are low.*

What is graphically demonstrated by this specific index is true in other respects. The task of educating children at every level is shared jointly by the home, the school, and other community institutions. A program of adult education will not only enrich the cultural resources of the home and the community, but it will help adults (and particularly parents) to gain an insight into the learning problems encountered by their children. Moreover, the child will observe his parents studying, and thereby learn to accept education as a normal lifelong activity.

Two other arguments for adult education are frequently advanced and are worthy of mention. It is said, first, that adult education will provide sound public relations for the schools, since it brings within their walls those who elect the public officials, vote on bond issues, and give vocal expression to beliefs about what the schools should do and be. This argument is valid, but only if the program offered to the

---

*1953-1963, Ten Years of Growing. Annual Report of the General Superintendent of Schools, 1963, p. 6.

citizens is a good one; if it is poor, it can have strongly negative public-relations consequences. It is said, second, that a program of adult education will provide for a more complete utilization of the school plant. To the practical citizen, it seems a great waste that the large and sometimes magnificent facilities of the public schools should stand idle so much of the time. This argument, too, depends upon the quality of what is offered. If a program is poor or pedestrian, a school system is merely increasing its costs without gaining any benefits; it would be cheaper to let the buildings stand empty.

The Board of Education and the General Superintendent should regard such arguments as these as valid—but as secondary in significance. The primary purpose of the school system is education, and this fact is as true of its work with adults as in its offering of childhood education. The only ultimate test of a program is the extent to which it can improve the quality of life of the individual and of his society.

The Board of Education does not need to provide all—or even most—of the education required by the adult citizens of Chicago. The city already has many resources—universities, libraries, museums, community centers, and other institutions—which offer services for the general public; and industry, business, labor, religious groups, and voluntary associations provide education for those who come within their orbits of influence. But as yet, this total offering does not begin to meet the needs of the city, as a candid look at its problems manifests. There are many gaps in service, partly because of meager resources, partly because there is little awareness of what results might be brought about by a total community program, and partly because the many separate institutions have never learned to work effectively together.

But while the public school does not need to do everything, it must occupy a central place in providing educational services for adults as is true in childhood education (where there are also many youth-serving agencies). In the United States, more adults seek classroom instruction in the public school than in any other agency, and its significance as an instrument of mass service is destined to increase. The advantages of the public school are many. Its buildings are close to the people wherever they may live. The physical facilities are empty and available at precisely the hours when adults need them most. The public school system is accepted as the central educational instrument of our society. Perhaps most important, the schools have staff members and administrative officers who are deeply trained in educational matters and who can readily learn how to design and conduct educational experiences for adults. These advantages make it seem likely that, in most cities, the public school will develop as the major service agency to provide organized instruction.

If the Board of Education is to be the central influence for adult education in Chicago, it must move forward constructively to strengthen its own offering and to take the initiative to bring about a stronger community-wide effort. The four most immediate steps which it might take are these:

First, the Board should adopt a clear-cut policy statement defining its interest in and support of a strong adult educational program. This policy should be drafted by the appropriate administrative group, transmitted by the General Superintendent when it meets his approval, and discussed and adopted by the Board of Education when its own views have been incorporated. This policy should then be used to guide the processes of annual planning and review of program by the General Superintendent and his staff.

Second, the Board and the General Superintendent should move as rapidly as possible to place full-time professionally trained administrators in the key positions which carry out the Board's policies concerning adult education. (Other functions—such as special education, guidance, psychological services, or medical and nursing care—have been built up within the Chicago School System because able people dedicated to their mission and well prepared for it have been given the opportunity to work on a full-time basis to discharge the responsibilities to which they have been assigned.) To choose but one example, though perhaps the most important, the principals of the evening schools should be on full-time assignment prepared to carry out the duties which can only be accomplished by those who can dedicate their whole time to them; and these principals should have special preparation for their work, either before they assume it or on an in-service basis.

Third, the Board of Education and the General Superintendent should work toward the establishment of a strong city-wide Center for Adult Education in its own building, preferably near the heart of the city. While the program for this Center should evolve in terms of emerging needs, various categories of purpose can be suggested.

a. In some cases the Center could serve as a demonstration and experimental center, trying out activities which might then be made more widely available in evening schools or other places of instruction.

b. In other instances, the Center could provide a place to highlight and dramatize certain activities which have first been tested elsewhere.

c. The Center could offer the kinds of special or advanced education which draw their students from the whole city and which can therefore not be carried on in dispersed neighborhood locations.

d. The Center could collaborate with other major educational and cultural institutions, such as universities, museums, and music-sponsoring groups.

e. The Center could provide education which is needed by those who work in the heart of the city. Some such people might come because the Center is convenient, and others because it provides specialized programs particularly suited to the needs of those who work at the control center of the urban complex.

These broad purposes, and others which might be added, could make of the Center a brilliantly highlighted capstone for the entire public school adult education program, and could serve as a model for other cities.

Fourth, the Board of Education should take the lead to provide a more effective program of coordination of adult education within the city. This effort might go forward on at least two fronts.

First, there is no reason why the Adult Education Council cannot become as powerful an instrument of community planning in its area of service as is the Welfare Council of Metropolitan Chicago in the welfare field. What is needed is strong citizen and professional leadership. If the Board of Education and the administrative staff of the Chicago School System made evident their desire to work through the Adult Education Council with other institutions and programs of adult education in a mutually developed program of collaboration, the Council could evolve into a powerfully significant means of community planning and execution of program.

A second form of profitable collaboration might come with the appointment of citizen or professional advisory committees in connection with various programs carried on by the Chicago School System itself. The principal of an evening school, for example, might have a rotating advisory committee in which interested people, either lay citizens or professionals, such as personnel directors or the heads of neighborhood settlements could serve to provide counsel, support, and public relations assistance. The director of a fine arts program might have a similar committee. A widespread pattern of contacts of this sort between the school system and members of its community would itself be a powerful instrument for public understanding and enlightenment.

These four immediate goals will not be sufficient to guide Chicago's public school adult education program for very long, but they will make an essential beginning on the great task which must somehow be accomplished. The actual nature of the program at any given moment is a product of the will of the community as guided by its leaders and as shaped by the philosophy and competence of its educators. It may be hoped that Chicago's Board of Education and General Superintendent of Schools will rise to the challenge which confronts them.

XV

Pupil Personnel Services and Testing Program

E very school system provides certain nonclassroom services to its pupils. A recognized term for these services is Pupil Personnel Services, generally including such areas as attendance, guidance, school health, school psychological, and school social work services. The obvious purpose is to help the student to derive the maximum benefit from the educational program by seeing to it that he is present, in good health physically and mentally, and that his individual needs and problems are taken into account in the planning of his school program. In other words, the nonclassroom services are very important in helping the school to recognize and provide for individual differences in pupils.

In many school systems, all of these services are combined in a special Department of Pupil Personnel Services often headed by an assistant superintendent. In this way, it is hoped that all of the

*   *   *

The material in this chapter is in large part based on reports by Edward C. Roeber, Professor of Education, the University of Michigan; Bruce E. Shear, Director, Division of Pupil Personnel Services, New York State Education Department; and Robert L. Ebel, Professor of Education and Psychology, Michigan State University.

322

information about pupils will be brought together and treated in a coordinated manner, and that the representatives of the different professional services, at every level, will work together, sharing skills and knowledge in planning for pupils.

In Chicago, historical and personal factors appear to have resulted in a rather Topsy-like growth of pupil personnel services, with the result that they are divided at the central office level among three bureaus, the Bureau of Pupil Personnel Services, the Bureau of Child Study, and the Bureau of Medical and School Health Services.

The Bureau of Pupil Personnel Services includes the following divisions: guidance, evaluation and pupil studies, school attendance, work experience and post-high school guidance, and the very new social work section. The Director of this bureau reports administratively to the associate superintendents in charge of instruction.

The Bureau of Child Study provides psychological services. It also staffs reading clinics and conducts a training program for adjustment teachers in the elementary schools. However, the testing program in the elementary schools, which is conducted by the adjustment teachers, is now under the direction of the Bureau of Pupil Personnel Services. The Director of the Bureau of Child Study also reports to the associate superintendents for instruction.

Finally, the Bureau of Medical and School Health Services includes the teacher-nurse service, medical examinations for teachers and pupils, and the hearing and vision conservation program. The Director of this bureau reports to the associate superintendent for administration.

Although the plan of organization seems complicated, the consultants were agreed in commending the caliber of personnel engaged in these services and were impressed by the interest and enthusiasm which they displayed. They suggested, however, that "in the long run, there should be developed a plan for pulling together central and district operations into a single, coordinated pupil personnel program."

At the local level, the consultants were favorably impressed by the trend toward regarding the representatives of the various personnel services—attendance officer, psychologist, teacher-nurse—as members of the local school "team". However, inadequate staffing makes the team approach to the needs of individual pupils possible only in exceptional cases. The teacher-nurse is in a single school from two to eight days a month; the psychologist even less. Social work services are available only in rare cases in a very few districts.

Attendance services

A total of 224 attendance officers serve the public schools and some parochial schools. This ratio seems fairly adequate, if not too much time is given to the parochial schools. However, in certain inner-city schools where attendance problems are severe, more time of attendance officers is needed. A more serious problem is the qualifications of attendance officers for the work they are doing. Their positions are Civil Service, and there are no educational requirements, although the examination is said to be fairly demanding. The consultants commended the effort on the part of the Bureau to define the job of attendance officers as remedial rather than punitive and praised the materials prepared for in-service training of these officers. However, they were agreed that effective carrying out of the philosophy required higher levels of preparation and training. In other large cities (New York and Los Angeles), a bachelor's degree and courses in certain appropriate areas are required for all attendance officers. The low requirements and correspondingly low salaries of Chicago attendance officers lead to considerable turnover, so that too much of the in-service training program is spent in basic orientation of untrained applicants rather than in improving the qualifications of experienced officers.

The provision for supervision of attendance officers on the district level by head attendance officers is good, and should be strengthened in districts where the caseload is excessive. These officers should be qualified by training and experience to provide in-service training and supervision on the job of considerable depth.

The guidance program

Until recently, counselors in Chicago high schools specialized in some particular guidance function—employment, preparation for college, discipline, etc. Several years ago the decision was made to reorganize and strengthen the entire guidance program and to change the emphasis from a function-centered to a student-centered program, with the goal of assigning a particular student throughout his high school career to one counselor, who would advise him in all guidance areas: educational program, post-high school plans, scholastic problems, behavior and adjustment problems, and so on. Continuous contact with someone who cares is an essential part of a school's holding power.

The consultants give strong support to this change and to the philosophy and objectives of the guidance program and other supporting materials prepared by the guidance division in the central office. They also approve the participation of local school guidance personnel in preparing these materials. However, weaknesses were seen at the point of putting the program into practice in the local school. Recommendations were directed towards implementing the stated objectives and making it possible for guidance people to do a better job. A summary of these suggestions follows:

1. *Orientation at the local level.* As yet, the new philosophy and goals are not being implemented at the local level in some schools. This lag may be due to lack of communication, but even more likely, it is due to resistance to the newer concept of guidance as a developmental process. The high school principals, teachers, and counselors will need considerable interpretation and assistance before they can play their parts in developing sound guidance practices. One way to expedite this would be to develop pilot programs in different types of schools at the elementary, upper-grade, and high school levels. Adequately staffed and organizationally sound, these pilot programs would serve as models for other schools with similar problems.

2. *Pupil load.* Although progress has been made in reducing the ratio of pupils to counselors, it needs to be further reduced. The average ratio in high schools at present is 1/500 or 1/370, depending on whether assistant principals in charge of guidance programs or only full-time counselors are included in the count. Whatever the base used, these loads do not give counselors enough time to counsel students or to work with teachers, parents, and others in improving the learning environment for each student. A counselor/pupil ratio between 1/300 and 1/250, not counting assistant principals, would provide adequate guidance services for all students in most schools. For schools with substantial numbers

of culturally disadvantaged youth, the ratio of 1/250 might be considered too high.

3. *Work load*. Consultants felt that too much time of guidance counselors is spent on clerical work which ought to be handled by nonprofessional personnel and on routine attendance checking which should go through homeroom teachers and attendance officers, except in special cases:

> Examples were observed where from 50 to 90 percent of the counselor's time appeared to be taken up with checking, issuing, excusing, making record notations and probably just cajoling in relation to class cutting, tardiness, early leaving, and truancy. Ten to 20 percent is too much for such routines, as there are more effective ways to use the time of well-qualified counselors.

Also, it was suggested that the amount of time which some counselors have to give to work experience programs should be given consideration in assigning pupil loads.

4. *Preparation and supervision*. Counselors need substantially more graduate preparation in guidance and counseling, including supervised practice in individual and group counseling, and the opportunity for observation of good use of group guidance techniques. Supervisors need more graduate preparation, including training in the direct supervision of individual and group counseling of pupils and parents.

5. *Physical facilities*. The work of counselors can be extended and improved by more adequate facilities in many schools. Privacy for counseling, more waiting and browsing space, and readily accessible telephones are needed.

6. *Upper-grade elementary guidance programs*. The extension of the guidance program to upper-grade centers is to be commended. But there is no reason why counselors in these centers should carry a heavier load than high school counselors, as is now the case. This is a crucial period for all pupils and even more so for disadvantaged pupils. Efforts should be directed toward strengthening the guidance program at this level and tying it into the high school guidance program by close relationships and exchange of information and insights between upper-grade elementary and high school guidance personnel.

7. *Guidance of disadvantaged pupils.* Guidance procedures and materials should be adapted to meet the particular needs of disadvantaged pupils and their parents. Potential early school leavers need early identification and attention, and continuing guidance and counseling assistance. Counseling and group guidance, if necessary to reach parents, should be taken from the school to the home and into the community centers.

Unfortunately, as in other fields, the staff in schools serving these pupils tends to include a disproportionate number of inexperienced personnel, including some who do not have the required preparation for guidance positions. An effort is made to give these individuals the more routine chores, but this simply increases the load on experienced personnel.

Weaknesses were noted especially in some of the counseling in schools serving mostly Negro pupils. Cases were cited of Negro high school seniors with very high IQ's who were guided to less demanding colleges although they might have succeeded in the best colleges and universities in the country. On the other hand, some pupils make college plans who should seriously consider technical, skilled, or semiskilled noncollege jobs in which there are good opportunities. It is especially difficult for counselors of Negro pupils to avoid pitfalls; on the one hand, they must help students to evaluate themselves objectively in the light of the competition they will meet; on the other hand, special efforts should be made to acquaint more able students with the widest range of opportunities available and to encourage them to accept the challenge.

One difficulty has been a tendency to identify any special concern with guidance for Negro pupils as somehow discriminatory. This is wrong. Negroes do face special problems and special efforts have to be made to deal with them. A good approach would be the assignment of a task force to examine the special guidance problems of Negro pupils and to develop relevant principles and techniques. The task force could then work directly with guidance personnel in schools serving large numbers of Negro pupils.

Adjustment teachers in elementary schools

The elementary adjustment teachers are a unique Chicago institution. They are classroom teachers who have been selected by the school principal, freed from classroom teaching, and given a short training program planned and carried out by the Bureau of Child Study. Their original function was to "adjust" the school to the child; that is, make recommendations for his grade placement and give remedial help to individuals who needed special attention. As the testing program in the elementary schools has expanded, it has claimed an increasing amount of the adjustment teachers' time. In schools with high mobility, adjustment teachers also spend much time assembling and checking records of children as they come and go. As freed teachers, they are also called on for many emergency tasks, such as taking over a class when the teacher is absent, hurry-up reports, discipline cases, and so forth. The remedial teaching program and any guidance functions have to give way to these more immediate demands.

The consultants were agreed that the adjustment teachers are useful, but that their role needed clearer definition and that too much of their time was taken up with duties which should not be theirs. Remedial teaching and supervision of testing appear to be their most important functions. They would be able to concentrate on these services if their burden of routine work could be reduced through further automation and clerical help and if more adequate psychological and social work services were available. It was also suggested by one consultant that, with a little more training and a little more time, adjustment teachers could screen out some unnecessary referrals to the psychologists, reducing the number of time-consuming full-scale psychological examinations.

Health services

The Bureau of Medical and School Health Services is a part of the Department of Administration and thus is under an associate superintendent other than the ones responsible for the Bureau of Child Study and the Bureau of Pupil Personnel Services.

There are 139 teacher-nurses in the bureau, a staff of four medical doctors, and a corps of clerical workers. Most of the doctors' time is taken up with medical examinations of applicants for school positions, teachers, and occasionally pupils. In addition, the Bureau administers a hearing and vision testing program and a few other preventive programs.

Teacher-nurses. The consultants commended the guide for teacher-nurses and the basic philosophy of the teacher-nurse program. They were particularly impressed by the fact that teacher-nurse services are an integral part of the school system, rather than administered and granted to the schools by a public health agency, as in some large city systems. In the schools, they found the teacher-nurses in general have good working relationships with other school staff members. The almost universal cry, especially in schools serving socially disadvantaged pupils, was not for any change in the teacher-nurse program, but for more of it.

Although the number of teacher-nurses has been gradually increased in recent years, it still falls far short of meeting the needs and should be increased. Each teacher-nurse can give only a fractional part of her time to any one school. Many health problems must be glossed over because there is time for only major health cases. There is also little or no time for other important activities: for example, participating in staffing of individual cases with the psychologist and other staff members; counseling with teachers about individuals or health education in general; group health guidance of pupils; and so on. Teacher-nurses in the experimental summer schools, where they were assigned to only one school of 600 pupils, found great satisfaction in being able to do direct educational work with pupils and teachers besides their usual full-time occupation of follow-up on major health problems. Too much clerical work and lack of adequate facilities, including easy availability of telephones in some schools, reduce the efficiency of teacher-nurse service.

Certain districts and types of schools face common health problems and could benefit from a health program which was district based as well as school based. Health-related aspects of the attendance program and the identification and counseling of pregnant girls are projects which could be considered and approached on a district or regional basis.

Health examinations. Present practices with respect to health examinations, as well as hearing and vision examinations, indicate insufficient staff and budget to maintain an adequate program. Preschool examinations, for example, are especially important, and yet nothing is currently being done about this matter.

Psychological services

Psychological services are centered in the Bureau of Child Study. Besides a Central Office staff of clerical workers who process records of pupil data, the bureau is responsible for the work of school psychologists and for the training of adjustment teachers in all elementary schools.

There are 113 authorized positions for school psychologists but only 85 positions are actually filled. Based upon an estimated enrollment of 532,000 pupils in K-12 and the services of 85 psychologists, there is a present average ratio of one psychologist to more than 6,000 pupils.

Psychologists process about one and one-half cases per day, including projective and individual intelligence testing and contacts with teachers, parents, and others concerned with individual cases. Few schools have the services of a psychologist for more than one day a week and most for considerably less than that. An effort is made to relate assignments to the volume of need, but the over-all load was so great that there was a backlog of 14,000 referrals in the spring of 1964. Hiring some psychologists during the summer months helps to reduce this backlog somewhat. Probably all the psychologists should be employed full-time.

The basic problem with regard to psychologists is twofold. First, it has not been possible to fill all the positions presently established; and second, even if all these positions were filled, there would not be enough psychologists to meet the need for their services. A more favorable ratio of psychologists to pupils would permit psychologists to contribute their unique skills to a wider range of activities, such as more consultations with teachers and parents and more participation in staffing cases. The professional insights of the psychologists are especially needed in schools which are trying to meet the educational needs of socially disadvantaged pupils. At present, psychologists have to spend almost all of their time in purely diagnostic work on pupils referred for some kind of special placement.

The reasons for the high turnover and numerous vacancies in psychologist positions seem to be principally the salary scale, the lack of opportunities for advancement, and probably the fact that there is little room for creative use of professional skills due to the endless backlog of diagnostic examinations. A careful study should be made of all these factors and an effort made to overcome them. If the requirement that all psychologists have teaching certificates were removed, many more candidates for the positions would be available and the positions would be more competitive with those in other Illinois school districts which do not have this requirement. If credit were given for outside psychological, not merely teaching, experience, some candidates would be eligible for higher salaries. Credit might also be given for the additional preparation time required for meeting the state requirements for "qualified psychological examiners." This includes a master's degree or higher and "at least one year of full-time supervised experience in the individual psychological examination of children." It does not include a teacher's certificate. The state reimburses local school districts in the amount of $5,000 for these "qualified psychological examiners," and many districts take advantage of this to pay higher salaries.

Some means should also be sought to provide opportunities for psychologists to advance to positions of greater responsibility and reward. If a training program for school psychologists were established in cooperation with some local university, it would not only help to fill vacant positions but would provide a certain number of supervisory positions and other opportunities for advancement.

Social work services

Social work services in the Chicago Public Schools are in their infancy, and have not yet had an opportunity to demonstrate their usefulness. The 1964 budget shows a Social Work Section in the Bureau of Pupil Personnel Services, providing for one supervisor of social work and 10 social worker positions. At the time of the Survey, two social workers had been employed and were assigned to the IMPACT program (for the "improvement of attendance and control of truancy").

Several factors have delayed the development of a social work program in the Chicago schools. The requirement that all applicants meet the Chicago prerequisites for a teacher's certificate in addition to a master's degree in social work greatly restricts the number and quality of possible applicants. This is not required under the state school social work program, and in fact many districts throughout the state have developed effective programs without such a requirement. There are other ways to insure that the social worker understands and respects the teacher's role. Less specific but equally important obstacles arise from two factors. First, there appears to be a lack of understanding and appreciation on the part of school leaders as well as teachers of how a trained social worker can help in making the educational program more effective. In answering the questionnaire, the majority of teachers rated the assistance of social workers seventh in a list of seven items which might help the teacher to do a better job. This is much more likely to be a reflection of teachers' lack of experience with such a service than a fair evaluation. Teachers in school systems which have a well-developed school social work program are enthusiastic about the help it gives them in meeting the educational needs of youngsters with problems.

Second, social workers themselves hesitate to enter a program which is so limited and yet so indefinite as to structure and job assignment. The two social workers who were serving at the time of the Survey were assigned to one and two districts, respectively. The tentative IMPACT plan indicated that their services were to be called upon after all other resources had been exhausted, including a home visit by the head attendance officer of the district. While this was not being strictly followed in all cases, one of the workers was working with pupils and their families only after the pupil had been transferred from his regular school to a special IMPACT room. Thus most teachers and principals in the district had little opportunity to see what a social worker could do as a member of a local school team. Supervision, interaction with colleagues, and other opportunities for professional growth are almost nonexistent. A very able social worker, now directing a field work program for a local institution, left the system a year ago in spite of general enthusiasm for her work among those who knew it. Her principal reason was the impossibility of doing justice to the job under the existing circumstances and the lack of progress toward a more effective plan.

The consultants felt that 10 social workers for a school community the size of Chicago could hardly provide enough service to assess their value to the pupil personnel team. However, if the

Board of Education seriously wishes to make the effort, constructive steps could be taken even without an increase in the present budget. The first step would be the creation of an advisory council composed of persons experienced in the direction of school social work programs and representatives of the social work training institutions in the area. There would be no difficulty in recruiting such a committee from the Chicago Metropolitan Area, with perhaps one or two from other parts of the state. With the help of such a committee, an experienced director could be hired and a program planned to use the 10 positions in such a way that there would be a fair opportunity to evaluate their usefulness. It is noteworthy that the consultants strongly stressed the value of making nonteaching personnel a part of the local school "team." In spite of the fact that they only spend a fraction of their time at any one school, teacher-nurses are so regarded at the present time, with a resulting enthusiasm for their work. This is also true of psychologists to a lesser degree. It is probably the only way in which social workers can demonstrate the value of their own professional competencies.

Another value of the advisory council would be the possibility of planning an in-school training program for school social work trainees in cooperation with local institutions. This would give added service at the same time that it would provide a framework for professional growth.

RECOMMENDATIONS

1 Efforts should be increased to give attendance officers training in preventive and casework procedures, and the qualifications for new attendance personnel should be increased.

2 There should be one fully qualified, full-time guidance counselor for each 300 pupils in Grades 7 to 12; variances of 50 in each direction might be planned for, with the more favorable ratios provided in the more "difficult" school situations.

3 Minimum pre-service preparation for counselors should be increased to a full year of graduate study in guidance and counseling, with supervised practice in individual and group counseling.

4 Adjustment teachers serving elementary schools should have more graduate education and continuing in-service education;

they should be freed from the routines of attendance, testing, and records to become child development consultants, spending most of their time working directly with pupils, teachers, and parents.

5   The number of teacher-nurses should be increased so that they may have more opportunity to develop the educational aspects of the health program and to relate their work to the special needs of the schools and communities they serve.

6   Immediate steps should be taken to counteract the decline in psychological services through constant loss of personnel by
  a) removing the requirement of a teacher's certificate;
  b) improving salaries through credit for outside experience and additional preparation, or other means;
  c) provision of more full-time positions;
  d) establishment of a career framework—"somewhere to go."

7   Services of a competent advisory committee should be sought in making plans for effective use of social workers in the Chicago schools.

In conclusion, we quote from one of the consultants:

Two important aspects of effective pupil personnel organizations are balance and coordination. With increasing provisions for school social work service a more balanced pupil personnel program would be possible—a program in which some presently imbalanced roles may be corrected. With all services represented the functions of each can be better defined and delimited and personnel in each service will be able to work more effectively within and up to the limits of their particular competencies and skills.

THE TESTING PROGRAM

A city-wide program of achievement and ability testing is essential. It provides a basis for quality control of the educational process. A program is a good one if good tests are given fairly frequently, under conditions which guarantee that all pupils have had an equal opportunity to do their best.

In the judgment of the visiting consultant, the Chicago testing program is a good one. The consultant was Professor Robert L. Ebel, now Professor of Psychology and Education at the Michigan State University, and formerly a staff member of the Educa-

tional Testing Service, an agency which has taken the lead in research on the quality and usefulness of tests in this country.

Professor Ebel has made the following evaluation and suggestions. His suggestions deserve careful consideration by the staff of
the Chicago public schools. He proposes that "in the long run" it
may be desirable to publish the average test scores, school by school.
While this should not be done today or tomorrow for the reasons
indicated in Chaper I, we recommend that the Board of Education and the school administration consider this possibility seriously
as a part of a long-term program of helping the public to understand and support the schools.

The tests used in the basic program are good tests. The students
are tested every second or third year during their progress through
school. Whether more frequent testing, such as annual testing, would
be advantageous is difficult to say with certainty. In schools, such as
the _____ Elementary School, where a close watch is kept on the
progress of a class in educational achievement, annual testing could
be justified easily. In other schools, where the test results are given
less attention, the present schedule may be reasonably adequate.

It appeared to this observer that the testing program may over-
emphasize tests of ability, perhaps at the expense of more adequate
testing of achievement. There is not the sharp and clear distinction
between these two concepts—ability and achievement—that popular
usage may seem to imply. For ability at any level of schooling is
largely determined by achievement at earlier levels. All learning builds
on prior learning.

If differences among pupils in native capacity to learn exist, as well
they may, it is impossible to measure those differences directly by
means of any tests currently available. All tests of ability and achievement measure only what the pupil has learned how to do. To attribute
score differences to differences in native capacity, one must assume
that opportunities and incentives to learn have been equal. For beings
as complex, as sensitive, and as autonomous as young humans, that is
quite an assumption.

Almost all test specialists now agree that the IQ should not be regarded as a valid measure of some biological gift. It may be largely
a reflection of educational opportunities and efforts. To their great
credit, the staff members of the Chicago schools strongly resist the use
of intelligence quotients to label pupils permanently. Perhaps they can

be persuaded to de-emphasize the distinction between ability and achievement, and thus avoid the half-truths about "underachievement" and "working up to capacity" that this distinction seems to encourage.

In the early grades tests of readiness and general mental ability provide useful, even indispensable, measures of background for learning. Accordingly, no suggestion is made that the use of ability tests be abandoned below Grade 4. But more frequent achievement testing in the upper grades could be justified. At the secondary level, achievement testing could and probably should go beyond the present tests of reading and writing, into the common general areas of subject matter—science, history, literature, etc.

In general, staff policies with respect to the reporting of test scores to students and to parents are guardedly conservative. The harm that might be done by naive misinterpretation is given greater weight than the good that could result from more complete and accurate knowledge, for all interested parties, of a given pupil's achievements and prospects, of his strengths and weaknesses. Some schools, such as the _____ High School make special, and commendable, efforts to communicate test score information regularly and efficiently. But the general view seems to favor reticence, and to treat the test scores as more or less confidential professional information.

But if a child's education is a cooperative enterprise involving active, intelligent participation of the child as well as the teacher, the family as well as the school, and if intelligent participation requires access to all relevant information, a policy of limited and carefully guarded release of quantitative data on achievement and ability seems open to question. Numerous school systems and numerous testing agencies have found that meaningful communication of test scores, and constructive utilization of the score information, can be achieved quite simply and with beneficial effects on the educational process. A program for improving public understanding of these test scores, and for making them readily available to a student and his parents, seems worthy of serious consideration.

There has been some pressure for publication of school average test scores. In the long run this too may be desirable. Reluctance to move in this direction is based on fear that the inevitable differences between schools in average scores on tests of educational *achievement* may be generally interpreted as evidences of inequality in educational *opportunity*. The reality and seriousness of this danger is hard to assess. Certainly the hazard could be much reduced by a well-planned program of public information. Most people can recognize that the quality of the school program is not the only factor that determines how much the pupils in that school actually learn. Enlightened public support of constructive educational programs is not fostered by withholding of essential data on educational accomplishments and problems. Hence, policies designed to create a climate of understanding, in which data on school achievements can be safely released, would seem to be desirable.

XVI

Teachers in Chicago Schools

This chapter will report some of the results of a study of classroom teachers made with a questionnaire. The technical details are presented in Supplement A. This chapter will concentrate on the attitudes of teachers toward the job of teaching in Chicago schools, and the sources of satisfaction and dissatisfaction in their work.

The questionnaire was given to all teachers below the rank of principal. Thus a number of people who are not now teaching a regular classroom were included, such as counselors, adjustment teachers, assistant principals, nurses, psychologists, librarians, physical education teachers, and teachers of special education classes. However, most of the analyses and tables in this chapter are limited to regular classroom teachers. This category included 75 percent of the teachers working in elementary schools, and 64 percent of those working in high schools. In the case of the high schools, the teachers of vocational and shop subjects were placed in a separate category, which includes 16 percent of all high school teachers, Their responses to the questionnaire are not included in most of the tables, but their responses were similar, for the most part, to those of teachers of the academic subjects. The limitation of the analyses to regular classroom teachers has the advantage of concentrating on the main body of teachers and bringing out some things about their attitudes that would tend to be obscured if all the teachers were lumped together.

Table 1
Years of teaching experience
and sex of teachers
(percentages, unless otherwise stated)

Years of experience	Elementary schools			High schools		
	Male	Female	Number	Male	Female	Number
1-2	16	84	801	41	59	428
3-15	18	82	2,738	59	41	1,243
16+	5	95	1,581	30	70	689
Total	14	86	5,120	47	53	2,360

The most general facts about the teachers are given in Table 1. The majority are women, comprising 86 percent of elementary school teachers and 53 percent of high school teachers. The teachers with the most experience are mainly women. Even in the high schools, where the total group is almost evenly divided between men and women, 70 percent of the teachers with 16 years of experience or more are women. Men are most strongly represented in the group with three to 15 years of teaching experience. Furthermore, it is clear that the proportions of men have been increasing since World War II, especially in the elementary schools. About 21 percent of the teachers are "substitutes" who are teaching full-time. That is, they have state teachers' certificates but have not yet passed the examination for a certificate in the Chicago system. Most of these people do pass the Chicago examination after a few months or a few years, if they stay in Chicago. The questionnaire was not given to day-to-day substitutes.

It is on the whole an experienced group, 68 percent of the elementary school teachers and 67 percent of high school teachers having six years or more of teaching experience. With respect to their training, about half of the elementary school teachers were trained in Chicago Teachers College and about half in liberal arts colleges and universities. Among high school teachers, 75 percent were educated in a liberal arts college or university, while most of the rest went to Chicago Teachers College.

Relations of age, sex, and teaching experience to socioeconomic area of the school

One of the most difficult problems of a big city school system is to equalize the quality of teaching among the many different types of schools. Teachers have preferences, and they have a right to consideration for their preferences. Teachers with the most service experience generally have some rights and priorities due to seniority.

Wherever there are some schools that teachers think are preferable to other schools in a school system, there will be a tendency to gravitate toward the preferred schools. Reasons for a school being preferred are generally the following: it is near a teacher's home; it has a principal whom the teacher likes; its neighborhood and its pupils are attractive. There are also other motives that influence a teacher to choose one or another type of school. A teacher may want a different kind of school than he has had in the past, for the sake of greater professional experience; or he may want a school where he thinks he can be of most service to people.

The net effect of these motives of teachers, together with the rules set up by the school administration regarding assignment and transfer, and the actual situation in the schools, is to produce a pattern in which the youngest and least experienced teachers tend to get the least desirable teaching assignments. This pattern is illustrated in Tables 2A and 2B. However, this pattern can be modified to get more mature teachers into the "difficult" schools by some of the devices suggested in Chapters IV, VIII, and X.

Teachers were asked, "In what kind of socioeconomic area is your school located?" They were asked to check one of the following: upper- or middle-class area; mixed middle- and working-class area; stable working-class area; lower-class or slum area. There was a difference between elementary school and high school reporting on this question, with 65 percent of elementary school teachers seeing their schools in stable working-class areas or in slum areas, while 39 percent of high school teachers reported their schools to be in these two categories. There is a real difference of this sort, because elementary schools are more likely to be located in slum neighborhoods than high schools are.

In Table 2 are presented the data on age, sex, and teaching experience in relation to socioeconomic area of the school. It will be seen that the younger teachers and those with least experience tend to be assigned to schools in the lower socioeconomic areas. On the other hand, the teachers over 50 years of age and with 16 or more years of experience are heavily clustered in the higher status areas and in the mixed middle- and working-class areas.*
It will also be seen that there is a tendency for men to be assigned to working-class and slum area schools more than women. This tendency is stronger in the elementary schools, where most of the men are younger and less experienced than the women teachers. Probably it is the factor of age and experience rather than sex that accounts for the difference.

Attitude toward present position related to teaching experience, sex, and socioeconomic area of school

The attitude a teacher has toward his present position is a matter of importance in his teaching. To secure some information on the matter, the teachers were asked, "What is your attitude, in general, about your present position?" They could indicate their attitudes by checking on a five-point scale as follows: very favorable, favorable, neutral, unfavorable, very unfavorable. Their answers were heavily "favorable" and "very favorable" with 72 percent of elementary school teachers and 71 percent of high school teachers giving these two responses.

However, there are some reliable differences between subgroups of teachers, as can be seen in Table 3. The older and more experienced teachers are more favorable than the younger and less experienced. Also, women are more favorable than men in their answers to this question.

The type of school area has the closest relation to attitude toward present position. Elementary school teachers in upper- and middle-

---

*The reliability of trends which are pointed out here has been tested by the usual statistical methods, but the statistics will not be given, since this is not a technical report. Whenever a difference or a trend is pointed out, it is statistically reliable unless a statement is made to the contrary.

Table 2
Characteristics of teachers related to
socioeconomic area of school
(percentages, unless otherwise stated)

	Upper- or middle-class	Mixed middle- and working-class	Stable working-class	Lower-class or slum	Total
A. Elementary schools					
Sex					
Male	10	9	12	19	14
Female	90	91	88	81	86
Age					
20-25	3	9	13	19	14
26-30	7	11	15	21	16
31-40	19	23	22	32	27
41-50	26	21	18	15	18
51-65	45	34	30	13	24
66+	1	1	2	1	1
Experience					
1 year	2	5	7	11	8
2	3	4	7	12	8
3-5	6	12	16	26	19
6-15	31	36	32	36	35
16+	58	44	38	16	31
Number	264	1,537	912	2,409	5,122
Percent of total	5	30	18	47	100

	Upper- or middle-class	Mixed middle- and working-class	Stable working- class	Lower- class or slum	Total
		B. High schools			
Sex					
Male	47	44	54	52	47
Female	53	56	46	48	53
Age					
20-25	14	16	17	23	18
26-30	18	15	22	21	18
31-40	23	22	23	28	24
41-50	12	17	14	12	15
51-65	31	26	21	15	23
66+	2	3	3	2	3
Experience					
1 year	5	7	11	11	9
2	5	8	11	14	10
3-5	19	20	23	29	22
6-15	35	31	28	31	31
16+	36	34	27	16	29
Number	242	1,187	391	504	2,328
Percent of total	10	51	17	22	100

Table 3
Attitude toward present position related to experience, sex, and type of school area
(percentages, unless otherwise stated)

	Elementary schools						High schools					
	VF	F	N	U	VU	Number	VF	F	N	U	VU	Number
Years of teaching experience												
1-2	20	42	19	14	5	806	19	50	16	12	3	428
3-15	25	43	16	12	4	2,768	21	48	16	12	3	1,254
16+	46	36	9	6	2	1,592	36	41	14	7	2	693
Total group	31	41	14	11	4	5,166	25	46	16	11	3	2,375
Type of school area												
Upper- and middle-class	65	25	6	4	0	264	35	46	11	5	3	242
Mixed middle- and working-class	41	41	11	5	2	1,537	29	47	13	8	3	1,187
Stable working-class	38	39	13	7	3	912	19	47	18	13	2	391
Lower-class and slum	17	43	18	16	6	2,409	14	45	21	16	4	505
Total group	31	41	14	11	4	5,122	25	46	16	11	3	2,343
Sex												
Male	9	14	19	20	21	720	41	47	53	49	65	1,123
Female	91	86	81	80	79	4,430	60	53	47	51	35	1,250
Number	1,576	2,083	731	541	185	5,150	581	1,087	363	246	66	2,373

Note: VF=very favorable; F=favorable; N=neutral; U=unfavorable; VU=very unfavorable.

class areas are 65 percent very favorable toward their present position, while those in lower-class or slum area schools are only 17 percent very favorable, with 22 percent unfavorable or very unfavorable. There is a similar difference, though not so striking, among high school teachers.

Why teachers request transfers

Among those who answered the questionnaire, 12 percent of elementary school teachers and 8 percent of high school teachers said their names are on the transfer list. That is, they wished to change to another school. They wrote out their reasons freely, and these were then put into the categories that seemed most appropriate. The results are shown in Table 4. The most frequent reason was one of personal convenience, which consisted mainly of such reasons as distance of the school from home. Next in frequency was a desire for professional advancement and growth through experience in another type of school. The category of professional dissatisfaction was equal in frequency to the category of professional advancement. This included such reasons as unsatisfactory working conditions, and relations with colleagues. The specific reason of dissatisfaction with the principal was given by 15 percent of elementary and 20 percent of high school teachers whose names were on transfer lists. Dissatisfaction with pupils and/or the local community was given by 16 percent of elementary and 12 percent of high school teachers as the main reason for wishing to transfer. Finally, there was the category of mechanical operation of the system which caused a person to transfer, usually because he was taking the place of someone returning from leave of absence, and therefore must move to another place.

The percentages of teachers on the transfer list from different socioeconomic types of school are also shown in Table 4. Lower-class or slum schools have about twice as many transfer requests as the middle- and upper-class area schools.

The major influence of the socioeconomic type of school

There is a deep ambivalence about teaching in a "difficult" school, which is a school in a high transiency and low-income area. Of the 82 percent of elementary school teachers and the 66 percent of high

Table 4
*Why teachers have requested transfers
(percent of regular classroom teachers)*

	Elementary	H.S.
Percent with name on transfer list	12	8
Socioeconomic area of school		
Upper- or middle-class	6	6
Mixed middle- and working-class	9	6
Stable working-class	12	9
Lower-class or slum	15	11
Number	616	164
Reasons given for requesting transfers		
Personal convenience	34	27
Professional advancement	15	17
Dissatisfaction with principal	15	20
Other professional dissatisfaction	16	21
Dissatisfaction with pupils and/or community	16	12
Operation of system	4	2

school teachers who have had experience in such a school, they divide almost evenly when asked whether they like working in such a school.

Some experienced teachers choose to work in such a school. Sometimes they do this out of loyalty and satisfaction with a principal who is competent and who gives them recognition and security. Sometimes they teach in such a school because they feel that they can be of most service there. Still, the median years of teaching experience of regularly assigned teachers in these schools is only four, compared with 19 for teachers in the most favored areas.

It is clear that the present situation works against a retention of experienced teachers in the schools in low socioeconomic areas.

This means that young and inexperienced teachers must work their apprenticeship in such schools—the most difficult schools in the city.

While the energy and the spirit of youth are desirable traits to bring to a difficult job, the job cannot be done well without more maturity on the staff as well as more help to the young and inexperienced. It is urgently necessary to make the work in the difficult schools more satisfactory to young teachers and to mature ones.

SATISFACTION-DISSATISFACTION WITH TEACHING

The questionnaire contained a list of 54 aspects of the teaching job. The respondent was asked to indicate for each aspect, whether he was "satisfied," "neutral," or "dissatisfied." A "job satisfaction" score was obtained by counting the number of items for which he was "satisfied" and subtracting one-half the number of items marked "neutral" or omitted. The scores for the total group were then ranked from high to low and divided into five equal-sized groups or quintiles. Thus each respondent received a score on a scale for 5 (high) to 1 (low).

The relative satisfaction of the various subgroups of teachers can be studied in Table 5, which shows the distribution of each subgroup along the quintiles. Thus, the male elementary school teachers are definitely less satisfied than the female elementary school teachers (as was also noted on the scores on attitude toward present position).

The most noteworthy findings in the table are:

Adjustment teachers have the highest satisfaction scores.

Assistant principals have high satisfaction scores.

Teachers of special education classes have high satisfaction scores.

Librarians have relatively high satisfaction scores.

Women have higher satisfaction scores than men.

Elementary school teachers have higher satisfaction scores than high school teachers.

The "job aspects" scores of Table 5 are generally confirmed by scores for the same groups on attitude toward present position. The only exceptions to this are counselors, psychologists, and remedial specialists.

These groups, who are not classroom teachers, tended to get "job aspects" scores in the middle three quintiles, probably because they

Table 5
Job satisfaction of various teacher groups
(percentages, unless otherwise stated)

	1 (low)	2	3	4	5	Number
Total group	20.0	20.0	20.0	20.0	20.0	10,956
All classroom teachers	22.2	19.7	20.3	19.1	18.7	7,592
Elementary school teachers						
Male	30.1	21.7	21.1	16.3	10.8	720
Female	19.1	18.5	19.1	20.7	22.6	4,430
High school teachers						
Male	28.9	21.4	22.5	15.2	12.0	1,123
Female	23.2	21.0	22.0	17.7	16.1	1,250
Vocational high school teachers	21.1	20.7	21.4	18.7	18.1	631
Adjustment teachers	8.8	16.4	15.3	26.5	33.0	294
Phys. ed. and recreation teachers	17.2	20.1	22.1	22.0	18.6	657
Librarians	18.7	17.1	17.7	20.2	26.3	316
Special education teachers	11.8	19.4	17.4	21.4	30.0	661
Remedial specialists	15.3	17.1	18.1	29.7	19.8	111
Counselors	12.7	24.2	19.3	25.0	18.8	260
Assistant principals	8.9	16.1	15.5	29.1	30.4	168
Nurses	13.3	25.5	24.5	24.5	12.2	98
Psychologists	13.2	45.3	24.5	15.1	1.9	53
Playground teachers	6.7	60.0	15.0	11.6	6.7	60

responded "neutral" to a good many items which did not apply to their job as fully as to the job of classroom teacher.

Specific sources of satisfaction and dissatisfaction

The specific aspects of the teaching job about which teachers are most satisfied or most dissatisfied are listed in Table 6. They have been classified under three headings: (1) those having to do with the teacher's work in the classroom; (2) those in which the teacher is acting as a member of a professional group; (3) those conditions that promote personal satisfaction or dissatisfaction.

Table 6A lists the items about which at least 50 percent of teachers (elementary *or* high school) expressed satisfaction. Table 6B lists items about which at least 20 percent (elementary *and* high school) expressed dissatisfaction. Taken together, the two lists contain 38 of the 54 items in the job aspects section of the questionnaire. They also contain seven items which appear on both lists, indicating high satisfaction felt by one group of teachers and relatively high dissatisfaction felt by another group.

The asterisks in Table 6 indicate items which 20 percent or more of the respondents picked among the five aspects with which they were "very satisfied" or the five which they marked as "very dissatisfied."

Aspects in which there was disagreement between elementary and high school teachers

While the general tendency was for elementary and high school teachers to agree on the level of satisfaction-dissatisfaction they felt, there were some interesting disagreements. These have been sorted out by looking for items in which there was a 10 percent difference at least between the two groups in satisfaction or dissatisfaction.

Aspects with which elementary school teachers are more satisfied than high school teachers:
Audio-visual services
Process of getting school started at the beginning of the school year
Materials and equipment with which to work
Relations with my principal
Leadership given by my principal
Availability of professional materials and journals

Table 6
Chief sources of satisfaction and dissatisfaction

	Percent satisfied		Percent dissatisfied	
	Elem.	H.S.	Elem.	H.S.

A. Sources of satisfaction

Role as a classroom teacher

Amount of pleasure I obtain from teaching	77*	74*	10	9
Relations with my principal	70*	59*	12	15
Freedom for innovation and experimentation in the classroom	69*	65*	10	10
Audio-visual services	58*	37	23	32
Process of getting school started at the beginning of the school year	57	33	19	45
Materials and equipment with which to work	53*	36	30	41
The library in my school	51	61	25	16
The textbooks available for use in my classes	51	44	31	36

Role as a member of a professional group

Relations with fellow teachers in my building	82*	79*	4	3
Degree of feeling that I am in an important profession	66*	53*	16	24
Availability of professional materials and journals	66	45	14	22
Leadership given by my principal	52*	38	27	32
My experience with the process of obtaining tenure in my job	58	55	10	12

*Was mentioned by 20 percent or more teachers as one of five aspects about which they were *very satisfied* or one of five aspects about which they were *very dissatisfied*.

Conditions promoting satisfaction or dissatisfaction	Percent satisfied		Percent dissatisfied	
	Elem.	*H.S.*	*Elem.*	*H.S.*
Provision for sick leave	53	55	22	20
The neighborhood in which my school is located	48	57	21	12
Extent to which I am consulted in the making of my teaching program	50	29	22	45

B. Sources of dissatisfaction

Role as a classroom teacher

Provisions for treatment of maladjusted, retarded, and disturbed pupils	9	10	79*	67*
Arrangements for teachers to learn what is going on in other schools	16	8	61	63
Behavior of pupils	27	41	51*	31
Size of my classes	40	48	43*	28
Process of getting school started at the beginning of the school year	57	33	19	45
The system of promotion of pupils in my school	40	35	40	36
The amount of time I spend outside of school hours on my job	33	25	35	43
Materials and equipment with which to work	56	36	30	41
The practice we follow for grading pupils in my school	43	37	35	40
The help I actually get from adjustment teachers and counselors	39	34	38	38
Availability of day-to-day substitutes in my school	37	42	40	18

Table 6 continued
Chief sources of satisfaction and dissatisfaction

	Percent satisfied		Percent dissatisfied	
	Elem.	H.S.	Elem.	H.S.
Role as a classroom teacher (cont'd)				
The textbooks available for use in my classes	51	44	31	36
The system of ability grouping in my school	40	37	32	33
Physical facilities of the building in which I work	44	34	37	42
Ability level of my pupils	36	34	37	35
Adequacy of day-to-day substitutes in my school	32	24	34	34
Leadership given by my principal	52	38	27	32
Audio-visual services	58	31	23	32
Extent to which I am consulted in the making of my teaching program	50	29	22	45
Assistance I have received from the Curriculum Department	35	28	21	30
Role as a member of a professional group				
Salary	47	35	29	41*
The way problems of racial integration and segregation are being handled in the schools	28	30	46*	39
Procedures for promotion of teachers within the school system	29	17	44	44
Official contacts with the Personnel Office	28	23	30	32
The system of teacher efficiency ratings	29	18	27	36
Leadership given by my principal	52	38	27	32
Faculty meetings	44	29	22	34

	Percent satisfied		Percent dissatisfied	
	Elem.	H.S.	Elem.	H.S.
Conditions promoting satisfaction or dissatisfaction				
The amount of time I spend on record-keeping and other clerical duties	14	8	67*	79*
Channels for discussion and settlement of grievances	23	15	46	55*
My work load	42	37	35	38
Opportunity to talk over my professional or personal problems with counselors in the Teacher Personnel Department	20	17	36	37
Activities of citizen and parent groups that are concerned about the public schools	22	18	39	30
The attention given by the newspapers to the schools	23	23	36	30
Provision for sick leave	53	55	22	20

Degree of feeling that I am in an important profession

Extent to which I am consulted in the making of my teaching program

Aspects with which high school teachers are more satisfied than elementary school teachers:

The neighborhood in which my school is located

The library in my school

Aspects with which elementary school teachers are more dissatisfied than high school teachers:

Provisions for treatment of maladjusted, retarded, and disturbed pupils

Behavior of pupils

Size of my classes

Availability of day-to-day substitutes in my school

Aspects with which high school teachers are more dissatisfied than elementary school teachers:

Process of getting school started at the beginning of the school year

Materials and equipment with which to work

Extent to which I am consulted in the making of my teaching program

Salary

Faculty meetings

The amount of time I spend on record-keeping and other clerical duties

Channels for discussion and settlement of grievances

Concluding comment

The sources both of satisfaction and dissatisfaction which teachers feel in their work can be extremely important in planning to make the teacher's job more effective and more rewarding. The sources of dissatisfaction especially point to some specific areas to which attention should be given by the Board of Education and the administration. For example, a large percentage of elementary and high school teachers indicate that they are very dissatisfied with provisions for treatment of maladjusted, retarded, and disturbed pupils and with the amount of time spent on clerical duties. These attitudes seem to reinforce the observations of consultants and the findings of the Survey as reported in other chapters of this report.

XVII

Educational Research and Development

A great deal of money must be spent by the citizens of Chicago on their school system. A great deal more than has been spent in recent years must be provided if Chicago is to have the quality of education it needs and wants. There must be an increase in the school budget of 10 to 20 percent, or somewhere between $30 and $60 million a year. This money must be spent mainly on new things—new ways of teaching, new materials for teaching, new ways of using the time of teachers and other people working in the school system. Very little of the extra money will go into sheer expansion of the school system, such as more buildings, more classroom teachers, more textbooks. It is *better* education that is needed, rather than *more* education.

The citizens of Chicago will pay the extra costs of better education if they are convinced they are getting better education for the money. The Board of Education will vote larger budgets, but

* * *

The principal Survey consultant for this chapter was Dr. Lorne H. Woollatt, Associate Commissioner for Research and Evaluation, The New York State Education Department. The middle part of the chapter is taken rather directly from his report.

only if its members are convinced that the money will buy better education. Consequently, there must be some system of reporting the results and evaluating the results of the new programs that will be developed.

Ideas will be more plentiful than the money to pay for trying them out. The past 10 years have been more fruitful of ideas and experiments in education than the preceding 30 years. When asked for proposals to improve the education of socially disadvantaged children in Chicago, the General Superintendent provided a list of new procedures as well as a program of expansion of present services that could cost more than the extra 20 percent on the budget just mentioned. And these proposals were for disadvantaged children—perhaps one half of the school enrollment. Those with average or better home backgrounds also need better schooling, which will cost more money. This all points to the need for a program of research and development in the Chicago Public Schools.

Research and development seems almost to be a magic phrase in America. Our enormous increase in productivity and income during the present century has resulted from the use of scientific research in the development of our technology. Industry and government spent 1 percent of the gross national product on research and development in 1950, 2.7 percent in 1960, and an economic analyst has predicted that the rate will exceed 3 percent in 1970.

The use of more money for research and development in education has been recommended by all of the major governmental and private educational organizations. For example, the President's Science Advisory Committee has created a Panel on Educational Research and Development which reports to the National Science Foundation, the U.S. Office of Education and the Special Assistant to the President for Science and Technology. This Panel published a report in March, 1964, entitled *Innovation and Experiment in Education*. This report says:

> The task of educational research and development is to learn how to provide for all students the education an exceptional teacher provides for a few. . . .

> This report seeks to give some intimation of how educational research and development can help accomplish this task. It seeks, also, to create a climate favorable to educational research and development,

for, to be effective, such work must enlist the services of many people already busy doing other things—outstanding scholars or practitioners at the frontiers of their art or science and outstanding teachers. Although the Panel is concerned with all levels of education, it has limited itself so far to elementary and secondary education and to the education of teachers. Necessarily, this report is concerned with only a partial view of the problems facing our educational establishment. . . . The aim is to increase the efficiency and efficacy of the entire educational establishment, and so multiply the effectiveness with which all funds are spent. . . .

   The Federal Government and private foundations currently spend about $25 million per year on curriculum development at the pre-college level. If curriculum development and teacher education are considered together and all the tasks of education are included, a sizable portion of attention being given the special needs of the deprived and the segregated, specific tasks and specific persons can be identified to warrant the expenditure of an additional $90 million per year. To this add $10 million per year to conduct an experimental school subsystem in a slum area, or N times that for N such experiments.*

Several estimates of the amount of money that could usefully be spent on educational research and development center around the amount of 1 percent of the total expenditure on education. The amount suggested in the Panel Report for expenditures by the federal government and private foundations on research and development at the precollege level is about $125 million, or .4 of 1 percent of the national expenditure on education.

One percent of the current operating budget for Chicago schools is approximately $2.5 million. There is no official figure for the amount actually spent currently on research and development in Chicago schools, but in a conference of the Survey Director with several of the associate superintendents, it was estimated that about $500,000 was spent in 1963-64 on research, and about $1,850,000 on demonstration and development. The largest share of the money goes into demonstrations of methods and materials which are judged

---

*The President's Science Advisory Committee, *Innovation and Experiment in Education* (Washington, D.C.: U.S. Government Printing Office, 1964), pp. vii-ix.

to be successful and which are scheduled for adoption generally in the system if the necessary money can be found.

What is educational research and development?

The use of the term research and development is a logical outcome of the scientific management approach to administration of school systems. This approach began over 50 years ago when Baltimore established a Bureau of Educational Research, closely followed by New York City in 1913. By 1917, bureaus had been added by Boston, New Orleans, Detroit, Cleveland, Chicago, and Los Angeles. The early bureaus concentrated on the assembly of statistical information concerning pupils, teachers, and expenditures. Later they added programs of testing pupil achievement and ability. With the great industrial development of pure and applied research since World War II, school systems have adopted a broader program of research, experimentation, and evaluation in recent years.

All the big cities are trying to use research and development, and all are having difficulties, Chicago included. Although Chicago has had a department of research headed by an associate superintendent for a long time, it has not been as successful with experimentation and evaluation of experiments as have New York and Detroit, for example.

The difficulties tend to cluster about stages 2, 3, and 4 in the following scheme which follows the process of research and development from beginning to end.

1. *Basic research.* Educationally this refers to finding out how children learn who come from various kinds of families and have various abilities and handicaps. It is a kind of research done typically by college, foundation, and private agency personnel with great depth of training and skill in the particular subject field and the application of the scientific method to the solution of problems.

2. *Invention (or application).* After the pure scientist has discovered a basic principle or generalization underlying a particular field, then he or some person closer to schools must invent a "practice"—a way in which the newly gained knowledge may be put into practical use in classrooms or counseling offices or laboratories.

3. *Experimental tryout.* After the new idea or practice has been

developed, it is tried out in a somewhat idealized situation or is applied to a sample of students and/or teachers.

4. *Field trial.* The next step is to make such adjustments in the application as have been revealed necessary in the experimental tryout. Field trial takes place in actual classrooms under actual conditions. Records are kept of what actually happens in the experiment; and often a complex design of experimentation must be used, including control groups in which pupils and teachers are matched with those in the experimental groups.

5. *Demonstration.* At this point there is no doubt left concerning the practice. One is sure it will work and can be put in certain schools in such a way that other schools and teachers may watch the demonstration.

6. *Installation.* To all practical purposes, this is a final stage in which the new practice is put into operation in all schools.

7. *Regularization.* After the practice is installed, there is a matter of keeping it continuously alive. This requires the training of student teachers in the use of the new practice and the development of courses in colleges for training in the use of the practice.

8. *Adjustment over time.* A watchful eye must be kept over a practice in order to insure that it makes adjustments over time to suit changing conditions in schools and in society.

In Chicago schools there are research projects at various stages in the process. The city-wide testing programs are in stages 6 and 7. The TV College is in stage 7. Projects on curriculum development are in stages 4, 5, 6, and 7 chiefly. Most of the projects for children with social disadvantages are in stages 2, 3, and 4.

The Chicago projects for the socially disadvantaged illustrate the difficulties that big-city systems face in the conduct of research and development. Several such projects have been carried on with funds from the Ford Foundation, the Wieboldt Foundation, and the U.S. Department of Health, Education and Welfare.

Although the projects were set up with enthusiasm and with creative originality, they were seldom accompanied by a careful design for collecting data on what actually happened to children and teachers before, during, and after the experiments.

For example, at the Doolittle Elementary School in 1959 there was started a "value-sharing project," in which a small group of teachers was given a considerable amount of in-service training by consultants, based on the application of Professor Harold Lasswell's theory of development of social personality. The Doolittle project was given favorable publicity, and there seems to be no doubt that the small group of teachers directly involved felt that they were able to do a better job with pupils and parents. Statements were made to the public that the reading level of the Doolittle pupils in the project increased remarkably. The *Response to Recommendations 4 through 10 of the Advisory Panel on Integration,* made by the General Superintendent in August, 1964, says, "The project at the Doolittle Elementary School . . . has spread to most of the schools in District 11." Yet the Survey staff has been unable to find a factual report of the results of the Doolittle project. Nor have the Doolittle teachers who were not actually in the project reported any change in their ways of teaching.

Another example is the "District 11 project" which was started in 1960 with Ford Foundation funds to improve the education of socially disadvantaged children in the elementary schools. A variety of experiments has been developed in the course of this project, and the observer is impressed with the devotion and the enthusiasm of many of the teachers and other staff members working on the project. Survey staff members all agree that the new things undertaken in District 11 are desirable. But which of these new things are most successful, and what improvements have they actually produced? What practices can be recommended with confidence for extension through other schools and districts, if money becomes available? There is some research going on in the District 11 project, but the Survey staff has not been able to find a clear statement of what new practices are being evaluated, and how they are being studied.

A contrast to this situation is found in the New York City school system where the Bureau of Curriculum Research has made a three-year study, with experimental and control groups, of the effects of the Higher Horizons program on socially disadvantaged children. It is now possible to make a decision concerning the future of the Higher Horizons program with some objective data on its effectiveness.

Of course it would be stupid to limit all innovation to things which can be recorded and evaluated with the utmost scientific rigor. Experienced teachers can generally tell whether a new practice is working better than an old one. When innovations are tried, certain ones seem to be just right, and they are likely to be continued by a kind of common consent, even though their value has not been established rigorously. Experimenting with socially disadvantaged children today is something like flying an airplane in the pioneer days of aviation, when a pilot flew "by the seat of his pants," using all of his senses and his intuition to guide him. Some good educational experimentation is done "by the seat of the pants" with the intuition and sensitivity of good teachers.

Nevertheless, if the public is going to be asked to contribute more millions of dollars to the school budget for new educational practices, it would be wise for the Board of Education to arrange for a thorough reporting and evaluation of these innovations so as to keep the new practices that work and to discard those that are not successful.

Staff organization. The superintendent for research should have a staff of persons trained and experienced in research and evaluation. This staff might well be organized into divisions and bureaus, each with its own chief. However, the total research concept should be maintained as against the fractional one; that is, a research person should not be responsible to an operational person, but should be part of the staff of the research superintendent. This will promote a coordinated approach and permit professional staff members in research to be in contact with each other in that kind of sharing of ideas which is so necessary for such personnel.

The superintendent for research would assign, at need, members of his staff to operational officers and offices requiring special assistance in research or evaluation. Alternately and in some cases, he might take on complete responsibility for a special project, as is done now, making sure that there are regular reports of progress to the operationally responsible officer.

The superintendent for research should be responsible for the data bank of key information. In this regard, he would coordinate information dealing with the files regarding students, enrollment and attendance, regular and city-wide testing data, plant and staff information. Staff members in the colleges who are in research should also have a direct relationship to the superintendent for research.

Resources. All the resources available within and without the school system should be tapped at need. These are rich and numerous, and include, for example, the following.

1. *Universities.* The universities of the area offer remarkably rich resources for working with the rich classroom and central office resources of the Chicago School System. This resource should be tapped or revived.

2. *Federal funds.* The U.S. Office of Education has funds specifically for research. Other federal agencies, such as the National Institute of Mental Health, have funds available.

3. *State funds.* The State Department of Public Instruction has a substantial amount of money to support research on gifted children and on mentally retarded and socially maladjusted children. Money is also available for research and demonstration projects in the field of vocational education.

4. *Foundations.* The various private foundations have funds available, some of which have been secured by the Chicago schools but in relatively limited amount.

A PROPOSED PROGRAM
FOR EDUCATIONAL RESEARCH
AND DEVELOPMENT

An organization of the magnitude of the Chicago Public Schools must operate from a framework of general policy implemented by operational rules and regulations. It is important for a modern school system to have a tone or climate that stresses the scientific approach to teaching and learning and to the related aspects of adjustment and administration. The climate and tone begin with the board of education and its general superintendent. Tone and climate are catching. They pass through the upper echelon of administration to staff and eventually to teachers. The outward expression of tone and climate lies in the stated policies of the board of education. The board policies should be examined to see if such a statement regarding the place of research and development exists. Further, if such a statement does exist, it should be analyzed in terms of its 1970 applicability in a forward-looking school system. It should be given publicity from time to time and be readily available. In its application through operational rules and regulations, it should include a clause which permits variations from standard procedures where experimentation and tryout are involved. It should include a statement concerning the ways in which a researcher seeking a population may proceed and ways in which the schools may identify problems and seek out research competence to help them in deriving suitable inventions and evaluations.

Organization

The research aspects of a great city school system require organization. It is not sufficient to rely solely on the good will of individuals in bureaus and divisions and the possibility of their "getting together." Structure is important.

Cabinet. The general superintendent of schools should have in his cabinet a person with a title of superintendent—either assistant, associate, or deputy. This position should be for research solely and not combined with other responsibilities. It would seem that in a modern school system of great size, at least one of the top 10 administrative positions should be of this nature. The incumbent of the position should be one who knows both research and administration. He should be more a manager of research, however, than a technician. His past experience may have covered a number of technical research positions, but he should have developed to the stage where he can locate and marshal resources for applying the scientific method to experimentation throughout the whole school system.

A council on research. Research and development could well be fostered by the organization of a city-wide Council on Research. The council could serve two functions, namely (1) the coordination of central office studies and facilities and (2) the encouragement and screening of proposals from schools and districts in the field.

Each of the districts might assign one representative to the council. A method could be developed so that in some cases the representative could be a field assistant superintendent, in others a principal, and in some cases perhaps a teacher. This membership would rotate on a one- to three-year basis, permitting different levels to represent a district at different times but still keeping some representation of the three instructional or administrative levels. The offices within the central office related to coordination of research programs would serve to add another six or seven persons. This would mean a council of 30 which could meet monthly or a total of seven or eight times during the school year.

Possible inadequacies of this program

Such a program, if adequately financed, would certainly strengthen the educational program of the Chicago Public Schools. Its main difficulties would be two:

1. Relations would have to be developed with great care between the research staff and the operational staff. The actual research projects would belong in the operational field—for example, evaluating a particular new mathematics course or studying the effect on teachers of a new system of teacher-aids. Research staff members would have to work sympathetically and constructively with the curriculum department and the department of administration in these instances, acquiring empathy with respect to the operational personnel and at the same time maintaining a kind of objectivity and scientific rigor that the operational personnel would not show.

2. Development of a competent research staff is a most difficult process in the research department of a public school system. The difficulty lies in the fact that there is not much opportunity for a career on a school system research staff under the circumstances generally prevailing. Promotion is apt to stop at the level of status and salary of an experienced classroom teacher, with only one or two or three positions above that level. Consequently, a research man is likely to shift over to a principalship, where there are many more opportunities for promotion.

An example of this problem in Chicago can be given. A young man, who completed a Ph.D. dissertation on a problem of interest to the school system, was offered a position at a salary of $9,000 for a full year, with one month's vacation. At the same time he was offered $8,000 for a nine-month service in a state university where he could expect to spend a third of his time in research. Since he was interested in a research career, he took the university job, knowing that he could be promoted rapidly and could give increasing amounts of time to research. In the school system he might have had to go into administration to get rapid promotion.

Related to the problem of making a career in research in a school system is the problem of freedom to publish. A research man must publish if he is to gain prestige among his research colleagues. In a university he can publish anything worthwhile, and is encouraged by the administration to do so. But in a school system he generally must submit his tentative publication to the administration for approval, and he may have to postpone publication or modify it because his findings might have an adverse influence on public opinion about the schools.

Whatever the reasons may be, the Chicago schools have had difficulty in recruiting and keeping even a small research staff. This suggests that alternative methods of conducting research and development should be tried. One alternative is to create a working relationship with local universities.

Research and development shared with universities

In Chicago there are several universities with strong departments or schools of education, which conduct a variety of research. Faculty members and graduate students are interested in doing research, and many of them would like to work in the local schools. In fact, a good deal of their research has been done in the Chicago or suburban schools.

The Survey Director conferred or corresponded with deans and chairmen of all the institutions that have graduate students in education in the Chicago area. He found them all appreciative of the opportunities they have had for research in the Chicago schools. Some felt that the restrictions placed by the school administration on the type of research instruments and problems were unnecessarily tight, and some also felt that the red tape and delay involved in getting permission for specific study was a source of discomfort which led some researchers to take their projects to other cities or to Chicago suburbs without even trying to do them in the City of Chicago.

On the other hand, members of the school administration made it clear that the demands of research projects on the time of school children and on the attention of teachers would quickly grow to be unbearable unless there was a strict limit on cooperation between the school system and the universities in this area.

Several of the Chicago suburban school systems have active and cordial relations with university research people. For example, the Evanston school districts, both elementary and secondary, have joint projects with Northwestern University.

If the need of the Chicago schools for a more highly developed program of research and development is seen in conjunction with the interest of local universities in conducting educational research and in training research students, the suggestion arises naturally that the school system might enter into formal contractual arrangements with local universities for research services. Thus, the total program of educational research and development might consist of two parts, one carried on by the research staff of the school system, and the other done by university research people in close cooperation with the school research staff.

For example, several experiments in the Chicago schools with gifted children are supported by research funds from the State of Illinois. Several professors in local universities are also doing research on gifted children. The Chicago schools might contract with one or more of the universities for part-time services of one or more of these professors, and might offer to pay for a certain number of research assistants or to supply school staff members as research assistants.

There are several visible advantages to the school system in such an arrangement. One is that the research activity of the universities would tend to be focused on problems and interests of the school system more than they are today. Another is that the university research people would bring a degree of objectivity and scientific rigor to research in the school system which is hard to achieve for staff members of the school system even though they are specialists in research. Another advantage is that university research professors have learned how to secure research grants from government and foundation sources, and would undoubtedly help to finance some of the research needed by the school system. In fact, several government research funding agencies will deal only with universities, and do not grant money for research to school systems.

The organization of cooperation between the Chicago schools and the universities might be something like the following: The Board of Education might authorize the appointment of an Advisory Commission on Research, consisting of the superintendent for research of the Chicago schools and one representative from each local university which trains four or more Ph.D.'s a year in education and related areas. This advisory commission would assist the research superintendent of the Chicago schools in drawing up a comprehensive plan for research and for dissemination of the results of research. The advisory commission members would invite suggestions and proposals from universities not represented on the commission. The research superintendent would coordinate the program with the school system's Council on Research. He would draw up contracts with several of the local universities, covering the research services to be obtained, the rules regarding publication, arrangements for recruiting and training junior researchers, and plans for financing specific research projects.

RECOMMENDATIONS

It is recommended that the Board of Education state a policy with respect to research and development, and implement this policy by allocating approximately 1 percent of the annual budget to this area of activity.

It is recommended that a Division of Research and Development be established with a staff adequate in numbers and in training to serve the operational divisions, and that a Council on Research be created.

Finally, it is recommended that the budget be planned so as to permit approximately one-half to be used for support of the research division and the remainder to be used for payment to local universities which will contract with the Board of Education for the conduct of the research that is important to the Chicago Public Schools, and for the training of research personnel for work in the Chicago schools.

XVIII

Schools and the Development
of the City

This is a critical period in the development of the City of Chicago. The city lost population between 1950 and 1960. The average educational level and the average occupational level of the adults of the city have been decreasing. Meanwhile the suburbs have been growing in population and in educational and occupational level. There has been a massive migration of middle- and high-income people from the city to the suburbs, to be replaced in the city by migrants from rural areas with lower education and lower occupational skills.

The city, through its Mayor and through its business and cultural leaders, is fighting to regain some of its former attractiveness as a place where all kinds of people, rich and poor, want to live and do business and raise their children. The official resources of the City of Chicago have been thrown into this fight, and have produced the Comprehensive Plan of Chicago.[1]

No doubt the foundation is here for further growth and continued greatness. The Chicago area is the largest diversified labor market in the country. There is relatively little unemployment.

---

[1]City of Chicago, Department of City Planning, *Basic Policies for Comprehensive Plan of Chicago,* 1964.

The metropolitan area is prosperous and growing. But the central city has lagged behind the suburbs. The same problems plague most of the other great central cities of the country.

To some observers the decline of the central city appears to be inevitable. They see the life of the city dictated by blind economic forces. But other students of the life of cities believe that the people who live in the city can control the direction and nature of its growth. People can make the city into the kind of place they want it to be. This is clearly what the leaders of the city believe. They are out to make the city a better place for human living.

The public schools are an important and indeed an essential agent in working out the fate of the city, since they largely determine whether people of middle and high income choose to live in the city.

Choices for the future

Chicago is choosing between two alternative futures.

Alternative A is the one Chicago will get if things go on as they have been since 1950. The proportion of manual workers to white-collar workers will increase. Nonwhite population will be about 33 percent of the total in 1970, instead of 23 percent as it was in 1960. Racial segregation will continue, with 300,000 more Negroes living in all-Negro areas in 1970 than were doing so in 1960.

Alternative B is what Chicago can achieve if people work for it. White-collar workers will stay in the city or move in from the suburbs. A majority of the population will be white-collar workers. The educational level of adults will rise. The proportions of whites and Negroes might be stabilized around 30 percent Negro. There will be a slow but steady movement toward residential integration, and the area of Negro residential segregation will not grow larger and will eventually begin to decrease.

This alternative is what the Mayor in effect has called for. This is the direction toward which the Chicago Committee on Economic and Cultural Development aims with its program for the development of industry and employment. The Chicago Commission on Human Relations is working toward this alternative.

The Comprehensive Plan of Chicago supports this alternative, with attention to social and economic policy. Major investments by corporations and individuals in new private housing lead in this direction. Religious organizations concerned with urban life are working toward this alternative, as are a number of civic organizations.

The role of the public schools

The public schools may be active or passive in this situation. They will be passive if the "four walls" school philosophy prevails. In this case the schools will do as good a job as possible for all kinds of students within the school, and will stay out of any direct involvement with community renewal programs. If they are passive, and follow the "four walls" principles, the effort at community renewal will probably fail.

If the public schools are active, they will adopt the "urban community" school philosophy. They will cooperate actively with the effort being made to achieve social and urban renewal in Chicago by the public and private agencies. They will develop programs and standards of instruction and attendance rules aimed at keeping middle-income people, white and Negro, in the city and encouraging them to live in integrated local communities.

The philosophy followed by the schools is crucial, as the following example will illustrate. In the vicinity of 83rd Street and Dorchester the Marynook Community is a modern postwar subdivision of middle-class homes which has been occupied by Negro and white families for several years. Their children attend an elementary school which is one of the most attractive schools in the city, and has a nearly 50-50 racial composition. But this school is in the Hirsch High School attendance area, which has become almost entirely Negro in recent years. Consequently the Marynook white children when they are ready for high school find themselves in a school that is more than 95 percent Negro.

Both the white and Negro residents of Marynook want integrated schooling for their high-school-aged children, and they have joined with other community organizations in the southeast area to petition the Board of Education for a clustering plan that would allow their children to attend the mainly white high schools in the vicinity. This the Board denied in 1963. The existence of an integrated Marynook is thus threatened by a rigid Board of Education attendance policy. The Board's policy in this case operates to increase segregation by driving the white residents away.

The Board of Education policy on integration

The Chicago Board of Education has affirmed its "belief that children in the Chicago Public Schools of different ethnic and racial groups should be integrated to the maximum extent consistent with the sound administration of the school system" and has approved in principle the recommendations of the Advisory Panel on Integration of the Public Schools.

The Board finds that integration in the schools is desirable as a means of improving our pluralistic democratic society. But integration depends on successful urban renewal, and school policies have a bearing on urban renewal. The report of the Advisory Panel on Integration (the Hauser Report) says,

> Finally, it cannot be too strongly stressed that programs to effect school integration must reckon with the fact that the white elementary school child is already in the minority in the public schools of Chicago and the time is not far off when the same will be true of the white high school student. Unless the exodus of white population from the public schools and from the City is brought to a halt or reversed, the question of school integration may become simply a theoretical matter, as it is already in the nation's capital. For integration, in fact, cannot be achieved without white students.[2]

The question of how many and what kinds of white students stay in the Chicago Public Schools depends on policies and practices in the Chicago Public Schools.

Are Negro children getting as good an education as white children?

One of the reasons this Survey was made was to answer the question whether Negro children are getting equal treatment with white children. There are several ways of answering this question.

---

[2]Chicago Public Schools, *Report by the Advisory Panel on Integration of the Public Schools,* 1964, p. 12.

Approximately the same amount of money is spent on a Negro pupil as on a white pupil. The Negro and white pupils in middle- and high-income neighborhoods are taught on the average by teachers of greater experience than the Negro and white pupils in low-income neighborhoods. Such teachers get higher salaries than younger and less experienced teachers get. Therefore there is a tendency for pupils in low-income areas to be served by less costly teachers, and the majority of pupils in low-income areas are Negroes. On the other hand, the low-income schools have certain extra services, such as master teachers and services of social workers. They also have an extra allowance for textbooks. All in all, probably the same amount of money is spent on a Negro as on a white pupil.

The schools in low-income areas, where the majority of Negroes live, have less experienced teachers. If this is taken to mean that the schools get inferior teaching, then many Negro children get inferior teaching. The cause for this condition is that many teachers, when they get seniority, choose to transfer to schools in middle- and high-income areas. However, the school administration is encouraging mature teachers to teach in the low-income areas, and it is recommended by the Survey that stronger measures be taken in this direction.

The schools in low-income areas, with exceptions when there is an unusually able principal, present the teacher with a problem of controlling the behavior of pupils which steals time and energy from the job of teaching. For this reason the learning that goes on in most schools of this type is inferior to the learning that goes on in schools where pupils are better behaved and have a stronger desire to study. In the course of this Report we have made clear that this is a fact, and it is one of the main problems recognized by the school teacher and principal.

To give a summary answer to the question, we shall say that pupils in low-income areas generally learn less than pupils in middle- and high-income areas, whether they are white or Negro. However, there is no deliberate attempt to give pupils in low-income areas an inferior education. On the contrary, the school staff work very hard to find ways to teach effectively in such areas. To date, they have not been as successful as they must be eventually. More money and more creative work must be spent to find out how to teach more effectively children who come from low-income and low-education families, whether white or Negro.

Another answer to the question has been given by the Advisory Panel on Integration, and will be repeated here. There is strong scientific evidence that growing up in a racially segregated society and going to school in a racially segregated school is harmful to Negro children. Therefore, Negro children who go to *de facto* segregated schools are getting an inferior education because of the fact of segregation.

The only way to reduce segregation of the schools substantially is to work for social urban renewal.

The school as an agent of social urban renewal

By social urban renewal is meant the physical and the social development of a city which make it a desirable place for all kinds of people, rich and poor, white and Negro, to live and raise their children. This means more than tearing down obsolete buildings and putting up modern houses and business buildings and factories. It also means developing a pattern of social relations and of cultural life which makes the city attractive as a place to live for adults and children.

In Chicago integration is part of the movement of social urban renewal, just as it is in most northern industrial cities. *But if Negroes were not present as a large minority there would still be an urgent need for social urban renewal.* This is the case in Minneapolis-St. Paul, for example, where there are few Negroes.

Social urban renewal will take a long time to accomplish. It means that people must get to feel at home in shopping centers, churches, schools, and parks, and in houses and apartment buildings where they did not grow up. They must get to feel themselves a part of the local community, and they must often become friends and neighbors with people who are different from those with whom they have been accustomed to live.

Progress toward stable social life will take a good deal of time in parts of the city which are now changing, while other parts are now stable and will probably remain so.

The contribution that good schools can make to the stability of a neighborhood is greater than that of any other factor. If the schools, both elementary schools and general and vocational high schools, offer high quality programs for different types and levels of students, the families of these students will want to remain in the area. In an area of mixed or changing racial composition, the quality of the local schools may well be the *determining factor* in retaining white families, or in retaining middle-class families.

PRINCIPLES OF INTEGRATION
FOR SCHOOLS

Since racial and ethnic integration is a stated policy for the Chicago Public Schools, and since this is an aspect of social urban renewal in a city like Chicago, it will be useful to summarize what is now known about the effectiveness of certain policies and practices through experience in Chicago and other cities, and what can be said on the basis of sound principles of community relations.

There is a considerable body of experience with attempts at integration in the public schools of other cities. New York City, for example, has had a deliberate and stated policy of integration for 10 years. Detroit, Baltimore, Philadelphia, and Los Angeles have been working at the problem longer than Chicago has.

The experience of failure or limited success

Much of the experience with attempts at integration has been one of failure. The existence of residential segregation in the big cities tends to defeat most efforts at integration, because nearness to a school is the determining factor in preference for a school with the vast majority of parents regardless of their skin color. *Residential segregation is the basic problem.*

Open attendance or permissive transfer. An obvious but generally unsuccessful method of promoting integration is to state a rule of open attendance—that any pupil may attend any school in the city if he can travel on his own responsibility to the school and if it is not overcrowded. Various adaptations of such a policy can be made in the form of permissive transfer under rules regarding the eligibility of a pupil for transfer and rules regarding schools available for transfer. For example, Chicago has tried a plan by which only the ablest high school students could transfer, but only to schools which were on a nine-period day or less. Another Chicago plan allows elementary school pupils from overcrowded schools to transfer to schools with vacant seats. These are severely limited plans compared with a general open attendance policy.

But no transfer policy has worked anywhere for large numbers of Negro pupils. This can be seen by examining Table 1, which shows the distribution of Negro and white pupils in schools in Baltimore, Detroit, and Chicago. Baltimore has had an open attendance policy for 10 years, modified by the closing of crowded schools to transfers. This policy was liberalized in September, 1963, to make nearly all schools open for all children. Detroit has a "permissive transfer" plan which is in effect an open attendance policy, not as liberal as that of Baltimore. Chicago in the autumn of 1963 had fixed attendance districts for all general high schools and elementary schools.

The three cities differ in relative numbers of Negro and white students in the public schools. They also differ in other significant ways with respect to residential patterns of Negroes and whites.

Yet the school attendance patterns are rather similar. There is a tendency for the number of schools with 50 to 90 percent white pupils to increase, as a number of Negro students transfer from the more highly Negro schools to ones not far from home which have some white children. There is also a tendency for the few white children in heavily Negro schools to transfer out, thus increasing the numbers of all-Negro schools. It is likely that if schools in Chicago were more widely open to transfer, 2 or 3 percent of Negro children would transfer to schools with a white majority. They would not transfer in large numbers.

A more positive administration policy toward transfers of Negro pupils would increase the numbers some, but not very much. In New York, where there has been a positive policy to promote permissive transfer, the result has not been striking. Only 6 percent of Negro pupils have transferred, even though their transportation was paid by the Board of Education.

Permissive transfer and open attendance policies result in more transfers where there is an active community organization to encourage the idea of transfer, to organize small groups of children

Table 1

Extent of integration in Chicago, Detroit, and Baltimore schools

Percent of student body Negro	Detroit 1961		Detroit 1963		Baltimore 1962		Baltimore 1963		Chicago 1963	
	Negro	White	Negro	White	Negro	White	Negro	White	Negro	White
A. Elementary schools										
99+	22.0	.05	36.3	.17	68.0	.10	66.4	.14	63.6	.16
90–99	47.4	1.71	37.0	1.45	15.9	.88	16.0	1.06	22.8	.76
50–89	22.6	7.34	18.0	7.21	9.8	6.4	10.3	6.3	10.1	3.5
10–49	7.4	16.3	7.6	16.6	5.8	17.7	6.6	32.1	3.0	8.0
1–9	.6	10.4	1.0	18.1	.53	17.6	.61	13.7	.46	12.0
0–1	.03	64.2	.09	56.4	.03	57.3	.04	46.8	.06	75.6
Total no. of students	94,000	106,000	101,000	98,000	66,000	45,000	70,000	44,000	200,000	183,000
B. High schools										
99+	0	0	26.6	.13	71.4	0	69.5	0	36.0	0
90–99	50.7	.95	20.7	.32	0	0	0.9	0	24.0	0.8
50–89	21.0	6.24	24.6	9.25	11.5	6.8	13.0	6.3	26.4	3.7
10–49	28.2	47.3	27.4	36.8	14.3	42.3	15.9	57.7	12.2	18.0
1–9	0	0	.5	21.6	2.8	43.2	1.1	26.6	1.5	23.7
0–1	.04	45.5	.12	31.9	0	7.7	0	8.8	0	53.8
Total no. of students	18,000	32,000	21,000	33,000	33,000	36,000	36,000	35,000	38,000	77,000

Note: Baltimore and Detroit have "open attendance." Detroit data are for senior high schools only, Grades 10-12. Junior high schools are omitted. Baltimore data include junior high schools with elementary. Chicago data for 1964 are only slightly different from 1963.

to transfer in a bloc, and perhaps to provide transportation for them. This has been done in New York City by civil rights organizations.

The attempt to combine a program of integration with one of relieving overcrowded schools does not succeed with both aims. One goal or the other will be missed. Generally the underoccupied schools are a long distance from the overcrowded ones, and children will not transfer unless they are assigned to do so by school authorities and given transportation. If the transfer is mandatory there is likely to be conflict at the receiving school between the local and the incoming pupils if they come from different socioeconomic levels, and often they are organized into separate class groups so that integration is minimal.

To summarize the conclusions from experience with open attendance policies, these affect at most a small group of pupils who are especially ambitious for what they regard as improved educational opportunity. These are often quite important pupils because they are likely to become leaders when they grow up. Open attendance is a desirable policy if it is not hedged in with restrictions on sending and receiving schools and if small numbers are acceptable as an indication of success.

The basic limitation on the effectiveness of open attendance policies is the fact that *the great majority of parents will send their children to the nearest school*, no matter how good or bad it is. There is no foundation for the fear felt by some people that their own familiar and satisfactory neighborhood school will be overrun by strangers of another color or economic level if open attendance or permissive transfer is adopted as a policy.

The tendency to send the children to the nearest school is greatest among the parents of lowest socioeconomic status, who are themselves busy with the pressures of everyday living, uncertain about their children if they are far away from home, and unaware of possible advantages of schools farther away. Therefore a policy of permissive transfer generally works to encourage the transfer of only the most ambitious and intelligent children or those who have ambitious parents.

It is a safe generalization that 80 percent of parents of public school pupils will send their children to the nearest high school, and 90 percent will send them to the nearest elementary school.

Open attendance also has the very important value of permitting white children and their families to remain in a neighborhood which has turned largely Negro and to go to a school which is not heavily Negro. Thus a degree of residential integration is protected by an open attendance policy. Open attendance is especially valuable in high schools, for the reasons just noted. A group of white parents whose children are in an integrated elementary school can remain in this local community even though it is the only white group in the attendance area of a high school that is 95 percent Negro, if there is an open attendance policy for high schools.

The Princeton plan. The Princeton plan is named after Princeton, New Jersey, where it has been successful. It consists of pairing elementary schools and sending all the children of half of the grades to one school and all the children of the other half of the grades to the other school. For example, Schools A and B which are close together would be paired, and all children from Grades 1 to 4 would go to School A while all children from Grades 5 to 8 would go to School B. If School A was largely Negro and School B largely white, there would be two integrated schools in their places. This plan has worked fairly well in Princeton because there are only two elementary schools in the borough of Princeton, the population is stable with no prospect of great change in the proportions of Negroes in the town, and the citizens of Princeton have studied their problems and have decided to support integration in their schools.

The Princeton plan is being tried successfully in a number of smaller cities, where conditions are rather similar to those in Princeton. But New York City is now trying it out in a different situation. The New York Board of Education announced early in 1964 that it would pair a number of elementary schools. Difficulties arose and the number was reduced to eight pairs. Currently, as the school year starts in the autumn of 1964, there is objection from some white parents, while others approve it, and the Negro parents seem generally in favor of it.

The plan is likely to run into difficulty in either of two situations. First, if children in one school are quite different in socioeconomic status from the children in the other school, parents of the higher socioeconomic group will feel that academic standards are threatened, even though they may favor integration. Second, if the schools are both in an area where there is pressure from Negroes for more housing, the effect may be to encourage first a few and then more white families to move away and thus to make the entire area a segregated Negro residential area. Both of these difficulties illustrate the need for careful study of the local community and for local community support of the plan before it is put into effect.

Necessary conditions for successful integration

The conditions necessary for a positive and sustained movement toward further integration in Chicago schools are the following:

1. A major program of opportunity or compensatory education should be placed in operation in all inner-city schools, with a substantial added expenditure between $100 and $200 per pupil. Some of these schools are now integrated, some are nearly all white, and some are nearly all Negro. This kind of program is a necessary companion to a program of integrated education. All schools in areas of low income need substantial added financial support.

2. The present ethnic complexity and diversity of the city should be respected. There are groups whose European or Oriental origins are so important to them that they want to live together and send their children to certain schools in their own neighborhoods. The strength of this desire is so great that it will defeat any program of immediate integration in the schools.

The achievement of integrated schools must be phased. The wise course at first is to work in the areas that most desire integration, and where there is a good prospect of stabilizing an integrated community. The next phase is to work in areas that can be prepared for integration on the basis of open and rational discussion of the problems.

The best policy is to maximize the extent to which integration is voluntary. It happens at times that efforts at compulsory desegregation actually retard integration.

This means that the Board of Education should carry on practices to promote integration more vigorously in some areas of the city than in other areas. Although some people may feel that such a policy is "unfair," it is the only practicable policy in a large, complex city which is just on the threshold of the great experiment of stabilizing an integrated population in a city which is renewing itself at the same time. There must be a "live and let live" spirit, in which parents in some parts of the city behave quite differently from those in other parts with respect to integration through the public schools.

3. The "neighborhood school" policy should be supported in principle, with some revision to fit the realities of life in a big city. The neighborhood elementary school essentially is a school which is near home for children, where the parents feel that the values of their local community are being supported, and where the parents take responsibility for supporting the school and its standards. It must be remembered that the large majority of all parents prefer to send their children of elementary school age to a neighborhood school.

At the high school level the limited neighborhood idea is far too restrictive to be useful in a big city. Chicago has a number of high schools open to students from the entire city. The big cities of the East have a tradition of city-wide high schools for students of special vocational interests and special abilities. For the sake of better schools in Chicago, it would be wise to put two or three or four high schools together into a cluster to serve an expanded neighborhood. This would allow for better high school programs and at the same time it might assist the process of integration.

The neighborhood school concept is inclusive, not exclusive. That is, it includes all children in a local area, but it does not exclude the idea that children from outside the area, in small numbers, might attend a local school because it serves their special needs.

Essential to the neighborhood school concept is the right of every child to attend a school near his home which has a program for him. Some pupils with special abilities or special handicaps may go to more distant schools which have special facilities for them.

The clustering of two or three elementary schools which are close together for purposes of improving their program, and the clustering of two to four high schools for the sake of better education, including integration, are in accord with the neighborhood school concept, provided there is a substantial consensus of parents and citizens in the local community that such clustering is wise.

4. The Board of Education should promote integration in large local areas of mixed residence, including two or more high schools. The most desirable size of the "local community area" is probably

200,000 to 300,000 in a big city. Such a community can have an all-Negro area, an all-white area, and an integrated area during the initial period of transition to a stable integrated community area. It will have several high schools, and a variety of other institutions. It can work out policies with respect to schools and other institutions that will lead to stable residential integration over its entire area. It can adopt a 10-year plan and work steadily toward the realization of such a plan.

Such a "home rule area" can proceed with its own enlightened approach to social renewal without frightening other areas of the big city that are not ready to move so rapidly. The other areas are likely to vote for bond issues and other means of school or civic improvement, if they are not "threatened" with forced social change in their own areas. Progress in the big city is most likely to come by means of progress in areas where the people are most nearly ready for it.

Such a home rule area should have a strong community council, with an education division made up of PTA representatives and representatives of other organizations. The Board of Education should set up a district which is contiguous with the defined area, and name a district superintendent who is positive toward integration and who knows how to relate the schools to the community. The Board of Education should encourage this district to develop its own educational plan within broad outlines approved by the Board, and should provide money for expansion of buildings and other facilities needed by the plan.

The Board of Education should work closely with urban renewal agencies of the city in the areas where it chooses to promote integration most actively. It should also work with the civic and religious organizations of the city, to secure their support and understanding of its program.

5. The Board of Education should not permit current lack of space and facilities to stand in the way of the active conduct of integrated programs of education in schools that are essential to the success of the program. Money should be provided to guarantee that overcrowded schools will not defeat the purpose of integration. This applies especially to high schools, which are so crowded now that they must be expanded anyway. The choice of sites for new

buildings and the decisions about additions to existing high schools should be made so as to facilitate the program of integration and in consultation with local community leadership.

Procedures for successful integration

If the conditions outlined above are met, there is every reason to believe that the Chicago schools will become an active agent for stable integration in the areas of the city where this is a real possibility. Chicago should be able to show the other big cities how a program of integration in the schools can support integration in the city rather than lead to the growth of segregation as has happened too often in the past.

The integration of the schools can only take place as part of a movement toward integration of the city, understood and supported by the city's leadership. As the Advisory Panel on Integration of the Public Schools said,

> The achievement of integration in the schools involves much more than modification of policy and program by the Board of Education. To implement a policy of integration requires a broad base of community cooperation and action, in addition to the adoption of the policies and programs recommended in this report. Mere admixture of white and Negro pupils does not constitute and will not produce integration unless other basic changes are achieved at the same time. Public and private policies and programs designed to retain and bring back middle-class white population to the City and to promote integration in housing, employment, religion, and society in general and attitudes of understanding and good will on the part of both whites and Negroes are as essential to the achievement of genuine integration in the schools as policies designed to eliminate *de facto* segregation in the schools.[3]

The program of the Board of Education aiming at integrated education should have two major aspects. One aspect of the program should aim to provide the opportunity for every white or Negro boy or girl over 10 years of age who meets reasonable conditions of school achievement to attend an integrated school. This

---

[3]*Ibid.,* p. 12.

may be called the *Program of Individual Opportunity*. It might be based on the following statements of intent by the Board.

1. Every Negro or white child at the fifth-grade level or over shall be permitted to attend a school which has at least 60 percent white pupils, provided he is not more than one year behind his age-level in reading ability.

2. The Board of Education will provide special remedial teaching (after school, summer school, tutoring, etc.) available to pupils who are more than one year below their age level in reading ability.

3. The Board will maintain elementary and secondary schools with at least 60 percent white pupils in sites which are well located for Negro pupils to reach them. However, in many areas these schools will be farther from home than other schools with greater proportions of Negro pupils.

4. Every pupil will have the right to attend the school of his home district or attendance area, regardless of his reading level, unless he is transferred to another school for a special class of some kind that he especially needs.

5. In the location of integrated schools (60 percent or more of white pupils) the Board of Education will cooperate with local community organizations to find or choose schools which are approved by the local groups. If there are areas where the consensus of sentiment is opposed to the location of an integrated school, the Board will respect this consensus, though it will also endeavor to help the people of the community meet their responsibilities in a pluralistic society.

The other aspect of the Board's program may be called the *Area Program for Stable Integration*. The Board should select three or four areas where stabilized integration is possible to achieve during the coming 10 years. The criteria might be: (*a*) the present population is between 40 and 60 percent white; (*b*) the area covers three to four high school attendance districts and has a population of 200,000 or more; (*c*) there is substantial local community organization which favors integration.

It is in such areas that integrated schools, astutely administered, can be used in a positive program to stabilize changing neighborhoods and achieve integrated neighborhoods.

Three such areas are described on pages 385-390.

Organizing Chicago schools to promote integration

With a program of the nature outlined, there would have to be some special arrangements made in the administrative staff of the school system. There should be an Assistant Superintendent for Integration and Community Development, responsible directly to the General Superintendent. This official should have a staff of one person in each district where there is an active program of integration of either of the two types mentioned. There would be at least 10 such districts, each with a district representative.

The district representatives would work with the district superintendent and the school faculties on behalf of integration. Each representative would help to organize a Community Education Council in his district, consisting of responsible leaders of civic, religious, and educational organizations. He would interpret the program of the schools to this group, and interpret the views of this group and of the community to the district superintendent and the central administration. He would be a specialist in school-community relations.

The Citizens Committee on Integration of the Public Schools. There is now in existence a committee to assist in implementation of the report of the Advisory Panel on Integration (the Hauser Report). This committee or its successor would be useful in the development of the plans sketched out here. Most of the major cities have citizens committees or commissions of this kind. They supplement the board of education, whose members are often too busy with other aspects of school affairs to give this one the attention it needs. Sometimes one or more board members serve on these committees. There are now active commissions, or there have been such commissions recently, in Detroit, Philadelphia, Baltimore, New York, Denver, and New Haven. They have been instrumental in getting public understanding and support for policies which the board of education was willing to adopt.

Such a group should take itself seriously. This means that it should employ an executive officer to get information, hold hearings, and prepare reports on behalf of the commission. Also it should define the central issues and focus on them. It should expect to make recommendations to the board of education and to the public.

DEVELOPMENTAL AREAS FOR PROGRAMS
OF INTEGRATED COMMUNITY DEVELOPMENT

There are certain areas where local sentiment favors integrated schools as part of a program for stabilization of an integrated community. Where such sentiment exists, the schools should enter into the closest cooperation with the organizations in the community that are working toward these ends. Such a matter as the location of a new school or the addition to an existing school should be discussed actively with a representative cross section of community leaders. The drawing of attendance areas is another such matter that ought to be discussed with local groups. The clustering of schools to promote integration and to stabilize the community should be a major goal of the school administration in such areas.

There are three geographical areas, each comprising a number of local communities, where conditions appear to be ready for an active program of integrated education as part of a plan for community redevelopment and social urban renewal. These areas are marked on the map in Figure 1, as A, B, and C.

A. *The Near North West*. This area is being called the Near North West, since it includes several of Chicago's 75 local community areas. With a heterogeneous population of 425,000 people, it has three general high schools, Waller, Tuley, and Wells which had, in 1963, a total enrollment of 6,800 white pupils, 990 Negroes, and 480 "others," largely Orientals. It also contains 41 elementary schools with ·a total enrollment of 36,340—22,580 white, 9,450 Negro, and 4,310 "other." This area includes all of the present District 7 and a part of District 6. Major building enterprises are being planned in this region, which can help to make it a beautiful and attractive as well as picturesque section of Chicago for decades to come.

This region can be stabilized racially. It has a number of community organizations of a civic and religious nature which have been studying their community and its needs, and they are in a position to represent it responsibly in discussions with representatives of the schools, the urban renewal agencies, and the Youth Commission. The Lincoln Park Conservation Association has taken a major interest in educational affairs for its own area, and might join in planning for this larger region.

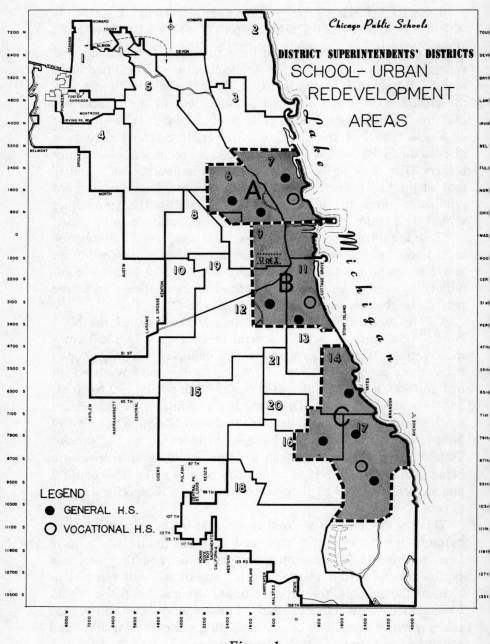

Figure 1

Among other things, this region needs a new high school. The location of this school and the nature of its program should be discussed with the community agencies, with the purpose of making it a major factor in the renewal and the integration of the region.

B. *The Near South West.* This area is great with tradition, now sadly disturbed by urban renewal, but great with potential for the future. It includes Chicago Circle, the site of the new University of Illinois which will become an internationally as well as nationally famous seat of learning. It includes Illinois Institute of Technology, soon to be expanded into one of the nation's three or four greatest centers of instruction and research in technology. It includes Michael Reese Hospital, one of the great research and treatment hospitals of the city. Facing Lake Michigan and McCormick Place are Prairie Shores and Lake Meadows, new high-rise integrated dwelling complexes. It also includes Chicago's Chinatown, which produces some of the brightest boys and girls in the public and parochial schools of the city.

The western boundary of this region should be determined on the basis of exploration with the present residents and those interested in the renewal of the area, which has been partly depopulated by the beginning of urban renewal. The region contains all of School District 11 and parts of Districts 9, 12, and 19. The population (corrected for the effects of recent urban renewal) is about 175,000 of whom 60 percent are white or Oriental, and 40 percent are Negro.

There are thousands of people already working or soon to be working in the scientific, educational, and research institutions of this area who do not feel that they can live here because the public schools do not offer what they want for their children. They will build homes on the vacant lots, and they will rent apartments in new apartment blocks to be built, once they know that their children can be sure of attending first-class integrated schools.

The present residents will welcome these neighbors. At the Board of Education budget hearing last December, a representative of one of the old residents' groups spoke as follows: "I am the chairman of the Pilsen Neighbors Education Committee. I am here representing the people of an area that 10 years ago had the possibility of becoming a slum. Our neighborhood has undergone tremendous change in the last years. Where the signs were once printed in Bohemian or Slovak they are now written in Spanish. Many of our people are newcomers to the city and many are new-comers to the United States. Our community has welcomed these newcomers as neighbors and has attempted to build a better com-munity with them. This is a task that can only be done with the cooperation of the citizens, the public agencies, and the city and national governments."

This region has a fascinating mixture of nationalities ranging from Hongkong to Warsaw by way of Mexico City. The three biggest ethnic groups are Poles, Italians, and Mexicans. There were census tracts in this region where 50 percent of the families had incomes of less than $3,000 in 1960, and there were other census tracts where more than 15 percent of the families had over $10,000 annual income.

There is no high school north of Phillips in this region, and a new school will be needed for the new population. The Board of Edu-cation might build here a model Central City High School, looking toward the Loop, which could become the finest general high school in the United States. It might be a semi-selective school, re-quiring a reading level of eighth grade at least for admission. It could have as strong a college preparatory track as any in the city, as well as a first-class commercial and mechanical arts pro-gram. The Board of Education should announce that the enroll-ment will not be allowed to go below 60 percent white and Orien-tal. Probably the enrollment would grow faster than units of the new school could be built. The school could be a vital element in demonstrating to the nation that it is possible to rebuild the inner city on a base that is not segregated by race or by income. As a fitting name for the new school we suggest it be called the Jane Addams High School.

C. *The South East.* This area includes School Districts 14 and 17 and a small part of 16. It has a population of about 350,000, about 60 percent of whom are Negroes. This region is nationally famous for its demonstration of a stabilized integrated residential area in the Hyde Park-Kenwood community. It is also unique in the extent of local community organization, and the amount of interaction between such organizations as the South East Commission, the Woodlawn Organization, the South Shore Commission, the Hyde Park-Kenwood Community Conference, and the Marynook Home Owners Association.

All the high schools are overcrowded in this area, and some new high school facilities are needed immediately. Here it is recommended that the leadership of the community be consulted on the matter of clustering of high schools so as to secure more integration and expanded high school facilities. Although the school administration should consult with community leaders on the matter, there has already been enough study and discussion in this region to suggest a procedure. Starting at the southern edge, it appears that Washington High School should remain as it is, since no great gain could result from clustering it with other schools. Then Bowen, South Shore, and Hirsch High Schools might be clustered into a single open attendance area. Here there would probably be some transfers out of Hirsch, but Hirsch is already overcrowded. South Shore and Bowen should get new facilities, either mobile classrooms, one or more new additions, or the opening or expansion of a branch. Probably a new high school should be constructed as soon as possible. The Board of Education should guarantee that neither South Shore nor Bowen will be allowed to become less than 60 percent white. This guarantee would hardly be threatened, since experience elsewhere indicates that at least 80 percent of students living in the Hirsch attendance district would attend Hirsch as the nearest school. Every student should be guaranteed the right to attend the school of his own residential district, unless he has a special need that requires his being assigned to a school elsewhere.

The Hyde Park High School is so severely overcrowded that something must be done there very soon to get more classroom space. Community organizations and the PTA have been studying the problem, and could work efficiently with the school administration. One possibility is to set up an integrated branch or even a new high school in the Hyde Park-Kenwood area, possibly making it semi-selective with an admission requirement of eighth grade reading ability.

The South East area has the greatest potential for early creation of a large stable integrated region, but it also has at present an uneasy equilibrium with the possibility of massive spread of segre-gated housing areas occupied by Negroes. It is not too much to say that the policies set by the Board of Education for high school attendance in this region will determine the outcome.

Concluding comments

The reader is reminded that the examples of these three regional developments are offered to give some concreteness to the idea advanced earlier of an Area Program for Stable Integration. We recommend that the Board of Education and the General Superin-tendent work at this task, with the aid of an Assistant Superin-tendent for Integration and Community Development, and that the Board agree to commit funds for needed new high schools to make these area plans work effectively. We have suggested that perhaps three or four new high schools would be needed in these areas. It was noted in Chapter X that Chicago urgently needs 10 new high schools to care for the 30,000 additional high school students of the next 10 years. Three or four of these schools could well be placed in these three regions, which have a third of Chicago's school population.

XIX

Administration and Organization
of the Schools

In every complex school system there is always the two-sided question whether: (1) the responsibilities of the people working in the various positions of the system are such that each works effectively and they all work cooperatively; (2) the geographical organization of schools into districts is accomplishing efficiently the work of the system.

Although the Survey did not include the use of experts on the over-all structure and administration of a complex school system, the experts in various aspects of school program pointed to certain desirable changes with such near unanimity that there was no missing the signal. Consequently, the following suggestions for administration and organization are offered to the General Superintendent and the Board members as a clear consensus from people who felt, each in his own area of competence, that certain general changes should be made.

DISTRIBUTION OF RESPONSIBILITY
FOR CURRICULUM AMONG PERSONNEL

What kind of decisions should be made by persons at the various levels of the school system? What initiatives should the classroom teacher take? What responsibility should the school principal take, and what decisions should he expect the district superintendent to make? Where does the district superintendent's authority extend into the separate schools, and what questions should the district superintendent pass on to the Central Office?

The general outlines and policies of the educational program and of the curriculum are determined by the Board of Education and the central administration. But there are many important decisions and initiatives which lie between this level and the pupil in the classroom. A visiting consultant, who is a university professor specializing in the teaching of a basic subject in the high schools, wrote the following paragraph, which was repeated in substance by nearly every subject-matter consultant.

> I think that Chicago needs curricula and programs by schools and not for the city as an entirety. This is based on both the need to adapt to the population and on the desire of creative teachers to share in and help shape the organizational framework within which they work. Administratively this seems possible now, but not greatly encouraged. To be effective, alert professional teachers must be hired, recognized, and retained in each school, and some leadership encouraged and developed in each school. The central administration could plan for such an organization with meetings of department chairmen and proffered assistance and recognition. This would get many more teachers involved in and thinking about curriculum and teaching matters.

Decentralization of responsibility and authority

This style of thinking would place the initiative and the responsibility for deciding what to teach (within the official curriculum) and how to teach it as close to the classroom teacher as possible. The teacher, the department chairman, and the school principal would share most of the responsibility between them. The Central Office would provide consultants and supervisors, but these people would be stationed in district centers and would operate as close to the classroom teacher as possible, holding in-service training sessions, giving demonstration lessons, and visiting and observing teachers a great deal.

The functions of the Central Office would be to draw up general curriculum guides and to bring in outside experts to consult on the general outlines of the curriculum and the plan of organization of the school, such as ability grouping, continuous development, and articulation of elementary school and high school for foreign language teaching.

Additional persons in the form of curriculum specialists have been recommended for work with teachers and principals in the fields of English, mathematics, science, and social studies, as well as in classes for the mentally handicapped and the socially maladjusted. These additional persons would be assigned to district offices or regional offices, where they would specialize in the curriculum for a certain type of school. One English specialist would work with the inner-city low-achievement kind of schools, adapting the curriculum to pupils who are lagging in reading ability and motivation for schooling. Another English specialist would work with the high-achievement schools, helping pupils, teachers, and librarians to develop lessons full of challenge to pupils who are quick learners and whose families expect them to achieve well in school.

This is also the recommendation of the team of suburban high school superintendents. They thought that there should be more differences between the programs of high schools serving different kinds of youth, and that such differences would arise if the principals, department chairmen, and classroom teachers were given more responsibility and authority.

This line of thought would result in the grouping of like schools together for curriculum planning and development of teaching materials. Several high schools with low-achievement pupils would work together on the program of Basic English, which many pupils in all these schools would be taking. It would also result in grouping districts together for work with elementary schools. Several inner-city districts could work together on the reading program, holding joint in-service training workshops.

The logical result of this kind of program making would be to group the 21 districts into a small number of regions, perhaps with some reorganizing of district boundaries so that they would be more homogeneous. This will be discussed later when we come to the matter of geographic organization of the school system.

Central Office authority and responsibility in certain areas of work

The foregoing recommendation in favor of placing the decision-making authority as close to the individual school as possible is made with certain clear exceptions, which will now be presented. These were noted in Chapter VI, on improvement of instruction, and also in several other chapters.

There are certain special areas of the school program which are not found in all schools, and for which the average principal or district superintendent is not well prepared to act wisely and efficiently. An example is the teaching of the deaf, in contrast with the teaching of the educable mentally handicapped. Few principals know enough about teaching the deaf to be able to supervise a teacher of the deaf in a special class. And few principals will have a class for the deaf in their schools. But most principals do have enough knowledge and experience to supervise the work of teachers of the educable mentally handicapped.

In the special areas the responsibility for directing the program and recruiting, selecting, and giving in-service training to teachers should lie with an assistant superintendent or a bureau director in the central administration. This person should have direct relations with the teachers and principals in the schools where the special program is offered. Examples of such special areas are:

Education of the deaf, blind, physically, and multihandicapped, and the trainable mentally handicapped

Educational television

Home economics

Industrial arts

Adult education

Foreign language programming combining elementary and secondary schools

Program of social workers in the schools

Educational and vocational guidance centers

Programs for preschool socially disadvantaged children

Programs for marginal adolescents

The responsibility and authority for major decisions in these areas should be located, for the present, in the central administration for one or more of the following reasons.

1. The program is so special or experimental that it needs to be supervised by a specialist for the whole school system, with authority to get things tried out in a variety of schools. The average principal is not able to handle this program wisely.

2. The program needs special support during a critical period while it is being reorganized, and before it is ready to be put into general practice.

3. The program is likely to run for two to 10 years and then be discontinued or substantially modified.

4. The program is not located in regular schools, but in special sites where it does not come into contact with principals and teachers of ordinary schools.

Integration and community development. Responsibility for this program should be in the Central Office, under an assistant superintendent, because this is a new function which will be performed most effectively in certain selected areas of the school system and in certain schools. Furthermore, this function should have the personal attention and commitment of the General Superintendent.

Research and development. The Assistant Superintendent for Research and Development should be responsible directly to the General Superintendent and should work directly through his own staff with projects located anywhere in the school system, some in individual schools, some in district offices, some in Central Office departments. He must maintain an objectivity and independence which permit him to report negative as well as positive findings to the staff, the public, and the General Superintendent. His is like the "quality control" department of a factory. He must be able to detect and report poor quality in the output before it gets into the hands of the public, who will then quit buying it. Therefore, he must not spare the feelings of production managers who want to make a good showing with top management.

THE SCHOOL PRINCIPAL

Again and again the staff and consultants of the Survey reported that the principal is the key person in the educational system. Sometimes they reported the principal as the source of success in a school, and sometimes as a source of failure. In order to increase the amount of success which comes from the work of principals, certain facts can be pointed out and certain recommendations made.

There are almost 500 principals in the Chicago schools. They range in age from the early 30's to the mid 60's. Their salaries range from $9,500 to $14,500. Some salary increases are automatic, depending on years of service, but others depend on being promoted by the central administration. Most offices in the central administration (assistant and associate superintendents, bureau directors, etc.) are filled from the ranks of principals within the system. Therefore the principalship is a complex hierarchy of positions, not a single position one holds for 10 or 20 years, as is the case in a small city.

By contrast, in a small or medium-sized city with one high school and 10 to 20 elementary schools, the career of a school principal is somewhat as follows. The high school principal comes from a position as assistant principal in the high school or is brought in from outside the city at the age of about 40. He works at this job generally for 20 years or so, becoming a legend in the community. His salary may be increased slowly and slightly. If he wants more responsibility, he applies for a superintendency in another city, or he may succeed to that position in his own city. Almost never does he stay less than 10 years in his post.

The elementary school principals are generally experienced teachers, frequently women, who have taught in several schools, often in high school, and become elementary school principals at the age of 35 or 40. They may change schools once in their career, from a less favored to a more favored school with perhaps a higher salary. They also become legends in their own neighborhoods, and sometimes remain long enough to have the children of former pupils in their school.

Thus the position of principal tends to be a stable one, at the top of the career line, and the principal has great authority and wins great trust from teachers and parents.

The principal in the Chicago schools leads a far different life. Starting at the lowest of the principals' levels, he has eight salary lanes above him to which he can be promoted by action of the administration (not automatically). Above that are four ranks, from district superintendent to assistant, associate, and general superintendent, if he aspires that high. If his job as principal starts at the young age of 35, he has a 30 year career, and is likely to be promoted between five and 10 times, which means he will average three years to six years at a particular school. Thus the Chicago principal is likely to be a mobile person.

There are some principals who deliberately choose and prefer the role similar to that of the permanent principal in a small city. They refuse promotion, except the annual salary increments which continue for two to 10 years, depending on the size of school. They do become legends in the local community. They often build up a corps of loyal teachers who stay with them even if the school "suffers" from a change of neighborhood. Or they may shift just once, to a bigger and "better" school, often followed by some of their loyal teachers.

Most of the Survey consultants rather preferred these long-sojourning principals, and suggested that a change should be recommended in the promotion procedure which would reduce the number of promotion lanes, and increase the number of automatic annual increments in salary. This, they thought, would have the effect of lengthening the term of a principal in a particular school, giving him a good chance to get to know the faculty and the community. The team of suburban high school superintendents also recommended a change of this sort, together with a system of initial choice which pays more attention to "the highly personal competence of working with people and eliciting the cooperative efforts of a professional teaching staff," in addition to proficiency in the academic examination for the principalship.

GEOGRAPHICAL ORGANIZATION OF SCHOOLS INTO DISTRICTS AND REGIONS

A kind of organization of districts for greater efficiency has been recommended that would require the grouping of schools into administrative districts aimed at accomplishing two things:

1. A greater measure of integration in three areas where the schools should assist in working for a stable integrated community. This would cover something like six of the present 21 districts.

2. A grouping of the remaining districts into three or four regions with schools of rather similar pupil characteristics. This might be accomplished on the basis of the three types of high schools described in Chapter X. The high schools with emphasis on college preparatory programs and high student achievement might be grouped in one regional administration, together with their feeder elementary schools. The high schools of the common-man type with their feeder elementary schools might be clustered in another regional administration, and the inner-city type high schools with inner-city type elementary schools might be placed under a third regional administration.

A glance at the map of Figure 1 in Chapter VIII will show that these three regional administrative units would each cover a wide area—including schools that would be many miles apart. They would be functional administrative units primarily, and not geographical units. The present system of 21 geographic districts should probably be retained, with slight boundary changes to fit the six types of regional units which have been proposed, or something like them.

This is not as complicated as it may seem at first sight. There are now two associate superintendents with regional responsibility, one for the north and the other for the south of the city. These might be supplemented by one more person and made into three regional associate superintendents. Then the three areas of integration and community development might each have two district superintendents, one senior and one junior, with the senior district superintendents working closely with the central administration through the Assistant Superintendent for Integration and Community Development.

Thus the organizational structure would be somewhat as follows:

Regional administrative areas

X High-achievement and college preparatory schools
  Three districts: two in the north and one in the southwest
Y Middle-level achievement and comprehensive schools
  Seven districts: north, west, and south
Z Low-achievement and inner-city schools
  Four districts: west and south

Integration and community development areas

A   Near North West: two districts
B   Near South West: two districts
C   South East: two districts

It will be noted that two different principles of organization are being applied here. One, which includes the XYZ regional areas, is based on the idea that schools which are alike in neighborhood characteristics and in pupil achievement will be put together for the sake of developing the best possible curriculum and school program for each of three types of schools. Specialists in a particular type of school program will be assigned to that region, and will be able to use their special knowledge fully and efficiently with the principals and teachers who can use best what they have to offer.

This will have the effect of highlighting the inner-city area as one with a very high percentage of Negro pupils. At the same time it will put more teachers, social workers, nurses, clerical aides, and preschool classes into this area than will be found in any other area. This will be the area of greatest expenditure of money and ingenuity in opportunity education.

Objections to this proposal will center around the fear that this form of administrative organization will result in more rather than less segregation by race and income. Admittedly, this is an important consideration. But, there also will be three areas where integration and community development are foremost. The establishment of one administrative district which specializes in programs for the socially disadvantaged has great possibilities for improvement in the schools.

We recommend that this form of organization be tried for five years, and then be reviewed thoroughly to find out what it has accomplished.

The other form of organization brings together in one administrative area a cross section of Chicago's population, by income and by race. There will be high-achievement schools and low-achievement schools in the same area. The aim will be to develop a stable integrated area of 200,000 to 400,000, which is moving toward community redevelopment patterns that may eventually be good for the entire city. Within each of the large areas there will of course be schools and smaller areas that are now segregated and will continue so for many years. But the processes of integration will be deliberately promoted.

The high- and low-achievement schools in these areas will be in communication with similar schools in the XYZ areas, and will get some help from them on curriculum adaptation.

Comparison with the new Detroit plan

This scheme of organization can usefully be compared with the *Detroit Program for an Integrated School System* which went into effect in the autumn of 1964 and is described in a statement formulated by the Detroit Board of Education. The Detroit plan is an outgrowth of about six years of relatively harmonious cooperation by various community organizations working with the Board of Education. In 1957 the Citizens Advisory Committee on School Needs was created by the Detroit Board of Education with George Romney, later governor of the state, as its chairman. This Committee made studies and recommendations over a period of two or three years. It was followed by a new Advisory Committee on Equal Educational Opportunities in 1960, which reported in 1962 with recommendations that would lead to greater racial integration of schools and staff in the Detroit schools.

Pursuing this goal further, the Detroit Superintendent of Schools announced a reorganization of districts which would make each of the nine districts a kind of cross section of the city's population racially and economically. (Detroit's nine districts are similar in size to Chicago's 21 districts, each with two or three high schools.) According to a memorandum from the superintendent's office,

Within the administrative district there should be a broad range in socio-economic, racial and cultural backgrounds of homes generally representative of the city so that as pupils progress through the school system they can gain common experiences, regardless of the area of the city in which they live.

The activities of pupils, as they progress through the school system, should increasingly broaden their range of contacts and experiences. Thus they start with the self-contained class in a neighborhood school, progress to the Detroit plan in the middle grades, then to a junior high school which brings together pupils from several elementary schools and then attend a senior high school which has pupils from several junior high school areas.

In order to make each district a cross-section of the city, it was necessary to make four of the nine districts combine areas that were not joined on the map. That is, there would be a high-status area on the edge of the city combined with an inner-city area to make a single district. Four combinations of this sort were made, together with five districts which are all one piece on the map but generally have peculiar elongated shapes. In other words, the essential thing is to get a cross section of the city's population into each district, rather than to define districts in the simplest and most convenient ways on the map.

Detroit has also created a School-Community Relations Division under an assistant superintendent, with a staff of intercultural coordinators, one in each district. Their assignment is to do the following:

1. Develop, advise, and conduct interschool activities of pupils of an intercultural nature.

2. Help teachers and administrators from areas of the city which differ racially and socioeconomically to cooperate in the resolution of school-community problems.

3. Conduct studies of programs, course offerings, staffing, housing, pupil supplies, school policies and procedures in relation to equality of opportunity and integration.

Similarities and differences between the Detroit program and what is recommended for Chicago are apparent. The important thing to note is that cities like Chicago and Detroit can work experimentally, flexibly, and explicitly to improve the learning that goes on within schools and at the same time to promote integration in the city.

For the next 10 years, at least, Chicago schools should be freely trying for the kind of organization and administrative structure that serves the purposes of integration and of community development, as well as the purpose of the most efficient pupil achievement within the school walls.

XX

Recommendations, Priorities, and Costs

This is a period of transition in the Chicago Public Schools. The theme since 1950 has been growth—getting *bigger*. The public school membership increased 57 percent between 1950 and 1964. The increase during the next 15 years will probably be less than 30 percent.

During the next 10 years the emphasis will be on getting *better*, or improvement in quality as well as in quantity. While quality programs have not been deferred during the past 15 years (this Report gives evidence of improvement in quality), the limited financial resources have allowed sheer growth to take precedence over quality at times. This is not to say that there will be no problem of physical growth in the future. There is now a critical shortage of high schools and at least 10 new high schools should be started immediately.

The history of the Chicago schools will almost certainly record that the period from 1965 to 1975 was one in which the schools concentrated on the job of improving the *quality* of education as part of the city's effort to make itself a better place for people to live and raise their families. History will also record that Chicago schools did many new things in the face of the new problems that confronted the great cities in this decade.

Basically, the task is to improve the quality of present-day education for three broad groups of pupils—the socially disadvantaged, the average, the intellectually superior. Another way to describe it is to say that the task is to reduce the numbers of disadvantaged and to increase the numbers of average and superior pupils. This will be accomplished over a period of 10 or 15 years, as the schools discover better methods for working with young children of the socially disadvantaged group. These children will do better in the later grades and in high school. Their parents meantime will learn to be more competent urban dwellers and citizens and will send later children to school better prepared. Furthermore, the numbers of newcomers to the city from rural areas will decrease.

Thus time is on our side if we work effectively on the problems of today. After 10 years it may be possible to reduce expenditures for the socially disadvantaged and to increase expenditures even more for the average and superior pupils if we wish to do so. But the present situation demands substantial increase of support for education of the socially disadvantaged child.

MAJOR WAYS TO IMPROVE EDUCATION

The many specific recommendations in the chapters of this Report can be summarized for the purposes of this final chapter into the following major recommendations.

Improvement of the staff

1. Substantial resources should be put into the in-service training of teachers.

2. Additional specialists in the basic school subjects should be assigned to work with teachers and principals so as to adapt the curriculum to the local schools.

3. The work of the school principal should be strengthened as an educational leader in the school and local community.

4. There should be substantial additions to the corps of auxiliary workers: psychologists, social workers, counselors, school-community coordinators, nurses, and clerks.

5. In the Teachers College and the Junior College, procedures for employing faculty should be simplified, and the present practice of examinations for certification should be discontinued. At the same time, faculty should participate more fully in the making of educational policy.

New and improved programs

1. Preschool classes for socially disadvantaged children should be expanded.

2. Class size in the elementary schools should be reduced to 30.

3. The program of classes in the field of special education should be expanded.

4. There should be more special classes in the local school for children who do not adjust well to the ordinary class.

5. Programs for marginal adolescents should be expanded.

6. Vocational education should be reorganized and expanded.

7. Adult education should be expanded and upgraded.

8. The Chicago Teachers College should become part of the state system as recommended in the State Master Plan for Higher Education.

9. The Chicago City Junior College should come under a new local Junior College Board, with more state support, as recommended in the State Master Plan.

10. Programs in the Teachers College and Junior College should be expanded: (*a*) toward preparation of more teachers to work in upper grade centers and high schools, in the Teachers College; (*b*) toward more emphasis on vocational education in the Junior College.

11. There should be a greater and more critical use of new technology in teaching, such as television and language laboratories.

12. There should be an expanded use of adult volunteers in the elementary schools.

Organization and administration

1. The present administrative districts should be organized into three different regions, each with elementary and high schools of a similar general achievement level. Each regional organization should have curriculum specialists working with teachers and principals to adapt the curriculum to the special characteristics of that region.

2. In possibly three administrative areas the schools should be organized to assist in a community-wide policy of stable integration and community development.

3. Administrative arrangements should be made to encourage

experienced teachers to work in "difficult" schools in areas of low income and high transiency.

4. A strong and technically competent research and development staff should be located in the central administration, to assist program divisions with research and evaluation techniques.

5. The present Citizens Advisory Committee should be continued at least through 1965, with an executive secretary, and should be asked to advise the Board of Education on programs of education for socially disadvantaged children and adolescents.

What can be done with little money?

Although the recommendations generally require new and added expense, some of them do not involve more than a reorganization or more effective use of present resources. They are:

Reorganization of and combinations of existing districts. This requires no more administrative staff than the numbers now on appointment.

Organization of three administrative areas for integration and community development.

Reorganization of special education services to give greater responsibility to central administration for directing programs for pupils with the less frequent types of handicaps.

Change in the conditions of tenure and promotion of school principals.

Reorganization of vocational education. Federal government money is available for expansion of new programs.

Expanded use of volunteers in the elementary schools.

More flexible and liberal program for the selection and procurement of textbooks and other teaching materials.

Reconsideration of the policy of standards and grading practices in low-achievement schools.

Transfer of the Teachers College to the state. This would save money.

Transfer of the Junior College to a new local Junior College Board. This would save money for the existing Board, but would not bring much saving to the local property taxpayer.

What are the areas of major needed expenditure?

The following changes involving major added expense are essential to any far-reaching improvement of the educational program.

Reduction of elementary school class size to average of 30 pupils
Addition of auxiliary services to elementary and high schools
Addition of new small classes for pupils with special disabilities and social maladjustments
A major program of preschool classes for socially disadvantaged children
Expansion of the staff of curriculum specialists who are attached to district or regional offices for work with pupils and classroom teachers
Expanded program of adult education
Expanded research staff
Expanded program for marginal adolescents
Expanded program of vocational education
Ten new high schools

A rough estimate of the amount of money needed for these improvements and additions comes to a little more than $50 million a year, as is shown in Table 1. This is a very conservative estimate. The $41,500,000 in Table 1 which is allotted to operating expenses amounts to about $80 per pupil, on the average. According to the recommendations of the Survey, this would be spent at a rate varying from about $50 per pupil to $150 per pupil, depending on the needs of the school. Every school would receive added support, and the inner-city type of school would receive more than the schools where the need is not so great.

This may be compared with what the New York City schools have done for almost half of the New York schools, which are in the *Special Service School* category. Those schools were selected more than five years ago on the basis of low reading scores, low IQ, high number of children receiving free lunch, high transiency, high number of pupils with a language handicap. These schools now receive special services of the kinds recommended for Chicago, at a cost between $150 and $175 per pupil above the per pupil cost in regular schools.

Table 1
Rough estimates of minimum necessary additional expenditures

Expenditures	Estimate
700 new teachers, to reduce class size to 30 in elementary schools	$ 4,000,000
1,000 new special classes, averaging 15 pupils	6,000,000
Additional classes in special education	1,000,000
Expansion of summer school and after-school programs	2,000,000
Preschool classes—200 classes—teachers and equipment	2,000,000
Additional auxiliary professional and clerical personnel (psychologists, counselors, social workers, nurses, school-community coordinators, school clerks, curriculum specialists) $45 per pupil in half of the schools; $25 per pupil in other half	18,500,000
Free one hour a day for department chairmen in high schools—400 chairmen	600,000
Additional vocational school program	2,000,000
Additional marginal youth program	2,000,000
Additional adult education program	1,000,000
Additional equipment for language, social studies, science	1,000,000
Additional for new media (TV, etc.)	200,000
Additional for research staff	1,000,000
Additional for central administration and related staff	200,000
Total operating expense	$41,500,000
New buildings, mainly high schools, but some elementary schools—outlay for direct cost and debt service on bonds	$10,000,000
Grand total	$51,500,000

In New York this extra expenditure is regarded as a basic essential for the kind of opportunity education needed by socially disadvantaged children. In addition, such programs as the Higher Horizons program are being supported by the Board of Education. Thus New York City has been spending more than is recommended as a minimum for Chicago.

Variations of expenditure in different types of schools

Questions will be asked about the Survey recommendation for higher expenditures in the low-achievement schools than in the average- and high-achievement schools. This is recommended because the need is greatest in those schools. However, it is also recommended that expenditures be increased substantially in the schools where children are better off educationally. Only in this way can Chicago schools keep up with the quality of education offered in most suburban schools, which spend as much as 50 percent more per pupil than do Chicago schools.

Parents of children in the more favored schools and areas of the city might reflect on the amounts of public funds spent for the education of children who reach different levels of the educational system. The annual cost per pupil in the various educational institutions maintained by the city and state for Chicago students is approximately $460 in elementary school, $600 in high school, and $1,100 in the Teachers College. A pupil attending inner-city schools for 10 years and then dropping out would receive education costing the city $4,900. A pupil attending for 12 years and graduating from high school would receive education costing the city $6,100. A pupil going on to four years of Teachers College or a state university would cost the city and state about $10,500 in total.

When the city adds perhaps $100 a year to its expenditure for socially disadvantaged children over what it spends for children who grow up in more favored circumstances, it still pays less for such pupils than it does for those who take advantage of free education for more years. And if the socially disadvantaged child then does better in school and stays to graduate or even to go on to college, this will be a very good investment by society in the increased earning power of the child, which means that he will pay higher taxes to the city and state when he grows up.

Where can the money come from?

It is well known that the tax rate for the Chicago schools is close to the present legal limit. For 1965 it can be raised three cents per $100 of assessed valuation without a referendum. The city voters can vote to raise the ceiling on the tax levy as much as 15 cents by means of a referendum. If the Board of Education can transfer the City Junior College to a new local Junior College Board in accordance with the State Master Plan for Higher Education, this will result in a saving to the present Board of approximately $5 million a year.

The Illinois Education Association is sponsoring legislation for a moderate increase in the grants by the state to local school systems which would add about $10 million a year to Chicago's share. This legislation can probably pass the State Legislature next spring if it is supported by Chicago members of the legislature.

Finally, three major federal laws will provide approximately $5 million more to Chicago schools than has been received in the past. These laws are the Vocational Education Act of 1963, the Economic Opportunities Act (Anti-Poverty Law), and the new National Defense Education Act.

These resources are summarized in Table 2. They add up to approximately $38 million, which is close to the amount needed for additional operating expense as shown in Table 1. Also, the Board of Education could go to the voters in a referendum with a proposed bond issue to pay for the construction of 10 or more new high schools and a few more elementary schools, which are badly needed.

Thus it appears that by stretching all of its resources for additional income, if supported by the voters in two referendums, the Board of Education could barely meet the cost of the minimum program here being recommended. This amount of money could be secured under existing and pending legislation and could have a substantial impact on the quality of education in Chicago.

Action is needed almost immediately if the Board wishes to undertake even this minimum program in 1965.

Perhaps the Board of Education will support a legislative

Table 2
Sources of additional money
for operating expense

Source	Amount
From additional state aid, if IEA proposal is adopted by the legislature	$10,000,000
From maximum raise in local tax levy, without a referendum (three cents)	3,000,000
From maximum increase in local tax levy, if approved by a referendum (15 cents)	15,000,000
From saving, if Junior College is transferred to a new local Junior College Board in accordance with the State Master Plan	5,000,000
From federal government for support of *new* programs under Vocational Education Act, Economic Opportunities Act, National Defense Education Act	5,000,000
Total	$38,000,000

program in Springfield, looking toward greater amounts of state support for school districts than is proposed by the Illinois Education Association. In any case, the Chicago Board of Education is severely limited financially, and is far below most of the suburbs of the Chicago metropolitan area in supporting the schools.

CONCLUSION

It is recommended that the Board of Education aim for a *balanced* school improvement, with more money and better quality in a variety of programs. Since the greatest need is in the schools which serve mostly socially disadvantaged pupils, a high proportion of new funds should be directed to this area. But added resources should be used to serve all areas and all ages, from adults to preschool children.

A

The Chicago Teacher Questionnaire

As part of the Survey it was decided to make a questionnaire study of teachers, with the following purposes.

1. To secure data about the way teachers view their jobs.

For this, a list of 54 aspects of the teaching job was made, and teachers were asked to say whether they were "satisfied," "neutral," or "dissatisfied" about each one. The range of aspects is indicated by the following examples: salary, relations with my principal, materials and equipment to work with, behavior of pupils, neighborhood in which my school is located, the system of ability grouping, amount of time I spend on record-keeping and other clerical duties, amount of pleasure I obtain from teaching.

Teachers were also asked, in other parts of the questionnaire, how they felt about such things as textbook supply, teaching in "difficult" schools, characteristics of a good teacher, opportunities to take part in research projects, etc.

Teachers were asked what might be done to make teaching in "difficult" schools more satisfactory.

Junior College teachers were asked how they felt about the new trimester plan, and also they were asked to rate their morale.

All teachers were asked a general question about their liking for their job.

2. To secure information on the usefulness of the curriculum guides produced by the Department of Curriculum.

3. To find out how age, sex, and years of experience are related to the ways teachers view their job.

4. To find out how the attitudes and characteristics of teachers are related to the socioeconomic area of the school and the race of pupils in the school.

One form of the questionnaire was made to serve for elementary school and high school teachers. This was found to require about 30 minutes' time by the average teacher. A shorter form was made for teachers in the Teachers College and the Junior College, but it covered much the same ground. Junior College teachers were asked in addition to respond to questions about relationships between faculty and administration, about their morale, and about the desirability of the new trimester plan.

The sample

After some study of the situation it was decided that it would be more useful and no more expensive to send the questionnaire to *all* teachers than to select a sample. Selection of a sample would have required either (1) a complete list of names and school assignments, from which a random sample could be drawn, or (2) a randomized procedure for distributing the questionnaire in the schools, which would have required a research assistant to go to each school and distribute the instrument. The first method was not feasible, and the second would have been as expensive as sending the instrument to every teacher.

The questionnaires were sent in the proper numbers to each school principal, who was instructed by the central administration to distribute the questionnaires to each teacher on June 25, which was "records day"— the next before the last day of school, when teachers were not meeting classes but were completing their class records for the year. This day was suggested by the administration on the ground that most teachers would have time to fill it out and mail it during the day, which would tend to maximize the returns. The directions requested the teacher to fill out the questionnaire anonymously and mail it in the prepaid envelope on June 25 to the research company in New York which would process the data.

The great bulk of teachers followed these directions. A few wrote notes expressing the following concerns.

1. In a few cases the questionnaire was not handed out by the principal until the following day, and some respondents were worried that theirs would not be counted.

2. Others complained that they were so busy on "records day" they did not have time to fill out the questionnaire properly.

3. Some wrote notes expressing their feelings about one aspect or another of the schools, as these were touched on by the questionnaire.

4. Some wrote notes expressing their opinions of the questionnaire. Though some of these were complimentary, others were critical either of the instrument from a technical point of view or of the idea that a fair and objective study would be made with the questionnaire.

There were 48 notes or comments of a paragraph or more, out of the 14,000 questionnaires. Their major themes were as follows:

Critical of the schools or specific administrators	24
Praising the schools or specific administrators	4
Critical of the questionnaire	10
Praising the questionnaire	4
Miscellaneous, mainly complaints about distribution of the questionnaire on "records day"	6

There were about 10 long and thoughtful statements about the teaching situation, which must have required at least an hour's writing.

The great mass of the teachers simply answered the questionnaire and sent it to New York. Only 49 questionnaires were so inadequately filled out that they had to be thrown away unused. The questionnaires continued to dribble in a few each day after the first two weeks, and a handful were received as late as August, after it was too late to use them.

Precautions were taken against one person filling out more than one questionnaire by sending to each school only the correct number for the number of teachers on the roster, plus one for the principal. Still, it may have been possible for a zealous person to secure copies from friends who did not fill them out, and thus to register his opinions more than once. In one case two identically completed forms arrived in one envelope, and one of them was discarded.

Although the questionnaire was not designed for principals, approximately 100, or one in five, filled it out and returned it, marking their teaching position as that of principal. Since this was only a 20 percent return, and since the questionnaire was not intended for principals, these were not tabulated.

The responses to the questionnaires were punched on IBM cards, and the questionnaires themselves were then destroyed.

The proportions of teachers in the various categories who returned the questionnaires are shown in Table 1. These proportions, varying from 65 to 85 percent, are reasonably high. Unless the respondents are

Table 1
*Comparison of respondents
to total teacher groups*

Teacher groups	Number returned	Number placed in hands of teachers	Percent returned
Total	14,226	20,472	69.5
Teachers college	212	289	73.3
Junior college	453	533	85.0
High school	3,792	5,825	65.0
Elementary school, plus supervisors and Central Office personnel	9,769	13,875	70.3

supervised while they fill out the questionnaires, and thus put under a certain degree of pressure, an 80 percent return is about a maximum.

In the actual processing of the questionnaires, about a third or 2,662 of the elementary school classroom teachers' questionnaires were set aside and not processed, so as to save time and money. The procedure for setting those aside was to place the questionnaires of elementary school classroom teachers in a pile as they arrived in the mail, and to go through the pile taking out every other one. This was not done for every shipment received, and consequently the number processed was more than half of the number received.

Is the sample representative?

It is important to know whether the sample of teachers who responded to the questionnaire is truly representative of the entire group. Was there any significant subgroup that did not respond or did not respond in proportion to their numbers? The fact that 70 percent of the total group responded gives fairly good assurance that the sample was a reasonably good one. It is also possible to compare the sample with the total group of teachers on age and sex, so as to find out whether the sample corresponded to the total group in these characteristics. The results of this comparison are given in Table 2. For a comparison with the data on the sample, we have used the Report of the

Table 2
Age and sex distribution
of questionnaire sample
compared with Retirement Fund

Sex	Questionnaire		Retirement Fund	
	Elementary	H.S.	Elementary	H.S.
Percent male	18	49	17	46
Percent female	82	51	83	54
Number	6,985*	3,770	9,614	4,286

	Questionnaire			Retirement Fund
Age (percentage)	Elementary	H.S.	Total	Total
20-25	12	14	13	12
26-30	15	16	15	18
31-40	27	22	26	26
41-50	19	17	19	18
51-65	26	29	26	25
66+	1	2	1	1
Total number	9,678*	3,775	13,453	18,118

*The difference between the two numbers of elementary school teachers is due to the inclusion in the age table of the 2,662 questionnaires from elementary school teachers which were not processed. This was necessary because the Retirement Fund data do not distinguish between elementary school and high school substitutes, and substitutes had to be included to get correct age distributions.

Note: Retirement Fund data show 6,755 teachers in substitute status as of August 31, 1963. The actual number of substitutes in June, 1964, was 4,033. This number was assumed to have the same age distribution as the substitutes in August, 1963, and was added to the age distribution of the regularly assigned teachers in order to obtain figures of this table.

Public School Teachers' Pension and Retirement Fund of Chicago, *Actuarial Statistics*, August 31, 1963. This report gives the age, sex, and other characteristics of the contributors to the pension fund, and these are all the teachers who were in the employ of the Board of Education during the year 1962-63. The report includes a small number of teachers who are on leave of absence. This particular report indicates that there were 6,757 "substitutes" in 1962-63. These were fully licensed teachers teaching in Chicago schools on a full-time basis, who had not passed the examination for a Chicago teachers' certificate. These people received the questionnaire, as did the teachers who were "regularly assigned." But in June, 1964, when the questionnaire was distributed, there were 4,033 substitutes. Accordingly, the age distribution of these 4,000 was assumed to be the same as that of the 6,757 on record in August, 1963. This means that the age data for the Retirement Fund group are not exactly accurate, especially for the younger age groups, which contain many substitutes.

Table 2 shows that the respondents to the questionnaire were very similar to the total group in sex and age. It appears that proportionally a few more men responded to the questionnaire than would have been expected, and slightly fewer people in the age group 26-30.

Some social characteristics

Not much is known about the social characteristics of American teachers, and the data from this study answer some questions that interest the social scientists who study the structure of American society. One such question has to do with the socioeconomic backgrounds of teachers. Do they still come largely from farm families, as used to be the case? How many of them were raised in homes of manual workers? How many of them are children of teachers?

Answers to these questions are given in Tables 3 and 4. Table 3 shows fathers' occupations, grouped into 14 categories. The respondent was asked to indicate his father's principal occupation, by checking the one on the list which was closest to his father's occupation. If he was uncertain, he was asked to write down the occupation, which was then placed in the appropriate category by a person who read the questionnaire and was trained to do this work. For example, if a teacher wrote down "policeman," this occupation was placed in the category "Foreman and similar." If he wrote down "truck driver," the occupation was placed in the category of "semiskilled worker."

In Table 4, the occupations have been grouped into four broad groups, as follows: A—professional and managerial; B—clerical and

Table 3
Occupations of fathers of teachers
(percentages)

Category	Elementary school	High school	Junior college	Teachers college
Farm laborer	0.5	0.5	0	0.5
Laborer, not farm	5	4	2	4
Farm renter	0.5	0.5	0	1
Semiskilled worker	12	9	10	5
Skilled worker	14	16	15	14
Foreman and similar	17	14	10	7
Office worker	5	6	6	5
Store clerk	1	1	1	0
Farm owner	3	4	6	4
Small business owner	16	17	18	21
Salesman of insurance, etc.	6	5	6	7
School teacher	4	4	2	4
Doctor, lawyer, other professions	12	13	18	17
Business manager or owner	5	6	6	9
Number	6,930	3,713	425	205

Table 4
Socioeconomic backgrounds of regular classroom teachers
(percentages)

Socio-economic group of father	Elementary school			High school			Junior college	Teachers college
	Male	Female	Total	Male	Female	Total		
D (low)	27	16	18	21	10	14	12	11
C	33	31	31	30	24	30	25	21
B	20	26	25	24	30	27	31	30
A (high)	20	27	26	25	36	29	31	37
Number	720	4,430	6,930*	1,123	1,250	3,713*	425	205

*Includes counselors, adjustment teachers, nurses, assistant principals, and other nonclassroom teachers.

small business; C—skilled work and foreman and similar; D—semi-skilled and unskilled.

Three things stand out in these tables. One is that the profession of school teacher offers opportunity for upward social mobility. Almost half of the Chicago teachers were reared in the homes of manual workers. A second point is that men are more likely than women to have been upward mobile. A third point is that the social origins rise progressively from elementary to secondary to junior college to teachers college faculty.

Before World War II it was generally true that school teachers were recruited heavily from farm families. But only 4 or 5 percent of present-day Chicago teachers were raised on a farm. As Table 5 shows, the majority of Chicago teachers grew up in Chicago and three-fourths of them grew up in a big city.

Validity of the attitude scales

Since a large part of the questionnaire deals with attitudes and questions of satisfaction and dissatisfaction, it is important to answer questions

Table 5
Geographical origins of Chicago teachers
(percentages, unless otherwise stated)

In what part of the world did you grow up?

	Elementary school	High school	Junior college	Teachers college
Chicago	70	69	51	46
USA outside of Chicago	6	8	9	9
USA outside of Illinois	23	19	35	41
Outside the USA	1	1	5	4

In what kind of residential area did you grow up?

	Elementary school	High school	Junior college	Teachers college
Big city (over 100,000)	75	74	64	59
Suburb of a big city	5	5	7	6
City of 10,000 to 100,000	8	8	12	12
Town of less than 10,000	7	7	10	16
On a farm	4	4	5	7
Number	7,019	3,782	428	207

that may be raised about the validity of the instruments that are being used. One way to answer this question is to compare the results of several different ways of asking questions about satisfaction and dissatisfaction. For example, the respondents to the questionnaire were asked the following question: What is your attitude, in general, about your present position? The responses were as follows, from the various groups of teachers, in percentages.

	Elementary	H.S.	Jr. Coll.	CTC
Very favorable	33	29	28	36
Favorable	40	45	46	46
Neutral	14	14	12	9
Unfavorable	10	10	11	7
Very unfavorable	4	3	3	2

We may ask, how does this measure of the teachers' attitudes compare with some other measure? If they agree, this is evidence of the reliability of the data, and some evidence also of the validity of the measuring instrument.

Another way of measuring attitude toward the job is to use the "job aspects" score. This is the amount of satisfaction expressed with the 54 "aspects of the job" that were listed on the questionnaire. The satisfaction scores were grouped into five equal-sized groups or quintiles. Thus each person had a score from 1 to 5 on his satisfaction with various aspects of his job. The "satisfaction with job" scores for college teachers are reported in Table 6, compared with scores on the "attitude toward job" item which was stated above. It will be seen that there is a close correspondence between the two sets of scores.

The "job aspects" score or "satisfaction with job" score is really a composite score which reports a teacher's satisfaction or dissatisfaction with a wide variety of conditions and circumstances in connection with his work. By grouping the scores into quintiles it is possible to distinguish clearly five levels of satisfaction-dissatisfaction, which is more convenient than the five-point scale for the general question about attitude toward the job, where three-fourths of the responses are clustered at the two highest points of the scale.

However, there is one disadvantage of the "job aspects" quintile score. It is designed for classroom teachers, and all the items do not apply well to nonclassroom teachers such as counselors, librarians, and nurses. On an item such as "the textbooks available in my classes," a person who does not teach a class will probably mark his attitude "neutral." Therefore the nonclassroom teachers are less likely to have

Table 6
Cross-validation of the job attitude question with the "satisfaction with job" score (percentages, unless otherwise stated)

"Attitude toward job" score

Junior college faculty

"Satisfaction with job" score	VF	F	N	U	VU	NR	Total percent	Number
1 (low)	5	15	34	50	75	57	20.5	90
2	6	22	42	21	25	0	19.5	86
3	20	28	19	18	0	29	23.0	101
4	28	21	4	7	0	14	18.6	82
5 (high)	42	14	2	5	0	0	18.4	81
Total number	120	204	53	44	12	7	100	440

Teachers college faculty

	VF	F	N	U	VU	NR	Total percent	Number
1 (low)	5	19	39	62	100	50	20.0	42
2	12	29	33	23	0	0	21.9	46
3	15	25	22	8	0	0	19.1	40
4	26	19	6	8	0	50	19.5	41
5 (high)	42	9	0	0	0	0	19.5	41
Total number	76	97	18	13	4	2	100	210

Note: VF=very favorable; F=favorable; N=neutral; U=unfavorable; VU=very unfavorable; NR=no response.

extreme satisfaction or dissatisfaction scores because they are probably "neutral" to several items on which classroom teachers have well-defined attitudes.

The measurement of socioeconomic area

Another important scale in the questionnaire is that which characterizes a school by the socioeconomic area it serves. Many of the comparisons in Chapter XVI used this scale as a measure of the "difficulty" of a school. The item read:

In what kind of socioeconomic area is your school located? The responses were as follows, in percentages:

	Elementary	H.S.	Elementary school types
Upper- or middle-class area	5	10	9
Mixed middle- and working-class area	30	49	19
Stable working-class area	19	17	20
Lower-class or slum area	46	23	52
Other	1	2	

The "other" responses that were written in were either "Chicago Loop" or "wide span of socioeconomic levels."

Since the responses to this item were used in many important tables, it is useful to ask whether the teachers understood the meanings of these phrases in the same way that a sociologist does. The most difficult distinction to make was probably that between "stable working-class area" and "mixed middle- and working-class area."

One way to check on the teachers' judgments is to compare the results of their responses to the questionnaire with the results of the analysis of elementary schools by the Survey staff member who studied such schools intensively and divided them into four categories (see Chapter VIII). His division was based as much on school climate as on purely socioeconomic factors. He grouped the elementary schools as shown in the table above (in the column headed "Elementary school types"). It will be seen that the largest discrepancy is in the category of "mixed middle- and working-class" which is the main-line type of school in Chapter VIII. The amount of agreement between the two sets of data is enough to indicate that the classroom teachers were probably being fairly realistic and fairly accurate in their descriptions of the schools' socioeconomic areas.

B

Teachers College and
Junior College

This supplement will amplify Chapter XIII, giving added information on faculty, students, buildings, and libraries.

TEACHERS COLLEGE

The faculty

Members of the Chicago Teachers College faculties in the winter trimester of 1964 numbered 348, of whom 235 were full-time and 113 part-time.

"At Chicago Teachers College South faculty members holding a Master's degree make up 19.2 percent of the faculty, Master's degree plus 36 hours are 36.9 percent, and 43.9 percent have earned doctorates. At Chicago Teachers College North the percentages are: 29.5 percent, 30.5 percent, and 40.0 percent, respectively.

"The doctoral degrees were earned at 29 different universities; the Master's at 33. In 1954, four-fifths of the staff came from Illinois graduate schools and only one-fifth from schools outside of Illinois. The only foreign school represented was the University of Ottawa (Canada). At the present time approximately two-thirds of the faculty come from Illinois graduate schools and about one-third from schools outside of Illinois including the Universities of Ottawa, Paris, and Lvov. This improved balance in staff is especially desirable in the Chicago Teachers

Colleges, which serve student bodies from a geographically restricted area."[1]

About half of the full-time faculty have come to the Chicago Teachers College from the faculty of another college or university, one-fifth directly from graduate schools, and one-fourth from teaching in secondary or elementary schools.

Students

"In order to be admitted to either Chicago Teachers College South or Chicago Teachers College North, a student must be a citizen of the United States and a graduate of a state-recognized, four-year high school. A declaration of intention to teach in Illinois public schools and evidence of ability to engage in teaching are also required.

"The faculty sets specific standards of admission with respect to scholastic status and ability. For a high school graduate without advanced standing two criteria are employed: namely, rank on a college level scholastic aptitude test, national in scope, and rank in high school graduation class. At the present time students above the twenty-fifth percentile rank on the national test are admitted. If scores fall within a band slightly below the cut-off point, admission is granted to those who are in the top quarter of their high school graduation class.

"For undergraduates transferring from accredited colleges and universities with 30 or more semester hours of credit a cumulative grade average of 3.25 (C=3.0, B=4.0) has been established. For a lesser amount of college credit, the rank on the national test is taken under consideration as well as college grades.

"Admission policies are constantly under study. Currently being considered are questions relating to the cut-off point on the national tests, to the language proficiency of prospective teachers, to the able student with weak academic background, and to a wide range of other factors which influence success in college. Before applying for student teaching or during the junior year, all students are required to take proficiency tests in speech, English, and mathematics. The results are an important factor in determining the competency of a student to enter student teaching.

"During the last ten years the total fall-term enrollment of undergraduates doubled, mounting from 2,086 to 4,039. The enrollment of Chicago Teachers College South and branches rose from 2,086 in 1954

---

[1]Staff Report, *Higher Education*. Chicago Public Schools, 1964, p.30.

to 2,305 in 1963. At Chicago Teachers College North, the opening enrollment of 979 in 1961 increased to 1,734 in 1963. In the same decade the proportion of men in the student body varied little. In 1963 at the southside campus 34.1 per cent were men whereas at the northside campus there were 16.4 per cent."[2]

Data on the persistence of students in Chicago Teachers College South are presented in Table 1. About one-fourth of the entering students completed degrees in four years. An unknown number completed their work in later years.

The average ages of day students enrolled in a recent year were: CTCN—20; CTCS—22; Crane—29.

The Teachers Colleges get most of their day undergraduate students from their immediate vicinities. (See Figures 1 and 2.) CTCS enrolls 34 percent of its students from nonpublic high schools while CTCN gets 26 percent from nonpublic schools.

It can be seen in Table 2 that 78 percent of the 1963 freshmen at North and 71 percent of the entrants at South came from the upper half of the high school graduating class.

Students at Crane Branch of CTCS are older and have more work experiences than those at the other colleges. They have all attended other colleges, and almost all are married, have children, and must work part-time, if not full-time.

What becomes of graduates? In the decade from 1954 to 1963, the Chicago Teachers College awarded a total of 4,152 bachelor's degrees and 552 master's degrees. In this 10 year period, the percents of graduates completing the various curricula are: Kindergarten-Primary, 12.8; Grades 3-8, 74.8; Physical Education, 3.4; and High School Major Sequence, 9.0.

"Several follow-up studies conducted during the past decade indicate that the great majority of graduates of Chicago teachers colleges pass a Chicago certificate examination and accept employment in the Chicago public schools. In the period from January, 1953 to June, 1959, approximately 85 percent of a total of 2,500 graduates were employed in the Chicago public schools. Nearly 1,800 of these had passed examinations for a Chicago certificate, and an additional 459 obtained temporary certificates to teach in the local school system. Many of the latter group, it is reasonable to assume, eventually passed the certification examinations.

---

[2]*Ibid.*, pp.9-10.

Table 1
Persistence for the class entering September 1959,
Chicago Teachers College South

	Number	% of total
Persisted less than one year	144	39
Persisted one but less than two years	80	22
Persisted two but not three years	37	10
Persisted three but not four years	15	4
Persisted all four years	95	26
Total	371	

Table 2
Percentage of freshmen entering September 1963,
*who were in each quarter of their high school
graduating classes*

	CTCN		CTCS	
	Number	% of total	Number	% of total
Top quarter	197	45	125	41
2nd quarter	145	33	90	30
3rd quarter	90	20	58	19
4th quarter	9	2	30	10
Totals	441	100	303	100

"A study of 601 June graduates for the years 1957–61 revealed that 436, or 73 percent of the total, passed at least one Chicago certificate examination. As of April, 1963, 70 percent of the 601 graduates were regularly assigned Chicago teachers. In the most recent follow-up, questionnaires were mailed to the December, 1962 graduates. Eighty-seven of the 101 graduates responded. Of the 84 graduates who were teaching, 78 had accepted positions in the Chicago public schools.

"One report has been made on the graduates of Chicago Teachers College North. Data on 187 students who graduated between September 1, 1962 and August 31, 1963 indicate that 150 were teaching. One hundred twenty were teaching in Chicago."[3]

A source of pride to Crane is the fact that, of its more than 200 graduates, 70 percent are now teaching on Chicago's West Side.

CHICAGO CITY JUNIOR COLLEGE

The faculty

As of September, 1963, the total full-time faculty numbered 539, while there were 185 part-time members. Fifteen percent of the full-time faculty held Ph.D. degrees, and 82 percent had a master's degree.

"Chicago City Junior College faculty members earned their highest degrees in 85 different colleges and universities throughout the United States and in nine foreign institutions of higher learning. Fifty-five percent of 75 doctoral degrees and 62 percent of the 281 master's degrees were awarded by Chicago area institutions. The University of Chicago leads in the number of degrees awarded Chicago City Junior College teachers, with 29 doctorates and 137 master's degrees. Next in order are Northwestern University, De Paul University, Loyola University, and the University of Illinois. Outside the Chicago area the University of Illinois leads with 23 graduate degrees. Foreign universities are represented by faculty members with eight doctorates and five master's degrees."[4]

The average teaching load for the Junior College faculty is 16 to 18 hours per week. In accordance with Board of Education regulations, faculty members are required to be in attendance at school for 30 hours a week. This factor of teaching load, among other things, probably contributes to the greater dissatisfaction of faculty of the Junior College

---

[3] *Ibid.*, pp.16-17.
[4] *Ibid.*, pp.21-22.

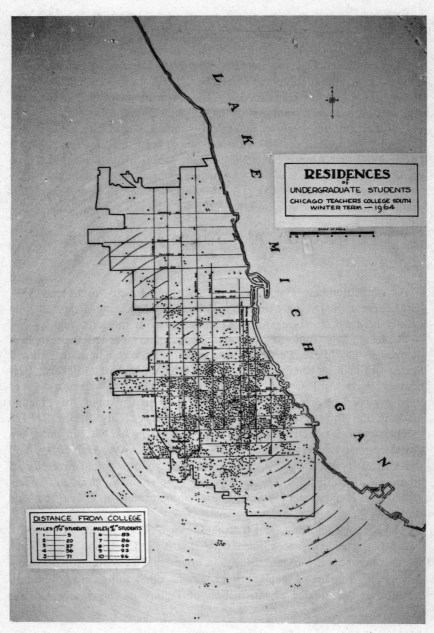

Figure 1

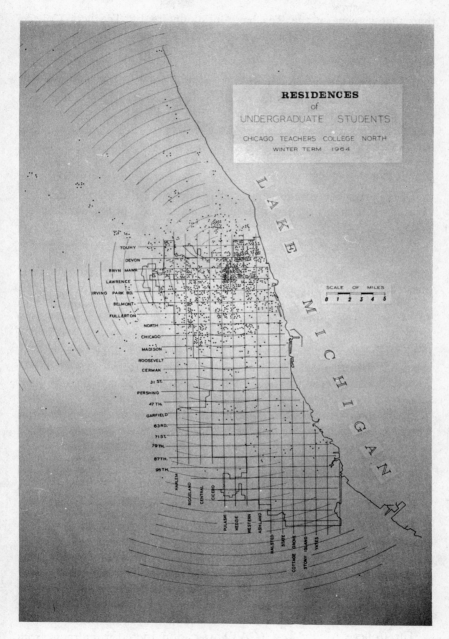

Figure 2

than that shown on the Teacher Questionnaire by Teachers College faculty. The Teachers College course load is 12 hours per week. Another factor is the difference between physical facilities, which favors Teachers College.

This is a period of growth and of challenge, with many opportunities as well as many frustrations for faculty members. With the establishment of the Faculty Council and with the physical and financial improvements that must come, the attitudes of faculty members will probably improve substantially during the next year or two.

Students

The Chicago City Junior College is an "open door" college. Graduates of accredited high schools, transfer students, and special students 21 years of age or older are admitted.

In the fall trimester, 1963, the College enrolled 29,700 students (14,820 full-time equivalents). Thirty-nine percent (11,500) were day students and 61 percent (18,200) evening students. In terms of full-time equivalents, 58 percent were enrolled in the day program and 42 percent in the evening program. There were 7,540 full-time students and 22,160 part-time students.

Each branch of the College draws its greatest proportion of Chicago Public High School graduates from schools nearest that branch. For instance, 36 percent of Southeast's new freshmen from Chicago Public High Schools entering in fall, 1963, were from the two nearest high schools.

Of the new freshmen entering in fall, 1963, 56 percent were from Chicago Public High Schools and 22 percent were from private or parochial high schools. Only 20 percent were from outside Chicago and 2 percent were admitted by examination or did not indicate their high school. A sizable proportion of the student body is made up of sons and daughters of working people seeking to improve their occupational and social skills.

The day students of the Junior College are younger than the evening students, and a smaller proportion is employed. The median age of day students was 19.7, of evening students, 22.9. While 15 percent of the day students were 25 years or older, 40 percent of the evening students were in this age group. The majority of the students are at least partially self-supporting. Approximately 88 percent of the evening students are employed, slightly more than 60 percent of the day students.

The College Ability Test (CAT) was administered to entrants from 1956 to 1963. Assuming that junior college entrants scoring above the

25th percentile on national college norms have the scholastic aptitude to succeed in the average college, it can be inferred that 50 percent of the Chicago City Junior College entrants have similar possibilities. But 25 percent score below the 10th percentile, probably indicating the necessity of precollege or remedial work. The 10th percentile has been used as the cutoff point for placing students in the precollege level Basic Program.

The levels of the general scholastic scores vary from branch to branch. The available median scores compiled over a period of several years indicate that from 10 to 50 percent of the entrants, depending on the branch, have not demonstrated the scholastic aptitude necessary to have much chance of success in regular college courses.

The proportion of students who complete a four-trimester course and qualify for a diploma or a degree of Associate in Arts is rather small. In 1962–63 there were 1,333 such graduates out of 29,700 enrolled (14,820 full-time equivalents). There is evidence that for every student who graduates and then transfers to a four-year college there are at least two who transfer before completing the Junior College requirements. A survey of 600 June, 1963, graduates of the Junior College indicated that over 60 percent planned to continue full-time academic work and 22 percent expected to continue on a part-time basis.

Student activities. The degree of student participation and the scope of student activities varies greatly among the branches. Indifference and lack of facilities and financing hamper the programs. A continuing problem in a two-year institution serving commuting students is the identification and development of student leaders. There is a lack of continuity in the student body. Student activities are financed mainly by student fees, which are also used for other essentials of the college operation.

Student government, and the various clubs, usually meet during an activity hour set aside one or two days a week. Originally there were no classes during this time, but overcrowding is forcing some branches to schedule classes during the activities hour, thus reducing the opportunity for participation in the activities.

Amundsen-Mayfair, Crane, Wilson, and Wright have intercollegiate athletics, but facilities are not available at Bogan, Fenger, Loop, or Southeast. Intramural programs are limited for the same reason.

Crane, Wilson, and Wright have active speech, drama, and music organizations. Plays, variety shows, and concerts are produced and presented to community audiences. Few outside cultural events are brought to the students because of lack of funds or the facilities to house the performers.

The knowledge, skills, and general cultural uplift gained through participation in extracurricular activities are important to junior college students. These activities provide students with an opportunity to gain the social skills that may mean success in later life.

The location of students and the distance they travel. There are no restrictions placed upon residence within Chicago for attendance at any of the branches, but the students tend to attend those near their homes. This fact is reflected in the racial and social composition of the student bodies, which resembles that of the neighborhood in which the college is located. Analyses show that the branches tend to serve a neighborhood or community reaching out about five miles from the site of the branch. The centrally located downtown branch has a wider dispersion of students.

Junior College building facilities

All branches of the Chicago City Junior College except Wright share facilities with other educational units. All branches except the Loop Branch are either housed in or share buildings constructed or reconditioned as elementary, junior high, or high schools. Fenger and Bogan are exclusively late afternoon and evening operations. Southeast has a relatively small day program limited by a lack of classrooms.

Each branch reported that students had been turned away because of limitations in budget, facilities, or course offerings. The record enrollments expected in fall, 1964, should drastically increase the number turned away.

Wright Branch. The Wright Branch, built about 1928, was a junior high school until 1934. It accommodated 1,800 students. With conversions and a $350,000 addition, Wright was offering junior college courses to 9,246 students in 1963. It is estimated that at least 1,500 students are turned away at each registration.

The Committee studying physical facilities for the Illinois Master Plan for higher education reported that Wright had the maximum average room usage of any institution in the state not sharing facilities: 38.9 hours per week from 7 a.m. to 5 p.m., and an almost equal percentage of scheduling during the 5 p.m. to 10 p.m. period. Wright should have at most about 6,500 students; 3,000 during the day and 3,500 during the evening.

Loop Branch. The Loop Branch has exclusive use of 11 of the 17 floors in a high-rise building. Begun in 1962, without facilities for offering a complete curriculum, the planned physics and chemistry laboratories will partially fill the need. There will be no physical education facilities. Two new elevators will be needed as enrollment increases.

Amundsen-Mayfair Branch. Located in the Amundsen High School building, the college has exclusive use of a converted classroom for administrative and faculty offices, and a room set aside for a small library. High school classrooms and laboratories are released to the college in the late afternoon but there are no lounges or counseling areas.

The Mayfair unit is in the Mayfair Elementary School, closer to Wright than to Amundsen. Biology, chemistry, and physics laboratories are scheduled for completion in the fall of 1964. A lunchroom accommodating 90 students and 24 faculty members is planned. The gymnasium was designed for elementary physical education.

Wilson Branch. Wilson Branch is a split operation, with facilities in the Arts Building of Chicago Teachers College South and the nearby Rock Island office building which had been reconditioned and found unsuitable for an elementary school. The building is a few yards from the railroad tracks and was built before 1900.

The Arts Building, built about 1915, houses laboratories for chemistry, physics, and biology, as well as various classes. The roof has leaked over the years, leaving water marks and flaking paint.

Crane Branch. Crane is located in a formerly abandoned section of Crane High School, built before 1890. Some of the areas used by the college have not been reconditioned. The Junior College shares a section of the gymnasium with the high school. Valuable chemistry balances are stored in a room which cannot be locked because of fire department regulations. The chemistry tables are 30 years old and the drains have leaked into the drawers so long that the drawers can no longer be opened. The student lounge is not ventilated. There is no sound insulation in the music room, and storage is completely inadequate.

Southeast Branch. The Southeast Branch is located in a wing of the Chicago Vocational High School. The College, cramped in the two rooms it used exclusively, recently moved into the unfinished, unheated, unlit, and abandoned portion of this wing. Gradually, with the assistance of NDEA funds, it is being rehabilitated. The facilities, including unfinished rooms, are used to the maximum during the day. English and literature classes are held in the electronics laboratories, with benches for desks and stools for chairs. Although there are six gymnasiums, only one has been released to the College on Tuesday and Thursday evenings. A girls' washroom nearing completion means that the college girls will no longer have to walk a quarter mile to and from the nearest washroom. The student lounge still lacks lights.

The day program has been limited by lack of space and the evening program by lack of funds. The College has been operating with five classrooms during the day. In the evening about 30 classrooms are available, with only about 20 being used because of lack of funds.

Bogan Branch. The Bogan Branch is located in the Bogan High School building. Facilities are released to the College after high school classes are dismissed. In September, 1963, the College moved faculty and administration offices into four mobile classrooms. No physical education facilities are released to the college. The streets around the building have been posted with "no parking from 7 p.m. to 10 p.m." signs.

The enrollment potential here has been estimated as high as 10,000 students, if facilities, funds, and adequate day programs are provided.

Fenger Branch. Fenger Branch opened in the Fenger High School building on Chicago's far South Side in February, 1958, and is in operation five evenings a week. The space used exclusively by the College consists of a converted foyer on the second floor, divided into two small offices, and a small room used as a library. A similar area on the first floor is used as a lobby. No gymnasium has been released to the College. Off-street parking is available for 60 cars. There are no student activities areas, or faculty or student lounges.

Faculty offices. There are few provisions at any of the branches for necessary faculty offices. Wilson, Crane, Wright, and the Mayfair unit of Amundsen use converted classrooms as offices. The overcrowding is a serious detriment to college-level efforts by the faculty. The English faculty office at Wilson is a converted classroom with 26 desks, 21 file cabinets, and six large storage cabinets. This facility is shared by 24 faculty members. The faculty office at Southeast is a large bay, originally used as a shop, now filled with 45 desks, numerous files, cabinets, duplicating machines, and other necessary equipment. Fenger Branch has no faculty offices, and faculty members share parts of file drawers. Bogan Branch has converted two mobile classrooms into offices, with 19 desks, files, and other essential equipment in each. Although Crane has four floors, several departments were unable to secure telephones from 1954 to 1963. In addition, the business faculty office can be entered only through a classroom.

Although the rules of the Board of Education require the college teacher to be in the building six hours a day, facilities that would enable faculty members to do the necessary work have not been provided. Course preparation and planning, serious reading and research, and the other numerous obligations requiring intensive concentration are impossible under the noisy, crowded conditions that prevail in most faculty

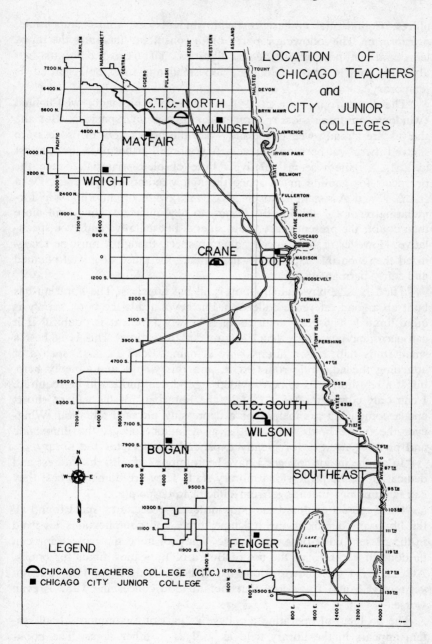

LOCATION OF CHICAGO TEACHERS and CITY JUNIOR COLLEGES

Figure 3

offices. Confidential conferences with students are almost impossible.

Libraries. The following report from a consultant illustrates the problems and the possibilities of the libraries. The report contrasts two libraries, both in quarters that are too small and must be regarded as temporary.

"The large room at _____ is extremely pleasant—well-lighted (windows on three sides), airy, and, to a point, spacious. But the shelves are already well filled, and when the books now in process are shelved there will be room for very few more. Furthermore, in contrast to _____, there seems relatively little obsolete material, hence the prospects for gaining much space through weeding do not exist. Dean _____ and Assistant Dean _____ are aware of this, and are formulating plans for shifting the library to new quarters which will more than double the present space. This is good, but tentative and even speculative. However, it is an encouraging prospect, though it must be recognized that even this expansion will not take the place of a well-planned and fairly permanent library.

"The _____ physical situation is all but hopeless. The librarian has built up a good reference collection, but beyond this the book supply is quite limited. The very small room is crowded, and it is doubtful if it can accommodate more than 8-10 readers at a time. This is at best a small study hall; it is a library only in name. Dean _____ speaks of attaching the adjoining room to it, and this would undoubtedly help, but if a real library is to be provided a good deal more will be required. I can only commend Mr. _____, the librarian, for his valiant efforts and accomplishments in face of a depressing physical situation. Whatever the future holds for _____ as a junior college, the immediate and pressing need is for greatly expanded quarters for the library.

"In all the junior colleges I have been impressed with the interest and dedication of the professional library staff. They are doing the best they can in situations that range from difficult to desperate.

"Once more I explored the book-ordering procedures and I found all the librarians deploring the red tape, time, and complications involved in the present book-ordering routine. They all hope that something can be done to decentralize the use of Board of Education funds for books. At _____ I was shown a long list of books ordered in 1961 but not yet received, and I was told that the situation concerning 1962 is even worse."

The problem of operating a college as part of a common school system appears in the library field as well as in other areas. The book-ordering process was designed for high school and elementary school libraries, which generally order books from a prepared list. But college libraries order a wide variety of books by the following cumbersome precedure:

1. The librarian submits a Requisition-Purchase Order in seven copies. One requisition must be prepared for each supplier, who may be the publisher, a jobber, or a book-supply house.

2. A copy of each requisition is sent to the appropriate supplier for a unit price for each book wanted.

3. Upon return by supplier, requisition is sent to Comptroller for encumbrance against the college library's allocation, becoming a Purchase Order.

4. The Purchase Order is sent to the supplier, who sends the books direct to the library, accompanied by invoice and packing slip.

5. The librarian is then responsible for checking for accuracy of shipment, omissions, etc.

Ordering books in this way takes from two to six months, and sometimes as long as a year passes before the books are received. The librarians generally feel that the situation would be improved if they could order books directly, although this would involve more paper work for them and might be less efficient than the Purchasing Office.

As the libraries of the Junior College and the Teachers College develop, book ordering may come to deserve a full-time purchasing official whose sole responsibility is the ordering, follow-up, and clearance for payment of books for these schools.

C

Adult Education

No examination of adult education can progress very far without some conception of its ultimate goal. Within a quarter century, adult education enrollment in Chicago public schools—or in some agency willing to meet the need—will be multiplied at least five times. Yet it is difficult to point to a program anywhere which is a clear-cut model of a satisfactory adult program. Adult education is fighting for the conceptualization of its role.

Enrollment statistics over the country are impressive, but everywhere quality is uneven, and frequently personnel are of uncertain ability. In short, the Advisory Committee on Adult Education is recommending expansion of an activity which has never shown quality and quantity simultaneously. It believes, however, that it errs only on the side of conservatism. It is asking others to join in an act of faith, a request that needs some explanation.

Functions of adult education

The Committee is convinced that adult education is the most effective means:

1. For overcoming the inequities which race, economic status, and luck often impose.

* * *

This supplement is a summary of a report by the Advisory Committee on Adult Education, consisting of citizens of the Chicago area who have an interest in adult education. Chairman of the Committee was Mr. George W. Overton. The Committee met several times, and also worked in subcommittees to prepare part of its report. Members of the Committee were: Russell Barta, Albert Y. Bingham, Louis Cheskin, Mrs. June Cook, William Cousins, Jr., Mrs. Newton Grobe, Mrs. Paul C. Harper, Jr., William Hartmann, Eugene L. Johnson, Theodore Jones, Mrs. Milton Krensky, Abner Mikva, George Philips, and Robert I. Shackford.

2. For helping the society as a whole to adjust to the impact on employment of constant technological change.

3. For the school system to affect the home environment and thus create a more supportive atmosphere for children's formal schooling.

4. For increasing the quality and quantity of citizen participation at all levels of government in community life.

None of these tasks can be undertaken by the regular education program designed for persons below age 18; these needs arise only with adult status. Each of the tasks is too big for a private agency, although fruitful experimentation may be performed by them, or they may reach specialized interests.

Findings of the Advisory Committee

1. Increasing leisure, more complicated technology, and high mobility will increase the demand for adult education in the next 20 years. There is already considerable evidence of growth.

2. Chicago cannot maintain its leading position as an industrial city without vigorous adult vocational and technical education programs.

3. Adequate adult education offers greater flexibility to the total educational program, increases opportunities for all persons within the school system, and is the sole means for even partially minimizing the great disparities within the adult population.

4. Chicago is hampered by a lack of tradition and of respect for and commitment to adult education on the part of supervisory personnel, so that in quality and quantity she lags behind other, comparable cities.

5. Chicago's adult educational program, taken as a whole, is static and isolated from the community. Its administrators do not have time or training to build a program which is responsive to the needs of the community it serves, which utilizes community and human resources to enrich its programs, and which serves as a bridge to other institutions and leadership forces in the community.

6. The disparity between Chicago and other cities is explained only in part by school finance problems. It is largely attributable to centralization of authority and isolation from other major community institutions. This is inevitable when adult education is in the hands of part-time personnel with other major jobs in the school system.

RECOMMENDATIONS, GENERAL

The following propositions underlie all recommendations of the Committee: (1) The functions of the public school system are to provide education for persons of all ages. Adult education should be recognized as a responsibility of the school system equal to the education of those below age 18. (2) The distribution of programs, course, and services among the various age groups should be determined according to this concept of equal priority.

The effects of such an assumption on the primary and secondary school levels will be extensive. At present, the school system reaches the student only within a limited number of years. There is no way of overcoming a tight, lock-step timetable and of avoiding at least some serious consequences to a student who gets out of step with that time-table. The felt presence of a vigorous and widespread adult education program would alleviate the problem and lead to greater effectiveness and flexibility of the whole educational program.

Short-range suggestions

1. Adult education activities should be administered by full-time personnel, whose enormously greater efficiency will obtain, within the same budget, more effective results than even the best of the "moon-lighting" supervision now operative. They should be educators who can develop continuity of skill and communicate with similar experts in other cities for the greater exchange of knowledge.

2. The adult program should constitute a division of the public school system with separate status, responsible to the General Superintendent or his immediate deputy.

3. The administrative structure of a Division of Adult Education should grant the widest possible autonomy to local administrators to devise the programs they find appropriate at the local level and to initiate programs on short notice.

4. School system personnel should determine the maximum potential of the public school system for the use of federal funds for vocational and adult education, and make prompt recommendations for such use.

5. The Board of Education should appoint a city-wide advisory committee on adult education consisting of, among others, persons prominent in industry and labor and able, by their own positions and influence, to advise the Board of Education on the best ways to deal with current adult educational needs. This committee should have a secretariat.

6. There should be citizen advisory groups geographically dispersed who will work with the administration on curricula, distribution, etc., for the specific area being served. These should include representatives of community and service organizations, religious groups, etc., to cover the entire spectrum of neighborhood life.

7. Certification procedures as applied to adult education personnel

should be flexible or, on occasion, suspended entirely. The aim should be to measure qualifications for the specific function. (For example, a good music teacher may never have attended college or taken formal teacher training.)

8. There should be prompt development at the local level of centers for adult use, possibly in the short range through changes in use of existing buildings.

Long-range aims

1. When, in accord with the short-range recommendations, a vigorous adult education program has been established, the program should be integrated into other public school offerings. This can be done through administrators of the local schools, who thus become responsible for all three phases of public education: adult, secondary and primary. This does not conflict with the recommendation that adult education should be directed by full-time personnel. It does recognize that adult education must become part of a continuing process; a strong and well-distributed adult program should profitably influence the other two divisions.

2. Funds should be made available for research in and evaluation of adult education.

3. With the establishment of a full-time staff, a career line for adult educators should be developed in order to attract persons who are committed and professionally trained.

SUMMARY OF PRESENT LEVEL OF CHICAGO PUBLIC SCHOOL ADULT EDUCATION

Because adult education activities in the Chicago schools have not been developed as a unified program, information on what is available is not organized. There is no single document summarizing Chicago's adult education opportunities. There are no current data on student characteristics other than those gathered by individual schools, and even these, gathered on registration cards, have not been systematically analyzed. Adult education activities[1] fall under the headings below and, except for TV, are in the Bureau of Education Extension.

---

[1]The Committee on Adult Education of the Illinois Board of Higher Education defines adult education as, "any continuing education for out-of-school youth and adults in courses and programs related to personal, vocational, cultural, or social interest or need. The courses and programs may be credit or non-credit, formal or informal; however, they are primarily a part-time activity. Such education should encompass persons of all educational levels, from those lacking a basic common school education to those with a high level of formal education."

Programs

Evening high schools. There are 20 evening high schools, 14 general and six vocational. Each evening school is administered by a part-time principal and assistants. Teachers, mainly from regular day school ranks, are also part-time.

The vocational evening high school curriculum is limited to vocational subjects. Regular courses cover a broad range, including academic subjects leading to a high school diploma; general education courses (languages, history, science, etc.); business education courses, typing, bookkeeping, business law, office practice, etc.), and physical education and recreation.

The evening high school also houses the special elementary education program, leading to an elementary grade certificate. The subject matter varies considerably to meet the special needs of the students, many of whom are handled on a tutorial basis, enabling them to proceed at their own speed.

Americanization program. This program serves adults who are preparing for citizenship and/or who wish to learn to speak and read English. The curriculum stresses English language, but it also familiarizes the student with United States history and various aspects of contemporary Chicago living. In general, it is an excellent means of integrating the newcomer into Chicago and often provides very practical assistance in such matters as seeking employment.

The students are not only foreign-born immigrants but also native Americans who read or speak English as a second language. Many Puerto Ricans who are, of course, citizens are enrolled.

Classes are often held in public school buildings but, for the convenience of students, may also be held in churches, settlement houses, factories, and other nonschool buildings. In June, 1963, there were 362 classes in 188 different locations.

Relief instruction program. This program, developed in 1962 in cooperation with the Cook County Department of Public Aid, provides for persons on relief a basic education curriculum as well as the opportunity to participate in the regular elementary and high school programs. This significant experiment is being watched throughout the United States because of its implications for education and public welfare. Presently, its student body is 85 per cent women and 15 per cent men. The high proportion of women is accounted for by the fact that the largest percentage of those on relief are women receiving Aid to Dependent Children payments.

Junior colleges and teachers colleges. These institutions, open to individuals who have obtained a high school diploma, provide a useful educational program for some adults. Although they do not now serve the general educational needs of adults, they are potentially rich resources. Imaginative use of TV programming could be extremely useful, particularly if it went beyond simply telecasting regular junior college courses.

Comparisons with other cities

Chicago's lag in adult education can be demonstrated by comparisons with New York and Los Angeles in significant areas:

	Chicago	New York City	Los Angeles
1 Full-time adult educators at local level	0	50	50
2 Use of local adult education advisory committees	0	25	27
3 Funds allocated to adult education (in millions)[2]			
a Total school budget	250	568	360
b Allocated to adult education (including vocational adult education)	2.5	5.4	8.5
c Percent of total budget	1	1	2.2
4 Number enrolled in adult education	54,000	206,000	185,000

5 Quality and scope of offerings in the three programs: Chicago offers much less curriculum variety than New York City or Los Angeles. This appears to be due to Chicago's emphasis on high school curriculum, vocational and remedial education. Such limited offerings attract a lower educational group with narrower interests. Pitching the curriculum at such a level restricts the growth potential of adult education. Recent research has shown that the more education a person has, the more he participates in adult education; the more he participates, the more education he acquires. Thus there is a cumulative effect if activities are provided for those with education beyond high school, along with adult education programs primarily designed for correcting the deficiencies of elementary and secondary systems.

---

[2]Because the budgetary systems for the three school systems are not identical, these figures are rough approximations.

Table 1
Facts concerning adult education
in Chicago

A. Enrollments*

Evening high school

	Regular	Vocational	Elementary	Totals
1953	12,486	8,124	3,736	24,356
1958	12,794	8,125	4,511	25,430
1963	22,233	9,876	4,812	36,921

Americanization

1953	9,101
1958	11,028
1962	8,676

Relief instruction

	High school	Elementary	Total
1962-63	2,116	6,398	8,514

TV College

	Credit	Noncredit	Total
1962-63	8,119	2,901	11,020

*Enrollment figures for adult education in the Chicago Public Schools vary from one report to another, depending on when the count is taken and whether "enrollment" refers to individuals or course registrations. The figures reported here can be thought of as maximum enrollment, as they seem to represent course registrations tallied early in the semester, before drop-outs occur.

B. *Budget and Personnel,*
Bureau of Education Extension,
1964

General office (Asst. Supt., staff, and expenses) Number of positions: 4	$ 55,486
Division of Evening Schools Number of positions: 992 (principals, directors and teachers: 950)	1,144,702
Division of Americanization Number of positions: 275 (teachers: 270)	313,769
Division of Relief Instruction Number of positions: 362 (teachers: 350)	439,232
Total	$ 1,953,199
Operations of plant, evening school	460,500
Total	$ 2,413,699
Total operating expenses, Chicago Public Schools, 1963	$250,793,367

RECOMMENDATIONS, SPECIFIC AREAS

Vocational and remedial education

The adult vocational training capability of the Board should be expanded enough to permit the training and retraining of at least 10 times the number now in such programs.

There were 6,663 adults enrolled in vocational training, day and evening, full- and part-time in Board of Education schools as of January 1, 1964. As of the first quarter, 1964, 2,918 trainees were enrolled in Manpower Development and Training Act courses in the City of Chicago; 531 of these were in Board of Education schools.

Comparable figures for private vocational schools are not available, but it is estimated that the 10 largest proprietary schools in the city have a combined capacity of 12,000 students, including some who may enroll from out of state.

Thus, only about 21,600 adults in Chicago are participating in institutional vocational education. In contrast, the number of unemployed in Chicago Standard Metropolitan Statistical Area as of July, 1963, was 136,000. Most are residents of Chicago. All could profit from training.

For adult vocational training, the Committee recommends top priority for unemployed and underemployed heads of household, with subpriorities assigned in terms of the number of dependents. Next priority should be for men in the age bracket most likely to become heads of households within a year or two.

In developing vocational programs for adults, their particular needs should be kept in mind. More attention should be given to on-the-job training and to searching out secondary skills of the trainees and building on them. Teaching materials and techniques should be more mature. Finally, there should be more adequate provision for living allowances and other family problems.

The resources of the regular vocational schools should be made available for adult programs. But separate facilities should be established where possible for training programs geared especially to the adult.

A revised and greatly expanded program of remedial education should include literacy training and other basic courses, plus a modern equivalent of the successful Americanization program. An estimate of the number now served by this program is as follows:

1. As of February 1, 1964, 7,893 persons were enrolled in the Board of Education's adult literacy program (ADC-sponsored relief classes), 6,021 persons in basic courses and 1,872 in the high school program. Ninety percent of those enrolled are women.

2. About 4,000 persons are served by Board of Education programs, not including those in category 1.

3. The Americanization program serves about 12,000, including those in category 1.

4. A Volunteer Tutoring Program has emerged in response to the great need for literacy training. The adult program, now serving about 850 persons, sprang from the original children's program.

5. About 2,000 Chicago residents are served directly and indirectly by the University of Illinois Urban Extension Program. It trains in millinery, sewing, child rearing, home management, credit management, etc.

At best, we have about 20,000 persons in literacy training and acculturation programs. Yet the Cook County Department of Public Aid estimates 192,000 persons who could profit from remedial education. We need a program with five to 10 times the capacity of current offerings.

The expanded programs fall into two categories: (1) basic remedial programs for men and women as a prerequisite to vocational training and job placement; (2) programs mostly for women who need training to function as homemakers. Both groups will profit in terms of their broader community responsibilities.

Remedial work should become an integral part of the vocational program. Such a merger will provide motivation for the sustained effort the trainee must make to reach his vocational goal. Supportive services, such as counseling and financial assistance, should also be available.

The fundamental justification for more broadly based literacy programs is Chicago's need for a literate and informed citizenry. To this end, we should build upon existing offerings, such as the Board's literacy program and the Volunteer Tutoring Program, and appoint a director and small staff to perform the following functions for such programming:

1 Serve as a central clearinghouse for research, information, and public relations.
2 Recommend areas of need.
3 Serve as a secretariat to bona fide volunteer training programs.
4 Provide technical advice and guidance.
5 Develop and provide teaching materials.
6 Develop and conduct tutor training classes.
7 Receive and dispense funds to help defray costs of administration, management, and physical plant and equipment.

Citizenship education

"Citizenship education" treats of problems involving the relationship of an individual to the city as a whole. Adult education in citizenship for the purposes of the public school system falls into three main areas: orientation to urban living; parent education; leadership.

Orientation to urban living. The public school system has a traditional responsibility for the adjustment of the citizen to urban living. The new element today is the presence of large numbers of city residents, who present all the problems formerly characteristic of immigrants, but who are American citizens, white and nonwhite. An adequate, decentralized adult education program can determine the special needs of residents of various neighborhoods for aid in adjusting to the urban setting.

Education for citizenship should stimulate independent thought and inquiry about community affairs. Programs are needed both to convey information about public issues and to help participants learn how to think about them, with emphasis on the skills of analysis and judgment.

Public discussion forums can be established to replace more formal instruction, with subjects covering issues significant to urban life. The Committee also recommends traditional courses in politics. These could include instruction on how the complicated machinery of government operates; the nature of legal and civil rights, etc. Such programs can hardly avoid "controversial" issues. Although it is not the function of the school system to take sides, it does have the responsibility of offering forums and courses in which the various aspects of such issues can be presented and discussed.

Parent education. Parent education programs are now being carried on by the Parent-Teacher Association, in cooperation both with the public schools and with other institutions. A tremendous potential lies in such cooperation.

The Committee recommends that the public school system:

1 Consider expanding the existing course, Basic Concepts for Parents, as part of its adult education program;
2 Make its physical facilities available for parent education, a practice now common throughout the country;
3 Tap the human resources already available in the community for such programs (older parents are an example);
4 Assign "parent coordinators" to schools in underprivileged areas, as was done in the special summer schools in 1964.

Leadership training. The special role of the public school system as both an activity of government and a stimulus to political activity can best be demonstrated in leadership training. The development of adequate community leadership among persons who are tied to their local communities and who can diversify the power structure of the city is essential. At present, the only leadership training program provided by the Chicago Public Schools is found in the Human Relations Department. Since 1960 it has completed 25 courses in nine locations. Total enrollment since 1960 is 886, of whom 521 (73 percent) finished the courses. The enrollment includes men and women from 17 to 70, a cross-section of the population. The courses, called Institute for Community Leaders, are co-sponsored by the League of Women Voters' Citizen Information Service.

Cultural adult education

The Committee starts with the assumption that Chicago is, as a center for dignified human life, a failure, as is New York or Paris or San Francisco or any large city yet constructed. The distance between what these places now offer and the level of human dignity and decency which can be anticipated in an affluent society is so immense that the differences between them seem trivial. What Chicago can become is going to depend upon the constructive and active interest of its citizens, their level of sophistication, their scope of imagination, and their sense of hope. Many things will affect this level of growth. However, the mechanism which can be most consciously encouraged, financed, and developed is adult education.

The primary purpose of a culturally oriented adult education program should be to develop a trained eye and ear, with a view to building a responsive clientele for existing institutions, such as the Art Institute, the Park District cultural programs, and the Chicago Symphony. The Committee also had in mind the development of community programs and activities which would encourage direct participation.

The Committee believes that, faced with the pressures of modern urban life, the individual can achieve greater balance and understanding if he is part of a society which provides a wide range of cultural opportunities.

The Committee does not recommend that extensive programs be offered in the development of professional and technical skills in the arts. It does believe that the adult education program should consider the arts as a point of contact in the community and that the administrator of the program must exercise considerable initiative in providing the program most appropriate for his neighborhood.

The school system is a suitable agency for decentralizing the programs of the several existing institutions, such as the Art Institute, the Chicago Symphony, etc. The Art Institute and Lyric Opera, for instance, will remain downtown, but the school program, working with them, will give them local roots which they presently do not have.

The public school can play a catalytic role in the fine arts. A specific assignment would be to build a great audience, in some cases for institutions which do not now exist, a repertory company being one example. Such an audience would surely encourage the financing of more artistic experiments. Thus the schools' role in cultural education is that of acting as a bridge between cultural institutions and the public at large.

Finances

The Committee is not convinced that adult education problems in Chicago result from dependence of the school system on the real property tax. More cogent reasons stem from (1) the unusual concentration of power in the central office, suppressing local initiative; (2) the isolation of the schools from other major community institutions; (3) the distribution of funds through part-time administrators whose main interests lie elsewhere.

Nonetheless it is true that further expansion of public school adult education on the present tax base is probably impossible. Funds should be sought from the state specifically for adult education, and separate from general education funds.

The Committee also recommends full utilization of all existing federal programs.

The private sector and other portions of the public sector must be encouraged to help finance adult education: for example, part of the state welfare budget should be so allocated, and private employers should be encouraged to finance vocational training.

Tuition should be treated not as a major source of revenue for adult education, but as a stimulus to attendance and performance.

Chicago is not an overtaxed city in support of its school system. The capital deficiencies which prevent full utilization of federal monies available could be met by additional bonded indebtedness. Chicago is already bearing through other budgets the cost of inadequate vocational and remedial training. In some areas, such as welfare payments, a direct monetary equivalent can be found, and in the meantime a steady deterioration of morale in large sectors of the community imposes an uncountable cost that is perhaps even greater.

The Committee concludes that maximum utilization of present resources for a more vigorous adult education program would gain support for broader financial aid for adult education in the school system generally.

E

Special Education for Handicapped Children

The survey of the program of Special Education was made under the direction of Dr. Robert Henderson, Chairman of the Department of Special Education of the University of Illinois. Programs for socially and emotionally maladjusted children were surveyed by Dr. Eli M. Bower, Staff Member, Research Utilization Branch, National Institute of Mental Health, U.S. Department of Health, Education and Welfare, and Dr. Jeanne Noble, Associate Professor of Education, New York University; programs for the auditorily handicapped were surveyed by Dr. William Desmond Phillips, Associate Professor, Division of Deaf Education and Mental Retardation, Institute of Rehabilitation, DePaul University; and programs for the orthopedically handicapped were surveyed by Mrs. Dorothy B. Carr, Supervisor, Special Education Branch, Los Angeles City Schools.

Dr. Henderson spent many days in Chicago, interviewing persons inside and outside the Chicago school system and visiting schools and classes for exceptional children. The other consultants also devoted from three to six days each visiting schools and classes, in addition to the time spent in reviewing materials and interviewing persons who are working in or are concerned with the various programs.

The general chapter on special education reflects the conclusions and principal recommendations of the Survey team and consultants in the various fields. The following sections on the programs for specific categories of handicapped children are in large part the work of the individual consultants in their respective fields. Dr. Henderson wrote the section on the educational program for trainable and educable mentally handicapped children, his principal area of specialization. He also contributed shorter sections on the visually handicapped, the multihandicapped, and the speech correction program. The recommendations in each of the sub-sections are those of the individual consultants and in some cases reflect differing approaches to particular problems.

PROGRAM FOR SOCIALLY AND EMOTIONALLY MALADJUSTED CHILDREN

Schools become concerned with the social and emotional problems of children when the child's behavior or attitude either prevents him from progressing satisfactorily in school or interferes with the educational program for other pupils.

The behavior which most obviously interferes with learning is absence from school. Therefore, it is not surprising to find that, soon after it became a matter of public policy that children must go to school, it became necessary to do something about children who were persistently absent or "truant." In Chicago, we find that the state legislature in 1899 required the Chicago Board of Education to provide "a place of confinement, discipline, instruction, and maintenance of children, both boys and girls, of compulsory school age, who may be committed thereto." To this day, children are committed to the Parental School by the Family Court, with the Chicago Board of Education responsible both for custodial care and for the educational program.

Some years later, first the Montefiore and then the Moseley School were established as day schools to which problem boys could be sent before they had reached the point of referral to the courts. Later, day-school branches for girls were established and "truant rooms" for younger boys 7-13 were opened in a number of schools. In 1911 the Illinois General Assembly provided reimbursement intended to cover the extra costs of special classes for pupils who were declared delinquent by the courts; and in 1915 this was broadened to include pupils who were truant and incorrigible.

While there have been many changes since 1915 in public and professional thinking about the behavior problems of children, the program in the Chicago Public Schools is still essentially one of referring truant or misbehaving children to special schools or classes which are partially paid for by state funds.

As long ago as 1932, the Strayer Report on the Chicago Public Schools made the following comment: "The personnel work now carried on in the special schools is most commendable, but it is nothing more or less than a recognition and an actual putting into practice . . . of principles that should be applied in every school. . . . It is regretted most seriously that the kind of personal study and guidance accorded the boys in these special schools is not available until after they have already developed habits of truancy and delinquency which are well nigh impossible to break."

In the intervening years, other school districts in the state began to experiment with the school social work type of program, intended to give this kind of "personal study and guidance" to children *before* they became intolerable in the regular school. In 1956, legislation broadened the law to include children who were "in need of special education facilities designed to prevent their becoming truant, incorrigible, or delinquent"; and in 1957, the word was changed to "maladjusted," meaning "children between the ages of 5 and 21 years who because of social or emotional problems are unable to make constructive use of their school experience and require the provision of special services designed to promote their educational growth and development." Since 1957, this legislation has made possible the establishment of school social work programs in a large number of Illinois school districts, with reported results which seem to confirm the wisdom of this approach. Chicago, however, has been very slow to take advantage of this aspect of the legislation, although the IMPACT program, mentioned in the following section, seems to represent a small beginning.

Before turning to the specifics of the Chicago program, a general word about maladjusted children in a big city is in order. The personal situation and conditions of life for many parents in the city are such that they are not able to give their children the kind of healthy and nutritious preschool experiences, emotional or intellectual, that send them to school ready to learn and grow as we would like to see them. Socially and emotionally maladjusted adults and communities produce socially and emotionally maladjusted children. The greatest hope for the community and the children is that positive factors in their school experiences can be brought to bear to counter or compensate for early deprivation or conflict.

It is rare, however, to find that schools or communities really believe this. Most school systems hope for a treaty of peace with the difficult child, in which tranquillity and avoidance of trouble can be secured for both parties, with the result that the child's emotional progress is minimal.

In this evaluation of the Chicago Public Schools' program for maladjusted children, the over-all measure for judging programs was the extent to which each program tended to increase the competence of the student for learning and for social effectiveness, and his eventual ability to function as an independent, economically self-sufficient adult. No city or state which expends vast sums of money to deal with incompetent, dependent, socially inadequate, or ill adults can overlook the possibility that this burden can be reduced or prevented by effective educational programs.

Overview of the social adjustment program

The Bureau of Socially Maladjusted Children is a part of the Division of Special Education. The staff consists of the director and three clerk stenographers. The Bureau serves in a staff rather than administrative relationship to the schools and classes for socially maladjusted children. All referrals are processed by the director, sometimes as many as 75 in a day, leaving little time for supervision of the program in the schools and classes, for recruitment, or for research. During the school year 1963-64, the Bureau of Socially Maladjusted Children received 3,069 school case reports from regular elementary and secondary schools, from special schools or classes, or through court referrals. In addition, 5,646 letters and requests for pupil placements and changes were processed. These included 283 girls and 936 boys being returned by the Illinois Youth Commission to the Chicago schools, and 549 girls previously excused from attendance who were requesting return to school.

The social adjustment schools and classes, with enrollment and number of teachers as of January 1, 1964, are shown in Table 1. To these should be added 22 classes for younger boys 7-13 in 17 elementary schools; two classes in regular high schools; and 11 recently established IMPACT classes in elementary schools. Total number of teachers in these decentralized classes is 35, serving about 500 boys. The children in the Audy Home and its branches are in the custody of the courts, and the Board of Education provides teaching services only. Children in the Parental School are referred by the Family Court of Cook County on petitions submitted by the schools. Therefore, the only control on the Parental School enrollment exercised by the Board is in the number of petitions presented to the court. But since cases are severe and have claimed much attention from the local school by the time they reach this point, restricting intake by this method has not been favored. Children in the local social adjustment centers and the special schools are referred on the recommendation of the home principal and attendance officer, and are assigned by the Director. A psychological case report is not required, but is customary in most cases.

The waiting list for local centers was 102 in March, 1964. For Montefiore, it was 155 at the elementary level, 41 for high school. For Moseley,

Table 1
Enrollment and number of teachers in social adjustment schools

	Enrollment, January 1964	Number of teachers
Arthur Audy Home for Children with 4 branches	211 (total, all branches)	18 (Audy)
Bartelme Home for Girls		1
Cook County Jail		11
House of Correction		15
Ridgeway Hospital		1
Montefiore (day school, boys)	487	39
Chicago Parental School (boys)	111	
Girls Branch	14	59
Moseley (day school, boys)	339	26
Motley (day school, girls)	352	25.5
Wells Branch, Motley	21	2
Bousfield Branch, Motley	103	10
Totals	1,638	207.5

it was 53 for elementary, 42 for high school. There are no waiting lists for girls. The fact that there are no centers for younger girls may have something to do with the lack of referrals. In the case of boys, the actual need is considerably greater than it appears from the waiting lists because principals, knowing the situation, do not go to the trouble of making out problem reports. Younger boys will no longer be eligible for local centers by the time their name is reached; and older ones will have passed school age.

Contrary to the situation at the Parental School, from which boys are released whether or not they are judged ready, in order to make room for new referrals from the court, boys are not being released from Montefiore or Moseley to return to a local school until a team at the special school determines that they are ready. This team consists of the principal, teacher, adjustment teacher, field adjustment teacher, and sometimes the psychologist. The field adjustment teacher visits the home, visits the local school to which the boy is to be returned, contacts social agencies that may be involved, and seeks job openings for boys who need them. In other words, he acts something like a school social worker, although he is a teacher who probably does not have social work training. A psychologist is supposed to be available full-time at the Parental School, three-fifths time at Montefiore and Moseley. But at the time of the survey, the psychologist was only visiting the Moseley School one day a week, due to shortage of personnel.

The newly established IMPACT programs in five districts involve classes similar to the regular local social adjustment classes for younger boys, but the intake procedure is more carefully planned and an effort is supposed to be made to select boys who have been merely truant, rather than those who present severe behavior problems. It is planned that a social worker will be assigned in every district which has an IMPACT program, but at the time of the Survey only two social workers had been assigned, one covering two districts. Referrals to IMPACT rooms do not go through the Bureau of Socially Maladjusted Children, although reimbursement is claimed from the state on the same basis as for the regular centers. Diagnosis and referral are made by a team consisting of the district superintendent, the head truant officer for the district, the psychologist, the principal of the local school, the social worker if there is one, and representatives of any agencies interested in the pupil and his family. Procedures have been established which are intended to insure that, before a pupil is referred to an IMPACT room, all other resources for treating the pupil in the local school have been tried, including a conference involving the head truant officer, district superintendent, the pupil, and his parents.

Certification requirements for teachers of socially maladjusted pupils include the usual teacher requirements plus 20 hours of courses deemed appropriate for working with maladjusted pupils. The state accepts these Chicago requirements as a basis for reimbursement. In fact, not all the teachers have met the requirements, and some who are not certified are doing a very good job with the boys. An effort is made to select teachers who show ability to understand and control the type of boy encountered in these programs.

The Chicago Teachers College North is now offering a master's degree program in the education of socially maladjusted and emotionally disturbed children, and this should help supply and train teachers for the centers and schools.

Observations and conclusions

1. *Special schools.* The Moseley, Montefiore, and Motley schools are well-run institutions with surprisingly competent and effective staffs. The program at each is aimed bluntly at enhancing the child's competence in basic skills. Discipline is firm but constructive. Many children travel great distances on city buses to get to school. Considering the fact that many are enrolled because of chronic truancy, the record of attendance is astounding.

Classes are small and well managed. In many classes, the program is so highly individualized that children get very little opportunity to work with others or interchange ideas in discussion. Although individual work is a necessity for such children, they need experiences in working with others, especially the ability to talk to others, to persuade and be persuaded and to test ideas in a group.

All three schools have a large number of young children in attendance and a long waiting list. Class size seems to be maximum for each of the classes visited. Although each of the schools has several teacher-counselors, assistance from school psychologists is minimal, and no professional social workers are available.

All three schools attempt some vocational training, although this is not the major focus of their programs. More should be done, including work experience programs, to develop educational and vocational skills.

The special schools are aware and conscious of their task to return each student to his or her home school as soon as possible.

As educational institutions, they seem to manage their difficult and less motivated students effectively. Yet none of the schools has any research resources or any hard data on the effectiveness of its program. It would seem almost as if no one wanted to know what happens to the children. Lacking such information, it would appear difficult to feed back information by which curriculum or program changes could be made. It would be extremely helpful to find out which children are best helped and which are least helped by special programs in special schools. It would also be helpful to find out what schools and children do while waiting for admission.

The Motley School and its branches, serving socially maladjusted girls, give unmistakable evidence of the lack of a plan, based on adequate research, for rehabilitating the girls and motivating them to achieve skills and jobs. The teachers are well prepared, on the whole, but they lack psychological and social work colleagues to work with them. One must also be concerned that such separate institutions for "failures" cannot give the girls role models who exemplify a different life style. The rehabilitation of socially maladjusted girls is a subject which has been seriously neglected, while attention has been devoted to boys, who are both more numerous and more troublesome. But these girls may easily become the mothers of future troublemakers.

2. *Chicago Parental School.* The boys' and the girls' branches of the Parental School were visited, including dormitories, bathrooms, kitchens, classrooms, recreation rooms, etc. The boys are housed in old buildings which seem clean and adequate. The classroom building is old but has been kept up nicely. The school program is well managed and the courses adequate.

The basic problem of the Parental School is that no one seems able to decide what it ought to be (detention home, school, residential treatment center, nonparental institution, etc.). Considering the mixed objectives and roles which the school is asked to accept, it is surprisingly effective in maintaining its management and educational programs. However, no one knows how effective a *change* agent it really is. It is doubtful that it can make any effective impact on its population for the following reasons:

a. The average length of stay is approximately eight weeks for initial commitments and 12 weeks for recidivous male students. This kind of rapid turnover makes program and rehabilitative impact possible only through the more difficult forms of magic.

b. The cottage or family instructor position does not attract professional personnel needed in this work. Present staff members are very inadequately housed and work long hours for minimal reimbursement. Fourteen of 21 family instructors are on the bottom step of the scale and receive $380 per month; 11 others get from $480 to $575 per month; 19 assistant family instructors get $275 per month. Some instructors have served many years in a helpful and positive manner. Nevertheless, their job as key adults for vulnerable children requires defining the job as a professional one rather than one needing a warm body. The position ought to be filled by a man and wife, one of whom should be a trained social worker or psychologist; they should not be on duty more than eight hours a day. Present dismal living quarters are an even stronger deterrent to competent applicants than the salary and hours. Only women are employed at the Girls' Branch, making it impossible for the girls to establish any healthy identification with men. At least one resident couple would be preferable.

c. There is a dearth of treatment resources available to the schools when measured against the fact that every boy or girl in the school is well on the road to delinquency or emotional illness, if not already there.

Interested groups, aware that something is wrong with the Parental School, have urged that the Survey make a "detailed study" of the school. But what is needed is not a detailed study, but agreement by the Board of Education and the Family Court that only boys and girls will be sent there for whom a stay of six months or more in a residential treatment-type school has been prescribed by a professional selection process; that no more will be assigned than the school can serve effectively; and that they will not be released until a professional team has determined that they are ready and until a postrelease plan has been made for them.

Administrative responsibility for the Girls' Branch of the Parental School needs to be clarified. The superintendent and school principal are located at the Boys' Parental School on the North Side of the city. The Girls' Branch now shares its South Side building with the Bousfield Branch of the Motley School for Socially Maladjusted Girls, which is on the West Side. Thus three administrators, none of whom is on the premises regularly, share responsibility in this building. Lunch is prepared for and served to the Bousfield girls by the kitchen staff located on the Parental School side. Plans are now under way to use some of the rooms on the Bousfield side as classrooms for the Parental School girls. As it is supposed to be essential that there be no contact whatever between the two sets of girls, this will create more problems. Since Bousfield, Motley, and the Boys' Parental School are located in three different districts, the theory of decentralization also requires the involvement of three different district superintendents in this picture. It seems highly desirable that some other plan be developed which would give more effective responsibility for the school and its program. Since more space could be used to good purpose by either the Bousfield Branch or the Girls' Parental School, the best solution might be to enlarge one or the other, appoint a responsible full-time director or principal, and find other quarters for the branch that is eliminated.

3. *Special class for unwed pregnant elementary school girls.* Approximately 700 girls are excluded annually from school because of pregnancy. Most are under 16 years of age and, without special provisions, most will not return to school after the baby's birth.

The regular school excludes these girls at a time when guilt, shame, and ostracism have already done a good job of depriving the girl of any semblance of self-esteem. The future for these girls and their children is sad and discouraging. High school counselors told members of the Survey staff that they were extremely concerned about the fate of girls who become pregnant, but that the lack of special provisions made it impossible to give these girls any effective help.

Chicago now has one class supported by a National Institute of Mental Health grant as a demonstration of how programs of this type can best be operated. It serves only children in elementary school. Programs for such girls have to be tailored to their special needs. For example, many need to keep medical appointments which should be available for them in the vicinity. Case work services must be an integral part of the program. The basic educational level of the girls needs to be raised, and some homemaking competence taught. The mother of the pregnant girl should be included in the program and the father, too, if available. Girls who wish to return to school should be helped to do so. A small demonstration of this kind in depth can help pave the way for expanded programs. Such programs are mandatory in a city like Chicago. Unfortunately, although the class is very well staffed by social work and psychiatric personnel, the classroom part of the program has suffered from a succession of rather poorly prepared teachers who have had to function in an isolated situation. The importance of the problem and of devising effective ways to meet it should be recognized by the assignment of well-prepared teachers with adequate supervision.

4. *Social adjustment classes for boys,* 7-13. The classes visited were well run and seemingly effective educational groups. One class was the only one of its kind in a large school (2,250) whose pupils were 90 percent Negro and almost all from a public housing project. The teacher seemed somewhat isolated but not uncomfortable in this position. The room, typically, had been intended as a book room and was small and cramped for 12 boys, even without the woodworking table which is provided for some of these classes. The teacher obviously took great pride in his work and, although his class program was highly structured, the boys seemed to enjoy it. An excellent feature was the plan for trying the boys out in regular classes in the same building before releasing them from the supervision of the social adjustment class. This is only possible with this kind of decentralized program.

Two other classes were in neighboring rooms in a school of about 700 in a middle-class white neighborhood. The two special class teachers (one qualified and experienced, the other fairly new to this work) seemed to function freely and easily. The advantages of two classes in a school are impressive. It permits greater flexibility in programming, interchangeability of teachers, and a chance to compare notes and ideas with a sympathetic colleague.

The teachers visited were all quite different. Visits to hundreds of special classes for socially and emotionally maladjusted children seem to indicate that there is no single type of best teacher. Many teachers seem to be able to work in this kind of program and do a good productive job in it.

The special classes, however, need professional supervision and assistance by mental health personnel. It appears that there are a small but significant number of severely emotionally disturbed children in each of the classes who could benefit by treatment, case work, mental health consultation with the teacher, or combinations of these services.

IMPACT classes as such are similar to the regular social adjustment classes, though because of their newness they are less likely to be taught by teachers who have met the requirements for social adjustment classes. They are different in that children are placed in them only after they have been studied through a team approach and various other procedures have been undertaken. According to the material provided by the Department of Pupil Personnel Services, only younger, less disturbed children are accepted.

It is hard to understand why such services and assistance are not required for the social adjustment classes. Why have second-class citizenship among special programs and two administrative units operating similar programs? If the differences between IMPACT and social adjustment classes are significant and important, they ought to be spelled out in terms of specific purposes, kinds of children served, and the needed auxiliary services. Programs of special classes should be administered cleanly and without administrative overlap.

RECOMMENDATIONS

1. Social adjustment classes and other services should be established in regular elementary schools in sufficient numbers so that elementary school-aged emotionally and socially maladjusted children can be helped closer to home. Such classes should be served by professionally trained social workers, psychologists, and psychiatric consultants. Services should be geared to early identification and prevention rather than to waiting for problems to develop to a point where little positive help can be given.

2. With the younger pupils kept in their own districts, the special social adjustment schools should be designed and utilized for high school-aged students and should include terminal vocational training.

3. Certification procedures and requirements for social workers and psychologists should be completely revised and redeveloped to encourage the development of a competent, well-trained staff of psychologists and social workers.

Although education is primarily a teacher-pupil transaction, other professions can assist the teacher to make these transactions more effective for more children. The myth that only those persons who have teaching experience can help teachers is just that—a myth. It is not the job of a psychologist or a social worker to tell a teacher how or what to teach just as it is not the job of the teacher to tell the psychologist how to test or the social worker how to interview. Each profession needs to employ its own training and competencies in an effort to plan educational programs for each child. In this relationship, the teacher never relinquishes her administrative responsibility for what goes on in her class. To insist that anyone helping her also know how to teach is to depreciate and undermine the teacher as a professional person and to confuse other professions trying to help. Partly as a result of this role confusion, the program for school psychologists in the Chicago Public Schools is highly demoralized and ineffective. The recruitment of competent school psychologists is seriously hampered by a certification system geared to the historical past rather than to building a sufficient, qualified staff.

The situation for school social workers is still more critical. There seems to be little attempt to incorporate well-trained social workers into the elementary schools for some of the reasons mentioned. The use of social workers by schools can be highly preventive and educationally productive.

4. The Bureau of Socially Maladjusted Children should be headed by a director with professional responsibilities for the content, direction, and over-all supervision of the special schools, the special classes, and all residential schools.

The staff should include three professional persons—one to supervise and coordinate the programs at Montefiore, Moseley, and Motley; one to supervise and coordinate the programs of special classes; and one to supervise and coordinate the residential programs.

5. Placement of children in special schools and classes should be administered by a coordinator for special education in the district, who would review and act on referrals and would coordinate special education programs at the district level.

6. A research and evaluation unit should be part of the Bureau. The over-all expenditure for just the special schools is over $2,270,000 per year. Almost no data on the effectiveness of these programs are available. It would seem that any organization utilizing special programs of this type could afford at least 1 or 2 percent of the cost of the program for its evaluation.

7. The branches of the Parental School should be adequately staffed with two resident staff psychologists and two social workers, with psychiatric consultation available once a week. Children released from the

school should be ready to return to their homes and school, and should not be sent home because space is needed for new admissions. This is a senseless and wasteful use of a residential program. Most important, living quarters and working conditions of cottage parents need to be made attractive and helpful in recruiting competent professional persons to these jobs.

8. Pupil personnel, health, special education, and child study services should be organized under one associate superintendent, with a director for each area. As now constituted, each is in a separate administrative structure of the school system. By placing them all under one administrative banner, it is conceivable that the mutual support and coordination of these programs could be enhanced.

9. No large city school system can suppose it has solved the problem of educating socially and emotionally maladjusted children by setting up special schools and classes for the worst of the lot. The Board of Education and the administrative staff should plan, develop, and support massive educational innovations in slum areas which include preschool enrichment nurseries, neighborhood programs for parents on how to increase their child's verbal powers, new and suitable books for reading development, Higher Horizons programs, and small kindergarten groups.

PROGRAM FOR PHYSICALLY HANDICAPPED CHILDREN

Scope of the program

There are four Chicago schools for the physically handicapped: Spalding High and Elementary School; Christopher Elementary School with its branch in Nightingale; Burbank Elementary School with its branch in Lovett; and Neil Elementary School. The last two have both handicapped and nonhandicapped children, as do the two branches. In general, the children served by these schools are either orthopedically handicapped or have cardiac difficulties severe enough to require special facilities; or they may be multihandicapped.

The total number of children enrolled in these schools in June, 1964, was 1,398, divided as follows: 39 classes in Spalding High School and 63 in Spalding Elementary School; 24.5 classes at the Burbank School and its branch in Lovett; 22 classes at the Christopher School and five more in its branch at Nightingale; and 22 physically handicapped classes at Neil School. A total of 67 teachers of hospitalized and home-bound children work out of the four schools, serving approximately 650 children.

Findings

1. *Staffing.* The ratios of pupils to teachers in these schools, and the provisions for attendants and other nonteaching personnel are generally satisfactory; but more effective use might be made of attendants' time in helping classroom teachers. No trained occupational therapists are provided and it is recommended that at least one be assigned to each school. State reimbursement programs could be more fully utilized in providing nonteaching help for classroom teachers.

2. *Program.* The educational and extracurricular programs on the whole provide for the varied needs of children according to their physical and mental abilities and interests. However, there is lacking a consistent program of prevocational and vocational training. This is particularly important for handicapped children and should begin in the elementary grades. It should also include on-campus work experience programs and cooperation with community organizations, unions, and employers in developing work opportunities for older students.

Multihandicapped pupils present an especially difficult problem and it is recommended that the school district cooperate with colleges or universities in Illinois to develop curriculum materials and methods especially planned for their needs.

3. *Research and evaluation.* Funds and personnel should be specifically provided for studies such as the following: (*a*) to learn how physically handicapped pupils in our schools get along after leaving school; (*b*) to experiment with a greater variety of types of programs for the handicapped, including special resource rooms or resource teachers in regular schools for less handicapped pupils; (*c*) to test and evaluate new equipment.

4. *Organization of facilities.* The branch schools set up to meet problems of overcrowding cannot give the full benefits available in the larger schools designed for physically handicapped children. They should be eliminated when possible. At the same time, Spalding High School might be made a six-year high school which could provide for better grouping, improved teacher assignment, and a strengthened curriculum especially in vocational and prevocational areas.

The location of the Burbank School is admittedly unsatisfactory and service to pupils would be improved if a new school large enough to serve both the Burbank pupils and those now in the Lovett Branch could be established in a location more central for North Side pupils.

5. *Administration.* There appears to be a need for more consistent policies in such areas as public relations, in-service training, and recruit-

ment of teachers of handicapped children. It would be desirable to develop a consistent program of counseling and group meetings for parents of handicapped children, and to set up evening school or extension courses for handicapped out-of-school adults. All these purposes might be served by centralizing authority for these schools in the Department of Special Education.

PROGRAM FOR DEAF AND HARD OF HEARING CHILDREN

In the education of the deaf child, there is no one method, no one way of education, which is agreed upon as the best. Some believe that lip reading and ordinary speech are essential; but others hold to hand language as necessary; still others favor a combined approach.

At the present time there is a dearth of empirical evidence as well as of educational research in this area, and for the most part subjectivity is supreme. However, all educators of the deaf agree that consistency of program is necessary.

Chicago's program

Classes for deaf, hard of hearing, and multihandicapped deaf children at the time of the survey were maintained in six high schools and 10 elementary schools. The eight high school classes were located in six different districts, with two classes each in two schools, one in each of the others. The 93 elementary classes were located in eight districts, with 28 classes at the largest center (Bell) and one at the smallest (Greene). It is understood that in the fall of 1964 the number of elementary centers will be reduced to eight in six districts by increasing the number of classes at three of the remaining centers.

Class sizes at the elementary level are six to eight for the deaf, eight to 12 for the hard of hearing, six or less for multihandicapped. Class sizes at the secondary level vary from 10 to 16.

On an over-all basis, the Chicago program for the deaf could be rated as average, in spite of excellent work in some schools and classes. The majority of the teaching staff observed were doing very well in their individual classes under certain circumstances. The minority could well be graded as poor or below average. However, regardless of the quality of the teaching staff, a sequential developmental program focusing on each child and the development of his potential while he proceeds with his education is missing.

Conclusions about the program were derived from three phases of the study: interviews with interested and competent people who are not on the school staff; visits and interviews with school staff members; analysis of questionnaires sent to all teachers of classes for the auditorily impaired.

Opinions of people outside the school staff

What others think of us is important whether or not it is accurate. It affects how they will work with us, and what we can do for and with them. Therefore, it was distressing that the one consistent finding in the first phase of this evaluation was that everyone interviewed was exceptionally critical of the Chicago program for the deaf and hard of hearing.

Space does not permit a summary of even the principal criticisms that were leveled at the program. Those having to do with administration, teaching methods, curriculum, and personnel were checked through interviews, direct observation, and the Teacher Questionnaire. Where the evidence seems to sustain them, corrective steps have been suggested in the recommendations.

Other criticisms indicated the need for a more systematic program of parent education and communication with parents, community groups, and public and private agencies dealing with the hearing handicapped. There was a strong feeling that deaf parents, especially, were looked down upon by the educators of the deaf and discriminated against because of their handicap. The need was expressed for educational programs for the adult deaf and for the provision of social workers to work with parents and children in meeting the problems arising out of their handicap.

In general, the critical nature of comments of nonpublic school personnel regarding the Chicago program for the auditorily impaired emphasizes the need for better public relations and for inviting outside agencies and individuals to learn more about the work of the schools and to advise on critical issues.

Visits and interviews with school personnel

For a period of one week, the consultant visited nine of the 16 centers that contain centers for the deaf and hard of hearing and spoke to the majority of the educational staff in these centers. Other school personnel from various departments were interviewed.

Organization of program. Several examples can be given illustrating the disadvantages of having supervisory authority for classes for deaf children vested in principals and district superintendents who do not have professional training in this area and whose major responsibilities lie elsewhere. One principal spoke of "your people and mine" in referring to the teachers of the deaf, adequately reflecting his divided allegiance. In other cases, trained teachers of the deaf were found to be teaching regular classes, although untrained teachers were manning classes for deaf children in other schools.

In one center, there were several questionable practices. These included placement of substitutes as teachers in classes for the deaf without any orientation and meager supervision with regard to teaching the deaf; early dismissal of teachers and children 45 minutes before the regular school dismissal time, taking almost four hours from the children's weekly education time; the placement of deaf children with normal intelligence in mentally handicapped deaf classes. In another school which had had four classes for the mentally retarded deaf, the principal, who was new to the school, stated that on checking the psychological records of these children he found that only one-fourth of them were legally classified and adequately diagnosed as mentally retarded. Since this practice was found to exist in two centers, it is conceivable that it was fairly common.

One of the main advantages to any large program for the deaf and hard of hearing is the possibility of establishing homogeneous classes. This had been done in several large centers, yet in the smaller centers appeared to be lacking. Classes containing hard of hearing, deaf, and retarded deaf youngsters with a reading-grade span of four years were uncovered. There were also some non-English speaking children in these classes. One child, when spoken to in Spanish, responded eagerly, even when addressed in a whisper from 20 feet. Undoubtedly, because of a foreign language background, this youngster had been misdiagnosed.

Identification and screening. The identification and screening program for the auditorily impaired seemed weak. Personnel in hearing conservation reported that children are screened at only the first and fourth grades. The identification of children at other years must rely on the alertness of the regular teacher. There is little reason to doubt that children with moderate hearing losses and even some with severe handicaps are overlooked in this screening program.

Administrative and teaching staff. The Supervisor of Deaf Education is to be commended for her efforts in the almost impossible position of sole advisor to 102 classes. Although her efforts must be spread so thinly, she exhibits an insight helpful to the administration of the program.

Several administrators including one who is not an educator of the deaf are doing excellent work; over-all, the quality of administration is uneven.

At the time of the Survey, 65 teachers were found to have met the official course requiremen-ts for teaching the deaf, while 37 teachers had not completed these requirements.

The number of unqualified personnel can be partly explained by poor recruitment practices and indifference or ignorance on the part of Central Office staff receiving initial applications.

It appears that only two individuals in the entire school system have actively undertaken to recruit teachers for the deaf, or to ease their way through the maze of application procedures. This, again, seemed to reflect the lack of centralized direction.

The requirements established by the Board of Education for teachers of the deaf are open to question. To teach the deaf in Chicago as a "qualified" person, a teacher must be certified to teach normally hearing elementary children and then must have all the necessary required technical courses to teach the deaf. The reasons underlying this stringent practice are obscure. One research study comparing teachers of the deaf who had elementary school training and experience with teachers of the deaf without the latter training found no significant differences between the two types. Some individuals enter programs for teaching the deaf after graduating from liberal arts colleges and, while having had an excellent education, are not qualified to teach the deaf in Chicago because they are lacking elementary education courses.

Integration of deaf with normal children. The practice of integrating a good proportion of deaf children into classes for the normally hearing, and, in some cases, into normal classes also containing other handicapped (e.g., blind) children, is questionable. Research has shown that only a very small percent of the deaf can profit from this practice due to disabilities imposed by the very nature of the handicap. The use of this practice should be restricted and should be allowed only after careful analysis of all aspects.

Curriculum and methods. The teachers, even in the same center, were using different methods of teaching speech and language to deaf children. Obviously, deaf youngsters progressing through the oral program cannot help but be confused by this diversity of method and technique. This may be the major reason for oral retardation of many deaf students.

Similarly, when teachers were asked if they were using a specific curriculum guide, many reported they were not; others reported that they were using the guide for the normally hearing; and others claimed to be adhering to the Chicago curriculum for the deaf which no one seemed to have at hand. A copy of the latter was finally uncovered and discovered to be quite antiquated and in need of revision. Here, too, is evidence of a lack of program consistency.

One school was pursuing an in-service program from 8:30 to 9:00 A.M., prior to school, in an attempt to devise curriculum guides for the center. This was stated to be exceptionally worthwhile, yet several teachers in the school were completely unaware of such a program. When asked why this could not be done in the afternoon, it was explained to the examiner that teachers would not attend, that they were "8 to 3" people and had home responsibilities.

Transportation. In several centers it was noted that some children had to travel as much as two hours on school buses as they wound their way through city streets picking up children for various schools. When one conceives of a deaf child awakening at 5:00 A.M., getting on a school bus at 6:00, attending school from 8:00 to 3:15, and then arriving home at 5:15 P.M., he must feel that better means of transportation could be organized. Secondly, it was noted that buses are manned by drivers only. In view of the normal hazards of city driving, added to attempting to control a bus load of 40 to 50 children, this seems a dangerous practice. The use of bus attendants is recommended, similar to the practice of the New York City Board of Education, allowing the driver to concentrate on traffic.

The program for the nursery school deaf child, because of the lack of flexible transportation practices, is maintained on a full-time basis. Many young children, both deaf and hearing, are only physically and emotionally capable of attending nursery school for a portion of the normal school day. Since the school buses are available only prior to 8:30 A.M. and after 3:15 P.M., these young children must remain in school full-time. If centers had an available bus in order to transport these very small children, this problem would be remedied.

Equipment. While every teacher seemed to be pleased with loud speakers contained in his room, the observer noted two peculiarities. No microphones were available for pupil use. This need for auditory feedback in the use of residual hearing, if any, was apparently overlooked in the classes observed. Similarly, a fairly standard practice of displaying the individual audiograms of the pupils was absent in the majority of the centers. This practice is used not only for visitors, but is recommended as a reminder to the individual teacher as to the residual hearing of each child.

Information from Teacher Questionnaires

Questionnaires were distributed to 102 teachers operating in classes for the deaf and hard of hearing. Candid comments were sought through anonymity. A total of 62 forms were returned. Of the program's 65 qualified teachers, 49 responded. Of 37 full-time substitutes only 12 completed the questionnaire.

Teacher qualifications and training. The following tabulation indicates from which preparatory program the Chicago qualified teachers of the deaf have graduated.

Institution	No. of teachers
Chicago Teachers College	26
Loyola University	8
Northwestern University	7
University of Illinois	3
DePaul University	2
Washington University (C.I.D.)	1
Milwaukee State Teachers College	1
Mississippi School for the Deaf (Normal Training Class)	1
Total	49

This tends to confirm the previous finding that little or nothing is being done to secure qualified teachers from preparatory programs outside the immediate area.

Of the 12 unqualified respondents, four had taken some course work in the education of the deaf.

The average years of experience with the deaf for the qualified teachers was 13.8 years, with the range extending from one to 45 years. The substitutes averaged three years, with a range of from six months to seven years.

Regarding methods of communication used in teaching, Table 2 indicates the current approaches.

It is interesting to note that officially only one manual class exists in Chicago, yet unofficially at least eight teachers are employing sign language.

The use of speech symbolization is of the utmost importance in the teaching of speech to the deaf. While the most common approach, used by 23 teachers, was the Northampton system and charts, the remaining teachers, qualified and nonqualified, were using various combinations. Again, it was revealing to see no consistent approach to the teaching of speech.

The actual content of teaching used in these classes is again revealed to lack uniformity. Twenty-eight teachers combined the use of the Chicago curriculum for the deaf with what they considered the immediate needs of their children; 26 just dealt with immediate needs; five used

Table 2
Methods of communication used
in teaching the deaf

Method	No. of qualified teachers	No. of nonqualified teachers
Pure oral	39	10
Pure oral with gestures	3	
Oral, sign language, and manual alphabet	4	2
Written, sign language, and gestures	1	
Written, sign language, manual alphabet	1	

immediate needs and curriculum guides for the hearing as well as for the deaf.

When asked about their feelings regarding various methods of communication, the teaching staff reflected a general diversity. A pure oral approach was deemed best or ideal by 25 teachers; 10 more stated they were in favor of this approach; 10 claimed it was worthwhile for some deaf children; and five teachers expressed feelings against this method. Concerning the use of sign language, 23 felt it was worthwhile for some children; eight were against any use of this approach; and three teachers were in favor of its use. Similar findings were apparent with regard to the use of the manual alphabet. The simultaneous use of speech and signs and/or manual alphabet was considered to be the best approach by six teachers; 14 felt it would have merit for some deaf students; seven made favorable comments; and six teachers were opposed to its use. The combined approach, speech in the first few years followed by the simultaneous method in the intermediate and advanced years, was listed as the best approach by six teachers; nine advocated this method for some deaf children; 10 teachers were in favor of exploring its use; while two were against its use.

RECOMMENDATIONS

The following principal recommendations are made:

1. One person, an experienced educator of the deaf, should be named to head and coordinate the program. An advisory board comprised of educators of the deaf (who are not connected with the Chicago schools) should be established to act in a consultant capacity to the director of the program. The coordinator should answer directly to either the Bureau of Physically Handicapped or to an Assistant Superintendent of Schools. In addition to administering and supervising the educational program for the deaf, his functions should also include the maintenance of a comprehensive public relations program, the recruitment of qualified teachers of the deaf, the coordination of the program with local, state, and national agencies and associations, and the development of good relations with parents of deaf children and others. He should also be charged with the supervision of research in this area, eventually providing the Chicago program with the national prestige it could easily earn.

2. It is recommended that the current 16 centers be consolidated into three schools for the deaf, one in the northern section of the city, one in the south, and one in the west. Each of these schools should be headed by a principal who has had experience as a successful educator of deaf children. At the present time the public school system employs 10 such people as principals, only one currently heading a school containing deaf youngsters. Based on present enrollment data, each school would contain approximately 280 children or approximately 47 classes. An advisory staff, comprised of a full-time psychologist, audiologist, social worker, and assistant principal, should be maintained and should advise the principal.

Adequate supervision and the resultant consistency of program should be provided for by the establishment of grade-level supervisors under the direct control of the school principal. One supervisor should be maintained at the nursery-preschool level, responsible not only for this program but also for a parent education program for parents of prenursery-aged deaf children. One supervisor should coordinate the program at the primary level. Another supervisor should be responsible for intermediate and high school levels. A secondary vocational supervisor would not only be charged with the supervision of his program, but could also act as coordinator of an adult education program for deaf adults. One supervisor should be established to formulate and maintain a special program for the multihandicapped children.

3. It is recommended that these centers contain only deaf children,

not to exclude the multihandicapped deaf youngster. While every effort should be made to integrate the deaf and hard of hearing child back into his community school, the scarcity of these children who can successfully integrate, plus the need of all deaf children for highly specialized teaching, indicates that the special schools should contain only auditorily impaired youngsters. This practice can be seen in successful operation in other large city schools (e.g., New York and Los Angeles).

4. It is recommended that the current oral methods be maintained for those children who succeed with them. However, for those remaining children (a large minority, who by the age of nine or 10 display no propensity for oral communication), a program utilizing the simultaneous method (speech and manual alphabet or signs) should be initiated to allow for the further education of these youngsters.

5. Classes for the multihandicapped deaf child should be established separately from classes for the normal deaf child. It is recommended that the teachers and supervisors of these programs be qualified in the education of the deaf and in at least one related learning disability area. Every effort should be made to establish communication with special educators in areas other than deafness to learn and adapt appropriate methods and techniques for use with these children. Teachers of the multihandicapped deaf should be aware of programs for these children in other sections of the country.

6. It is recommended that a unified and consistent testing policy be established. Achievement test norms for the deaf have been established and a yearly achievement test program should be initiated, administered by either the teaching staff or the grade level supervisor. It is also recommended that the teachers of the deaf conduct the audiometric testing of the pupils in their classes yearly. This would insure the awareness of the teacher of the pupils' loss and residual hearing, and would further substantiate the findings of the school audiologist.

7. With regard to certification standards and recruitment practices for teachers of the deaf in Chicago, the following recommendations are made.

Because of the immediate need for teachers of the deaf in the Chicago Public Schools, the present requirement of elementary certification should be temporarily abolished. If this is not thought feasible, a special salary increment should be provided for teachers of the deaf since they have dual certification.

Every effort should be made to insure the expeditious processing of applications by qualified teachers of the deaf. Personnel at the Central Office should be made aware of this need.

PROGRAM FOR VISUALLY
HANDICAPPED CHILDREN

Three types of services are provided for visually handicapped children in the Chicago city schools: special classes for the blind, and special classes and itinerant teachers for the partially seeing. The older the visually handicapped child, the greater the need for absorption into the regular program, and the corresponding decrease in need for special services. Once the blind child has acquired Braille and typing skills and has developed good mobility, he should be incorporated into the regular stream of education, with only the special education services needed to maintain his proficiency, to obtain the special equipment or services, and to provide special counseling and guidance.

Incidence of visual handicaps has varied considerably over the years. Retrolental fibroplasia, a major factor in etiology during the period 1947-53, has now almost been eliminated as a contributing cause of blindness. Most of these children will have completed their schooling by 1970. However, it cannot be estimated with certainty that there will be a correspondingly large drop in visually handicapped children needing special educational services. Medical science is finding ways to save children who would otherwise be stillborn or expire during the neonatal period, but often at the cost of some handicapping condition such as blindness. Also, the wide array of new drugs with unknown side effects will continue to contribute to the population of handicapped children.

The over-all program

At the time of the survey, 706 blind and visually handicapped children were being served by 75 teachers in a total of 14 districts. There were seven high school classes for partially seeing pupils; 39 elementary classes; and 11 itinerant teachers serving visually handicapped pupils in regular classes. There were four high school classes for the blind and 18 elementary classes, located in six districts.

Findings

The present plan of special classes at the elementary level and resource rooms at the high school for the blind seems to be satisfactory. If improvement is sought, it should be in the extension of the preschool program so as to counter the overprotective efforts of the parents to do for the child what he must be taught to do for himself. Additional staff, preferably school social workers trained in parent counseling in the area of the blind would strengthen the parent counseling and training so needed in the preschool years. Considerable evidence on the value of such a program is available in the literature.

Most rooms provided for visually handicapped divisions are excellent. One need observed was that special "dictation" booths were missing. Such sound-conditioned areas would permit a sighted student or adult volunteer to tape needed materials while other activities were being conducted in the room. Such booths are relatively inexpensive and could be constructed by woodworking shops or the building custodians, as were the ones for the brain-injured in the Cook School.

At the high school level more attention needs to be paid to the vocational needs of the noncollege preparatory blind student. The prevocational counselors recommended for the program for the educable mentally handicapped would also serve a valuable role here in providing for work experience, work orientation and evaluation, and placement assistance.

Rooms for the partially sighted seemed to be well equipped and staffed by qualified teachers. In one room it was noted that new large-type typewriters were of questionable value because of the poor spacing of letters which made the print difficult to read. Purchase of all special equipment should be made only upon the recommendation of the supervisor for that program after study and trial use in the classrooms. Small differences between models, not covered by specifications, will render the low bid method of purchase the most expensive possible, if after purchase the item has little or no utility.

While it is not known how widespread the practice is, there is some evidence that children whose vision is within normal limits, after correction, are being placed in the class for the partially seeing because of emotional problems. Although the school principal may rationalize such placement as the best for all concerned, it is both illegal and educationally unsound.

RECOMMENDATIONS

1 Maximum integration of visually handicapped children should be fostered by placement of special classes and resource rooms in buildings which do not contain several other divisions of handicapped children.
2 The program for the partially seeing should be expanded to provide services in every district. Where no program now exists because of shortage of rooms, special resource rooms should be given high priority at the blueprint stage in new buildings in that district.

3 Expansion of the program for the blind should be at the preschool level, and should include provision for school social workers to aid the parent in extending the school's efforts into the home, and to provide parent counseling in terms of realistic developmental, social and vocational potentials.

4 Additional attention to the vocational needs of the terminal high school student is needed. Prevocational counselors are needed to provide work experience, work orientation and evaluation, and placement assistance. Multihandicapped visually handicapped youth needing sheltered workshop training would also be served by these counselors. State reimbursement of $3,000 per prevocational counselor is available.

5 Additional supervisory service should be provided to (*a*) aid in the expansion needed; (*b*) select, develop, and test new furniture supplies and equipment; and (*c*) provide for placement conferences to determine initial placement and re-evaluation of visually handicapped children, thus providing for return to regular programs of all those qualified as soon as feasible.

PROGRAMS FOR MENTALLY HANDICAPPED CHILDREN

Two types of reimbursable programs are authorized by the Illinois School Code: special classes for the Educable Mentally Handicapped (EMH) and special classes for the Trainable Mentally Handicapped (TMH). Eligibility for placement in either program requires individual examination by a qualified psychological examiner employed by the Bureau of Child Study.

Special classes for both EMH and TMH children are found in the Chicago city schools. During the decade 1954-64, total enrollment in all special class programs for the mentally handicapped grew from 4,582 in April, 1954, to 6,977 in April, 1964—a 52 percent increase. It must be noted, however, that the total public school enrollment during this period also increased, from 377,423 to 519,096 (40 percent) so that much of the special education increase represents growth needed to maintain the *same* level of service. Also, a small portion of this increase in number being served is due to the addition of special classes for the TMH in 1954.

In his report to the Board of Education of July 8, 1964, the Superintendent indicated that some 4,574 handicapped children have been identified as needing special educational services, but cannot be placed because facilities are not available. It is safe to assume that many of these are EMH and TMH, and further, that many more children are in need of services but have not yet been identified.

Two situations exist in Chicago which act to increase the need for special classes for the educable mentally handicapped: (1) the skewed distribution of socioeconomic levels in the Chicago population produces a larger-than-normal percentage of EMH children in the school population, and (2) the high proportion of school-aged children attending parochial schools serves to increase the proportion of handicapped children in the public school population, as these are often returned to the public schools for special educational services. Thus the over-all estimate for prevalence of mentally handicapped children in the Chicago Public Schools needing special educational services will be significantly higher than the 2.3 percent figure used nationally, and for planning purposes should probably be set at 3 percent. In those districts with a high proportion of families with low income, this figure could rise as high as 10 percent. Conversely, high socioeconomic areas will have a considerably lower-than-average prevalence of EMH children.

Figures supplied by the Special Education Office for November, 1963, indicate that "true membership" was as follows:

EMH elementary special classes   5,727
EMH secondary special classes   454

This shows that there are almost 13 elementary EMH children enrolled in special classes to each EMH child enrolled in a secondary class, compared with the two to one ratio which would be expected if all EMH children were enrolled in a secondary program. The lack of adequate numbers of special class programs at the secondary level constitutes a clear and undeniable weakness in the Chicago's program for the EMH. This lack tends to negate the positive efforts of the elementary EMH classes and serves to lower the morale of the teachers at that level.

Elementary EMH programs

Three levels of special class programs are provided in the elementary schools: preprimary, primary, and advanced. The terms "preprimary" and "primary" refer to the relative academic level of the EMH children enrolled, as compared with normal elementary pupils, and not to their chronological ages. Thus the curriculum for the "preprimary" classes is essentially readiness activities for formal academic learning in the tool subjects. Similarly, the primary EMH classes are concerned with beginning reading, writing, and arithmetic instruction, as is true with primary level classes for normal children. Since only seven classes with 75 children at the preprimary level existed in November, it can be seen that identification and placement of the EMH usually waits until the child has demonstrated clearly his inability to profit from the regular class.

Teachers qualified to instruct classes at the preprimary level are also in very short supply.

Location of classrooms. Decisions concerning location of special classes for the EMH appear to be made too often on the basis of "space available" and administrative convenience. In some cases the building principal indicated that he had requested that the classes be located in his school; in other cases, the principal could offer no reason for the existence of special classes at his school, except that there were so many vacant classrooms available.

Another problem concerned with location of EMH classes was the number of other special education programs existing in one building. Availability of space and the interest and willingness of the principal were the two reasons found for this situation. Such concentration of special education facilities within one building violates several principles of good administrative organization of special education programs. If handicapped children are to have opportunities for some integration with normal children, it follows that they cannot be herded together to such an extent that they equal or outnumber the normal children in that school. While it is desirable to have two to three EMH classes located at the same elementary school (preprimary, primary and advanced) so that the proximity of teachers will permit easy articulation between levels and mutual support, additional EMH classes and/or other special educational programs in sizable numbers are undesirable. A division into regular and special schools tends to occur and opportunities for integration of handicapped children with nonhandicapped drop far below the desired level.

The physical location of EMH classes within each building is of considerable importance. Placing the classrooms in the least desirable locations creates the impression that EMH children are not only different, but inferior in terms of their worth as individuals. The retarded child placed in a special class usually remains there for three years. Thus classroom location for EMH classes should tend to minimize the stigma of being "special" by placement in the same wing or corridor as children of similar chronological age. While the location of EMH classrooms visited varied from good to poor, it seemed that too often the location was determined by some chance factor, such as a particular room being vacant at the time it was decided to place an EMH division in that school.

Another facet to location of special classes for the EMH is the matter of permanency. Retarded children are characterized by their inability to adjust to new situations. If special classes are shifted from school to school each year on a space available basis, considerable educational efficiency is lost. Prime consideration should be given to the needs of the pupils to associate with their neighborhood peers, and not the location of vacant classrooms not needed for other purposes.

Educational program. The environment within the classroom also varies from one extreme to the other. Several of the elementary EMH classes visited were in attractive rooms equipped with functional furniture and containing adequate supplies of equipment and materials. On the other hand, a few classrooms were found to be barren, dark, and depressing—the teaching materials consisting of old regular textbooks which were either excessively difficult for the EMH children, or were inappropriate to their interest level. Since many examples of excellent classrooms were found, the question must be asked why the teachers (and principals) with grossly inadequate room environments were not subjected to some interaction with the good ones; why competent, professional supervision didn't detect these inadequacies and take steps to overcome them. Part of the answer lies in the decentralized organization, which presupposes a level of understanding and acceptance of special education in the line administrators—the principals and their district superintendents.

Curriculum is the heart of any educational program. Unfortunately, there is only spotty evidence that teachers are using the newer approaches in special education. In several of the classes visited, the teacher and her principal seemed content to utilize a watered-down approach, despite the existence of the 1963 "Overview Charts for the EMH Programs." This may be partly due to the fact that admission to the secondary program requires a certain level of academic achievement.

Secondary EMH programs

The program at the secondary level is grossly inadequate in terms of the number of children served. Chicago limits enrollment of the EMH in secondary school programs; pupil achievement in reading and arithmetic as measured by standardized achievement tests must be at or above the fourth-grade level to enter a high school program. Furthermore, EMH students are not permitted to remain in special education for more than two years, at which point they are dropped from school or, if they show unusual academic ability, are permitted to re-enter the regular school program.

These constitute unreasonable and arbitrary restrictions. If the elementary EMH program has followed the curriculum guides supplied by the Chicago schools and the State of Illinois, the EMH children should not be expected to achieve at the level indicated. Thus the elementary

EMH teacher is "forced" to use inappropriate graded materials to enable her students to pass the achievement tests at a level sufficiently high to qualify for transfer to a secondary program. Furthermore, study after study has shown that the real goals of the EMH program—to produce economically efficient and socially independent citizens—are not positively correlated with academic ability as measured by standardized achievement tests. Thus, a false standard is imposed to block the admission of many EMH children to high school programs, when children of the same ability are successfully completing four year EMH high school programs in other cities throughout the United States.

This entrance requirement, plus the lack of any functional curriculum goals, and the restriction on time in the program, has produced a totally unrealistic program of questionable value, in spite of ample documentation of the need for and the framework of an adequate secondary program for the EMH.

In only one high school was any concern for vocational training expressed, and that through a "back door" approach. The EMH pupils who had spent the two years permitted were being dropped from the high school, but were being advised to apply for the "Double T" program. State law permits enrollment of EMH pupils up to 21 years of age. School programs should enable EMH pupils to remain in a secondary program as long as needed to achieve sufficient economic and social competency to become tax-paying, contributing, independent citizens. Little of what is being done in the present EMH secondary program contributes to that objective.

A wide variety of community facilities exist to assist in the development of an adequate program. Federal vocational rehabilitation funds will soon be available to support on-going programs involving occupational education and prevocational training for the EMH, in addition to extra support for experimental and demonstration projects in these areas. For the EMH pupil with special problems such as multiple handicaps, such agencies as the Jewish Vocational Service have already conducted pilot programs in other cities such as Milwaukee, and have indicated their interest and willingness to participate here.

All of this indicates that the time to initiate a complete and thoroughgoing revision of the secondary program for the EMH is *now!*

Programs for the TMH

Pilot programs for the TMH were begun in 1954 under state sponsorship. An enrollment of 289 was reached in April, 1964. Conservative prevalence figures of 1.5 per 1,000 school children indicate that some

750 TMH children live in Chicago who would profit from public school special educational programs. Thus the public schools are serving less than one half of the TMH children needing special classes. (The actual waiting list was 400 in June, 1964.)

At present, 33 classrooms are scattered in 22 buildings in 16 of the 21 districts. Over half the buildings have only one class, and the largest concentration in any building (or in any district) is three classes. Why this wide distribution of TMH classes?

Certainly the answer cannot be found in the laws and regulations governing the program for the TMH. Included in the definition in School Code Section 14-1(4) is the statement: ". . . who may be expected to benefit from training in a group setting designed to further their social adjustment and economic usefulness in their homes or in a sheltered environment." For almost all other categories of handicapped children integrated experiences with nonhandicapped are desirable as a part of the process of learning to become a producing, independent adult. No such need for articulation between school and the general structure of society exists for the TMH since this individual will be operating within a limited, sheltered environment throughout life. Similarly, the opportunities for TMH children to participate in the regular—even extracurricular—activities of the school are extremely limited.

All these factors point to the lack of need for scattered classes. On the other hand there is considerable reason for concentration of TMH classes. Since the low prevalence of TMH children (as compared with the EMH) and the severity of their handicap will require transportation, it would seem desirable to obtain the best results from the transportation by having it go to concentrated units. Furthermore, the program for the TMH is less like that of the nonhandicapped than any other group served by the public schools. Teachers of the TMH, therefore, have little in common to discuss professionally with their fellow teachers in regular schools. No neat shelf of textbooks with teacher's manuals exists for these teachers—most of their teaching materials are teacher-made. All this necessitates considerably more teacher interaction and curriculum building than is the case for teachers of the nonhandicapped, or even the other areas of the handicapped. Supervision can assist but not replace such interaction. At the present time, not one of the 22 building principals with TMH classes is known to have ever taught a class of TMH children, or even taken course work on curriculum, methods, and materials for the TMH. Thus it must be assumed that their supervisory assistance is minimal.

Visitations disclosed a range from good to very poor classroom programs for the TMH. No program seemed to have enough of the quality ingredients to be rated as excellent or outstanding. While programs for the TMH are the newest program added to the Chicago schools, other cities and other states have had programs for some time—San Francisco since 1920 for instance—and thus considerable evidence is available on what constitutes a quality program.

In several cases, the principals of the buildings to which TMH classes had been assigned were of the opinion that TMH children were not the responsibility of the public schools. In this state, however, the people, through their legislature, have designated the public schools as the agency responsible for the community day program of education and training for the TMH. While one need not agree with such a position, it is academic to argue that the TMH "do not belong" in the public schools, and improper to take measures designed to limit the quality of the TMH classes assigned. In all fairness it should be noted that this attitude is not universal, and that in some cases, principals who stated they did not believe TMH children to be the responsibility of the public schools were providing the maximum support possible to their special classes for the TMH.

For all of the above reasons, it is clear that a major revision of the program for the TMH is needed.

RECOMMENDATIONS

1. The Bureau of Child Study needs considerable augmentation in order to more adequately screen for, diagnose and retest educable and trainable mentally handicapped children for special educational programs. Screening programs should extend down to the kindergarten and first-grade levels, in addition to teacher referrals. The present salary level is insufficient to attract needed psychologists.

2. More adequate screening will disclose large numbers of children eligible for EMH and TMH classes. This, plus revision of the requirements for admission to the secondary school program for the EMH, will necessitate increased number of classes, especially at the EMH secondary and TMH levels.

3. Location of EMH special classes should be thoroughly restudied. The need for integration of EMH children with their nonhandicapped peers dictates that two to four elementary special education classes for the EMH be located at a school with children of similar chronological ages (CA's), near the geographical center of the population of EMH children to be served. Sufficient inducements must be maintained to

recruit and keep the highly qualified and highly motivated teacher in special class programs in poorer areas.

4. The furniture, equipment, supplies, and teaching materials should reflect the "special" aspects of this program, and not be such that the teacher is restricted to a watered-down version of the program for normal children. At the intermediate level, for example, practical instruction in homemaking skills requires a kitchen stove, refrigerator, sink, and cabinets, plus the cooking and serving tools and supplies.

5. Curriculum development by teachers as an in-service training technique should be greatly expanded to meet specific needs within each district. High school and elementary school teachers of the EMH who will have the same children in their classes need to clarify elements of the program dealing with sequential development of skills and articulation between levels.

6. The secondary program for the EMH needs a complete overhaul. A strong occupational emphasis is needed not only at the high school level, but in classes at the advanced elementary level too. A work experience program to aid in articulation from school to the community is an essential ingredient. Prevocational counselors are used with good results in many communities in Illinois, and are included as special education personnel for state reimbursement.

7. The special education program for the TMH is likewise in need of considerable revision. Essential features are:

a. Centers should be planned to house eight to 12 classes with sufficient space and facilities to carry out a complete program for TMH children with chronological ages from six to 18. These centers should be carefully located in terms of geographic centers of the area to be served and easy access to road nets. Prevalence figures indicate that Chicago should plan on developing eight to 10 such centers.

b. Transportation by school bus is indicated. Because many of these children are multihandicapped and younger ones have little sense of self-direction or ability to avoid common dangers, an attendant would also be needed. These attendants would also serve as teacher-aides for classes of younger TMH children. Approximately half the cost of each of these services is reimbursable under the Illinois Plan for Exceptional Children.

c. The program in these centers should provide for a sequential development of functional skills needed by the TMH child to become as capable of self-care as possible, and as competent in sheltered workshop production and assisting with home duties as his limitations permit. This necessitates a special school environment, facilities, equipment, supplies, and techniques. All of the essentials of a home must be included if training is to have carryover. For the older child, practice in caring for a garden, trimming hedges, sanding icy walks, should be included in the curriculum. Language development is extremely important, and tape recorders should be available for teaching purposes and providing a record of improvement.

PROGRAMS FOR MULTIHANDICAPPED CHILDREN

One of Chicago's unique programs for handicapped children is the variety of special classes for the multihandicapped. In April, 1964, there were 696 multihandicapped pupils in 75 classes. The four classifications with more than 25 pupils were: deaf EMH, 145 pupils; socially maladjusted EMH, 137 pupils; crippled EMH, 224 pupils; and severely crippled, 105 pupils.

These children, usually excluded from eligibility for other programs for handicapped children by rules or regulations, offer the most difficult challenge to educators. Special education is partly based on the premise of exploitation of remaining capabilities with any particular handicapped group. Thus, we teach the deaf to use their vision to "read speech," and the blind to use their hearing to develop avoidance of obstacles. The blind-retarded or the deaf-retarded may never be able to acquire these needed skills, however. Likewise, the physically handicapped child is usually expected to make maximum use of his other assets in order to compete successfully with his nonhandicapped peers. The addition of vision or hearing handicaps or mental retardation or brain injury provides for a resultant handicap which is far more serious than just the addition of the two.

The greatest danger to programs for the multihandicapped is that they become "dumping grounds" for pupils who for one reason or another are not wanted in the special class program for their major handicapping condition. At one school a new principal reviewed the records of the multihandicapped children assigned there and discovered that many failed to meet the criteria for eligibility.

Probably most multihandicapped children should be initially assigned to a special class program for the category of children with the same handicapping condition as the child's major educational problem. In some cases—for example the physically handicapped blind—the child can succeed if itinerant services from one specialist can supplement the special class teacher of the other handicapping condition.

RECOMMENDATIONS

1 Tighter administrative and professional control of programs for the multihandicapped should be exercised by the Central staff. Programs should be centered in the four schools for the physically handicapped, and in the three centers for the deaf (see recommendations under programs for the auditorily handicapped).
2 Placement procedures for determining eligibility for such classes should require a professional staffing by the diagnostic personnel, teaching staff, and administrator responsible. More frequent re-evaluations are required, and recognition of this should mean a higher allocation of diagnostic personnel to such schools.
3 Other specific recommendations are to be found in the sections of this report dealing with the various handicapping conditions.

PROGRAM OF SPEECH CORRECTION

Since effective communication is essential to learning and to successful functioning as an adult, the school is concerned with speech defects of children which are too serious to be corrected through the usual classroom techniques.

In the Chicago Public Schools at the time of the survey, 92 speech correction teachers were giving individual or small group help to 8,873 pupils. It is estimated conservatively that 2.5 percent of the school population generally need speech correction services. This means that in Chicago 12,500 children probably have a speech problem needing special service. Using a caseload of 100, this would require 125 speech correctionists. This would be minimal, especially when taking into account the need for speech teachers to provide classroom teachers with assistance in speech and language development. While the present level of service is about 75 percent of this minimum, it should be noted that there has been no increase since 1959, so that the program has not kept up with increasing population.

Correctionists are assigned to district offices and are given several schools to cover. Included in their services should be itinerant services to the less severely hard of hearing who can, with some assistance, succeed in the regular class. Many of the present correctionists do not have sufficient training to provide this needed service.

All beginning pupils are screened by the speech therapists in elementary and high school, and additional referrals are made by the local school staff. By far the largest number of referrals (83.8 percent in elementary schools, 65.3 percent in high schools)[1] are for faulty articulation which is functional rather than organic in origin. About 23 percent[2] of the total caseload is dismissed annually as no longer requiring special services.

Physical facilities for the conduct of the speech correction program in the various schools vary widely. Directions provided by the Central Office are clear and explicit, but represent an impossible demand to some principals of buildings which just do not contain the space needed. Because of their size, the high schools have apparently been able to find the space more easily than the elementary schools. Future buildings should incorporate the need for such facilities into every building, including sound conditioning, storage space, mounted mirrors, etc.

RECOMMENDATIONS

1 Recruitment for speech correctionists should be stepped up, with authorization for at least 10 additional positions per year until the 125 minimum number is met. Further expansion after this should be based on diagnosed cases and extension of services to children not now receiving them, such as the moderately hard of hearing. Movement into the latter field will need to be done carefully, as many of the present staff of correctionists are not qualified to teach speech reading and aural rehabilitation.

2 At least one additional supervisor for the speech correction program should be employed to permit more active recruitment, adequate orientation, and in-service training to the new correctionists.

---

[1]*Handicapped and Socially Maladjusted Children*, Staff Report, 1964.
[2]*Ibid.*

F

Some Observations Concerning
Certain Chicago High Schools

Our understanding of Dr. Havighurst's instructions concerning our assignment was that the committee was to make a limited visitation of a few selected high schools. The purpose of this phase of the Survey was to answer the single question, *"If more resources were available to the high schools, how could they best be expended to improve the quality and extend the services of the Chicago public high schools?"* We did not understand our task to include an evaluation of the strengths and weaknesses of the selected schools.

Our procedure

Our committee conferred on two occasions with members of the Survey staff to discuss our tasks and to receive information about the secondary schools. At the second session the high schools to be visited were determined. Factors considered in the selection process were socio-economic background, ranges and levels of ability, races and ethnic

* * *

Prepared by a committee of three superintendents from suburban school districts at the invitation of the Chicago Survey Committee: Dr. Lloyd S. Michael, Chairman, Evanston Township High School; Dr. LeRoy Knoeppel, Proviso Township High Schools; Dr. R. Bruce Allingham, York-Willowbrook Community High Schools.

backgrounds, drop-out rates, percentages of graduates going to college, pupil achievement data, and type of school. Four schools were selected for a day's visitation at each by the committee. The characteristics of the general schools (special and vocational high schools were not seen) visited were:

1. A school where the socioeconomic background is high and where a high percentage of graduates go to college.

2. A school where the pupils are of average and above-average socioeconomic background, with an average number of college-bound graduates.

3. A school with a large proportion of Negro pupils, below average and average in the socioeconomic category, and with a smaller number of graduates going to college.

4. A school with a changing ethnic population, below average and average in socioeconomic background, and with a below-average number of college-bound graduates.

An afternoon was spent with the principals of these four high schools to discuss the committee's task, to make plans for the visitation, and to arrange for materials and data that could be studied prior to the visit to the school.

Each visit was carefully planned and executed. Interviews were held with the principal, usually with one or more of his administrative staff and counselor groups. Conferences were held with a number of department chairmen in the schools. Classroom visitations were a part of the schedule in each school as was a tour of the school plant. Individual and small group conferences were held with students. Special attention was given areas of concern, innovations, and new programs that were identified by the principal and his staff.

A fifth day was spent in visiting three other comprehensive high schools that differed from the four high schools in several respects. In these schools a great deal of time was spent in discussion with the principal.

A final day was spent by the committee in discussing and analyzing the data that had been received, reviewing together our observations and recommendations, and finally preparing the first draft of our report. The final report has subsequently gone through several revisions.

In assembling the final draft of the report, it was deemed advisable to identify the 11 most significant recommendations which would logically stem from the observations of the committee. No effort was made to rank these in the order of importance either to the committee or in relation to their possible implementation in the schools.

RECOMMENDATIONS

1. *There is a clear need for more extensive secretarial and clerical services in the school.*

Such supportive services would release teachers from many non-teaching responsibilities so that they may give greater attention to classroom preparation and development of their essential teaching competencies; such services would also assure more efficient office operation and broader measures of assistance to the teaching staff in preparation of materials for classwork.

For instance, there should be clerical service for counselors to permit them to give undivided attention to working with student problems. There should be an efficient office duplicating service for all teachers. Also, most attendance matters should be handled by clerical personnel.

2. *Nonclassroom "duty" assignments of teachers should be significantly reduced.*

If the ultimate need in administering a school is to assure a maximum effort on the part of teachers *in the classroom learning areas,* where pupils with any reasonable curiosity and desire to learn can be stimulated and challenged to pursue new learning experiences, then one must question the practices now followed by Chicago high schools in teacher assignments.

Basically, each teacher is assigned five classes in the field of his competence. He is also assigned two "duty" periods and a "division," the latter being a sort of administrative homeroom.

The duty periods are assigned by the chief school administrator to handle such responsibilities as:

Corridor supervision
Cafeteria-lunchroom supervision
Attendance office clerical work
Registrar's office clerical work
Bookroom supervision
Class adviser
Visual aids supervision
Adviser to school newspaper staff
Adviser to school yearbook staff
Special disciplinary duties in assisting
    administrative personnel
Clerical work for counseling office
Study hall assignments

It is reasonable to suggest that many of these assignments are clearly within the range of competence one may find in carefully selected, noncertificated personnel. The small clerical staffs of the high schools (four or five clerks per school) are entirely inadequate under present personnel practices, and the theory seems to be that to get the necessary work done, a certain measure of teachers' energies and attention to the classroom process must be diverted to these "duty" assignments.

There is a limit to the physical endurance and mental acuity of a teacher. When too large a portion of this is drained off in nonclassroom assignments, the classroom work has to suffer. If the full competence and enthusiasm for teaching is to be utilized by a school system, every possible device must be used to free teachers of many of the duties *during the school day* which detract from their primary assignments as well-prepared, highly stimulating, professionally competent teachers of boys and girls.

3. *Greater flexibility should be explored in establishing teacher assignment quotas (and classroom facilities) for specific high schools with clearly varied needs evident in the character of student bodies and communities served by each.*

In the truly comprehensive general high school, provision should be made for emphasizing learning experiences and activities most appropriate to the needs of the students. If, for instance, it is evident that a more extensive remedial reading program is necessary to help students in a specific school reach a satisfactory level of performance, it should be possible to seek greater assistance in this area.

If a particular school has clear evidence of an unusually strong demand for more extensive offerings in foreign languages, science, industrial arts, business education, or homemaking, it seems reasonable to suggest that there could well be provision for justifiable modification of facilities and personnel quotas to meet such a need.

It seems sensible to recognize, also, that a particular school might need a more realistic quota of counselors and social workers to help with an unusually difficult school-community situation.

In summary, the committee feels there should be recognition of the desirability of greater flexibility in staffing and providing certain facilities and learning materials to schools in which circumstances warrant special attention.

4. *The role of the department chairmen should be enhanced by granting them more time for the performance of their duties.*

The turnover of teachers and the need to supervise the work of all classroom teachers point up the desirability of a reduced load for the department chairmen. The practice of assigning various teachers as department chairmen recognizes the need for leadership in various curricular fields, but the Chicago high schools provide no opportunity or incentive for them to have more than nominal status. Department chairmen, selected for classroom competence and leadership qualities, and reassigned annually on *performance only,* should be limited to a maximum of four classes daily so that they might assume greater responsibility for orientation of new teachers, classroom supervision of all teachers, requisitioning of and accounting for supplies and equipment, assisting the principal in selection of new teachers, chairing all curriculum work of the department, and assisting the principal in teacher assignments.

Judicious use of the department chairmen in a school as an advisory council to the principal will assure greater staff acceptance of all undertakings of the school, and will produce an "administrative and supervisory team" approach to all school policies and procedures that can well result in high morale and a feeling of belonging "on the team" for all school personnel.

It is further suggested that there be some monetary recognition of the responsible position of the department chairman, particularly in those departments with the most teachers.

5. *The high school administrative office should be staffed during the summer. The principal should be on a 12-month contract and assigned to his/her school for 11 months' duty. Some counselors and a portion of the clerical staff should be available during the summer recess.*

This time should be available (11 months) to plan, organize, and evaluate the school's program. If a summer school operates in the building, administrative assistance should be assigned.

It is especially important that a strong effort be made to have classes ready to function the first day of school, but, more important, the school must function effectively every day in the year.

6. *The desirability of continuity of educational leadership in a school would seem to call for a recognition of the high school principalship as a position of increasing importance.*

It has become axiomatic in secondary education that the level of effectiveness of a high school and its impact upon the educational development of its pupils are inclined to be directly related to the administrative and educational leadership of the principal and his staff. It might be well, therefore, to evaluate the frequent changes in the top leadership of a school, and to suggest that a greater effort might be made to induce principals to establish themselves in a school and community as an acknowledged educational leader. Thought could well be given to consideration of a compensatory salary schedule for principals which could obviate the need for principals to seek transfers to schools of larger enrollments as a means of improving their salaries. For example, they all might be paid salaries within a basic administrative range, but larger high schools could be allocated proportionately greater administrative and supervisory assistance.

It seems reasonable to suggest, also, a selective process for principals which requires that candidates for principalship demonstrate not only proficiency for passing academic tests, but also the highly personal competence of "working with people" and eliciting the cooperative efforts of a professional teaching staff.

We recognize the impossibility of administering a huge, unwieldy school system without clear and generally objective guidelines for curriculum, finance, personnel, maintenance, etc. However, it seems to us that firm consideration must be given also to the subjective criteria by which principals are selected, and to the scope of their duties and responsibilities as instructional leaders in their schools.

7. *The curriculum in each high school needs to reveal greater adaptation and adjustment to the needs of the pupil population it serves.*

Course offerings among most of the high schools show striking similarity regardless of levels of pupil ability and future educational and vocational plans. More extensive curriculum development, particularly in industrial arts, home economics, business education, art, and music, are urged. The recent efforts to develop work experience programs in a number of high schools are to be commended. The policies and procedures in ability grouping have been other efforts to adapt course offerings and content to pupil needs and abilities.

8. *There seem to be marked deficiencies in certain categories of learning materials and equipment.*

Although efforts have been made for marked increases in expenditures in some categories for the coming school year, it is suggested that this factor will still require more intensive evaluation as to the need for more materials and equipment.

a. Basic textbooks are supplied to pupils in the Chicago schools free of charge. Yet, the massive logistics of the task, plus a recognizably legitimate desire to avoid wasteful spending for materials which might not be fully utilized, have resulted in unnecessary delay in many schools at the beginning of semesters when many pupils have been without textbooks.

b. Each high school is allocated budgeted amounts, based upon enrollment, for requisitioning of library materials, classroom supplementary materials, classroom equipment, and limited office and teaching supplies. The budget also includes some funds to be spent for music department supplies, athletic equipment, and the like. Some of these amounts, especially those allocated to textbooks and to the libraries, seem unusually small. Those of us who feel that the library and the coordinated departmental supplementary reading libraries should be the learning materials centers of our schools can only suggest that much more should be provided in this area if students are to be confronted with inducements to read and study in *depth*.

c. The high schools visited seem to be generally well equipped and supplied in the science departments. Much has been accomplished in this direction through the assistance of the NDEA. However, the general high schools are very sparing of equipment and facilities in business education, industrial arts, and homemaking. In our judgment, the business education departments could be "beefed up" with business machines of considerable variety and with transcription equipment for more intensive training of secretarial trainees. Much more could be done with these departments. The industrial arts classes do have a legitimate place in a high school general education program, but the schools we visited simply do not provide a sufficient number of adequately equipped pupil stations. Every student should be fully occupied with clearly defined project work that challenges him to learn something significant every day. Homemaking areas were generally well maintained but ancient and discouragingly unattractive. Although it has become popular for high schools to be academically oriented in recent years, it is interesting to note that well-equipped, attractively arranged home economics departments with eager, competent teachers do attract an astonishing number of girl students who want to know more about homemaking, particularly those phases related to interior decoration, food preparation, sewing, and family living. The homemaking department definitely can be a legitimate part of a general high school.

d. There seems to be a clear need for the provision of a well-trained supervisor-consultant in audio-visual services in the school. In a very real sense, trained specialists in this area can be as important to a faculty as are librarians, who regard their prime responsibility as that of a specialist in providing resource materials for teachers and pupils. Much more equipment and materials and extensive assistance in lesson planning can be made available to classroom teachers if the audio-visual department becomes a resource center in the school.

9. *The daily schedule should facilitate the realization of the best instructional program. It should not deter the effectiveness of the teaching-learning process. It should be a means and not an end in school organization.*

Greater flexibility in the schedule should provide more differentiation of teaching assignments, reorganization of instructional groups, including large groups, small class discussions, and independent study, and other schedule arrangements to improve instruction. Methods of schedule-making are generally outmoded and should be changed to include computer programming and other efforts to utilize new media available to schools. The similarity of programs in the high schools raises the question of whether it is necessary for each school to continue its own scheduling staff, at least to the extent that is currently the case. More effective procedures to balance classes and to add or reduce divisions of classes at the opening of school are most essential.

10. *Basically, schools grow and improve in direct relation to the opportunities provided for a high school staff to become more professional and to work cooperatively at the task of all-school improvement.*

General faculty and departmental meetings are not the end-all of professional growth and school improvement. However, they may be the means of generating concern about educational needs and problems and an opportunity to plan, organize, and evaluate programs aimed at staff growth and school improvement. Means should be found to schedule such professional meetings. The staggered sessions in most high schools should afford time during the first and tenth periods for monthly meetings with the two groups of staff members. In addition, faculty committees concerned with curriculum, instruction, student activities, in-service education, lay participation, and the like could also work at the task of school and community betterment.

A marked reduction in the teacher load, particularly "duty" assignments, would provide the time within the school day for teachers to become more "scholarly," confer with other teachers and counselors, work with students, plan and prepare their teaching programs, and accomplish many other professional duties.

11. *Greater autonomy of "districts" in the Chicago system could be reflected in more flexible curricular possibilities in the various general high schools, and probably would result in a markedly higher morale among the professional staff.*

With so much of the decision-making concentrated at the Central Office, District Offices seem to be primarily functioning as action centers carrying out directives of the Central Office. Of course, it is quite natural that the Central Office, confronted as it has been with the urgency to meet the demands of overwhelming enrollment increases and the lack of classroom facilities, should have tended to assume extreme regulatory powers "to get the job done."

However, it is suggested that consideration be given to expanding the size of districts to include at least four or five high schools (and the "feeder" elementary schools), and drawing district lines to encompass certain appropriate geographical and sociological areas in the city. These area "districts" could then be delegated greater powers, within a sensible administrative plan, to establish budgets, allocate personnel, organize operation procedures, determine curricular offerings for all their schools, and encourage change and innovation.

Such a strong "district" organizational plan, providing greater powers and responsibilities for the district superintendents, could be a major factor in encouraging initiative and greater creative efforts of the professional staff at the "grass roots."

Suggestions for upgrading the position of the high school principal as a leader of the instructional program in his school would seem to fit in with a strong district organization, for the principals would then become part of the district superintendent's administrative team for effective operation of the schools. It seems clearly desirable to have the decision-making function closer to the professional staffs of the schools.

Concluding remarks

The committee commends the Chicago Public Schools for their progress in meeting their problems. The administration and teaching personnel in training, experience, ability, and motivation are reasonably satisfactory. The physical facilities—buildings, furnishings, custodial and maintenance services—are generally adequate for at least an acceptable minimum program.

Pupils' learning abilities and achievements reflect the tremendous range one would expect to find in any very large city with diverse cultural and ethnic backgrounds and varying concepts of the nature and importance of a high school education. The high schools of Chicago have generally shown a determined effort to recognize the ranges of ability, talent, and interests in developing courses and ability groupings to facilitate better instruction and improved learning. The recent efforts to reduce class sizes also have tended to improve the teaching-learning situation.

The high schools visited by the committee are good secondary schools because they have competent staffs working to improve their programs and services to their pupils. The teachers and administrators are aware of and speak frankly about their problems and needs. The Chicago high schools will be better schools when more resources—ideas, materials, and people—are available to them, and if public confidence and support are sustained.

G

Appendices

1. *Computation of the socioeconomic ratio (SER)* Chapters II, III, X

This is a crude socioeconomic index, based on easily obtainable census data on occupations in the male labor force, aged 14 and over. The occupations are placed in four categories, as follows:

A. Professional, technical, and kindred
   Proprietors, managers, and officials
   Farm owners and managers (one-fifth of total)
B. Sales and clerical occupations
   Farm owners and managers (two-fifths of total)
C. Foremen, craftsmen, and kindred
   Operatives and kindred
   Farm owners and managers (two-fifths of total)
D. Service workers, including private household workers
   Laborers, including farm laborers

There are some obvious errors in these categories, if a true hierarchy of occupational prestige is wanted. For example, policemen and firemen are included in service workers, but they rank above factory operatives in occupational status. However, the errors tend to neutralize each other, since semiskilled workers such as truck drivers are included in category C but probably should be in category D. In order to test the SER's, the ratio was computed more exactly for the male labor force of the USA aged 25 to 64 in 1960. Farm owners and managers were distributed between A, B, and C, according to their levels of education. Men with occupations unreported were distributed between the four categories according to their incomes. The resultant SER was .80, quite close to the value of .82 obtained with the cruder method.

The SER for the Chicago communities and for the high school attendance districts was computed from data for census tracts in Chicago. The formula was:

$$SER = \frac{2A + B}{C + 2D + 2U + NR}$$

where U is the number unemployed and NR is the number who do not report on occupation.

Categories A and D are given a double weight because they represent more fully the upper-middle and lower-working class characteristics.

SER for high school attendance areas

The tables in Chapter X contain SER data for each general high school attendance area. These were computed from census tract data for 1960. They are multiplied by 100, to avoid decimals. For comparison with a high-ratio suburban high school, the SER for New Trier Township, including Winnetka, is 563. The coefficient of correlation of SER with achievement score is approximately .8.

2. *Population projections for Chicago and suburban area Chapters* II *and* III

The estimates of total population and of school age population come from the Population Research and Training Center of the University of Chicago, in a bulletin issued in 1964 entitled "Population Projections for the Chicago Standard Metropolitan Statistical Area and City of Chicago, 1970 and 1980."

It was assumed that there would be a slow reduction in the numbers of whites moving out of the city, and a somewhat faster reduction in the numbers of Negroes moving into the city. At the same time it was assumed that the numbers of Negroes moving into the suburbs would increase slowly.

For school age population estimates it was necessary to make some assumptions about the birth rates of whites and Negroes. Taking the 1962 birth rates as a base, it was assumed that the birth rates would decline after 1965, the Negro birth rates declining more than the white birth rates.

3. *Possible vocational programs*

	Program and duration	Admission achievement criteria	Levels of classes	Drop-out readmissions
Group I (above average)	Diploma 4 years	Above 9.0	Honors Regular	Admit to regular vocational high school if over 16.
Group II (average)	Diploma 4 years	Between 8.9-7.5	Honors Regular Essential	If under 16 admit to regular vocational high school. If over 16 admit to Certificate Program or Adult Program.
Group III (below average)	Certificate 3 years	Below 7.4	Regular Essential Basic Remedial	Admit to Certificate Program

Freshmen

English
Algebra
World History
*General Shop
Mechanical
   Drawing
P.E. or ROTC

English
Algebra or Math
World History
*General Shop
Mechanical
   Drawing
P.E. or ROTC

Combination
   English and
   Community
   Civics with
   Reading Clinic
Math
*General Shop with
   Vocational Infor-
   mation
Music or Art
P.E. or ROTC

Sophomores

English
Geometry
U.S. History
Vocational Shop
Mech. Drawing
P.E. or ROTC

English
Geometry or Math
U.S. History
Vocational Shop
Mechanical
   Drawing
P.E. or ROTC

Combination Eng-
   lish and Social
   Studies with
   Reading Clinic
Math
Vocational Shop
Music or Art
P.E. or ROTC

Juniors

English
Physics
Civics
Vocational Shop
   or Related Tech-
   nical Training
P.E. or ROTC

English
Physics
Vocational Shop
Music or Art
P.E. or ROTC

Vocational Shop
Optional Electives

Seniors

English
Related Techni-
   cal Training
Electives
Music or Art
P.E. or ROTC

English
Related Voca-
   tional Shop or
   Related Tech-
   nical Training
Music or Art
P.E. or ROTC

*Admission to Exploratory or Vocational Shop after half a year in General Shop.

Index